ACTIVIST AFFORDANCES

ACTIVIST AFFORDANCES

ARSELI DOKUMACI

How Disabled People Improvise More Habitable Worlds

Duke University Press   *Durham and London*   2023

Library of Congress Cataloging-in-Publication Data
Names: Dokumacı, Arseli, [date] author.
Title: Activist affordances : how disabled people improvise more
habitable worlds / Arseli Dokumacı.
Description: Durham : Duke University Press, 2023. | Includes
bibliographical references and index.
Identifiers: LCCN 2022033073 (print)
LCCN 2022033074 (ebook)
ISBN 9781478019244 (paperback)
ISBN 9781478016601 (hardcover)
ISBN 9781478023876 (ebook)
Subjects: LCSH: People with disabilities. | Chronic diseases—
Social aspects. | Disability culture. | Discrimination against
people with disabilities. | BISAC: SOCIAL SCIENCE / People
with Disabilities | SOCIAL SCIENCE / Anthropology / Cultural
& Social
Classification: LCC HV1568 .D64 2023 (print) | LCC HV1568
(ebook) | DDC 362.4—dc23/eng/20221020
LC record available at https://lccn.loc.gov/2022033073
LC ebook record available at https://lccn.loc.gov/2022033074

Cover art: An activist affordance for cooking. Photo by author.

Babanneme . . .

To my grandmother, Lütfiye Dokumacı, whom I deeply miss
every single day

CONTENTS

ACKNOWLEDGMENTS

The acknowledgments was the hardest part of this book to write. I have so many thanks to give to so many people, and I feel and fear that my words can never be enough. First, my greatest thanks to my participants who generously opened their homes to me and shared their stories, insights, and knowledge. There is no way I can reciprocate. I wrote this book in the hope that it can be my way of thanking you. I want the whole world to know all the brilliance you are, to respect and learn from all your wisdom and your ingenuity. Çok sağolun varolun! Merci beaucoup! Thank you!

Although rarely mentioned, ethnographers *do* have bodies too—bodies that can be impaired, sick, and chronically ill. Mine is one of those, and I am indebted to my care network. There are no words to describe my gratitude to Hasan Yazıcı (aka Hasan Hocam). Back then, when other rheumatologists gave up, saying there was nothing more they could do for me, you took on my care and gave me hope, which I desperately needed. For years, you have taken care of my ill health and have seen me through the most difficult times of my illness. When I left Turkey and became an academic nomad (moving from country to country and getting lost in unfamiliar healthcare systems and bureaucracies), you always answered my calls for help, making sure I would find the care I needed regardless of where I was. You have been not only a relentlessly meticulous rheumatologist, a most caring doctor, but also an unwaveringly supportive mentor. (Not everyone gets to have a genius scientist both as their doctor and mentor!) From the first time I mentioned my project on the daily lives of people with rheumatoid arthritis, you entirely believed in it and, of course, challenged it! From its beginning to its end, you did everything you could to make this project happen, for which I am forever grateful. I could not have done this project if it were not for your generous support and mentorship all the way through. Mine Batumlu (aka Mine Abla), I do not know how to thank you for all the things you have done for me on a personal and a professional level. I remember many hospital visits where I was in pain, angry and in tears, and you were always there to listen to me with deep care, which meant the world to me. You have been my emotional line of support, and I know for a fact that I am not the only one to say this. During my fieldwork you were a key facilitator and a mentor, and it is thanks to you and your amazing skills that I was able to meet so many fascinating participants. You are an amazing nurse, a gifted researcher, and a steadfast problem-solver who touches the lives of so many people. I also want to thank the entire rheumatology team and staff at İstanbul Cerrahpaşa University Hospital, in particular Dilşen Abla. I am thankful to Dr. Henri Menard and Dr. Elizabeth Hazel at McGill University Health Centre for their support during my fieldwork in Montreal. Finally, I am eternally grateful to my rheumatologist, Dr. Inés Colmegna. You are a brilliant scientist, a scrupulous and fearless researcher, and an exceptionally caring doctor. I am in awe, and I am continually inspired by your sharp mind, your fierce mentorship, your endlessly caring sprit, and all the love your enormous heart holds for the world. You always went above and beyond in taking care of my health, and you also supported me professionally, emotionally, and academically. I do not have words to thank you enough. Were it not for you and your unwavering care, I would not have been able to finish this book.

This book draws from my doctoral and postdoctoral research materials, and I am grateful to everyone who supported this project, whether as a supervisor, advisor, mentor, or committee member: Mike Pearson, Margaret Ames, Heike Roms, Alan Read, Kim Sawchuk, Lisa Stevenson, Tobias Rees, and Ayo Wahlberg. It was a gift for me that I completed my PhD journey under the supervision of Mike Pearson. It hurts to write these lines in past tense: Mike was an extraordinary human, a brilliant artist, creator, thinker, teacher, and yet *the* embodiment of humility. I wish I could have shared and celebrated this book with you. I wish you could have seen for yourself how deeply your work affected my thinking . . . You and your work will continue to live in this and many other books.

My gratitude to Lisa Stevenson is boundless. There is no way I can thank you enough for your generosity, your extraordinary supervision, and everything you have done for me. Your "Anthropology of the Self" graduate course was in many ways an eye-opener. I learned so much from the most generative discussions you led. (Not to mention that I got to meet wonderful people!)

Over the years I benefited enormously from being in dialogue with your brilliant mind, which has nurtured this book project in so many ways. Your never-ending feminist line of support made me survive the precarity of academia. You have always and always *been* there, and for that I am forever grateful. You are my role model of what a feminist supervisor and mentor is—one that I can only hope to become. I would also like to give a very special thanks to Ayo Wahlberg for his amazing supervision and mentorship during my time at the University of Copenhagen. Thank you for bringing me into the Vitality of Disease—Quality of Life in the Making (VITAL) team. Those two years have been the most intellectually nourishing and delightful time of my academic life, and I felt completely welcomed and at home. It is thanks to you, Ayo, and the VITAL spirit you created, that I was able to experience what a sincere collaboration was and felt like. Your humility as an academic, heartfelt commitment to supporting early career researchers, and dedication to collective work have given me so much hope. I vow to emulate your leadership style, support for others, and collaborative commitments in my own work in the future.

I cannot begin to thank Faye Ginsburg enough for her unwavering support, enormous generosity, and the intricate feminist care webs she gently weaves around her. I was lucky enough to be enveloped by them. (May all early career folks be as lucky as me!) You are the definition of brilliance. Your mentorship opened my eyes to so many things that I would not have otherwise thought of. I adore your fearless feminism, commitment to disability justice, and all the good vibes and energy you radiate, which make the world more welcoming, accessible, and hospitable. Thank you for being so smart, inventive, and hilarious. You are a gift to the world.

At Aberystwyth University, where I completed my PhD, I was so lucky to have wonderful colleagues. Esther Pilkington, Daniel Ladnar, and Jazmin Llana, you made Aber-times so fun and unique, and that deserves so much thankfulness. Esther, I am indebted to you for being such a caring friend and endlessly fun coconspirator. I deeply miss our days at the National Library, all our conversations, and all the joy we shared. My postdoctoral time at the University of Copenhagen Anthropology Department was hugely transformative. My colleagues there were very welcoming and kind. The entire VITAL team has been wonderful, and I am especially happy that I met the amazing Rebecca Journey and Thomas Scott Hughes. Thank you Peter Fini Henriqucs for inviting me to lunch tables.

I would like to thank Francesca Meloni, Katherine (Katie) Zien, Jonathan Sterne, David Howes, Janet Gibson, and Kate Maguire-Rosier, who read drafts of the introduction, offered extremely generous feedback, and talked through ideas with me. My special thanks to Jonathan Sterne for his press matchmaking role. I am deeply grateful to Francesca Meloni, Janet Gibson, Katherine Zien, and Dörte Bemme for being such wonderful and supportive friends. We had so many conversations about this book, and you sharpened my thinking with your priceless feedback. You also listened to my worries and encouraged me along this path endlessly. Katie, thank you also for inviting me to your graduate class, "Interdisciplinary Approaches to Improvisation," at McGill. I am thankful to your students who read the introduction and generously engaged with my work and provided incisive feedback. I am grateful to Michele Friedner, Faye Ginsburg, and Rayna Rapp for inviting me to contribute to the special issues they edited. Your feedback was extremely helpful, and it was such a privilege to work with and learn from you, and of course, be involved in the same issues with amazing scholars whose works I admire.

The ideas in this book developed over the course of several years and have been nurtured by many gatherings, events, and conversations. I cannot thank enough the participants of the Wenner Gren Disability Worlds Symposium that took place in 2018 in Tucson, Arizona. This was the most nourishing, most intense, and at the same time the most delightful event of my academic life. To this day, I still think about and remember all the enriching conversations. My deepest thanks to the organizers, Rayna and Faye, for inviting me. I am grateful to all the wonderful participants whose commentaries immensely helped me and this book: Ayo Wahlberg, Beatriz Miranda-Galaraza, Cassandra Hartblay, Danilyn Rutherford, Devva Kasnitz, Herbert Muyinda, Laurence Ralph, Michele Friedner, Pamela Block, Patrick J. Devlieger, Renu Addlakha, Roy Richard Grinker, Susan Reynolds Whyte, Tom Boellstorff, and Tyler Zoanni. Also, my thanks to Laurie Obbink for making everything run smoothly. I am thankful to the amazing participants of the Performing Disability/Enabling Performance Working Group that took place in Montreal as part of the Hemispheric Institute's 2014 Encuentro. This was in many ways a foundational event that led to establishing of Critical Disability Studies Working Group (CDSWG) at Concordia (2014), which in turn set the ground for the Access in the Making Lab. Finally, I want to thank the past and current members of Performance and Disability Working Group at the International Federation for Theatre Research. I much enjoyed being part of the working group and deeply appreciate the vital work this group is doing. I would like to thank my colleagues at Concordia University in the Department of Communication Studies and beyond. I would especially like to thank Kim

Sawchuk for her ongoing and generous support, and Krista Lynes for her kindness and mentorship.

I am grateful to my editor, Courtney Berger, as well as Sandra Korn, Lisa Lawley, and the staff at Duke University Press for all the care they put into their work. I cannot thank enough my developmental editor, Claudia Casta-ñeda, for her generous, generative, and brilliant feedback, and for thinking together with me throughout the writing process of this book. Thank you for always challenging and pushing me further, Claudia. I immensely benefited from your most meticulous and caring editorial work which, to me, is feminist editing.

As this book was in its final stages, Access in the Making (AIM) Lab came into being, and I am filled with gratitude to the following amazing team of hard-working, bright, creative, and generous students, research associates, postdocs, and community members who brought this lab into being: Alaina Perez, Amy Mazowita, Diego Bravo Pacheco, Dresda Emma Méndez de la Brena, Jessie Stainton, Nicholas Goberdhan, Prakash Krishnan, Raphaëlle Bessette-Viens, Roï Saade, Sabrina Ward-Kimola, Salima Punjani and Yolanda Muñoz. You all are extraordinary humans and I learn from you every day.

I am grateful to my friend Senem Göçtü for our longtime friendship and for her continual helping hand that was and will always there for me. I am so lucky to be friends with Janet Gibson. You are such a friend that, even if we are at the two other ends of the world, whenever we meet it feels as if we have been friends forever and were seeing each other every day. Thank you for being who you are, the beautiful soul and mind. I am deeply grateful to my longtime friend Özcan Vardar, who so generously helped me with filming during my fieldwork in İstanbul. Without your amazing skills and kind help, I would not have been able to do this fieldwork. I am so proud to have such a gifted artist as my friend. Your friendship is irreplaceable, and I am so thankful that we can still meet in different parts of the world and take up where we left off. I would also like to thank Melike Sungur, who opened her home to me during my fieldwork in İstanbul and helped me along the way. I also want to thank Geneviève Vincent, all of her kind colleagues, and Benoît Laroche for helping me during my fieldwork.

Dearest Francesca Meloni, you have a very special place in my heart reserved for you and you only. No one can take or replace it. It is only with you that I can enjoy the deep darkest corners of humor. It is only with you that I can go into endless ramblings about literally anything. It is only with you that I can feel supported at all times regardless of time, place, and boundaries, and most importantly, with zero judgment. Your care, love, brilliance, and friendship are magical. If anyone is lucky enough to be touched by that magic, I know that they would be transformed by it forever. I am forever grateful to the universe that I have you in my life. I couldn't have walked all this journey, or any journey, without you.

My parents have been very supportive of my research all the way, and I know that they would do everything they can to help me. Thank you so much, *Anne* and *Baba*, for all your love, support, and care. I also want to send a heartfelt thank you to Guy Vincent and Louise Bastien, who always care for me and François. We care so much for you, too. Thank you Bruno Vincent and Melissa Viens for all the good and fun times we have had together, and for your support. My brother (Abi), my sister-in-law (Arzu'cum), and my nephew (Arel) and my niece (Arya), I love you all unconditionally. You are not only my kin; you also are my dearest friends with whom I have endless fun and the best of times. Abi, bi tanesin. You mean the world to me. You have always been and will always be there for me and for anyone you love. You deeply, truly, and inexhaustibly care, and I have no words to describe your caring spirit. You are the best of brothers, and I have loved and continue to love every moment of growing with you. You have made and continue to make my life beautiful. Arzu'cum, you are the sister I never had and could only have wished for. I am forever grateful to have you in my life, in our lives. . . . Arel and Arya, you are the light of my world. To see you grow into the beautiful human beings you are has been the most precious gift of my life. Your generous hearts, your gentle and caring souls, your extremely curious and sharp minds, and your joyful spirits nourished each and every page of this book. You always asked about this book, and when I explained to you what it is about, you immediately got it. Not only that, you even kept feeding me new ideas for new books I should coauthor with you. What a gift you two are . . . Thank you for making me your auntie. I love you endlessly.

And finally, François, there are no words that can describe what I feel for you. Since you came into my life, you transformed it so much so that I cannot imagine a "me" or a life without you. You made me understand love. This book is in so many ways the story of us. You enabled this book in ways that you even don't realize. I could not have and would not have done this or anything without you. Thank you for being who you are—the beautiful, caring, kind, and most gorgeous human I love. Thank you for gifting me the life we share. I couldn't have asked for more, and I cherish every second of it.

I would like to acknowledge the generous funding that allowed me to complete this book. The writing of this book was supported in part by funding from the Canada Research Chairs Program (Canada Research Chair in

Critical Disability Studies and Media Technologies); the Social Sciences and Humanities Research Council (SSHRC Insight Grant: 435-2021-0869, Mobilizing Disability Survival Skills for the Urgencies of the Anthropocene, PI Arseli Dokumacı); a Fonds de Recherche du Québec–Société et Culture grant (FRQSC Établissement a la relève professorale: NP-296720, Disability Creativity, PI Arseli Dokumacı); a European Research Council grant (ERC-2014-STG-639275, The Vitality of Disease—Quality of Life in the Making, PI Ayo Wahlberg); a Fonds québécois de la recherche sur la société et la culture postdoctoral fellowship.

An earlier version of chapter 8 appeared as "People as Affordances: Building Disability Worlds through Care Intimacy" in *Current Anthropology* 61, no. S21 (2020): S97–108. Copyright © 2019 by The Wenner-Gren Foundation for Anthropological Research. All rights reserved. An earlier version of chapter 5 appeared as "A Theory of Microactivist Affordances: Disability, Disorientations, and Improvisations," in *South Atlantic Quarterly* 118, no. 3 (2019): 491–519. Copyright © 2019 Duke University Press. Earlier versions of some sections in chapter 3 appeared as "Disability as Method: Interventions in the Habitus of Ableism through Media-Creation," in *Disability Studies Quarterly* 38, no. 3 (2018). Earlier and much condensed versions of some of the material interspersed in chapters 5, 6, and 7 appeared as "Vital Affordances, Occupying Niches: An Ecological Approach to Disability and Performance," in *Research in Drama Education: The Journal of Applied Theatre and Performance* 22, no. 3 (2017), 393–412, and as "On Falling Ill," in *Performance Research: A Journal of the Performing Arts* 18, no. 4 (2013): 107–15.

INTRODUCTION

Arseli's Story

One morning, I was in the bathroom. I stood up from the toilet and pulled my jeans up in the slowest of motions. My hands, elbows, and shoulders were inflamed, tender, and painful (as they often are). Then came the hardest part: my fingers were swollen to the size of mini-bananas. I could not bend them even to the slightest degree needed to grasp the zipper. How the hell was I going to zip up?

Everyday life is full of such negotiations for me because, since my early teenage years, I have been living with chronic diseases that damage my joints, causing pain and gradual disablement. None of this is immediately apparent to an observer.[1] Because the diseases in question affect joints, and because joints mean movement, my everyday life turns into a stage for what I would describe as *choreographing the dance of avoiding pain*—a dance that is sometimes done solo and at other times with another, or others. In this solo "dance," in order to zip up, I kneeled down a bit, put my right knee on top of the left one, positioning my legs in the shape of a crooked X. I bent slightly forward, and exhaled a big breath. The distance between the two sides of the zipper was now almost erased. The button on top and its buttonhole were now almost overlapping. All that was left to do was to slide the zipper up. I did so not by grasping the zipper but by pushing it up from the base with the nail of my thumb that I rested on my other fingers. This is a routine choreography that I rehearse whenever I have to wear trousers. I now also minimize the need for this dance by maximizing my time at home, where I can wear loose clothing like PJs or, indeed, anything without zippers.

Henri's Story

Henri has lived most of his adult life with rheumatoid polyarthritis, which has ended up damaging the joints in his hands, arms, and feet, among others. On a languid Sunday morning in Montreal, Henri and I were sitting around his kitchen table while my life partner, François, filmed us. Beautiful sunrays and a light breeze were coming through Henri's kitchen window, filling it up with all the distinctive smells and senses of the fall. As Henri slowly sipped his coffee, we got into a deep conversation about lives lived with a chronic painful disease, what this living does to us, what we do with it. As Henri slowly but skilfully stood up for a refill (figure 1.1), he suddenly turned back to me and said, "Do you want to see how I put a full mug on the table?" After explaining that he has a very limited range of motion in his wrists, which affects their flexion and extension, Henri described with almost mathematical precision how he puts a full mug on the table without spillage.

Henri: [When] I put a cup on the table, if I don't bring that elbow to the same level as the table [figure 1.2]. You know, it's gonna, see, it's gonna drop, it's gonna go like this [figure 1.3]. So gotta bring down the elbow to put the cup on the table [figure 1.4].

The dance of zipping your trousers in crooked limb angles. The dance of putting a full mug on a table in bent bodily curves. The dance that lets you avoid pain and relieves your impaired body parts of their presumed functions by making the rest of your body move with ordinary objects, together in extraordinary union. In and through the dance (see chapter 5), the fixed, rigid, and obdurate materiality of the environment becomes something else, as if it were alterable and bendable, as if it were alive, sensing, reciprocating and caring for your sick, impaired body in pain.

This book is a visual ethnography of such largely unnoticed choreographies performed in the most fleeting of movements, the most ordinary of everyday actions. It traces how chronically ill, "oddly" formed, and debilitated bodies carve out niches for themselves—though the material world bears no record of their pains and vulnerabilities, remains impervious to the

FIGURE I.1 IN THIS AND THE FOLLOWING THREE IMAGES, HENRI, WHO HAS RHEUMATOID POLYARTHRITIS, DEMONSTRATES HOW HE STANDS AND SITS WHILE HOLDING HIS COFFEE MUG SECURELY. HERE, HE IS CLUTCHING THE MUG WITH HIS RIGHT HAND WHILE LEVERAGING HIS WEIGHT AGAINST THE TABLE AS HE STANDS.

FIGURE I.2 AS HE STANDS AT THE TABLE, HENRI'S LEFT HAND MOVES ACROSS HIS BODY TO SUPPORT HIS RIGHT ELBOW AT THE SIDE OF HIS RIBS.

FIGURE I.3 AS HENRI BEGINS TO SIT, HIS RIGHT ELBOW HAS STRAIGHTENED AND HE TILTS THE COFFEE MUG ONTO THE TABLE AND AWAY FROM HIS BODY; HE PLACES THE THREE MIDDLE FINGERS OF HIS LEFT HAND ON THE TABLE TO BALANCE.

FIGURE I.4 LEANING TO THE RIGHT WITH HIS RIGHT SHOULDER ANGLED DOWNWARD, HENRI LOWERS HIS BODY BY BENDING AT THE KNEES AND PLACES THE MUG FLAT ON THE TABLE.

diseases they live with, and offers no gesture of recognition for the unusual shapes, scales, and abilities that their bodies and minds come with. This book is an account of how disabled people build accessible worlds in and through the unspectacular choreographies of the everyday that I call "activist affordances."[2] I mobilize the terms "activism" and "affordance" in specific ways: "affordance" means an action possibility shaped by the reciprocal properties of the organism and the environment,[3] and "activism" means world-making. I consider performances like mine and Henri's as kinds of actions that are inseparable from creation. These affordances are performative: they say and do, do and make at the same time. Activist affordances are performative microacts/-arts through which disabled people *enact* and *bring into being* the worlds that are not already available to them, the worlds they need and wish to dwell in.

The mode of activism in these performative acts is less about opposing or disrupting existing worlds than about "being the change you want to see."[4] To pun on J. L. Austin's famous phrasing "how to do things with words,"[5] activist affordances are about *how to build worlds with acts* (rather than with words and slogans). It is not the persons who change the world, but their actions. Their activism does not entail the intermediary action of asking for change but involves making the change itself. These affordances may be neither hailed as activism in the traditional sense, nor celebrated as art or recognized as design. In fact, they may go entirely unnoticed. But they are acts of world-building nonetheless. This is precisely the point of my intervention. These performative affordances *can* and *do* transform the world. These are acts that we, as disability studies scholars as well as scholars and practitioners of design, need to name, trace, and theorize.

In theorizing activist affordances, I build upon and expand the emergent literature on disability maker-cultures, their histories, and the resourcefulness, ingenuity, and expertise that contribute to a broader recent emphasis on design and making across the humanities and social sciences.[6] This conceptualization involves a transdisciplinary blending. The term "affordance" originates from a subfield of psychology founded on the mutuality of organism and environment, or organism-environment relations. Disability, performance, and activism have not been a concern among those who use the term. Disability studies has not paid much attention to affordances either, apart from a few cursory mentions that do not take up its rich ecological grounding.[7] This is where I intervene: What happens when we think of disability, affordances, and performance together, as related terms? What can this conceptual work allow us to do? What new openings can it provide us with when it comes to the intersection of disability and design? And how does this intersectional attention turn us toward a further intersection with environmental (ecological) justice?

Activist Affordances

In the words of its coiner, James J. Gibson, affordance refers "to both the environment and the animal in a way no existing term does."[8] It describes how the animal's (organism's) action and perception are shaped through the dynamics of its relation to the environment. Affordances are possibilities of action that emerge from the reciprocity between the properties of the organism and those of the environment. A round, stiff object fits the shape of my palm, just as my palm fits the shape of the object, and with the strength of my fingers added to them, this environment-organism interaction offers grasping.

My term "activist affordances" differs from Gibson's "affordances" in that it describes possibilities of action that are almost too remote and therefore unlikely to be perceived, and yet are perceived and actualized through great ingenuity and effort to ensure survival. To perceive an affordance that exists in the actual and to perceive an affordance that is too distant a potential to even be perceived are not one and the same. When the two are treated as equals by being lumped under the rubric of "affordances," then we lose track of the tremendous labor, struggle, and creativity that it takes to discover and actualize the latter. I propose the theory of activist affordances in order to name and recognize the tiny, everyday artful battles of disabled people for more livable worlds that otherwise remain unaccounted for. I propose the concept of "activist affordances" as a way to understand how disabled people literally *make up* whatever affordances fail to readily materialize in their environments (or otherwise be immediately available for perception) and at the same time must *make up for* that failure.

The Question of Necessity

In a sense, this book focuses not so much on the possibilities for action as on the *constraints on* action, and what follows from those constraints. No doubt the material world offers possibilities and constraints to any living being, disabled or not. No doubt we all create affordances that contravene normative directives. One might then wonder: What about any of this is specific to disability? Given that affordances are so variant, is an affordance created by a disabled person any different from a daily trick invented by a nondisabled person, like Henri's "different" way of putting a mug on the table? If the idea of activist affordances always implies that affordances take different forms depending on the particularities of the perceiver in question, then what specificity, if any, is there to the affordances emerging from the experiencing of disability? By extension, do we actually need a new vocabulary and theory of activist affordances?

I argue that we do. We do because activist affordances are like no other affordance in the sense that their generation is necessitated by "shrinkage" (a term that I will discuss in full later on). It is not that Henri has a choice among multiple affordances that would allow him to deal with the mug's design limitations. Henri can manage the full cup and the liquid only through a particular affordance; and herein lies the very urgency and indispensability of the world-making acts that I call activist affordances. Impaired, sick, painful bodies, mad selves, debilitated populations, vulnerable beings—and threatened organisms, as I shall discuss later on—live in environments that for them are shrunken and shrinking. The activist affordances that they create from within this shrinkage are not a question of choice or preference, but of necessity. It is exactly this *necessity* that I want the concept of activist affordances to articulate.

Let me say this loud and clear: I am not attempting to reject restrictions, lack, negativity, and loss in the experiencing of disability; I acknowledge and take them quite seriously. My proposed theory of activist affordances is a response to Alison Kafer's yearning for "stories that not only admit limitation, frustration, even failure, but that recognize such failure as ground for theory itself."[9] In fact, activist affordances can emerge only in the face of constraints, failures, and losses that I broadly conceptualize as "shrinkage." As I will demonstrate throughout the book, when the environment's offerings narrow, and when its materiality turns into a set of constraints rather than opportunities, the improvisatory space of performance opens up and lets us imagine that same materiality otherwise. The emergence of activist affordances in an improvisatory space of performance is the subject of this book.

Performance

Performance, Diana Taylor writes, is what "moves between the AS IF and the AS IS, between pretend and new constructions of the 'real.'"[10] Performance has to do with what Victor Turner described as the "subjunctive mood."[11] That is, while "the indicative" concerns "normatively structured social reality" (the

AS IS), the subjunctive concerns the world of "'if it *were* so,' [AS IF] not 'it *is* so.'"[12] Performance enacts a world of counterfactual wishes and possibilities. In this book, I mobilize performance precisely in this subjunctive sense. I argue that whether it takes place on stage or in everyday life, performance allows us to perceive the environment AS IF it were a someplace else that already provides the affordances that we need, desire, and wish for. This is especially so, I argue, when material constraints stifle our actions—when we find no world-counterparts for our bodies, needs, vulnerabilities, and wishes in the current ordering of the world. In this book, I develop a theory of activist affordances by mobilizing this concept of performance together with disability: the imaginary space and subjunctive mood of performance opens up for the creation of affordances exactly when the normative order in which the environment has been occupied suppresses and pushes these affordances beyond the boundaries of the plausible.

Think of actors on stage. The actors have to operate within the constraints that the materiality of the stage or site (AS IS) puts on their actions. In fact, it is within these constraints that the work of imagination (AS IF) unfolds. As actors relate to the stage and its props within the imaginative layer of performance, they transform this materiality into an elsewhere and else-when through their actions. I argue that the same transformation takes place in everyday lives of disabled people, which are lived within a shrinking world of possibilities. When the existing ordering of affordances leaves no room for their nonnormative bodies and minds; when the world's surfaces become most unresponsive to the impairments, diseases, and pains they live with; when the world's offerings become unreachable in states of extreme deprivation and debilitation, it is exactly the imaginary space of performance that opens up. In this space, disabled people *make up* and *make real* action possibilities AS IF those missing world-counterparts were present. Like actors or dancers on stage, they may bring into being affordances that the environment's form, layout, and materiality did not initially seem to allow. They come up with highly inventive choreographies such as putting a mug on a table without spillage, and putting on pants, as well as combing without combs and leaving shirts partly buttoned in order to take them off later as though they were pullovers. They stand up from sofas by minimizing the use of their knees, turn light switches on and off with their heads, and improvise many more micro, ephemeral affordance-creations that this book extensively documents. Activist affordances bend the seemingly fixed forms, sand the hard edges, and give movement to the rigid layering of the world AS IF it were habitable, in as yet unimagined and undreamed-of ways.

The "What if?" framework of critical design, speculative design, and other related approaches is similar to the subjunctive (AS IF) mood of performance.[13] If, as Charles Eames suggests, "design depends largely on constraints,"[14] then we can think of activist affordances as *a mode of designing* that emerges from the constraints of the AS IS and moves toward "What if?," bringing possible futures to life. The difference between a critical design framework and my framework is that activist affordances are not created in design studios or makers' labs with specialized tools and materials. Instead, they are choreographed in our everyday lives, in and through our bodies, and with whatever we find around us. In fact, let me revise my definition: activist affordances are about *making up* and *making real* worlds that we were not readily given by *making do with* what we have. The worlds that we build with our activist affordances do not require blueprints, pillars, or concrete to exist. They come into being through our bodies and imagination as we engage with the material world. In contrast to normative design and making, we design without having to possess, produce, or consume things. Our designing involves speculating about the kinds of worlds we want to live in through *making up* and *making real* within the limits of the spaces and situations we have found ourselves in and the bodies that we have to live with. While we may create a material object in this process, this is less likely rather than more likely, and in any case the creation of objects is not an important question here. Instead, the focus is on the provisional, the feat of creating something out of nothing, and the necessity of finding a way through, under constrained circumstances. Accordingly, the three defining phrases of activist affordances are *make up, make real*, and *make do with*.

To claim that disabled people *make do* does not, however, mean that accessibility features and services, assistive tools, adaptive equipment, and devices are redundant. Absolutely not. (This would be a serious misreading of activist affordances that would eventually lead to their co-optation within a neoliberal logic of austerity.) As I discuss extensively in chapter 10, this claim means only that the modesty of improvisatory performance can enable survival in the least likely of circumstances by allowing their creators to *make up, make real*, and *make do with* what they have, which at times can be only their bodies and whatever happens to be in their surroundings.

My theory of activist affordance concerns disabled lives, but it is not simply "about" or "for" disabled people. At a time when colonialist, capitalist, extractivist depletion of the world's offerings has brought life on earth to the brink of catastrophe, we desperately need nonexploitative ways of designing and making, and in particular ways that respect limits on available resources of all kinds.[15] Understood as the *art* of economizing our bodily and environmental resources, activist affordances provide one such kind of making. Activist affordances are ways of acknowledging the limits of our bodies and the environment, and of bearing "response-ability" for those limits.[16] They are matters of how to make things work within constraints. They are ways of building liveable worlds against all odds. In short, a theory of activist affordances turns disabled experiences of surviving under conditions of shrinkage and constraint into ways of living for us all. The seeming narrowness of that experience, as I will show throughout the book, can become a mode of our very survival.

Research-Creation, and Disability as Method

This book is the product of a continuous twelve-year ethnographic engagement with disability. It starts with my own experiences of living with nonapparent disability, and it continues into my engagement with disabled people and activists. It spans the different geographic locations of my everyday life across time, including Denizli, a (then) small city in southwestern Turkey; İstanbul; Florida; North Wales; Montreal; Copenhagen; London; and Montreal again. The different geographies and living conditions I have encountered in my macro/migratory movements across these sites affected my own micro/everyday movements as a disabled and (in the past) precariously employed researcher. Crucially, in each of these locations, I encountered varying meanings and valuations of disability and engaged with local disability communities (or came to realize their absence). Each site, each encounter, and each dwelling have gone into the experiential groundwork for the arguments I make. Each one was also formative for my networks, affinities, and so also for my field sites. The book's ethnographic fieldwork sites are located in Western Turkey, where I was born, raised, and spent most of my life as a disabled person; and in Quebec, where I immigrated, built a life, and became part of a growing disability community.

The theory, methods, and modes of analysis that I propose in the book have evolved both from these ethnographic encounters and from my ongoing experimentations with "research-creation." Research-creation, which also goes by the names of arts-based or practice-led research, refers to a diverse set of academic practices whose research questions "could not be addressed without engaging in some form of creative practice."[17] In my case, the challenge at the beginning of my research journey was: How do you study nonapparent disability and render perceivable the almost imperceptible choreographies of world-building to which they may give rise? I turned to visual ethnography and practiced it as a form of research-creation by deploying what I called "disability as method."[18] Disability as method names a creative approach through which research methods are informed by, modeled after, and tailored to the situated knowledges of disabled people. It involves attuning and sculpting research methods and modes of analysis to the particular ways of relating to the world that disabled living entails.

Photography and the camera in general have the notorious history, precisely in the history of anthropology, of being utilized as tools for othering and for control and containment with respect to people with disabilities and many other groups. In response, disability artists and activists have mobilized visual media to subvert and upend that tradition of representation, to "stare back" and perform, what Rosemarie Garland-Thomson calls "visual activism."[19] The design of my visual ethnographies builds on this genre and extends it to disability research through "disability as method."

In my visual ethnographic work, disability as method involved harnessing photographic and video editing technologies to seize what otherwise disappears in the ephemerality of performance, providing images of moments viewers may otherwise miss. I zoomed in on and magnified movements and gestures that might have remained too microscopic to be noticed. Whatever choreographies of survival got buried in the everyday, I sought to unveil and map through creative deployments of visual media. I used these methods to forge a form of what disability justice activist Mia Mingus calls "access intimacy," or "that elusive, hard to describe feeling when someone else 'gets' your access needs."[20] While Mingus's concept relies on direct access, putting media affordances to creative uses during fieldwork, analysis, and dissemination allowed for what I would call "mediated access intimacy." The photographs that I offer in the book provide images of my participants' "access needs" in the sense that they document and describe how they "make do" by creating activist affordances. To render perceptible the often almost imperceptible and largely ignored creations of disabled people and to bring them close to others was a process not just of theorizing activist affordances, but also of initiating access intimacy. It was a means of doing activist research, turning the camera into a "care device," as it were, a technology for "making kin."[21]

In this book I am focusing on the stories of "noncrips," so to speak, in the sense that my participants do not fit the description of "the paradigmatic person with disability."[22] Their stories do not necessarily belong to the bodies with which disability is typically associated, or the identities through which disability has traditionally been reclaimed. I have chosen them because their world is my world as well, and there is no reason *not* to start with this group. My ethnographic work primarily concerns people living with inflammatory types of arthritis that are marked by chronic pain. I also bring in the stories and everyday lives of people living with a variety of impairments, including other forms of chronic pain, depression, cancer, thyroid disease, and blindness. Many of these people appear quite able-bodied. Only a handful would call themselves disabled. A majority of them may not even be familiar with politically informed terms of identity like "crip," and I doubt that the people I visited in remote suburbs of İstanbul would even have heard of disability (*engelli* in Turkish) as a specific identity category, let alone had the choice to identify with it or not. I say have "the choice" because to identify with certain categories or not (or to consider them as fluid or reject them altogether) still requires a degree of exposure to and familiarity with identity-based discourses. And we need to take into account the fact that this exposure and familiarity may not be available to subjects whose subjection occurs outside of North American discourses, geographies, and histories from which identity politics (and its subsequent critiques) have emerged. Given these variations in the level of exposure to and fluency in politicized discourses, which can be indicative of the privilege of English-speaking, educated, networked, urban classed people and of the different local, cultural understandings and valuations of disability, I have difficulty calling my participants "crip," although the term's fluidity might grant it the capacity for such designation. I am more interested, along with Kafer, in "making room for those who do *not* or *cannot* recognize themselves in crip,"[23] and crucially, for those who are not even part of such a system of recognition. It is exactly these "nots" that I am interested in. What kind of a disability story emerges from these experiences that do *not* fit the normative narratives around disability? What do these stories tell us about disability itself? How do they complicate and "disorient" the category,[24] and multiply its becomings?

As an ecological concept, activist affordances can be used to understand the acts/arts of survival of any being who is made to live in an inherently shrunken and shrinking world. The creation of activist affordances requires neither group identification nor belonging to a category (nor even to a certain species for that matter). Activist affordances can be undertaken by any disabled organism at any place and time. I am not suggesting, therefore, that my participants' activist affordances can arise only from their particular cultural and geographic location or from some kind of "not" identity. In fact, my ecological approach does not—and cannot—take disability as "a category inherent in certain minds and bodies"[25] but instead considers it as a particular *mode of inhabiting* a constrained or "shrunken" world of possibilities. In taking this approach, I seek to join Kafer, Julie Avril Minich, and others in thinking of disability relationally, as a way of forging collective affinity. Locating disability *somewhere* would always require us to identify where that somewhere is, creating boundaries that would inevitably need to be policed. Taking up critical disability studies "as a methodology," I seek to align with Kafer's political/relational model of disability "as a site of questions rather than firm definitions."[26] Are people with rheumatoid arthritis (RA) disabled? If so, how and under which conditions? What sort of shared affinities can be found among, say, people living with chronic pain, people in wheelchairs facing a flight of stairs, people undergoing severe mental suffering, and people whose lives are debilitated by "slow violence"?[27] Can a tree, the air, or the environment itself be disabled? If so, what does it mean to talk about the disability of the animate and the inanimate? Crucially, how can the concept of affordances allow us to navigate this messy territory?

An Ethnographic Journey

Let me rewind the process of my ethnographic journey and research-creation experiments through which I came to question and trouble the traditional theory of affordances, moving toward the theory of "activist affordances"—a term that I use only in retrospect. This journey started from my engagements with autoethnography, in which I visually documented and analyzed my own daily movements. During this pilot project, I encountered specificities in my everyday movements as a person living with rheumatoid arthritis. At the time, I was fascinated with the theory of affordances for what it could offer as a theory of movement and perception. Still, it did not fit well with the movement-related specificities of the disability I live with. This incongruence led me to ask: What possible affordance could there be for me in my "ecology," when living in constant pain from joint inflammation is often so profoundly limiting? But then I also wondered: If to be disabled is to "realize that . . . the world is not [your] dance floor," as Vivian Sobchack puts it,[28] what if disabled people imagined new floors to be danced on? What would these disabled reimaginings of the world do to the theory of affordances? What if I started with my experience and adapted the theory of affordance to it?

To find answers to these questions, I engaged in a visual ethnography. Fine-tuning the methods I had previously developed, I conducted field-work in İstanbul and Quebec (2009–2010), tracing the (potential) appearances of nonapparent disabilities related to rheumatoid arthritis. I worked with twenty-three participants, whom I recruited through two local hospitals, community organizations, and my own networks.[29] I visited them at their homes and explored how they went about their everyday lives. During these visits, I filmed my participants as they undertook a series of "simple" daily tasks that I chose beforehand (such as dressing or cooking) plus any other tasks for which they had developed special "tricks." During the same visits I interviewed my participants, along with any family members and friends who were present. When we met in person, my participants and I, right from the beginning, knew that we had a shared experiential knowledge base that we could move past to more in-depth issues. I was by no means a "distanced" ethnographer, "objectively" observing the field. Our meetings were less semi- or unstructured interviews than the conversations of two longtime friends who had so much to share. But it was not only the shared experiential knowledge; the recognition that we supported each other—a recognition that we could hardly have in our routine lives, and a recognition that we have long desired and hoped for—created this space of relating, belonging, and sharing. For a group that is used to being perceived and treated as not disabled, as not disabled enough, and as too disabled, there was indeed a delight in finding that you and your group are none of these things that you are said to be in an ableist world and its rigid categories. As soon as I asked my participants about their everyday "tricks," as they often called them, or what I am calling "activist affordances," their eyes often sparkled with joy as if this was the moment they had long waited for. Of course, not everything we talked about was joyful; there were many moments of frustration, anger, and sadness and the acknowledgment of loss. Nonetheless, a process of elated exchange unfolded during which my participants shared their art/acts of getting by in the everyday with someone who finally understood these acts and who appreciated their value to their everyday survival. During the interviews our positionalities became rather fluid; at times, I was the one being asked questions rather than the one doing the asking. This means that as much as I talk about my participants' stories in the following pages, I also talk about mine. Hence the interchangeable uses of the pronouns "they" and "we" when speaking of my participants.

During fieldwork, I used the following research-creation methods. I positioned the camera to try to capture whichever affordances escaped the public gaze not sensitized to recognize them. During editing and analysis I replayed the footage, slowing it down to allow me to pay attention to the details that I may otherwise have missed (some of which I was able to spot in the moment, some only during editing). I selected clips frame by frame in order to identify where and how exactly activist affordances occurred. I then captured the images of these critical moments and juxtaposed them with what my participants said about their own movements in the moment of undertaking them, or with descriptions of the creativity that I came to notice about them later on. In my writing, I use these image/text collages as a multimodal documentation of an activist affordance that once was, of a performance that once took place. This, again, is what I mean by disability as a method of creative practice: to reappropriate the affordances of any medium for our own subversive purposes, which in this case was to capture and freeze the fleeting and micromoments of everyday survival of disabled people, and render them recognizable, archivable, and shareable.

At the end of my first fieldwork period there were questions left unanswered, and more to explore. Did the affordance-creations that I encountered in the field result from the specificities of the mobility-related disability that I focused on? Would I have found something else had I explored the lived experience of another kind of disability? What if I moved beyond the sphere of homes to public places? What activist affordances would there be, if any? To seek answers, I pushed my critical interrogation of affordances further in a second visual ethnography, using the creative methods I developed in the first one. In 2013 and 2014 I conducted fieldwork in Montreal, Canada, a city that is known to be highly inaccessible because of its harsh winters, uneven geography, and strict architectural codes for historical buildings.[30] Using participatory approaches, I collaborated with differently disabled individuals living in the greater Montreal area, filming their everyday practices at home and following their daily mobilities through public places over the course of a year. In this book I reflect on my collaborations with two of these individuals: Jérôme and Anna. Jérôme is blind from birth, and Anna has a mobility-related disability (unrelated to rheumatoid arthritis). I contacted Jérôme through the association for students with disabilities at a local university. We met as participants of the Megafone.net project at Concordia University—the Montreal leg of a worldwide digital mapping project by marginalized communities.[31] I met Anna at a conference aimed at raising awareness of disability in Montreal, where she was one of the co-organizers. Given our shared commitment to disability and access issues and the highly personalized nature of the research, we decided I would not anonymize their names. At our initial meeting, I explained to Jérôme and Anna the purpose of the project, and in line with participatory methodologies, they chose the time and place of filming. Our meetings depended on which locations, events, and time periods mattered to Jérôme's and Anna's everyday lives and movements in public places. At times we were in the metro taking the train; other times we were at home baking muffins. As I expected, activist affordances were still present, but they were not always in the places that I was used to finding them. This time, an activist affordance was not an ingenious way of putting a full mug on the table but lay in placing the tips of one's fingers on its brim in a "blind style of perception."[32] Further, I accounted for how multiple variables, including technologies and the mobilities of other humans and nonhumans, have factored into affordance-creation.

Redefining Affordances

Psychologist James Gibson proposed the theory of affordances in the 1970s as part of his broader project of framing action and perception in ecological terms, and in so doing he questioned psychology's binary thinking. "The dualistic separation of a physical and mental environment," as Edward Reed writes, "has always been one of the basic philosophical tenets of psychologists, from experimental psychologists to phenomenologists."[33] "Knowledge of the world," the field's scholars assumed, "must come from somewhere; the debate is over whether it comes from stored knowledge, from innate knowledge or from reason."[34] But what if, Gibson asked, no such source is necessary?[35] What if what we perceive is not a stimulus that needs to be processed but an always already meaningful environment? Knowledge of this environment "surely . . . develops as perception develops . . . gets finer as [the observers] learn to scrutinize . . . gets richer as they notice more affordances." But "knowledge of this sort does not 'come from' anywhere; it is got by looking, along with listening, feeling, smelling and tasting."[36]

As this brief review suggests, Gibson's ecological approach attempted to bring the body and its agency back into psychology. Organisms, Gibson argued, do not perceive their environments indirectly, through the mediation of some mental system (be it memory or input-processing), but *directly* by way of their engagements with it. Crucially, they are able to do so because *self-perception and environment perception are complementary processes.* That is, we cannot perceive the world without coperceiving ourselves at the same time. It is exactly this relation that led Gibson to the idea of affordances. If we can perceive the environment *directly* as such, he wondered, then why should not we also perceive which action possibilities it affords to us? Upon seeing a flat, rigid, and knee-high surface, for instance, I see not only the surface but also the possibility of sitting, which is embodied in its materiality. But the possibility I see at the same time depends on my embodiment: I am bipedal, sighted, of a certain body weight and scale, and possibly in need of rest at that moment. Affordances describe how actions are shaped by such emergent correlations between our bodies and the environment.

Affordances are material, relational, and emergent. But they are also objective and invariant in the sense that they are "always there to be perceived," independently of whether we actually perceive them or not.[37] This is how Gibson distinguishes his ecological approach from a phenomenological one: affordances are not the sole products of our subjectivity. They reside neither "in the world of matter" nor "in the world of mind," such that "the theory of two worlds is rejected."[38]

Finally, we do not just go about doing anything with anything in our daily lives. Things have social and "canonical affordances" that have been chosen long before us[39] and that are sustained within a habitus into which we have already been enculturated. Ultimately, affordances are historicized. Some have already been taken advantage of, others not. Gibson's use of the concept of "niche," which he mobilized to refer to a set of affordances, implicates this historical transformation of the world, setting those environmental affordances that societies have already made use of apart from those that they have not yet occupied.[40]

My theory of activist affordances begins with Gibson but takes a different path. No doubt any action of the organism is shaped by its reciprocal relations to its environment, and if the organism has survived it is because that reciprocity exists. And that reciprocity is always there, as Gibson correctly surmised. But do we all find those reciprocal relations the same way, with the same amount of effort, and thereby ensure our survival? Or do some take more labor, energy, and, in fact, some creativity to discover? What does it take to actualize an affordance? What happens on the way to this discovery and actualization? What takes place in the space between the here/the actual and there/the potential; between the niches already occupied and those that are yet to be found? These are the questions that drive my theory of activist affordances.

Describing Disability Ecologically: A Shrinking Environment

In this book, I propose that disability can be described as the shrinking of the environment and its existing set of affordances for a given body or bodies, regardless of the cause of shrinkage. I use the concept of "shrinkage" to refer to the process in which possible affordances are reduced in a given body-environment relation.[41] Shrinkage makes the field of possible affordances *smaller*. Smaller than what? In the case of a congenital disability, the field is smaller than for the normate. In the case of the onset of an illness, pain, or disablement, the field is smaller than it used to be. Shrinkage is a lessening or diminishing in relation to the scope or range that was available before for the person in pain, the person who falls ill, the person who becomes disabled. Irrespective of the differences in the starting points of shrinkage, all cases share the common denominator of having *fewer* options. The environment does not afford as many possibilities as it once did, or as it currently does to privileged coinhabitants. It is exactly this scarcity of opportunities and the exigencies that it creates that I want to capture with the idea of shrinkage.

I admit that shrinkage is a risky concept. Read too quickly, it might sound like another iteration of the social model of disability, and the first thing it brings to mind can be barriers to access. Indeed, "the cripple before the stairs," "the amputee before the typewriter," and "the dwarf before the counter" all strikingly illustrate how the barriers of the built environment shut disabled people out by design.[42] The concept of shrinkage surely involves such situations of "misfitting,"[43] but it is not limited to those, and this is the nuance I want to introduce. Differing from the social model, rights-based frameworks, and demands for access—the staples of early disability studies and movements—the idea of a shrinking world goes beyond environmental barriers and encounters of misfitting to a range of other situations, processes, and experiences in which the environment and its sphere of possible actions narrow down. The world's shrinkage can arise from bodily experiences of pain and illness that cannot be alleviated by environmental changes; lack of access despite the (seeming) presence of accessibility; regimes of debilitation; and finally, the ongoing disablement of the environment itself. Let me begin with chronic pain and disease—two areas that disability studies have been slow, if not reluctant, to analyze and theorize.[44] I then move on to discussing what I call, after Pierre Bourdieu, the "habitus of ableism," and how it reduces the world's opportunities for action in unnoticeable ways.

Of all our bodily states, Elaine Scarry writes, pain is the only one without a world-counterpart. While fear, desire, and thirst can have corresponding objects, there is no *thing* in the world outside that can match this unique bodily urgency. Pain, she writes, is utter "objectlessness."[45] But I would argue that pain still involves a relation to the world, albeit one that is negative. Upon touching a hot surface, for instance, a person feels what is called "acute pain," and—contra Scarry—that acute pain still takes, and in fact (given its essentiality to biological survival) *must* take, an object (in this case, the hot surface). Acute pain still offers an affordance, consequently, the affordance of avoiding what could bring harm. We can think of its affordance as avoidance, an "ill" or negative affordance.[46] When pain becomes chronic, such negative affordances inundate the person's space for action, making it shrink in direct correlation to the amount of pain the person experiences. The more pain you are in, the more the parameters of the environment narrow down, even (at its extreme) to the confines of a bed. From an ecological approach, chronic pain can be thus defined as the shrinking of the environment and its existing set of affordances. To experience chronic pain, I contend, is to experience the scaling down of the environment and the ever-widening distance between the body in pain and its previously available affordances.

Chronic pain's neighboring condition, chronic disease, may as well be described in similar ecological terms. Disease, Georges Canguilhem writes, "is characterized by the fact that it is a reduction in the margin of tolerance for the environment's inconstancies."[47] A sick person does not have a plenitude of *opportunities* at her disposal with which she can easily respond to and handle the fluctuations in her environment. Her already compromised immune system has reduced the biological resources her body has available to deal with an invading virus. A person with chronic kidney disease cannot *just* drink more. A person with osteoarthritic knees calculates every step needed to reach the next bus stop. The sick person does not want to "spoon out."[48] She does not want to take any chances, because her body can at any moment let her down. At any moment it can *fail*. Living in a state of precarity, the person begins to inhabit an environment that is more and more protected, more and more narrowed, so that no surprises will occur in the environment that the person is not ready to tackle. An immunocompromised person refrains from occasions of contact with the outside world (as made so much more evident in the current COVID-19 pandemic). Likewise, a person with osteoarthritis tries to minimize the walkable paths in her daily life. This is how the parameters of the existing environment diminish when living with a chronic disease.

The *constraining of the space of affordance from which an action can arise* is evident in the following, where Drew Leder reflects on a depiction by Herbert Plügge of the "reduced sense of time and space" experienced by cardiac patients:

> A landscape is viewed not as a field of possibility but of difficulties to negotiate. The ordinary sense of free and spontaneous movement is now replaced by calculated effort: one does not want to take chances. Etymologically, "ease" comes from the French word *aise*, originally meaning "elbow room" or "opportunity." This experience of world-as-opportunity is precisely what dis-ease calls into question.[49]

Amending Leder's description, I argue that chronic disease calls the existing affordances of the world into question. To experience chronic disease is to experience a shrinkage of otherwise readily utilized ecological affordances.

Shrinkage: The Habitus of Ableism

Of course, there are many other ways in which the environment contracts and becomes less reachable. A major one is related to how ableism functions as a form of habitus, that is, an "embodied history, internalized as a second nature and so forgotten as history."[50] The idea of the habitus of ableism does not focus on the social creation of disability by barriers and discrimination (as does the social model) but on how a collective system of beliefs, habits, and dispositions that are deeply ingrained in our ways of acting, perceiving, and behaving can automatically make the affordances of the world more available to some bodies/minds than to others. By the term "the habitus of ableism," I refer to an unknowingly incorporated set of bodily dispositions and skills and, necessarily, their affordances that have become established as *the* way of moving, sensing, and behaving in the world, negating all other alternatives. Take walking. Walking, anthropologist Tim Ingold writes, is a "skill" that humans get to incorporate during their development "within an environment that includes skilled caregivers, along with a variety of supporting objects and a certain terrain."[51] Walking is one possibility among many (including crawling and wheeling) in which the environment can be traversed by humans. But because the affordances that complement walking have been carved into landscapes by those that came long before us (with roads, stairs, and so on), and because walking has been endlessly repeated, normalized, and naturalized, walking comes to appear as an innate "ability" that we are all supposed to have rather than a skill into which bipedals have been "enskilled."[52] Walking, in other words, becomes normative, and so turns into walk*ism*.[53] I propose the "habitus of ableism" concept in order to capture precisely this "performative magic of the social," which renders the environment only *singularly* habitable, erasing other possibilities of habitation as those "'not for the likes of us.'"[54] Those "unlikely" habitations may be called "issues of access" (which may or may not be noticed, which may or may not be provided) or "assistive" this, "adaptive" that. But those other possibilities may only ever be add-ons in relation to the hegemony that the habitus of ableism holds over the world's affordances. Here is how we are brought to the situations of shrinking, which I explore in chapter 3, where accessibility features may exist but not properly function, where accessible spaces may be thoughtlessly occupied by those who do not need them, and where lack of access may be excused away or not given attention in the first place.[55]

A Shrinking Planet

The environment shrinks and becomes less and less available for action to certain populations because its affordances have been denied them historically and systematically and weaponized against them. As histories of colonial occupation, neocolonialism, imperialism, militarization, nuclearization, capitalist expansion, extractivist operations, environmental racism, and many other atrocities tell, the colonizer, the state, disaster capitalism, and other systems of oppression wield their power over the world's affordances—seizing, exploiting, and ultimately exhausting them. Through the control they hold over the land and its affordances, they can produce and perpetuate impairment and death through direct and explicit forms of violence, as in slavery and police brutality; and through less direct and apparent forms of "slow violence,"[56] whose attritional effects manifest only over time. We can recognize the former in how the US police, in putting Black and Brown people in chokeholds, deprive them of the most fundamental of all affordances, the air. We can trace the latter in how racial segregation and the deliberate placement of polluting industries, landfills, and other toxic sites in Indigenous, Black/Brown, and other racialized, low-income neighborhoods contaminate the air, land, and water and expose these communities to prolonged intoxication. During such attritional violence, not only are colonized, racialized, classed, and gendered subjects injured physically and psychically, as Jasbir Puar unveils in her analysis of "debilitation" in Palestine; they are left without the affordances of the land, air, water, and infrastructure and state sustenance that they desperately need to recover, survive, and thrive.[57] Debilitation can be understood as the deliberate withholding of the affordances of a land, and at times weaponizing them against its inhabitants, to the degree of making the land uninhabitable and life as unlivable as possible for them. Globalized forms of power materialize themselves as domination over the world's affordances, rapaciously utilizing, usurping, and depleting them until they produce conditions of utter uninhabitability. This takes me to my final point: the shrinking of the planet and its livability.

In this age of the Anthropocene, Capitalocene, and Plantationocene,[58] we cannot decouple the disablement of humans from the disablement of other species and their lifeworlds. All lives are entangled. All livelihoods are interdependent, as the COVID-19 pandemic has most recently proved. What many Indigenous peoples, environmental justice activists, feminist scholars of science, and climate scientists have long recognized was instantiated in a matter of months in disastrous ways. The ongoing destruction of forests, lands, and natural habitats of various species has (once more) enabled the transmission of deadly pathogens from wildlife to humans and ended up disproportionately affecting already disenfranchised minorities and impoverished regions.[59] In a pandemic world, where the direct and indirect effects of human-induced environmental degradation will only increase, we need a disability theory that goes beyond human exceptionalism and addresses the environment in all its complexity, as a matter of multispecies habitation. We need a disability scholarship that moves beyond the question of how the built environment disables people, as the mantra of the social model goes, to how humans themselves injure and disable the environment through their crippling and destructive activities of *building* and *unbuilding*—activities that exacerbate the precarity of already disabled and debilitated lives. This alternative approach, I argue, requires an *ecological understanding of disability*.

The Communality of a Shrunken Environment

I have now drawn a scratchy map of a variety of situations in which the environment shrinks and becomes less and less habitable. The culprit may or may not be an explicit form of discrimination. There may or may not be a barrier, a disease, or even an actual impairment. The disabled may or may not be human. The ecological understanding of disability that I am after is not concerned with a place to locate disability, whether it is the body or the environment or one's identity (as the binary social/medical and minority models, respectively, suggest).[60] Rather, it is concerned with the commonality of environmental shrinkage with its correspondingly contracted affordances. And it is exactly this shared shrinkage, I argue, that can offer us a way to build coalitions and to approach critical disability studies "as methodology."[61] For sure it matters where, how, for whom, and under which conditions the shrinking occurs; each occurrence of disability is geographically, culturally, historically, and materially specific, and as such requires a discussion of specificities rather than "a tendency to talk of universals."[62] Nevertheless, from the perspective of an ecological understanding of disability, disability occurs as the contraction of the environment and its existing affordances, whether or not those who are affected are categorized as disabled.

An ecological understanding of disability raises the question: At what point will the environment become so shrunken that it disables all action, all life, and how can we prevent this?

Accessible Futures

Recall that the opening of the imaginative space of performance in the face of a shrunken and shrinking world is a core argument of this book. When the environment shrinks and constrains the actions of sick, impaired, nonstandard, and debilitated bodies, it is exactly this imaginative layer of performance that falls on the "actual" world and allows us to make it afford otherwise or more precisely, as Sara Ahmed puts it, "slantwise": a generative disorientation to the "right" angles and "right" order of things.[63] Let me show you what I mean in an example. When the design of a zipper asks my fingers to perform actions that they cannot accomplish, I then bend my knees inward, exhale a big breath, and push the zipper up with the nail of my thumb, making use of only a distant potential in the form and materiality of the zipper (AS IS). In so doing, I create an activist affordance that minimizes my joint pains; that somewhat counteracts the shrinking and intolerance that the diseases I live with bring about; and that correspondingly transforms what previously was a hostile object (the zipper) into a welcoming and even an accessible one, however momentarily, ephemerally, and counterfactually.

If the odd body-object pairing that makes my pants zip-up-able were to be given a material form, perhaps it would result in self-zipping trousers or garments with magnets that are yet to be thought of.[64] If the slanted positions that Henri uses to put his mug on the table were to be contoured, perhaps it would concretize in an arthritic mug that is yet to be designed. But these future objects were already actualized, and their affordances were already foreseen in and through our improvisatory affordances. The creation in and through our bodily performances of such potential "assistive" devices *in* their absence, and the making of "inhabitable worlds" whatever their unlikelihood,[65] are exactly what *Activist Affordances* describes.

Activist affordances arise from the remoteness of ecological complementarities—affordances—between bodies and their environments: the activist affordances that disabled people enact make a given environment into a livable and habitable elsewhere. These affordances, no matter how small or modest, open up room to move, create, and live onward in the absence and distance of a more readily workable affordance. Activist affordances are inherently the products of a shrunken world that multiply its conditions of livability against all odds.

Let me bring in the story of Ahmet. Ahmet fell ill when he was about ten years old, with his feet and arms completely inflamed and swollen. He could not walk without support or do much on his own. Ahmet and his family lived in a small Turkish village in the early 1990s, where his primary school was far from his home, with only a rough country road (a *patika*—literally, "a path to be walked upon") connecting the two. I asked Ahmet if he was able to attend the school regularly. He replied: "Of course. But my dad helped me. He carried me in his arms." Ahmet's father did this every single school day, back and forth, for three years, until Ahmet had to take a five-year break from his education due to intense flare-ups.

Let me put Ahmet's and his father's story in its historical and local context. Rural 1990s Turkey lacked basic infrastructure and services, and in their absence, Ahmet's father lent his arms to be carried within, and his feet to be walked with, becoming the very affordance of what would have, in ideal circumstances, been a wheelchair, together with an adaptive public transportation system or a smooth-surfaced road on which the wheelchair could easily travel. The way that Ahmet's father met the incontrovertible need to move Ahmet's impaired body from his house to the school in the absence of an adequate and accessible transport system exemplifies exactly what I mean by the *exigency* of activist affordances.

In the current shaping of the environment we may not live in accessible spaces or have "adaptive" tools, "assistive" devices, and technologies at our disposal; we may not be readily provided with infrastructures or services that would sustain our movements and activities; we may not live in an accessible world, and perhaps we never will. (Even assistive devices cannot meet the needs of every body that might otherwise make use of them. It also seems unlikely that assistive devices for every body's needs could be made generally available, given that in the current economy, custom-made productions are prohibitively expensive.) But when an activist affordance is choreographed, it is as if "inhabitable worlds" were already built, as if such "accessible futures" already existed, except that they exist in our actions, performances, and unfinished makings, not in some concretized object or infrastructure that may or may not be available in the locations that we happen to inhabit.

In *Cruising Utopia*, José Esteban Muñoz writes, "Queerness is that thing that lets us feel that this world is not enough, that indeed something is missing." Muñoz suggests that we consider embodied queer performances as actualizations of that thing missing, as "a future in the present," as "outposts of actually existing queer worlds."[66] Following Muñoz, I propose that we consider activist affordances as the outposts of already existing accessible futures. Whichever accessible presents we have not found ourselves in, whichever opportunities we have been denied, whichever inhabitable worlds a stultifying present has failed to provide for us we make up and make real in and through our ephemeral acts of world-making that I term "activist affordances." Activist affordances are "a future in the present"—a future in which the very same environment becomes habitable otherwise. Activist affordances bring "accessible futures" into life, AS IF those futures were of the here and now, AS IF they had already arrived.

For sure, an already existing accessible world might save us from having to continually and laboriously rehearse a "danced" version of it.[67] But a fully accessible world, as I have noted, is a sheer impossibility. Access is not a competition with a finish line, which, once crossed, would complete the mission. As long as life goes on, we will keep bringing accessible worlds into life in and through our activist affordances. Crucially, as we do so, we might not have all the resources at our disposal. This is exactly why I want to elevate our acts of making to the level of performance. Because when all other means of making become unavailable, when all other possibilities of articulating our sick, impaired, and atypical bodies slip away, the improvisatory space of *performance* is always there, requiring nothing more than our bodies and our imagination. And sometimes—particularly in times of deprivation, as in the case of Ahmet and his father, and in the current state of ecological devastation that threatens all living beings—our bodies are, indeed, all we have.

The Structure of the Book

The book is divided into two parts. In part I, I go back to the original theory of affordance and then trouble it by bringing in disability and proposing the concept of shrinkage. In part II, I turn to performance and gradually elaborate the theory of activist affordances.

I begin chapter 1 by tracing the lineage of the ecological theory of action and perception and the conditions of intellectual history under which it emerged. Drawing on Gibson's theorization of affordances and subsequent commentaries, I introduce the concept of affordance, foregrounding the potential it holds for disability scholarship, disability justice, and environmental justice. Then I turn to my ethnographies to bring in a series of situations in which existing affordances of the world fail, and the environment AS IS becomes a set of constraints. Each chapter in this part addresses the varying ways in which the existing environment and its affordances may shrink. Chapter 2 focuses on chronic pain and disease. In chapter 3, I consider situations in which accessible spaces and services exist but are not actually available to particular bodies, or where such spaces and services simply do not exist because the normative environment goes unquestioned. Drawing on these encounters, I introduce the "habitus of ableism" as a concept that accounts for how the absence of accessibility *and* its existence arise from a normalized environment that privileges some affordances over others. In chapter 4, I discuss the shrinking of the environment as a corollary of colonial, extractivist, and capitalist power. Through these four interwoven chapters, part I maps out disability in the ecological terms of shrinkage as the overall consequence of the failures, denials, deprivation, and diminishing of the environment's socialized/materialized affordances.

Part II asks: What happens in the face of shrinkage? This part's six chapters bring in a range of ethnographic materials to demonstrate how the shrinking of the environment, when not a complete blockade, becomes an opportunity to inhabit that environment otherwise through the improvisation of activist affordances. In chapter 5, I build upon Scarry's theory of "making" to conceptualize activist affordances as a form of creation emerging in and through the ephemerality of performance.[68] Chapters 6 and 7 present a detailed inventory of activist affordances that become evident as participants enact and explain why, how, and under which conditions they came up with improvised solutions to the shrinkage they encounter in their everyday lives.

Activist affordances can take different forms. At times we may imagine and actualize a more hospitable world in and through our ingenious movements. At other times, when our bodies reach a limit and can no longer do things on their own, other people may enable, facilitate, or directly become our affordances (as in the case of Ahmet's father), creating a subset of activist affordances that I term "people as affordances." I introduce this concept in chapter 8 and bring in various ethnographic situations where "people as affordances" materialize (or fail to do so, for that matter). In chapter 9, I think about the cumulative effects of activist affordances over time and discuss how performance and activist affordances may persist through *transformations* in the places we inhabit, including their furniture, wardrobes, kitchens, social relations, and so on. Drawing on Diana Taylor's concept of "repertoire,"[69] I refer to this persisting power of activist affordances as "disability repertoires." Disability repertoires describe the set of everyday survival techniques that disabled people create within the very constraints and normative environments that are imposed on them. Put differently, disability repertoires can be thought of as a collection of activist affordances, like a recipe book of how to go about reinventing the everyday in the face of restraints, failures, and losses. In the final chapter, I emphasize why the creation of activist affordances is an *urgent need* and speculate about the possibilities that this form of creation and way of living may offer for saving a shrinking planet.

The Affordances of This Book

This book is not an academic exercise in creating yet another theory. Instead, it emerges from the *ethical responsibility* to understand how accessible futures can be imagined and actualized in the face of enduring constraints and how livable lives can be dreamt and brought into being against all odds. Disabled people's imaginative everyday acts are acts of *activism* that need to be acknowledged, named, articulated, and theorized in themselves because they provide an important resource for living into our future as inhabitants of this shared planet. The theorization, analysis, and investigation of activist affordances are not high-minded academic tasks but pressing social responsibilities.

Like all things, this book has its own affordances. Nancy Mairs wrote a book because she wanted to offer other chronically ill and disabled people a place in which they could recognize themselves.[70] Alison Kafer wrote a book because she desired "crip futures," that is, "futures that embrace [not erase] disabled people."[71] I wrote this book because I do not want our activist affordances—the *making up*, *making real*, and *making do*—to go unrecognized anymore. I offer activist affordances as a critical vocabulary, a theory, and a method we can use to identify, trace, and appreciate the ways in which our radical affordances—no matter how ephemeral, discrete, or momentary—*can* and *do* bring livable worlds into being. This book affords a companion to those *worlds-in-the-making*, to those accessible futures, by whomever or whatever they are being made and wherever and whenever they are being inhabited.

PART I. SHRINKAGE

1   AFFORDANCE ENCOUNTERS DISABILITY

Prepare for a bumpy journey in this transdisciplinary encounter. Cruising across disciplines and their subject matter is bound to be disconcerting. Get ready for two sharp transitions that will throw you from one discipline and topic to another. These jolts and jerks will be worthwhile, I suggest, because they offer opportunities to dislodge well-rehearsed arguments in our fields. In those very shocks we can discover ways of seeing long-standing issues and debates in ways that can better account for disabilities in terms of how they manifest in bodies and in the worlds they inhabit.

One way to describe disability is that it concerns the relation between body and environment, a concern that has long occupied disability studies. Various concepts and frameworks have been developed to address this relation, such as the social model, which attributes the cause of disability to environmental and societal barriers, and "misfit," which describes "the discrepancy between body and world."[1] But at this contemporary juncture, when the planet is facing ecological collapse and becoming *less* and *less* habitable, we need new approaches to articulate the body-environment relation—hence the two sharp transitions that will follow. I begin the chapter with a brief historical survey of how disability studies has articulated this core concern since its emergence as a field, in particular through the social model and debates about its analytic value. Then the first transition occurs: a turn to ecological psychology and its theory of affordances as a more effective account of the body-environment relation for disability studies. Then comes the second transition: I return to disability and bring in my ethnographic materials to stage an encounter between affordance and disability in which disability rubs against the standard theory of affordance. The concept of "affordance," I argue, has a significant potential for disability studies in that it can provide a nondualist and nonanthropocentric framework to address its core concerns. But for that potential to be realized, it needs to be tweaked, bent, and altered, which is what I set out to do at the end of this chapter (and what I continue doing throughout the rest of the book). Drawing on my ethnographic vignettes, I offer the concept of "shrinkage" to name the ways that disability is experienced as the constraining, diminishing, and at times complete deprivation of available affordances. It is within a shrinking world of possibilities that it becomes a *necessity* to create affordances in their physical absence, and it is precisely this necessity to create affordances, and all the *labor* and *ingenuity* that it takes to make things work within constraints, that the traditional theory of affordance omits, and that I want to account for in my theorization of affordances.

Mapping the History of "Disability" in Disability Studies and Politics

Disability activists and scholars in the Global North—and more specifically Britain, the United States, and Scandinavia—have long argued that people are not disabled as a function of their bodies; they are disabled by built environments that act as a materialized form of exclusion and discrimination. Known as the (British) social model, this argument focuses on the *social creation* of disability, which it separates from "impairment" as a bodily phenomenon.[2] Mike Oliver, the founder of the social model, defined impairment as "nothing less than a description of the body," while "disablement"—that is, the means by which disability comes into being—"is nothing to do with the body."[3] In this model the body may be impaired in its lack of limbs, but it is disabl*ed* by the lack of ramps—the failure of the society to provide access for the impaired body.[4] Disability is not the "lack" of sight, but the lack of braille; not the "absence" of hearing, but the absence of sign language.[5] Because it is social processes and barriers that cause disability, what must change is not the impaired body but the environment that the society creates for impaired bodies.

The social model has endured, proliferated across geographies, and provided the foundation for disability politics as well.[6] For example, what came to be known as the US "minority model" built its civil rights and politics of access on the understanding that "disability is in the environment," so that as disability rights activist Harlan Hahn observed, "in order for us to have equal rights, we don't have to change but the environment has to change."[7] Disabled people did not require their bodies to be "fixed" but instead needed political action in the form of improved access (ramps, parking provisions, accessible bathrooms and educational facilities, for example) and legislation to ensure its provision. This politics has culminated in the passing of the Americans with Disabilities Act, which is counted as a major success of the US disability rights movement.

While the social model clearly provided an effective way of depathologizing disability and attributing the responsibility of disablement to the society, the model also became subject to various critiques within and beyond the academy.[8] One critique came from feminist disability scholars who challenged the field's failure to consider impairment as a subject worthy of investigation in its own right, particularly because of its parochial focus on the social creation of disability, or "disability as 'all.'"[9] Grounded in the feminist refusal of the mind/body, public/private binaries, and insistence on the personal as political, these scholars argued that the body, and particularly the bodily experience of impairment, was a fundamentally political matter that should be central to disability studies.[10] "If pain, by definition, hurts," Liz Crow asks, "then how can it be disregarded?"[11] Impairment was also an important subject of study because even if the social model's goal of removing all barriers were complete (arguably an impossibility), the bodily/mental experiences of impairment, such as illness, suffering, depression, and fatigue, would remain. For these scholars the experience of impairment was not simply given; it was precisely a phenomenon that needed investigation. As Simi Linton wrote, "Impairment . . . is as nuanced and complex a construct as 'disability.'"[12] Ultimately, feminist scholars argued, a disability studies and politics that failed to acknowledge the bodily experience of impairment would be inadequate and incomplete.

A second aspect of the social model that came under criticism was not the understandable goal of depathologizing people with disabilities but the way it achieved that goal. In separating impairment from disability, the social model not only shifted responsibility for addressing disabled people's needs from that group to the society but also refused any association between disability and illness or disease: there could be nothing "wrong" with an impaired body; it was just different. But as Susan Wendell bluntly put it,

"Some people with disabilities *are* sick, diseased, and ill."[13] In truth, impairment takes many forms, some healthy, some "unhealthy disabled,"[14] and can fluctuate between these variations. A further corollary to the separation of impairment from disease or illness was that if the problem of disability lay in the environment, then treatment—and the desire or support for treatment—would only reinforce the impaired body's pathologization. But critics of the social model have argued that treatment was not necessarily a betrayal of disability politics. As Alison Kafer has cautioned, "A desire for a cure is not necessarily an anti-crip or anti-disability rights and justice position."[15] People with disabilities might seek treatment in addition to fighting against ableism exactly because of the bodily experiences of impairment that exist regardless of environmental conditions[16] or their improvement.

Further, impairments are locally experienced, shaped by the material/social conditions under which they are lived. Considering these specificities, the meaning of medical and rehabilitative interventions may differ depending on the local context in which the impairment has to be lived with. For example, an amputee woman in rural Botswana, as Julie Livingston's work reveals, may wear an "ill-fitting prosthesis" not because she embraces a deficit or a medical model, but because the device simply helps her "to farm her fields," and hence to survive.[17]

In chapter 4, I will be drawing on additional criticisms of the field's "first wave" that attend to its failure to address social differences and inequalities among bodies produced through histories of colonization and racialization.[18] For the moment, though, I want to focus on the theoretical requirements that arise from the criticisms already reviewed. These critical interventions call for what Tobin Siebers names "a theory of complex embodiment," one that would provide a means of addressing the disabling effects of the environment and factors that "derive from the body" such as pain, aging, and illness.[19] Such a theory would in turn allow for treatment as compatible with disability politics rather than as a capitulation to ableism.

This book proposes that through an encounter with disability (and, as I will discuss later on, performance), my theory of affordance offers just that. To stage this encounter requires care, as Sara Ahmed has cautioned about doing transdisciplinary work. When we borrow concepts and do not "return" them to their home disciplines, Ahmed proposes, we need to work with care. We need to first understand what it is that we are borrowing and what it enables us to do before we question or trouble the original work, shift it to another domain. Ahmed calls this consideration of the original work in its own terms "the act of following."[20] In the rest of this chapter, I follow the original theory of affordance proposed by US psychologist James Gibson. This is especially important in that the theory of affordance has "travelled light,"[21] as Bloomfield and his colleagues put it, in its transdisciplinary movements, meaning that it has been cut off from its ecological and evolutionary roots. Only after following the theory, including its roots, do I stage the encounter between the theory and the experiences of disability that I bring in from my ethnographic research.

Theories of Affordance

> The *affordances* of the environment are what it *offers* the animal, what it *provides* or *furnishes*, either for good or ill. The verb to *afford* is found in the dictionary, but the noun *affordance* is not. I have made it up. I mean by it something that refers to both the environment and the animal in a way no existing term does.[22]

When I encounter a solid horizontal surface, I see not only the surface but also the possibility of sitting, which is embodied in its materiality. I am able to see this possibility because I am bipedal, sighted, of a certain body weight and scale, and possibly in need of rest at that moment. "Affordance" refers to such possibilities of action whose actualization depends upon the complementarity between the organism and its environment. As the quote makes clear, the term "affordance" is meant to name a relation between the animal and the environment. It does not lie in, or belong to, either one alone.[23] Further, to say that the environment "offers" or "provides" an affordance to the animal is a claim not only about a property or feature of the environment but about the animal's perception of that environment as providing something that it needs or wants. The animal cannot perceive what is not already there, but what is there does not become an affordance until the animal perceives it as such. An affordance becomes perceivable as such only through this *mutuality* between the environment and the animal.

Gibson established the subfield of ecological psychology that emerged in the 1980s precisely to center this mutuality as a critical response to the field's long-standing separation between humans (whether as mind or as body-mind) and the world they share with all other organisms.[24] The field of psychology, like other modern sciences, was shaped by dualisms of Western thought and, in the case of human psychology, specifically, by Cartesian mind/body dualism. In other words, from the very beginning, the field has been trapped in the fundamental division of mental processes from the body and from the physical world. In the case of perception, ecological psychologist Edward Reed argues, available theories offer two equally problematic accounts. The first describes "embodied observers who live in isolated phenomenal worlds," while the second proposes "disembodied observers whose knowledge of physical reality is disconnected from the tasks of life."[25] In the first group the mind and body are not separate, but the human's perception creates for it a self-referential world that cannot be shared with any other. In the second, perception takes place in the mind as separate from the body, creating knowledge about the world that is useless for functioning as a body in a material reality. Gibson's "science of the animate,"[26] influenced by evolutionary theory, sought to account for human behavior as arising from the human organism's relation with an actual material world. He proposed that perception involved the nondual human mind/body and the environment together.

What Is There to Perceive?

"There has been a great gulf in psychological thought," Gibson wrote, "between the perception of *space and objects* on the one hand and the perception of *meaning* on the other."[27] Meaning has traditionally been understood to be the product of our mental operations, couched in our minds rather than in the actual material world of things. But what if, Gibson asked, it need not be so? What if meaning is already there in the very physicality of the environment that we perceive? This environment is not an abstract, geometrical space on top of which meanings need to be added. Nor do we live in a phenomenal space, the meanings of which can emerge only from our subjective experiences of it. Instead, we *live in* and *perceive* a terrestrial environment that is consequential to our actions and behaviors. The environment, in other words, is not incidental to the event of perception; on the contrary, it is at its core. This environment is earthly, grounded, and relational. It is made up not of geometrical lines, atoms, and energies, but of a triad—of *substances*, *surfaces*, and *medium*—that matters to its inhabitants. Accordingly, "substances, media, surfaces, layouts and events are what there is to perceive, that is, know directly."[28]

The Medium, Substances, and Surfaces

The medium is relational, meaning that what counts as the medium changes depending on the properties of the organism in question (the medium for humans, for example, is the air, while the medium for marine animals is water). The medium is insubstantial and homogeneous. It has "no sharp transitions" within it,[29] and this uniformity allows animals and things, including light and sound waves, molecules and particles, to move through it. In other words, the medium allows locomotion and movement along with seeing, smelling, touching, and respiration.[30] What the medium allows in terms of movement, substances forbid because they are "more or less rigid . . . more or less impenetrable by solid bodies."[31] But substances manifest a great degree of variation in their rigidity, density, strength, elasticity, and plasticity as well as in their viscosity (resistance to flow), their cohesiveness (resistance to breakage), and their susceptibility to chemical reactions. Accordingly, substances provide animals with a variety of possibilities for action: food to eat, ground to move upon, and materials with which to build and make things. The last part of the triad, the surface, is what separates the medium from the substances, and it is of great importance because the surface is "where most of the action is."[32] The surface is what touches the animal, what reflects or absorbs light and transmits vibrations. The surface is also where ecological events, mechanical actions, and chemical reactions happen.[33]

By describing the materiality of the world in terms of surfaces, substances, and mediums, Gibson was able to account for human bodies as neither separated from nor identical to the environments in which they exist. In this version of the world, perception becomes a bodily process, something like feeling into arrangements of surfaces, substances, and mediums at the interface between the body and the rest of the environment. Perceivers *actively* generate information in their engagement with a given stimulus, such that perception is an "achievement" of "a keeping-in-touch with the world."[34] The form of this in-touchness, as I explain in the following, is quite literal.

Perceiving through In-Touchness

Once the environment is described in terms of the medium, substances, and surfaces, it becomes a seamless continuity of matter. First, surfaces, as Tim Ingold points out, do not separate "materiality from immateriality" but "one kind of material . . . and another."[35] Surfaces are "interfaces between . . . for example rock and air—not between what is material and what is not."[36] Second, the medium does not indicate immateriality: "We are tempted to think of the medium, air, as being space but this misleads us."[37] The medium, Gibson writes, "might be called *room* but it is not *space*" for the very reason that "there was no such thing as empty space to begin with."[38] The environment is dense with matter, and so is the medium as a core constituent of it (whether it is the air humans breathe or the seas in which fish dwell).[39] Once we understand the medium as packed with matter, vibrations, and waves, then no hollowness can be presumed to exist between the perceiver and a world to be perceived. Between my body here and the substances over there—both separated from the medium by surfaces—there exists no emptiness but a *medium* (air) filled with particles that are more or less lighted by those surfaces, that more or less transmit vibrations from and to those surfaces, and volatile molecules emanating from and traveling toward those surfaces.

Considering that the environment is dense with matter, Gibson concludes, "we do not see the light that is *in* the air, or that *fills* the air."[40] Instead, what we perceive is *the structuring of light* by the surfaces of the environment. The medium has a materiality and this materiality is given a particular chemical, acoustic, mechanical, and optical structure by the substances of the environment from which surfaces separate the medium. Most importantly, because this materiality and its components (including lighted particles, as well as vibrations and other forms of energies) are already structured by substantial surfaces, they come to contain *information* about those surfaces. In "the sea of physical energy," at any given moment, perceivers are surrounded by "information about things that reflect light, vibrate, or are volatile."[41] Accordingly, what we perceive is *not* a stimulus as such, as traditional theories of perception assume,[42] but one that has already been structured by the surfaces of the environment. Gibson terms this "stimulus information," which is necessarily "itself environmental."[43]

Unlike stimuli, which are received by special senses that can only receive particular energy (such as the receptor in the eyes receiving light), "stimulus information" is picked up by systems operating in tandem with one another, which Gibson calls "perceptual systems."[44] In the perceiving of light, for instance, it is not only the visual system that operates. The other sense organs and their activities, and in fact the entire body and its movements, partake in the optimizing of visual information. "The stimulation of retina," Gibson argues, cannot be thought of separately "from the ocular adjustments of accommodation, of intensity modulation, of stabilization, of fixation and exploration, that determine what the retinal image will be."[45] During the act of perception, the entire perceptual system adjusts, acts, optimizes, and explores. In brief, stimulus information is not *passively* received (as in the classic stimulus-response formula) but is *actively* picked up by the perceptual systems. Crucially, perceivers are able to do so because self and environment perception always go together. The "dynamic interrelation between a living thing and its environment" is the "sine qua non" of the ecological theory that Gibson proposes,[46] and it is to this interrelation that I now turn.

The Reciprocity of Self and Environment Perception

Information about the self accompanies information about the environment, and the two are inseparable. . . . Perception has two poles, the subjective and the objective, and information is available to specify both.[47]

In the triad of medium, substances, and surfaces, the body is a substance, and like all substances, it is separated from the medium by a surface. Like all others, the body's surface contributes to the structuring of stimulus information. This means that any point of observation in the environment carries information for the perceiver not just about the surfaces of the environment but also about its body: "Information about a world that surrounds a point of observation implies information about the point of observation that is surrounded by a world."[48] In other words, organisms pick up stimulus information about the environment's surfaces that is always already imbued with information about their bodies—and more specifically, about how their bodies are positioned in relation to those surfaces.[49] We cannot perceive the world, or more precisely the incoming flow of stimuli, without simultaneously perceiving our bodily selves.[50] The perception of self and the perception of environment are, in short, complementary processes. It is precisely this mutuality that enables perceptual systems to remain *in touch with* and *tuned into* the incoming flow of stimulus information. It is also what allows Gibson to claim that organisms *directly* perceive the environment without the need for a "high-order" operation such as decoding signals or applying memories to them.[51]

An important aspect of this arrangement is that the exploratory activities (among which locomotion is but one) that perceivers engage in do not simply generate stimulus information but also cause "disturbances" in the overall optical, chemical, and acoustic structures of the medium. Each of these millisecond disturbances creates variations in the ceaseless flow of perceptual information. Gibson terms this variation "the perspective structure."[52] Precisely because the variations (or disturbances) that the perspective structure entails were instigated by their own exploratory activities in the first place, perceivers detect what remains persistent in the changing flow of stimulus information by resonating it. Gibson terms the persistent aspects of this flow "the invariant structure."[53] "Perspective structure" is caused by the exploratory activities of the perceiver, and invariant structure is created by the environment. While the perspective and invariant structures specify two different sources of information—one "locomotion through a rigid world" and the other "the layout of that rigid world"—Gibson likens them to "two sides of a coin, for each implies the other."[54] For the invariances to emerge, there has to be continuous flow of changing stimulation: "The moving self and the unmoving world are reciprocal aspects of the same perception."[55] Stimulus information inherently points both at the world and at the observer. Precisely because it does so, perceivers can tune into the incoming flow of changing stimulation in order to discover what remains the same in them. In brief, perception occurs as the detection of invariances within variance; it is a process of discovering what remains constant in an otherwise changing flow of stimulation.

Crucially, tuning, resonating, exploring, adjusting, discovering, modulating, and so on—that is, action, no matter how infinitesimal—are part and parcel of perception.[56] Perception is not a passive input-processing but an action, "an achievement."[57] Perception, in short, is not something that *happens to* organisms but something that organisms *do*.

Affordance

If perceptual systems are "capable of extracting invariants from a changing optic array," Gibson reasons, then why should they not be able to "extract invariants that seem to us highly complex"? That is, there can be not just one type of perceptual invariant relating, say, to visual perception, but "a unique combination of invariants, a *compound* invariant."[58] Perceiving, he writes, "is extracting the information in ambient light, sound, odor and mechanical contact. The invariant combinations of features . . . are what the animals pay attention to."[59] These combinations constitute an affordance—what the environment offers the animal in terms of possible actions. For example, as we see, touch, smell, and taste things, the information that we pick up about their surfaces is replete with information about their underlying substances. The texture, form, and color of a ripe apple, for example, differ from those of an unripe one because they embody different kinds of states (ripe vs. unripe), which make their stimuli materially different. This difference also necessarily enables what we can "do" with a ripe versus unripe apple, while also setting limits on our doing.

Gibson's reasoning behind affordances goes as follows: just as a persistent structure can be detected by the individual in what is otherwise a changing flow of stimulus information, the observer can also perceive all of the invariant properties of an apple's surface (including its substance, layout, texture) in the form of a single compound invariant, that is, its "palatability."[60] The surfaces of the environment structure the stimulus information, and the "compound invariant" that we perceive by way of that structuring informs us not just about the surfaces and substances but also about which action possibilities they allow in relation to our bodies. "To perceive a surface is level and solid," for instance, is to perceive that it is possible for me to walk on it, or as Gibson puts it, it "is also to perceive that it is walk-on-able."[61] Or the perception of "a break in the continuity of the supporting surface" is, as in more common language, that the ground crumbles underfoot at the edge of a precipice, or in Harry Heft's terms, the "shearing of the texture of the ground on the surface below by the edge of the surface of support." Our perception of the light reflecting off of the relevant surfaces carries for us the *meaning*: "Here is a falling-off place."[62] Note that although it is described in words, this meaning is not a matter of higher-order thinking. It is a direct *perception* of the meaning that that the surface at the edge is definitely "not-walk-on-able."

As these examples illustrate, the reciprocity of exteroception (environment perception) and proprioception (sense of self movement and position) that renders the perception of a surface possible (in the last case, the surface of a cliff) also allows the perception of what it affords (a fall-off-able place). In brief, direct perception applies not only to what the surfaces of the environment *are* but also to which *actions they offer us*. Are they walk-on-able? Wheel-over-able? Sit-on-able? Climb-up-able? Throw-with-able? Collide-with-able? Edible? The term "affordance" refers to such possibilities for action that emerge from the interlocking of multiple environmental properties that the organism perceives and has the option to realize. This option arises from the particular correlation between the organism's attributes and those of the environment. Affordances concern complementary *"relations between an animal and its environment that have consequences for behavior"* and action.[63] For example, a round, stiff object (a ball) that I perceive to fit the shape of my palm and the strength of my fingers offers grasp-ability, and its grasp-ability, together with the well-lubricated joints that connect hand to elbow, shoulder, and torso, offers throw-ability.

While the language of affordance might seem to address solely the physical body, the theoretical concept encompasses all kinds of behavior, including emotions, needs, desires, intentions, and all other affective and intellectual behaviors.[64] For example, a blanket is an environmental object that affords warmth. But if that blanket was made by a beloved late grandmother for a grandchild, it may also afford fond memories and love. So too the environment is made up not only of things and places, but also of other beings, like the grandmother for the grandchild. In fact, for humans, "the richest and most elaborate affordances" are the "mutual affordances" that are "provided by . . . other people."[65] Mutual affordances are evolutionary and socially conditioned reciprocal behaviors between humans, including social—communicative, sexual, and economic—ones.

Affordance: A Material/Relational Concept

Again, an affordance is a characteristic neither of the world nor of the perceiver but of their interrelation. It refers to a relation between organism-as-perceiver and environment, not to a property that belongs to one or the other. "There are dynamics," as Thomas Stoffregen writes, "that are unique to 'this animal if it climbed these stairs' or 'this animal when climbing these stairs,' but that do not inhere in the animal or the stair"; these dynamics inhere in "the animal-environment system" instead.[66] Affordances are, to borrow a phrase from William James, "double-barreled."[67] They point "both ways, to the environment and to the observer."[68] This means that when we perceive an affordance, we are not "perceiving a value-free physical object" first, and only then interpreting *what it could do for us*. Rather, by way of the very organism-environment reciprocity built into perception, we are "perceiving a value-rich ecological object" to begin with.[69] With the concept of affordances, we refer to the same concrete reality that we all share (i.e., the environment), but for any organism, the affordances that arise within this single physical reality are particular to the organism-environment relation in which that organism exists.

Because affordances arise from a relation in which both the organism and the environment can change at a given moment or over time, they are also always emergent rather than predetermined. When I see the knee-high, stiff surface of a bench, say, its surface is "sit-on-able" only in relation to my bodily properties and needs in that moment (e.g., I may be in need of rest, my knee is more or less the same height as the bench, and my body bends at the hip and knees, so that I can lower my buttocks and upper thighs to the level of the bench's surface and rest on it, with my feet touching the floor to support me, possibly using my arms to steady myself, and so on). A dog, among other organisms, does not have the bodily properties that would perceive in this bench the same affordance but might perceive another, such as lying on its surface. The bench might also afford step-on-ability for me in another moment, when I need to reach something on a high shelf, or my bodily pain might not allow me to perceive that as an affordance. For a person without sight, the bench's surfaces can also be bump-into-able (remembering that affordances can be "either for good or ill").[70] For a toddler, it might be climb-on-able, or for a worm, get-underneath-able. Particularities and situatedness matter for what an affordance *is*, or can be.

The fact that we need to specify the bodily and environmental components of a relation before identifying an affordance demonstrates that the concept is not only relational but, as John Sanders argues, fundamentally *ontological.*[71] That is, ontology is determined by the perception of affordance, and affordances *are* the ontology of a given organism-environment relation. Multiple affordances mean multiple ontologies. Accordingly, when we think of affordances, the environment and perceivers must be conceptualized in the broadest sense possible. As I discuss in chapter 4, this breadth will be especially productive for taking disability beyond the human.

Single Environment, Multiple Ontologies

Affordances emerge in relation to the particular properties of an organism, but they do not need to be perceived, actualized, or desired by an observer in order to exist.[72] This nuance is what prevents affordances from being reduced to a mere subjective phenomenon.[73] Affordances, Gibson notes, are not "bestowed upon" the environment by our experiencing of it. They are "invariant" and so "always there to be perceived" or available to a particular organism's perception, whether or not it engages in that perception.[74] The surface is sit-on-able, bump-into-able, or climb-over-able whether or not the organism that can perceive it actually does so, and even if the organism is not present to engage in perception at all. To give another example, "an apple is a real food object, even if it is uneaten and even if it does not afford eating to a dog."[75] Affordances exist in the environment as a host of potentialities that can be actualized by organisms with the capacity to perceive them as such. But they "do not disappear when there is no local animal to perceive and take advantage of them."[76]

Let me then put it this way: affordance refers to the offerings of the environment that exist independently of their actualizations; and, those actualizations themselves emerge *strictly from the complementarity of organism-environment relations.* The materiality of the environment is an affordance only in relation to a specific organism, while continuing to have an existence of its own. And an organism's relation with the environment may be an affordance that does not exist for another. Affordances are *"facts of the environment,"* so that while that environment may be inhabited by many perceivers, a given affordance *"can* [only] *be used by particular observers."*[77]

Affordance theory allows for plural ontologies among different organisms, but this is not based in the dualism of matter and mind, because its multiple ontologies are not simply creations of the "world of mind" separate from the physical "world of matter." The multiple ontologies do not presuppose correspondingly different environments. "There is only one environment," Gibson writes, which "*contains* many observers with limitless opportunities for them to live in."[78] The multifarious, disparate, and even *conflicting* affordances that different organisms perceive and the behaviors they enact do not either constitute or arise from multiple physical worlds. Instead, each organism's ontological "reality" is contingent on what it perceives as affordance out of all the possible affordances and lack of affordances that the single physical world offers. As we will see, this is what differentiates the world of the normate from the disabled but can also bring them together—albeit in highly disproportionate ways—under conditions of radical environmental change.

The Sociality of Affordance

How does affordance theory address social aspects of human existence such as norms, values, and ways of relating?[79] Some scholars argue that they function like any other environmental feature or property.[80] More precisely, material things (including bodies) are embedded with symbolic, aesthetic, economic, religious, and other intangible properties, as the blanket discussed previously affords memories and love along with physical warmth. In this context, R. C. Schmidt gives the example of a mug given to us as a gift by a beloved family member, which may offer a different action possibility than a mug that happens to be on the counter of our workplace, even if both mugs afford grasping in the strict sense of the term. The "gift properties" of the mug may invite its recipient to use the mug on a daily basis, while the workplace mug's properties may not.[81] Similarly, people do not just grasp and take with them whatever object they find in a convenience store because, Schmidt adds, "ownership properties" of the objects displayed in the store that are created and sustained by "all of the cultural structures (institutions of commerce, currency, other people's behaviors that breathe life into these structures)" demand that we pay for them first.[82] Again, we relate differently to a chair displayed in a museum than the chair in our living room,[83] such that although each may afford sitting in a physical sense, institutional properties of the former chair disallow what its physical properties might (outside of a human-museum relation) otherwise afford. As these examples illustrate, though we may speak of physical and social affordances as separate, in fact they never are: there are no physical properties that are not already saturated with social properties (ownability or not), and there is no social property that can be perceived without material properties (ownability *of* something).

The social, in turn, carries its own histories, and perception is socially and historically contingent. In other words, perception (of affordances) is learned through social interaction, according to the terms of a physical world saturated with social worlds and their historicity. To learn to perceive objects as graspable (throughout our developmental process) is to learn to perceive whether they are take-with-able or not, depending on where our encounters with the object take place (at home, at a store, or at someone else's place). That is, they are not simply graspable but also ownable, and only graspable-as-ownable. More broadly, our environment is such that we never encounter physical properties outside of a historical context that figures in our perception. Further, in our encounters with necessarily social environments, we as human organisms bring the whole of our past and perceptual learning process, which then also necessarily figures in the affordances that arise.

Learning to Perceive Affordances: "The Education of Attention"

Perception is not innate. Instead the infant "does *learn* to perceive."[84] Perception involves what Gibson terms the "education of attention,"[85] and as such, perception is something that is *improved* with practice. Accordingly, all affordances are necessarily learned through this education[86] because they all involve social properties. The learning also carries with it a history of learned perception that is not only our own but also transmitted to us through education. "Each object," Alan Costall writes, "has its own definite, relatively enduring meaning, which, though not independent of 'us,' transcends whatever individual transactions I might have with it."[87] This "enduring meaning" and what other scholars have called its "extraindividual" historically embedded properties establish a certain normativity or "normative structure" to affordances.[88] Costall uses the term "canonical affordances" to name the "normative character of the meaning of things."[89] The chair, he argues, does not just happen to afford sitting to sitters. Instead, the chair "is *meant to be* a chair." It is *meant to* afford sitting. Its meaning "is defined by its name, sustained and revealed within certain practices, and realized in its very construction."[90] This means that there is a certain normativity to the sit-on-ability of the chair. Similarly, "forks afford skewering food and trans-porting it to the mouth, pens afford writing and drawing, mailboxes afford sending correspondence."[91] All of these use-meanings are associated with the physicality of objects in fork-using, chair-sitting, letter-mailing, and pen-writing societies. Through the explicit and implicit influences of other people who are already skilled in the perception of canonical affordances, we learn to perceive *what things are meant to be* and/or what they afford—or are meant to afford.[92]

In taking up the ecological concept of "niche," Gibson prefigures an account of the social that subsequent theorists have elaborated. "In ecology," Gibson observes, "a niche is a setting of environmental features that are suitable for an animal, into which it fits metaphorically."[93] Whereas a single affordance might offer an animal the possibility of a single given behavior, a cluster of affordances becomes a habitat, a place with its ways of dwelling for the species—a niche that fits that particular kind of organism or animal. Gibson writes:

> There are all kinds of nutrients in the world and all sorts of ways of getting food . . . all kinds of locomotion that the environment makes possible. . . . These offerings have been taken advantage of; the niches have been occupied. But, for all that we know, there may be many offerings of the environment that have *not* been taken advantage of, that is, niches not yet occupied.[94]

While this quote does not immediately suggest that a niche has social dimensions rather than just, say, multiple possibilities for sheltering, eating, and so on, Gibson also notes that an affordance becomes valid for a species "when [the affordance] is part of a niche." Socialization, in affordance terms, takes the shape of children's growing perception of affordances not only for themselves but also for others with whom they share a niche.[95] Ultimately, based on the difference that Gibson draws between "niches that have been occupied" and "niches not yet occupied," the occupation of niches by organisms must necessarily transform the environment over time.

TRANSITION 2

Situation 1

An early spring day. After a journey of almost two and a half hours and four types of transport, my cameraman friend and I arrived at a spot on the outskirts of İstanbul in a poor neighborhood. It was pouring rain. We took shelter at a coffee shop (*kırathane*). My participant's son, as previously arranged, came to pick us up in his van. After a short bumpy drive, we arrived at a farm-house. The sprawling farm was barren after the winter, with leafless trees and bushes, buckets dangling on their branches. We went into a house furnished with a few basic items. Arif Amca and his sons welcomed us with excitement, and upon noticing our soaked clothes, quickly ushered us into a warm living room.[96] They immediately served us tea and biscuits and gave us slippers to warm us up. We sat around the burning stove, drank tea, and began talking about illness, pain, and life. Arif Amca is a devout man who visits his farm-house often to spend time in nature with his pets and to read the Koran, which he said takes his mind off of his pain. Arif Amca was in his sixties or seventies and said he had been living with this agony (*ızdırap*) of various diseases and disability since 1971. He had undergone four surgeries and suf-fered three episodes of gastrointestinal bleeding. He had been diagnosed with rheumatoid arthritis in 2006 and experienced periods of intense pain. He told us he had already taken pills to be in good enough shape to welcome us. Whatever "good enough" meant for him in those moments, he described agonizing pain that stretched throughout the night and day:

> For example, at night, you lie in bed, I pull the duvet, and when turning around, the duvet falls, and I cannot stay still because of pain. If I wake up around three thirty, four thirty, or five a.m., because of medication side-effects, I can never go back to sleep. Today, it was either ten or fif-teen minutes to five a.m. I have been awake since. Even the bed feels like thorns to me. I mean, I cannot even rest.

Situation 2

From the author's pain journals:

> Fluffy sheets covering my body at night feel like a slate of iron that my arms feel too weak to lift. The toilet paper feels like a stone to roll, pull and manipulate. Sleep is the most limitless of all actions. But every position, every move hurts. I do not move. It still hurts. All I can afford to do is to breathe. Even that. Breath. It hurts.

Situation 3

I was interviewing Sevim at her home in İstanbul, together with her hus-band. Sevim, a tall well-groomed lady in her early fifties, has had rheumatoid arthritis for the last twelve or so years. I asked her what type of toilets she preferred, knowing that in Turkey, toilets are typically squat and hardly ever accessible. She answered:

> Seated wc. Squats are a no-go. When I go for tests at the clinic [where the toilets are squat], we look around and ask people, "Please do not go in," and then my husband comes in to lift me up. . . . Once in Tekirdağ [a city in Northwest Turkey], there was this woman who used to be a colleague of my husband's. She asked, "Would you like to go for a bit of a walk?" We walked around, grabbed a bite, and at some point, I had to go to the toilet. We went inside an arcade, and she said, "Oh, no these are all squat my dear. So we either go home . . ." I said, "Well anyway, let me give it a try." I went in, sat down [squatted] and I could not stand up again. The poor girl was waiting by the door. She waited and waited, and in the end, she called my name. I answered, "Oh dear, I cannot stand up." She said "Oh, why didn't you tell me!" and came in. You know, there was no single thing to hold onto for support. There was nothing on the walls. It was simply impossible to stand up. I was demoralized. I told my friend to lift me up. Poor girl came inside, she held my two hands and lifted me up.

Situation 4

On a beautiful sunny spring day, I accompanied Anna as she left her home and drove to the university where she was studying at the time.[97] Anna was in the driver's seat, with me filming from the back seat. We entered an urban campus with some Victorian-style buildings. As we drove through roads cluttered with trucks, construction machines, site fences, and barbed wires, Anna complained about the increased amount of construction on the campus and how it had been taking up disabled parking spaces lately. She said this in quite a gentle tone for someone who had been affected by it routinely. "I often have to call Parking Services and ask them if I can park in a different location because the handicap spot is taken. These are the real problems with parking on campus," she said, and while smiling added, "You'll get to experience that too." It turned out that Anna was right. As we approached the building where she was supposed to hold her office hours, Anna noticed that the disabled parking spot was already taken:

> Normally I park where that car is there. But then also, they have this, like, um, they have food trucks, which, like, is really nice for the students, . . . but then that [the space where the food truck is parked] used to be,

like, a space that I could park in if someone was parked [in the disabled parking spot] but now I can't park there [either]. So, I usually try and find, um, like, the closest space that is out of the way. It's not normally a parking spot here [the awkward spot where we temporarily parked]. But I think that cars can get past me, so I just kind of park here and call Parking Services and tell them.

With the speakers on, she dialed a number. A woman's voice answered: "Parking Services."

Anna: Hi, I'm a student that has handicapped parking on the downtown campus.
The woman: Anna?
Anna [smiling]: Yeaaah.

The woman's immediate recognition of Anna, a student that she had never met in person, was enough proof to understand how many times Anna had encountered problems parking on campus before.

Having gotten the approval of Parking Services, we left the car where it was and walked toward a big building. From our previous interviews I had a rough idea about what kinds of environments could be troubling for Anna because she had once told me: "I get really nervous in big crowds. Because, like, I have issues with balance, and with, like, standing in one spot for a long period of time, um, without, like, any support. So um, like, I guess in big crowds I kind of get nervous that someone is gonna, like, knock into me. Or that I'm just gonna be, like, stuck there, and I won't have anything to, like, hang onto for support."

We entered the building. I followed Anna with the camera as she walked through a crowded corridor. People (presumably students), carrying their bags, drinks, and coats, walked past her on both sides. Some, engaged in conversations, walked side by side even though the space was narrow. Anna managed to walk through this minefield without losing her balance. She climbed a flight of stairs; reached an elevator and took it up; walked through a rather long corridor and arrived at a different segment of the building; took a second elevator (this time down); and arrived at a new level, from which she passed through another corridor cluttered with cleaning buckets and wall-mounted tables with their chairs on the floor. We finally reached an old wooden door with some posters on it. This was the room where Anna was supposed to hold her office hours that day, and yes, the circuitous route we had taken was the shortest one. As Anna approached the door with a five-digit pushbutton lock on top of a round, goldish-metal doorknob, I asked:

Arseli: Do you have problems opening the locks?

Anna: Sometimes . . . [*she pauses as she enters a code, turns the knob, and pushes the door, but it does not open*] like right now, in a frenzy.

She tried again and again, first entering the code and then turning the doorknob forcefully. The door did not open. Positioning her hands differently, and with many "arghs" and "uhs" in between, Anna kept trying and trying in vain. At some point, she started doubting herself: "I'm also . . . I'm trying to think, do I have the right number?" She entered the code and tried turning the knob once more. She took her phone out of her pocket and scrolled down a few seconds to find the code. Once she confirmed that the code was right, Anna continued trying. The same cycle repeated again and again: enter the code, turn and turn the knob, and push the door to no avail. "Why is it not working?" Anna muttered disappointedly. "I cannot get the job done!" Frustrated, she gave it another try, this time by pressing the buttons very slowly and holding her finger on each, as if with more time they would have less trouble understanding her. As this attempt also failed, Anna burst out, "I don't know if this is me or the door!" She turned the doorknob one more time in vain, and with the exhausted voice of a defeated soldier, she murmured, "Oh . . . is it closed?" At that point, I offered to help. The footage stops as I shift from filming to helping Anna. It took us about five minutes until Anna somehow finally managed to open the door. I do not recall how many times I myself tried opening the door. Anna's hands and my hands were equally refused by the doorknob that knew nothing either of her impairment or of my arthritic joints and pain.

Kinds of Affordance?

Because Anna was eventually able to open the door, can we, by that very fact of accomplished action, assume the presence of a body-environment reciprocity, an affordance? How can the traditional theory of affordance account for all that labor that it took Anna to turn that doorknob again and again before finally being able to open the door?

In each of the four situations, impaired bodies are part of environments—a bedroom, clinic bathroom, office—in which actions are necessary. Humans get into bed, go to the toilet, unlock the door. Affordances that offer the possibility for such actions are perceived by each of the four of us as they arise from the relations of body and environment: human-sheet-bed, human-toilet, and human-hand-lock-doorknob, respectively.

We could say, alternatively, that in each situation there is no affordance. The beds and sheets do not offer the action of sleep, the squat toilet does not offer evacuation and exit, and the door does not unlock in a reasonably efficient and timely way.

These are the options that the existing theory of affordance allows: *either* the presence *or* absence of affordances. The theory accounts for the complex relation of these four particular human "bodyminds" with similarly particular environments,[98] as well as for the perception of different affordances in each case, and the enactment of different behaviors and actions that correspond to those affordances. Affordance theory can also account for the absence of the affordances that would make other behaviors possible. But it does not have any way of accounting for actions and behaviors that take place yet correspond to affordances whose possible behaviors or actions require enormous amounts of *effort, endurance,* and *ingenuity* to be realized by impaired humans. This is the first friction that has emerged from the encounter I have staged between affordance theory and disability. It tells me to find a way to account for these seemingly partial or incomplete affordances—affordances that don't work smoothly or according to some notion of adequate time and effort—and especially to account for all of the labor, effort, endurance, and ingenuity, that sometimes include collaboration—that these affordances require to be perceivable at all.

Staying with the friction that has arisen mainly with regard to rheumatoid arthritis–related impairments, I turn to the second friction, which concerns a particular feature of those impairments, namely that they come and go, change across time, and (unless the disease is fully controlled) progress over time. For one person, progression may happen within a matter of days or weeks, for another across a lifetime. But eventually one ages with rheumatoid arthritis and, hence, into disability. Along the way of gradual disablement, active inflammation may follow remissions, and relative stability can turn into intense flare-ups. That is, impairments are not necessarily static and definite, nor are relations of impaired bodies to their environments.

The theory of affordance addresses children's learning as a process that develops across time, but otherwise there is no discussion of how the concept of affordance works when bodies can change over short and long periods of time, and sometimes idiosyncratically, erratically, and unpredictably. In kinship with earlier feminist critiques of the social model as inadequate to the aspects of impairment that could not be addressed by the removal of barriers, I suggest that this variability/unpredictability that can take shape within the "same" impaired body cannot be captured by the traditional theory of affordance. This is because that theory does not engage with time. Nor does it distinguish among the different amounts of labor and creativity needed to actualize a particular affordance.

To address variability across time I offer the concept of "shrinkage," meaning that as the body's impairments shift—changing, deepening, spreading—previous affordances no longer offer anything useful. Shrinkage names the ways in which affordances can diminish over time, under conditions of impairment. Shrinkage also captures variability in labor and creativity exerted by more- and less-abled bodies in the actualization of an affordance. In other words, in making affordances and disability meet each other through the term "shrinkage," I am concerned with articulating the body-environment relation in *comparative* terms rather than as an either/or formula. Traditional affordance theory focuses on the *moment* of encounter between the body and the environment, where an affordance either exists or doesn't, and where—using Rosemarie Garland-Thomson's terminology—we can only "hope" to find either a "fit" or a "misfit."[99] I suggest instead that we think of affordances in *processual* and comparative terms. This requires us to ask, for instance, what happens to the affordances of the environment when one falls ill, or when one's disease and disability progress further and further. What affordances are available to a disabled person *as compared to* the affordances of her non- or less-disabled coinhabitants in a particular place at a specific point in time? My answers are, respectively: affordances shrink, are shrinking, and have shrunk.

Shrinkage

In this book I am focusing largely on mobility disabilities, specifically those related to rheumatoid arthritis. This is evident already in the situations I have presented, which in turn shape the questions I raise about affordance theory. Still, the irritations that arise as affordance encounters disability suggest that affordance theory can be torqued to effectively address the labored and ill-fitting affordances that arise for a broad range of impairments—those that involve a living being who is sick, impaired, in pain, debilitated, mad, or otherwise disabled.

In this part, I mobilize the concept of shrinkage to articulate the conjuncture of disability and affordances in an open-ended, nondualist, and nonanthropocentric way. While the bulk of this book elaborates affordance theory through RA-related disabilities, the concept of shrinkage and its ecological foundations also extends its usefulness to other disabilities and other ecological issues.

Disability, I argue, can be understood in affordance theory's ecological terms as the shrinkage of the environment and its existing set of affordances, *regardless of* the cause of shrinkage. By shrinkage I mean the shrinkage of the available affordances, of the opportunities made available for action. The reasons for shrinkage might differ. It may be that a person in a wheelchair is facing a flight of stairs. It may be that a diabetic person can no longer benefit from the affordances of a certain type of food. It may be that a person is in such pain or so depressed that she is not able to get out of bed. It may be that there are so many sensory stimulants around that a neurodiverse person needs to retreat to a secluded place. It may be that a pandemic hits and populations have to "confine" and go into "lock-downs" for months. As these examples illustrate, the "who or what," "why," "how," and "how much" of the shrinkage vary. But the fact that the environment affords *fewer* possibilities of action (as compared to the normates, to the neurotypicals, to the times prior to the onset of illness, to the prepandemic or pain-free days) does not change. In the experiencing of disability as shrinkage, what the environment affords diminishes *in comparison* to [x]. The environment becomes a *less* habitable place than [x], whatever [x] may be (what the environment once used to afford, or what the environment now affords to the non- or less-disabled). This commonality of "fewer" and "less than" is exactly what I wish to capture by defining disability as a form of ecological shrinkage.

Because shrinkage shifts our focus from objects/subjects to processes and comparisons, it can enable us to apply disability as a framework and a methodology, rather than as an object/subject of study. We can think of shrinkage as a way to practice critical disability studies "*as* methodology,"[100] as Julie Avril Minich advocates (see also chapter 4), rather than as a methodology *in* and *of* critical disability studies. Shrinkage can perhaps be a way for us to foster coalitions across variegated experiences, processes, and states of living that may or may not be recognized as disability. While these variations are extensive and certainly beyond the scope of this book to address, the following three chapters consider some of them, including the embodiments of chronic pain and disease, particularly the kind of less obvious and tangible forms of impairment that makes it harder to refute the negativities, losses, and restrictions that may come with it (chapter 2); the daily realities of inhabiting an ableist habitus, which cannot simply be remedied by the removal of barriers (chapter 3); and species that are losing their habitats and, ultimately, a planet that is literally melting away (chapter 4).

I have pain in my joints.
Because pain happens to be in my joints, at the exact place that allows me to move,
I cannot move without being conscious of my movements at the same time.
I cannot act in the world without being aware of that world, of its surfaces and substances, of
    its weight and textures.
I would call this "the bodily cost" of doing even the simplest of actions.
The bodily cost of lifting a coffee mug to your mouth;
the bodily cost of putting on your socks;
the bodily cost of turning the key in the lock;
the bodily cost of hugging a friend.
And even, yes, even the bodily cost of pulling the feathery sheets over your body
    while sleeping at night.
—Arseli Dokumacı, pain journals

Pain can be many things. Pain, Ronald Melzack and Patrick Wall write, entails "different, unique experiences having different causes, and characterized by different qualities varying along a number of sensory, affective and evaluative dimensions."[1] There is physical pain, mental pain, emotional pain.

While each of these kinds of pain can be experienced on its own, different kinds of pain can co-occur and affect each other to the point of being indistinguishable from one another.[2] Some forms of pain are known to be utterly aversive and negative, while others may be at least partially positive, beneficial, and "even 'desirable.'"[3] There is pain that brings great torment, which one seeks to avoid at all cost. There is also pain that one takes pleasure in, and willingly undergoes, as in masochism.[4] Pain can be something to be "saved from," but also something to be "saved through," as in religious rituals, spiritual practices, and rites of passage.[5] To endure pain can therefore be an act and a spectacle of devotion at once. In durational performances, pain can also be the artwork in and of itself. Pain can be "a passive state" of suffering but also "agentive," as an "action itself" (not to mention that suffering itself can also be actively handled, "without passively sinking into it").[6] Pain comprises many kinds of experiences and many different responses, meanings, and values linked to particular material, historical, and social conditions.[7]

In this chapter I focus on "chronic pain," which is pain to be *lived with* exactly because it is chronic: it endures over time. But rather than focusing on what chronic pain *is* (and like all pain it is many things), I am more concerned with what chronic pain *does* when considered in terms of affordance theory. In this case, pain is a quality or condition of the body. How does pain enter into the body's perception of the environment's affordances when the body from which that perception emerges is a body in persistent pain? What happens to affordances, in other words, when the environment is inhabited *by* a body in chronic pain?

To address these questions, I begin with conceptualizations of pain from Elaine Scarry and Drew Leder. Scarry identifies two main qualities of pain: 1) its capacity to unmake the world, and 2) its capacity to push one into creative action.[8] Because chronic pain is a subset of pain as a general category, these qualities accrue to it as well, albeit slightly differently. In this part, I focus on how chronic pain does not "unmake" the world, as Scarry would claim, but *shrinks* it. In part II, I turn to chronic pain's capacity to generate creativity, specifically the new livable worlds that are brought into being from within the shrinkage.

Pain: A Negative Affordance

What is pain—the painful body—in the dynamic of affordance? In *The Body in Pain*, Elaine Scarry argues that all of our physical and emotional states, all of our perceptual capacities and needs, all of our bodily events, claim a counterpart in the world, *except* the state of pain: "We do not simply 'have feelings' but have feelings *for* somebody or something. . . . Love is love of *x*, fear is fear of *y*, ambivalence is ambivalence about *z*."[9] We see surfaces, we smell odors, we hear vibrations, we touch textures, we taste substances, we breathe air, we desire or need something. All of these actions (desire, need, sensing, etc.), or the transitive verb forms that we use to name them, must take *objects*. Pain, on the other hand, as Scarry tells us, is just pain. It has no object; it "is not 'of' or 'for' anything—it is itself alone."[10] It does not reach out beyond itself to anything else. There are no words, no things, no symbols or events that can reciprocate this bodily state. Pain is a condition of utter "objectlessness."[11] At the same time, pain is "the very concretization of the unpleasant, the aversive."[12] It negates everything that is not itself so that "the very content of pain is itself negation."[13]

Because affordances owe their emergence to a particular organism's perception of the environment it encounters, the definition of pain as negation would seem to suggest that a body in pain perceives nothing, affordance or otherwise, outside itself. This body is not just without an affordance in one or the other environment (which might be true of any body). Instead, its environment is utterly affordance*less*. Pain becomes the antithesis of affordance because it would seem to insist on the absence of relationship altogether; it would negate all possibility of affordance.

Though it may be that pain has no counterpart in the world, this does not mean that it has no relation to anything in the world. To be in relation to another as counterpart is a positive relation, which is to say one of connection. But there are also negative relations, or relations of aversion. Put differently, while pain itself does not take an object, the body does have an aversive relation to pain. It hurts. Pain gives discomfort. But pain is also, as Scarry puts it, "an immediate sensory rendering of 'against,' of something being against one, and of something one must be against."[14] It produces a relation of separation between "one" and the "something" that is "pain" (the pain I feel in/as my body). So too, Scarry writes, pain "cannot be felt without being wished unfelt."[15] Pain is so essentially aversive, so "alien" and so much "against" oneself, that it "must right now be gotten rid of."[16] In the same moment that we feel pain we wish it were gone, so much so that, for Scarry, pain is both the message that harm has been or is being done and the imperative to get rid of that harm, or what Leder calls a "*telic demand*" to escape it.[17] The very aversiveness of pain pushes us into action: we must *avert pain*.

What might all of this have to do with affordance, or how can we understand it in those terms? In Scarry's and Leder's formulations, pain produces a relation of separation between "one" (me) and the "something" that is "pain" (the pain I feel in/as my body). These formulations require a subject who is in some sense *not* the body, or not the experience of pain. But affordance theory precisely refuses such superordinate abstractions. Instead, the body perceives the environment's affordances directly through its perceptive capacities. When the body experiences pain as a result of contact with some aspect of the environment, avoidance arises as a possible action, that is, the action of *moving away*. That is the very meaning of affordance: the environment affords the organism a possibility for action of one kind or another, which may engender anything from survival to death and everything in between.

Remember that an affordance can be positive or negative ("for good or ill," in James Gibson's words),[18] and that while a positive affordance provides some kind of support to the organism, a negative one affords something that is detrimental to its existence. When we feel burning pain at touching a hot skillet, we commonly withdraw from the hot plate immediately, avoiding a degree of injury that we might suffer if we did not move away. When I (as a person living with rheumatoid arthritis) feel the unpleasant friction in my joints brought on by standing up in the same position for a while, I am engaging in the act of perceiving pain in my particular body, at the same time that I am perceiving a particular aspect of the environment—the hard floor— associated with that pain. Together, these perceptions make up the perception of a negative affordance, something like a "painfully-stand-on-able hard floor." Some action to avoid the hard-floor-pain necessarily arises from the affordance precisely because it is negative, or aversive. Moving my legs to switch to another position is a kind of avoidance. Though it is a slight movement, this action can change the body-environment relation so that it affords me not a stand-on-able hard floor but a somewhat-less-painfully-stand-on-able hard floor, at least for a while.

More broadly, the experience of pain in affordance terms involves pain and environment as objects of perception that together constitute a negative affordance characterized by its "pain-make-ability." Negative affordances give rise to avoidance in a variety of forms. The experience of pain in the scenario functions as a warning signal that at one level or another, the organism's survival is at stake. At the same time, the avoidant action—the moving away from pain—that arises from such an affordance may transform the existing elements of body and environment into a new relation that provides a more hospitable affordance (a somewhat-less-painfully-stand-on-able hard floor), however temporary or slight it may be. Avoidance can arise as an action of moving away and as a transformative activity oriented toward alleviating or even eradicating pain.

What is perhaps most important about this formulation is that it exposes the ableism of affordance theory itself. In accounting for pain in the affordance scenario, it becomes clear that the nonpainful body functions as the unmarked standard for affordance, against which the painful body must be laboriously accounted for: it is necessary to warp the theory so that pain becomes an object of perception along with the environment. What is taken for granted, remaining unmarked in affordance theory's ableism, is the body as always already "able." "The body" or "the organism" is taken for granted as having characteristics of ability, which is to say that they remain unmarked.

Affordance theory posits that an organism perceives only those affordances (whether negative or positive) that are significant for its particular body. While these affordances may exist in the environment, they come into being as such only as the organism perceives them. The importance of the organism's particularity would seem to account for bodies in all of their diversity. But affordance theorists tend to consider affordances in terms of how particular environmental features accord with or negatively affect a generic—meaning assumed able-bodied—(human) organism. They tend to mark the environment while leaving the body unmarked. For example, a hard floor might be described as a stand-on-able surface, taking for granted a body that is able to stand. This is the case even though—or maybe because—the concept of affordance as a body-environment relation seems to account for the particularity of both the body and the environment: a body does not perceive an affordance unless it is an affordance *for* that particular body. And yet accounts of affordance do not describe a body's particularity as a factor in that perception. Instead, the able body functions invisibly as a general or universal body, and it thereby exerts a normative force in the theory. In this way, affordance theory contributes to what I call the "the habitus of ableism" (see chapter 3).

Clearly, the alternative to affordance theory's ableism (and perhaps to many other ableist approaches) is to describe bodies and environments in the body-environment relation as particular—to leave no body unmarked— and to consider the body as active in that relation, just as the painful body (of mine) is active in what I have described. As is often the case for the privileged category in a social hierarchy, the able body is marked by its ease and the ways in which this ease appears to be simply given, rather than something that is actually a historically and socially conditioned attribute. A radicalized affordance theory would need to disrupt this order of things by providing an account of bodily ease as well as of impairment in body-environment relations of affordance. For example, in the case of the relation between a body with pain*less* joints and a hard floor, it would be necessary to include the body's lubricated joints as an active element in the affordance. The affordance that would be named a "stand-on-able hard floor" within an ableist approach would become something like a "painless-stand-on-able hard floor." It would exist alongside other affordances perceivable by different bodies, such as the "painfully-stand-on-able hard floor" detailed in this section.

When Pain Becomes Chronic

> *Arif Amca:* The pain in my shoulders . . . I mean this excruciating pain (*dehşetli ağrı*) when it is there! Swelling! Look [*pointing at his swollen hands*], it [the swelling] started to go down by itself, it is going by itself now, diminishing. But when that pain comes, it feels like it is wearing me down.
>
> *Arseli:* Do you feel like lying down then?
>
> *Arif Amca:* No, not at all. I don't feel like lying down. Not lying down. I should walk, I should do something so that it [the pain] would go away from me. . . . When that pain strikes, what can I tell you [*pauses in silence, with his eyes fixed*]? My mind goes in one direction [*makes a swift hand gesture, as if he is losing it*].
>
> [*Later, during the same interview*]
>
> *Arif Amca:* Last year I was better than this. But this year I am not good. I intend to water the garden, with the hose, the flowers and all. The act of pulling the hose, oh my God! Once you release it, I am dying of pain!
>
> *Arseli:* What other things bother you?
>
> *Arif Amca:* My pain, nothing else. Pain!

Arif Amca does not want to lie down when the pain comes. He feels the need to walk. He feels the need *to do something* so that the pain will go away. But pain strikes. Over and over. It gets worse over time. Pain resists its telic demand to "be gotten rid of." When pain keeps coming back as in rheumatoid arthritis, or when it never goes away, it becomes something else: "bad pain," "pain-disease,"[19] or what I will from now on refer to as "chronic pain." The medical definition of chronic pain is "pain that persists or recurs for more than 3 months."[20] Chronic pain differs from acute pain in its *staying power*. How does the *chronicity* of pain affect the perception of affordance?

A Shrinking World of Possibilities

During my fieldwork in Montreal, a participant, Mariana, was showing me how she usually cooked. She took out an onion, a pack of bacon, and some canned food. (Mariana and her disabled husband were living in the basement of an apartment in a low-income neighborhood without much income, and I thought this was probably the food that they could afford—a point that I return to in chapter 6.) After peeling and cutting the onion with much difficulty, Mariana began slicing the bacon. She had to pause a few times because the movements were painful. During one of these breaks, she explained that the force needed to cut with the knife was very hard on her inflamed wrists. Indeed, each hand's back-and-forth movements was accompanied by frowns, grimaces of pain, and exclamations of "ouch." I reminded Mariana a couple of times that she could stop altogether. But she went on. Perhaps it was pride, perhaps it was her generosity, or perhaps it was something else.

She went on until it became impossible to ignore the pain. She had to let go of the knife, extend her arms down, and shake them a bit—movements I recognized from my own life. Whenever I feel my joints have "frozen" because they have been in a certain position for a while, I have to shake them to "unfreeze" them. After shaking her arms, Mariana brought both of her hands toward her chest, gently rubbing them against each other. Her unbending wrists looked stiff as a board. These movements show the bodily cost of preparing a meal when your body is inflamed and in constant pain.

In another participant's kitchen, having finished peeling the potato I gave her, my participant says: "After each potato, I have to do this [*forces her right hand to switch from the closed position it was in while holding the knife, to an open position, and shakes her hand afterward*]. Because it [*keeping her hand in the fist position while holding the knife*] is tough, eh! So, I have to do this [*forces her hand to open*]." Pain not only interrupts the undertaking of the action but also requires further movements following its completion, such as forcing one's hand to open after peeling a potato.

Many of my other participants with rheumatoid arthritis told me about instances in their daily lives when they were unable to open water bottles, cut, chop, slice, peel, or otherwise prepare food, or bring it to their mouths, or even to chew. "Like, one time," a participant recalled, "I went to a restaurant and I wasn't able to, um [*points at her jaw*], eat my steak. It [her jaw] was not working." Another interlocutor told me of a similar instance:

You know, like, when you eat soup and you have to extend your chin forward [*imitates the microgesture*]. Oh, my God! That's very hard. Sometimes I forget, and I'm, like, after [the] second or third [time of trying the same gesture]. Ah man [*grimaces*]! I forgot to be careful and the pain is there, that's it. That's not gonna go anywhere.

Another interlocutor remarked,

What I am afraid of—I'm afraid of shaking people's hands since I have this. . . . Because some people shake very strong. And a couple of weeks ago . . . we were going out for drinks with friends, and this lady, she knew a lot of people there. So, this gentleman came and [*imitates the man extending his hand*], "Oh, nice to meet you" and . . . he really squeezed my hand hard and I jumped. I was so embarrassed and he was like [*imitates the shock on the man's face*], looking at me like, "What's wrong?" And I said, "Oh, I just have problems."

An elderly interlocutor, with some sense of regret, told me that she cannot even hold her newborn granddaughter in her arms because the action is too painful. It was not only actions such as cuddling, hugging, shaking hands, and chewing but also sleeping—the supposedly least strenuous of all human actions—that could be painful for my participants:

Last summer, it was really bad. I used to wake up in the middle of the night constantly two, three times because the pain was so bad on one hand [*points at her hand*], it would wake me up. . . . Just the pain wakes you up. It's like a throbbing pain [*imitates throbbing*], it wakes you up. It's just, you can't [do anything].

In the case of chronic pain, the experience of pain in one instance affects the capacity to withstand pain in those that follow. As pain accumulates, it grows exponentially. Chronic pain hurts and continues to hurt. It spreads from one movement to another so that at some point, one cannot even *breathe* without *pain*. In affordance terms, every bodily state of pain whose corresponding affordance gives rise to the behavior of avoidance *shrinks* the space within which other affordances can come about. The sit-on-ability of a chair, the sleep-on-ability of a bed, the drink-with-ability of a spoon or a bowl, and many other affordances that in the traditional theorization assume an able body become affordances *with varying levels of* pain and degrees of restriction.

Affordance is less a matter of being negative or positive (or "for good or ill," as Gibson suggests)[21] and more a matter of a *ratio* between negative and positive. This is particularly the case for the kind of chronic pain caused by mobility-related diseases such as rheumatoid arthritis. When the experiencing of each tiny daily movement is painful, it gives rise to a tremendous effort and colossal negotiation *to avoid pain.* There is some positive affordance in this encounter, or there would be no impulse to move at all, but the degree of negative affordance is also extremely high, making the ratio of negative to positive high as well.

Echoing Scarry, Leder writes that pain seizes our attention in a way no other corporeal experience does, to the extent that "in the face of pain, one's whole being is forcibly reoriented," and "the new world into which we are thrust by pain has a constricted aspect."[22] That is, as an organism perceives more and more negative affordances for its painful body, its world becomes smaller. Put another way, the continual behavior of avoidance that arises as negative affordances proliferate increasingly constricts the world that the body in pain can inhabit. The world shrinks.

It is precisely this *constriction* that becomes clear in my interlocutors' accounts. Drawing from their experiences as well as from my own, I propose that chronic pain is the experience of shrinkage: a diminishing environment, a contraction of the positive affordances, and the expansion of the negative affordances that one may have experienced before the onset of this pain, so that the space of action comes closer and closer to the body itself.

Chronicity of Pain, and Chronic Disease

Chronic disease and chronic pain oftentimes co-occur,[23] as in the case of rheumatoid arthritis and many other diseases. But there also are chronic diseases without chronic pain (such as HIV and diabetes, provided that they are well controlled), and chronic pain without chronic disease (such as intergenerational trauma and lower back pain). Thus, when I address the chronicity of pain and chronic disease together in this chapter, it is not because they overlap at all times but because their respective affordances constitute *shrinkage* with respect to a normative space of action.

To suggest that under conditions of chronic pain and disease the environment shrinks can seem to assume an understanding of the environment as static, in relation to which the body experiences a reduced set of affordances. But as Tim Ingold suggests, the environment is not even a thing that is or is not static; it is "a total movement of becoming," of change, "which builds itself into the forms we see."[24] The environment as becoming is an environment that is alive, continually moving and transforming. It is under continual construction due to ecological events such as fire, snow, waves, and winds, "thunderbolt and hailstorm, rabid bat, small pox microbe and ice crystal,"[25] as well as to changes such as a bus stop removed due to construction or the contamination of a river by sewage, agricultural runoff, and industrial pollutants. What is shrinkage for a body with chronic pain or chronic disease if the environment is constantly changing?

Health, Georges Canguilhem writes, "is a margin of tolerance for the inconstancies of the environment."[26] It is not simply a matter of establishing harmony with the vital and habitual "norms of life" or "the momentary normal" and "tolerating [their] infractions." It is also a matter of "instituting new norms in new situations."[27] In this regard, health means feeling "more than normal"; being "normative, capable of following"—or instantiating— "new norms of life."[28] This means that for Canguilhem health is not just a state of wellness but "a set of securities and assurances" that have "the double sense of insurance against risk and [the] audacity to run this risk."[29] Health is defined by the capacity to risk establishing new norms in the face of environmental change (audacity) and to survive taking that risk should the attempt fail (insurance). When living circumstances change, like when a virus spreads, a heatwave hits, or a bus stop disappears, a body is healthy if it can respond to those changes by firing up an immune reaction, increasing liquid intake, or going to the next bus stop.

Disease, on the other hand, involves the *loss* of these capacities. Disease, Canguilhem writes, "is characterized by the fact that it is a reduction in the margin of tolerance for the environment's inconstancies."[30] From the perspective of affordance theory, the organism-environment relation allows for fewer positive affordances and more negative or totally absent affordances. So, too, a change in the organism, the environment, or both can give rise to a different set of organism-environment relations, or affordances. Chronic pain and disease most obviously involve a change in the organism. The resulting body-environment relation is like that of the heart that once broke down and can at any moment break down again.[31] When the body undergoes exertion, it right away produces increased pulsation, sweating, and dizziness, behaviors that indicate a reduction in the positive affordances available to it—which is also to say that there is a shrinkage in the environment from which actions other than aversion can arise for this sick body.

Chronic Disease's Shrinking World

Consider the following story in terms of shrinkage. Henri and I were sitting at his kitchen table, talking about how his early adulthood had seen the onset of a chronic, painful, debilitating illness. Henri, who was (at the time of filming) in his sixties, was twenty-five when he was diagnosed with rheumatoid arthritis. In 1994, at the age of forty-eight, he had a period of intense flare-ups that led him to take a six-month leave of absence from his job as a store manager, where he worked almost sixty hours a week and managed about twenty employees. He returned to work for a brief period of time only to realize that he could not continue because of his illness. He then decided to quit his job:

> [*Mother tongue French, speaking in English*] In 1995, the inflammation was so bad, and those days I used to smoke. And just bringing the cigarette from the ashtray to my mouth was incredibly painful then. I remember that day [when he had intense inflammation] I only smoked three cigarettes, and, uh, that was nothing [for him]. And I wouldn't even get up that day to go to the kitchen to eat. The pain was so incredible.

When Canguilhem describes disease in terms of a *reduced* capacity to weather environmental changes, "reduction" means "being able to live only in another environment and not merely in some parts of the previous one."[32] On falling ill, the person does not "adapt" their existing environment to make it better suited to the new condition of their bodies. Instead, the sick person begins to inhabit an environment that is reduced relative to a previously available environmental space or, in my terms, *shrunken* (and if the disease is progressive, further *shrinking*), *and* altogether different from that former space. The environment that Henri began to inhabit with the onset of illness was shrunken in that it did not extend as far as the one before, but it was also not just a part of the previous environment because it had to function for him in a different bodily state. At times of flare-ups, again a different bodily state, a newly shrunken environment takes shape inside the walls of Henri's house. Henri's environment can even shrink to the degree that parts of the house, such as the kitchen, become inaccessible. That is, they offer no affordances for Henri. In each new configuration of inhabitable space new sets of positive and negative affordances become perceivable, even as they are shrunken relative to a previous one. What does Henri eat in each one? Where does he eat it? These continual shifts are the stark realities of having to live in another—differently constricted—environment. The onset of a chronic painful disease and its ongoing flare-ups translate, on the level of lived experience, not just as the *contraction* of the environment that Henri once used to inhabit, due to the *withdrawal* of affordances that he could once perceive, but as the repetitive transformation of the negative and positive affordances that he is able to perceive.

Now consider how Yasemin described her experience of navigating the hospital where she was treated:

> We—the rheumatoid arthritis patients in the hospital—need to go for blood tests. That day, this was pure torture for me. I was about to cry. . . . Going up and down those stairs was like a death sentence for me. You can climb one or two perhaps, but you really don't have any energy left for the third one. We have to go up and down the stairs. Plus, I am a thyroid patient too. If I walk too much, my throat begins to hurt. And then because of rheumatoid arthritis, I feel like I could faint when walking. . . . I feel like falling down on the ground right at that second.

Yasemin's choice of the metaphors "death sentence" and "torture" is not incidental. These metaphors, and her overall account, illustrate exactly how chronic disease can be experienced as a drastic increase in the level of negative affordance and a miniscule degree of positive affordance that together make this environment only barely tolerable—a place of pending death, torture, and potential loss of consciousness.

Although many of my cases are about people living with rheumatoid arthritis, I am offering the concept of shrinkage for the experiences of chronic disease and pain more broadly, with the understanding that the environment can shrink in many different ways, depending on the specificities of the chronic disease in question. Consider Mel Chen's account of living with heavy metal poisoning. In a vividly evoked memory, Chen describes how molecules, particles, and sound waves moving in the air can suddenly trigger a series of intensely felt physical reactions within their body that were not there before, so that their environment shrinks (my term) dramatically in a matter of seconds. The account begins with a sense of freedom in moving through space due to Chen's feeling fairly well and living in a new place:

Today I am having a day of relative well-being and am eager to explore my neighborhood on foot; I have forgotten for the moment that I just don't go places "on foot," because the results can be catastrophic. Having moved to a new place, with the fresh and heady defamiliarization that comes with uprooting and replanting, my body has forgotten some of its belabored environmental repertoire. . . . It is for a moment free—in its scriptless version of its future—to return to former ways of inhabiting space when I was in better health.

For a short while, the conditions of Chen's body in relation to what is at most other times likely a more hostile environment affords ease, freedom, and spontaneity. But it is clear that for Chen this experience exists alongside the more familiar experience of navigating the environment as hostile—as one that affords limited action and that requires what they call a "belabored environmental repertoire." They describe their experience of shifting from a prior experience of ease to this repertoire in excruciating detail:

Some passenger cars whiz by; instinctively my body retracts and my corporeal-sensory vocabulary starts to kick back in. A few pedestrians cross my path, and before they near, I quickly assess whether they are likely (or might be the "kind of people") to wear perfumes or colognes or to be wearing sunscreen. . . . In an instant, quicker than I thought anything could reach my organs, my liver refuses to process these inhalations and screams hate, a hate whose intensity each time shocks me.[33]

In the case of living with rheumatoid arthritis, shrinkage occurs as painful, impaired, and inflamed joints encounter surfaces—the concrete floor, a multitude of stairs, an object with small parts, and so on—that make the environment less habitable. In the case of a body with environmental injuries and chemical sensitivities, it renders an environment (more specifically, the medium) filled with toxic particles uninhabitable, the world dramatically shrinking in a matter of seconds.

Chronic Disease as Shrinkage

If health involves risk-taking with assurance and insurance, as Canguilhem argues, then disease can be thought of as risk avoidance and the search for security—whether these are done consciously or instinctually—due to the absence of assurance and insurance in the face of such unknowns. The sick person does not want to take chances because she does not have a plenitude of assurances and possibilities at her disposal that she can use to respond to the demands and vagaries of the environment with ease. For Chen, a whiff of perfume, cologne, soap, exhaust, detergent, sunscreen, or any other type of fragrance can make their liver "scream hate" in a matter of seconds. For that not to happen, they have to inhabit a well-protected space within which their movements remain heavily scripted and where exposure to threat is minimized. For Henri and Yasemin, a large portion of their energy goes toward dealing with pain and inflammation, leaving very few bodily reserves that could enable them to tolerate whichever challenge their environment may bring in the future. This inability to deal with fluctuations and take chances turns an environment of possibilities into an environment of contractions, negotiations, and calculations, or what Leder calls "calculated effort."[34] Recall that etymologically, "'ease' comes from the French word *aise,* originally meaning 'elbow room' or 'opportunity.'" It is precisely "this experience of world-as-opportunity," Leder adds, that "dis-ease calls into question."[35] Disease calls the existing affordances of the world into question. Drawing on the etymology of the word "disease" and Canguilhem's work, I argue that to experience a chronic disease is to experience the shrinkage of the environment as its otherwise realizable affordances recede. The environment shrinks in comparison either to what it was prior to the onset of disease, or (if the disease in question is progressive) to what it used to be at each previous stage of progression, or (if the disease is congenital) to the environment inhabited by normates. "As the body breaks down," Scarry writes, "it becomes increasingly the object of attention, usurping the place of all other objects, so that finally, in very very old and sick people, the world may exist in a circle of two feet out from themselves."[36] Scarry's depiction vividly illustrates the contraction I am talking about. The environment does not extend outward toward the horizon as it once did; it, instead, pulls in toward the body, affording fewer and fewer possibilities for action.

Shrinkage: Pluralizing Disability Politics

For sure, Yasemin's body would hurt less, and the environment she describes would shrink less, if the hospital where she is being treated had well-connected buildings with elevators and minimal walking spaces in between. But this does not mean that the environment would stop shrinking once such access features were put in place. This is what differentiates the ecological conceptualization of disability that I am putting forth from the concept of "misfit"[37] and the social model of disability's environmental determinism.

My concept of shrinkage is meant to recognize that there is a limit to the environmental adjustments that can be made. There is no end, ultimately, to what kind of access may be needed in an environment even for one body, let alone for all bodies with so many different impairments and their different (and potentially changing) access needs. Even the most accessible of environments can still be experienced as shrinking when one falls chronically ill (rather than periodically so), or when the body suffering from a chronic disease progressively degenerates.

The fact is that bodies get sick and become impaired. At times they get sicker and sicker, and life continues within the confines of the shrunken environments that they have to inhabit. These bodies neither fit nor "misfit" entirely. They are not "square pegs in a round hole,"[38] nor do they fit without friction. We need new vocabularies for the ill-fitting and in-between experiences of disability that do not neatly fall under the designations of "fit" or "misfit," "accessible" or "inaccessible." The concept of shrinkage that I am proposing accounts for a more nuanced and flexible account of sick and debilitated bodies with potentially fluctuating and progressive impairments.

To be clear: the environment shrinks both when we are facing staircases in a wheelchair and when living with a chronic disease that turns climbing into a torturous act. Indeed, the concept of shrinkage is meant to bring this common denominator into focus. But it is also important to acknowledge that the responses to a particular case of shrinkage may vary, such that each shrinkage may require its own politics. It would make sense that disability activists agitated for ramps so that someone in a wheelchair would not experience the shrinkage of their environment in the face of stairs alone. It would also make sense for someone experiencing chronic pain in movement to agitate for an escalator in the same location where the ramp would be placed. These differentiations would not divide or fracture disability politics; on the contrary, they would enrich and further pluralize it. The apparent solutions of ramps and escalators might evolve into an entirely new approach that would address both kinds of impairments, or in a less traditional social model of change, reconsider what it means to care for people in the redesign of architecture. Reckoning with the fact that life has to be lived within *limits*, *losses*, and *shrinkage* would not go against but only nuance our ongoing efforts to redefine disability, and to rethink it beyond the boundaries of how it has previously been understood.

When one lives with a chronic, painful disease that exhausts the bodily resources needed to face the inherent inconstancies of the world, disability politics may not take the form of explicit, concrete, and conclusive demands (such as demanding access and civil rights). And we cannot succumb to measuring the political value of one's life choices as a person living with impairments in ableist terms. It may be desirable and even liberatory for some of us to find value and joy in living according to the limits and losses of our bodies and our shrinking environments rather than forever struggling to reach beyond them. As I shall discuss in part II, a politics reoriented to this way of living with disability may take the form of more subtle, nonvocal, inarticulate acts of world-making that transform the very definition of a livable life. And all of these multiple politics have value in their own right, whether they allow us to just simply survive or to mobilize rallies for grand social change.

Jérôme is blind, and he uses a white cane to navigate. At the time of our collaboration he was living on the south side of Montreal and pursuing a university degree in the city. This distance meant he had to commute almost every day, which included encountering bus stops indicated by poles and without shelter. In the winter the poles were halfway buried under snow, which made it impossible for blind pedestrians to locate them. Jérôme also had to travel in buses without audio cues and cross streets without adaptive traffic lights. During our interview at his home, I asked Jérôme how he finds the transportation system in Montreal, including buses and the metro. Based on my previous collaborations with other disabled people who use wheelchairs, I assumed that the metro, most of whose stations are without elevators, would be the least accessible. To my surprise, Jérôme replied (in English, though his mother tongue is French): "Metro is fine. Metro is accessible, metro is the more accessible way of transportation that has ever existed. Why? Because we fight in the past to have the announce of all the stops and we won that."

A few weeks later I met Jérôme again to film his path from home to the university. We took the bus that has no audio cues and then arrived at Longueil metro station. As we were standing at the entrance, a big hall without much nonvisual indication for where to go, I asked Jérôme whether it was easier to navigate in the metro with people around to ask for help, or without. He replied:

[*Mother tongue French, speaking in English*] It's easier when there are some people but not, er, too important [a] crowd. It's important to have, er, some people because they can indicate to me the way to go. If I'm not sure, I can ask someone to help me. And if there is just some people . . . they would have the tendency to take their time, and they are not as stressed as during the rush hour. And the problem, um, when the crowd is too important, um, more the crowd is big, less they are civilized [*smiles*]. Er, the more they are going fast, they are stressed. They are not, um, paying any attention to, to other people, um, and it's really dangerous because they are going in every way [in all different directions].

We then took the metro and arrived at Berri-UQAM station, which is one of the busiest stations in Montreal's metro, with three of its lines intersecting. As people were rushing to catch the waiting train (figure 3.1) or as they got out of a crowded train (figure 3.2), most of the time they did not pay any attention to Jérôme and his cane. Immersed in their own actions, they left almost no room for him, often invading the periphery Jérôme needed to sweep his cane, blocking his path, and ignoring or tripping over his cane (figure 3.1).

The metro, as Jérôme told me, is the most accessible mode of transportation for him. Unlike the buses,[1] the metro has audio announcements for each stop. It is also safer, he adds, because it is free of cars and does not require him to walk in or to cross streets. But it's clear from following him on his path, as captured in the images (figures 3.1 and 3.2), that even the most accessible and safest of places can shrink for Jérôme. This is not because of the lack of access, but because of fellow travelers who invade his space as Jérôme-with-cane, and who tend to casually and heedlessly take up Jérôme's space for action.

This invasion is not simply a matter of attitudes. If deliberate discriminatory attitudes were to blame, then the same commuters, as Jérôme attentively observes, would not be hostile obstacles in one situation and attentive and even helpful guides in another. Attitudes and prejudices know no rush hour. But the fact that fellow travelers can be facilitators to access in one situation and barriers to it in another, or "civilized" when it is quiet but "uncivilized" as soon as there is a fight for space or a race against time, tells me that there

FIGURE 3.1 IN A MONTREAL METRO STATION, JÉRÔME, WHO IS BLIND, EXPERIENCES
THE SHRINKAGE OF SPACE. AS THE TRAIN DOORS OPEN AND HE WALKS DOWN
THE PLATFORM, WHITE CANE IN HAND, A WOMAN DIRECTLY IN FRONT OF JÉRÔME
VEERS TO THE LEFT AS SHE HEADS TO AN OPEN DOOR.

FIGURE 3.2 ON ANOTHER OCCASION IN A MONTREAL METRO STATION, THE TRAIN
DOORS OPEN AND A HORDE OF PASSENGERS SWARM ACROSS THE PLATFORM
TOWARD THE EXIT, SURROUNDING JÉRÔME, WHO HAD BEEN MAKING HIS WAY
ACROSS AN EMPTY PLATFORM WITH HIS CANE.

is something more insidious, something beyond the reach of consciousness, something that is in fact deeply ingrained in the reflexes of the body. I call this "the habitus of ableism." In this chapter, I explore how the environment and its actualized affordances shrink for those with disabilities despite the purported provision of access in policy (e.g., legislation or architectural codes) and in material practice. I situate this approach to access in what Aimi Hamraie calls "critical access studies,"[2] which rejects earlier formulations of access generated from the social model of disability in favor of attending not only to access provision in itself but also to how a given form of provision is built, received, and negotiated by different actors.

I begin with some of the key works in critical access studies in order to lay out the theoretical groundwork that the habitus of ableism is built upon and to which it is contributing. I then explore how the (human) body takes on this habitus, starting with the form-generating relationship between bodies and their niches at birth, continuing with the naturalization of skills and abilities that are developed within the material/social specificities of those niches, and ending with what that naturalization process can do. I move on to three ethnographic instances where I trace the habitus of ableism and how it makes the environment and its affordances shrink for those with disabilities.

Critical Access Studies

Access has been a primary mobilizing force and a major political success for the disability rights movement of the last half-century in the United States and, more recently, globally.[3] Bess Williamson argues that identification of disability and its politics with access has largely been "a response to a lack" (lack of ramps, curb cuts, etc.), and that in the early process of making access a legitimate topic of academic study, the work "seemed to be more about establishing the category than defining it."[4] Aimi Hamraie characterizes access studies as rooted in the idea of access as a "self-evident good," as in "the social model, along with crip theories that treat accessibility as an alternative to medical knowing."[5] More recently, however, scholars have begun to question the category of access itself, asking who or what decides *what access is* and by what means this is established. What kind of work does access do, in which settings, and what happens to access when it travels globally?

As its name suggests, this newer "critical access studies" questions all that has been taken for granted or assumed in access studies and in disability politics concerning access. One of its aims is to expose the political, ideological, and social enactments of access. In questioning the concept of access as always good or desirable, critical access studies scholars find themselves working across a wide range of sites. Much of this work concerns rhetorical uses of access that are not coupled with actual benefit to people with disabilities.[6] Studies examine how within the neoliberal political economy access can become "a form of outsourcing"; how "the aesthetic of access" can be a way for businesses to stage access for promotional purposes, often without actual outcomes for disabled customers; how state welfarism can lead to the emergence of "an 'access industry'"; and how access can be taken up as "a sign of modernity" by nation-states that, in line with progress narratives, aspire to claim such status, but whose rhetoric does not necessarily translate into action.[7]

In disrupting established ways of imagining access, theoretical approaches in critical access studies also seek to disrupt earlier notions of access's normatively limited political imagination by opening up more expansive possibilities for living in human bodies with all their differences. Hamraie suggests that we rethink access as a historically entrenched knowledge-making process, a set of habits and practices, and a "regime of legibility and illegibility."[8] Similarly, Tanya Titchkosky argues that the occasional, partial, and limited provision of access should not be "taken as normal, sort of expected," and instead become a source of frustration and "wonder."[9] Titchkosky's "politics of wonder" displaces the conventional approach to access as a matter of material certainty (is there a broad-handled faucet or not?), with an understanding of access as an act of perception through which we recognize bodies as viable human beings (or not).[10] In these reformulations, access is considered a site of "political friction and contestation," a knowledge category, "an act of perception," and a product of social relations and values.[11]

In this chapter, I join these theoretical approaches in questioning the limits of access as traditionally conceptualized and exposing its normative aspects. As Jérôme's testimony clearly demonstrates (and as the daily experiences of many other disabled people would corroborate), purportedly "accessible" services, places, and technologies are not as readily and as smoothly actualizable for those that they are supposed to (bene)fit. But it is even more significant that no matter how many barriers are removed, no matter how improved access becomes, no matter how comprehensively legislation is crafted, an accessible environment cannot actually benefit all disabled people at once, nor can it benefit any single disabled person whose conditions change over time.

This is not to say that accessibility legislation, policies, architectural codes, and guidelines are redundant. To the contrary, they are extremely important and necessary—but they are *not enough*.[12] As critical access studies scholars point out, despite the progress that postindustrialized nations may have made since the early days of disability movements, they have not created, nor will they create in any near future, a postableist world.[13] I argue that this is because ableism is first and foremost a matter of entrenched and established ableist normativities with regard to the body and not just a matter of beliefs, attitudes, and mindsets that can be changed or fixed with access codes, legislation, and objects. What I call the "habitus of ableism" is the reason that the environment and its space for action can shrink for disabled people even in the presence of "accessibility." I argue that this *bodily* habitus can diminish the environment and its affordances for people with disabilities, whether or not that environment has been fitted with particular forms of access.

The Habitus of Ableism

What is the habitus of ableism, and what is its relation to affordance? "Environments," Georges Canguilhem writes, "offer man only potentialities for technical utilization and collective activity. Choice decides." Of all the "collective norms of life [that] are possible in a given milieu," the ones that have been actualized appear as natural and given, and they gain this power due to their endurance over time, or their "antiquity."[14] This account is uncannily similar to Pierre Bourdieu's concept of habitus. A habitus is that which "ensures the active presence of past experiences, which, deposited in each organism in the form of schemes of perception, thought and action, tend to guarantee the 'correctness' of practices and their constancy over time, more reliably than all formal rules and explicit norms."[15] Gibson addresses the perpetuation of selective affordances at the level of psychological development in suggesting that children are socially conditioned to perceive those affordances that give rise to normative actions and behaviors. But he does not address what constraining effects this social conditioning may have on the availability of affordances for perception and actualization to the diverse inhabitants of the same environment. This is what the habitus of ableism can allow us to unpack. When the concept of habitus is brought together with affordance theory, it becomes possible to propose that the habitus is created by the conditioning of perception toward those affordances that conform to historically established norms. The power of this conditioning is that it makes the actualization of all other available affordances unthinkable by way of the most apparently spontaneous of actions and behaviors and the most neutralized of its perceptual schemes, entrenched through their repetition over time. That is, the characteristics of the habitus fashioned by affordances actualized by those who came before us come to appear as facts, necessities, and urgencies of life because they appear to be the only ones in existence at all, when in reality there may be (and have been) any number of others.

For Bourdieu, the habitus is fundamentally bodily, a "social necessity turned into nature, converted into motor schemes and body automatisms,"[16] and as such, the "habitus of ableism" refers to a bodily habitus constituted under the conditions of ableism. This habitus is comprised of the "motor schemes and body automatisms" that pertain to the able body, meaning those that conform to ableism, and whose necessity, urgency, and sensibility go unquestioned; they are taken as given.

Take, for instance, the act of walking. Walking, or "the capacity for bipedal locomotion," Tim Ingold writes, "can only be said to be innate by presupposing the presence of the necessary environmental conditions for its development."[17] Walking is not innate but, rather, an ability that we *learn* in an environment shaped by the existence and selection of walking affordances. Children are conditioned by already practiced walkers (who enact the historically entrenched bodily behavior of walking) to perceive walking affordances available in an environment, whether "natural" or built, that provide walk-on-able surfaces (sidewalks, paths, floors, etc.). The capacity for bipedal motion would not be actualized were it not for these available environmental affordances that are both social and material. Or in Ingold's words, the fact that an infant "comes with a built-in developmental schedule which ensures that it will eventually walk upright" is no guarantee that it will walk no matter what. It will do so only *provided that*—and this proviso "is absolutely critical"—"certain conditions are present in its environment,"[18] or to be more precise, certain material/social walking affordances are present in its environment. In fact, whatever abilities humans can enact, those actions develop because they are *born into* an environment (or a niche, to be more exact) equipped with the very affordances—already *materialized* and *socialized*— that actively enable their development.

From this perspective, no one is born able-bodied; rather those who count as able-bodied become able to perform the action possibilities that their niches' socially and materially entrenched affordances provide. Able-bodiedness is ultimately contingent on the historical processes that define *which* affordances of the world will be utilized, *how,* and to the benefit of *whom.*

There is a recognition of power built into the concept of habitus, and so also into the habitus of ableism, that is important to highlight. If the habitus is social necessities converted into matters of bodily nature,[19] then the habitus of ableism is not only a selective set of bodily actions. It is also an embodied form of ignorance that oppresses those bodies that are unable to actualize those actions and make use of the relevant affordances. In fact, those sets of environmental features are not even affordances for them (or diminished affordances), because there is not a mutuality between them as organisms and that environment. As becomes evident in Jérôme's story, the habitus of modern city life requires efficiency, productivity, speed, and particular bodily abilities. If you are unable to benefit from the affordances that give rise to those requirements, then your space for action will be "taken"—or more precisely, it will simply not exist in the form that affords the fulfillment of your needs. The habitus of ableism enables niches that make inhabitable space for some while diminishing that space for others.

True, the environment is full of opportunities for action, as Gibson wrote.[20] True, its affordances can be actualized in so many different ways. But where the habitus of ableism prevails, what was once chosen among many appears as if it is *the* only choice, as if it is *the* way of living, moving, sensing, and being in the world, suffocating all other potentialities. Walking thus appears to be an innate ability that we all are supposed to have, not a skill, among many, that we have incorporated through what Ingold calls "enskillment,"[21] in a niche that actively enables its development. In other words, where the habitus of ableism takes hold, walking, a historically contingent skill, turns into "walkism": the expectation that everybody can and should walk, and that those who walk have an entitlement to take space and utilize the offerings of the world at the expense of those who do not. Likewise, we can speak of bipedalism, audism, visionism, sanism, and so on.

Why Define Ableism as a Form of Habitus?

Ableism, according to Fiona Kumari Campbell's oft-cited definition, is "a network of beliefs, processes and practices that produces a particular kind of self and body (the corporeal standard) that is projected as the perfect, species-typical and therefore essential and fully human."[22] Jay Dolmage similarly writes that ableism "positively values able-bodiedness," representing it "as at once ideal, normal, and the mean or default."[23] It is possible to take a critical distance from, to challenge, and to eventually abandon some of these beliefs, practices, and valuations. But some resist that denormalization. Ableism is a profound embodiment, which is not the case for a set of ideas or the built environment, at least not to the same degree. This deep entrenchment in the body is exactly what I wish to emphasize by defining ableism as a form of habitus.

Ableism is "learned by body," and "what is 'learned by body,'" Bourdieu writes, "is not something that one has . . . but something that one is," and what one, I would add, *does* casually and ordinarily.[24] When a certain body-mind is *enacted* as species-typical, it is not necessarily through a conscious enactment but through cultivated dispositions, sensibilities, and motor-perceptual schemes that run deep and that do not rise to the level of awareness: "The body believes in what it plays at: it weeps when it mimes grief."[25] So do the bodies that bring able-bodiedness into being "believe in what they play at." Recall the fellow commuters in the metro who, in a hurry to catch the train, block Jérôme's path during rush hour. Hardly any of them would consciously do so. When they occupy Jérôme's space for action to the degree of making it shrink, making it less available or completely unavailable to him, they do so not by way of outright discrimination but by way of the most naturalized of actions and perceptions that I am calling the habitus of ableism. Consider the following stories.

"They Consciously Chose Not to Do That"

Anna and I were at her home, talking about accessibility in Montreal's public spaces and events. At the time Anna was a US citizen studying in Canada and was well versed in disability rights discourses and the Americans with Disabilities Act (ADA):

> Yesterday, I went to this store. . . . It's, like, an American store. . . . It's, like, a woman's clothing store that is, like, popular in the US and the Montreal branch just opened. And the store was literally vertical! Like, I have never seen that many stairs in a store before. There were, like, no railings and no elevator. And, um when my friend went up and asked if they had an elevator and they were just like [*mimicking*], "Are you crazy for asking? Why would we have an elevator?" . . . Whenever there is [one] of these stores, all of the interiors of this store kind of look the same. So you know that they, like, ripped out everything and redid the whole interior. . . . So they could have added things to make it accessible. They could have added an elevator. They didn't. And, um, it's an American store so, like, in all of their American branches, um, they, like, had to think about these things because of the Americans with Disabilities Act, like, it's a lot stricter in the US with the building codes. So, like, you have to make your store accessible, and so then, like, not doing that here

makes you feel like they consciously made a choice *not* to make it accessible. 'Cause you know they have to think about this in all the other
stores! . . . And it's a popular enough store! You know they have the
money to put in an elevator. They just chose *not* to. So, things like that
really bother me, get me really frustrated. . . . I know there is probably
other issues at play and, like, it's the building codes here. But just as a
shopper that's what it feels like: that they consciously chose *not* to do
that [emphasis added].

While the ADA counts as the hallmark of the US disability rights movement, it is not Anna's reference to the ADA that stands out in her account but
her repeated frustration with what seems to be the store's willful refusal to
acknowledge—"they had to think about it"—the possibility of making the store
accessible to disabled people. Anna's friend receives an insulting response to
the request for an elevator because the default mode of social consciousness
is set to ignore disability, and this in turn sanctions disrespectful interactions. The absence of access in an actual material encounter is not the central
problem for Anna, it seems. It is the lack of consciousness to identify this
lack as a problem in the first place. As Titchkosky writes, the elevators, push-
doors, or washrooms are not missing in the environment; rather, *"what is
missing is any need to attend to such a barrier to participation."*[26] She argues
that this is because the "collective sensorium" (posited by Paul Gilroy) has
been "dis-educated" from perceiving the disabled participants as missing
from so many sites and aspects of public life.[27] Where disability is perceived
as that which "basically does not belong,"[28] and where the collective sensorium has been numbed and desensitized to its absence, the lack of access (or
its halfway provision, as in the case of malfunctioning push-doors or ramps
leading nowhere) not only fails to puzzle people, it is also somewhat normal.
It is for this reason that it takes very little for a store's agents to not provide
an elevator in a Canadian store, even though they had already done so elsewhere. Drawing on Titchkosky, and following the habitus of ableism concept,
I emphasize that what is missing is the *perception* of the need to address the
absence of access.

The habitus of ableism is what "makes possible the free production of all
the thoughts, perceptions and actions inherent in the particular conditions
of its production—and only those."[29] The very history that agents are born
into—a history that they have incorporated as their "bodily automatisms"
and "perceptual schemes"—comes to appear as if it is *the* way of occupying
the environment's niches. At the same time, all other possible embodiments

and ways of inhabiting the world become less and less likely *to be perceived.* This is not because they are physically impossible to undertake, but because the embodied history that the habitus is does not allow these affordances to appear as legitimate and viable ways of moving, sensing, and behaving in the first place. "'Without violence, art or argument,'" the habitus "tends to exclude all 'extravagances' ('not for the likes of us'), that is, all the behaviors that would be negatively sanctioned because they are incompatible with the objective conditions."[30] Climbing by means of an elevator and crossing streets with the mediation of traffic lights with audio cues are affordances that would benefit not just disabled bodies, but all bodies. But once the bare minimum set of affordances is provided for the nondisabled (such as stairs and traffic lights), other affordances (such as elevators and audio cues) tend to be excluded as "extravagances," as "not for the likes of us." Those affordances, in other words, may as well be done without, and without their absence even being perceived.

"For X, Y, Z Reason"

Jérôme is involved in blind communities and activism, sharing knowledge and expertise, and he is well-informed about the histories of blind people and the discrimination they face on a daily basis. He is an observant, analytic person with a wry sense of humor about things that do not function in life:

> [*Mother tongue French, speaking in English*] I think that the most universal problem for our safety is ... the circulation [traffic] lights. ...
> We fought for a lot of years and we continue to fight to have more and more, um, *feux sonores* [audible traffic lights]. But the problem is that, er, cities consider that it's ... really expensive and they are not really interested in installing a lot of them [*his voice reflects a sense of weariness*]. They installed some ... eh, but it's not systematic. ...
> There is not a conviction that it's important. ... So it's really the most difficult aspect, the most unsafe aspect of our traveling in urban areas. Because, for example, here in Longueuil, we have, er, more than twenty priority, er, intersections that are considered dangerous by our rehabilitation center. ... So there is unanimity to say that in Longueuil, more than twenty intersections are priority to be adaptive and that are dangerous. One of them is just [in front of] ... the Charles-Le Moyne hospital. It's probably the most dangerous and the most "significative" because it's just, er, beside a hospital. But the problem is that the city, er, goes, turns around and turn around, and turn around from few

years and they don't do anything [with an increasing tone of tiredness in his voice]. "Yes, we will install one or one or no, we will not install them this year for *x*, *y*, *z* reason, and . . . next year, we will see . . . we do another *appel d'offre* [tender] and we will . . ." It's a constant area of beginning, and during this time, we put our safety in danger at . . . any time that we have to cross one of these intersections.

For sure, the city officials' decision to not install adaptive traffic lights (even at dangerous intersections) is a conscious choice, as was the US company's decision to not install elevators in their stores in Canada. But again, the problem is not (only) "rational" decisions and "conscious" choices per se but the entirely embodied, casual, and habituated ways underlying such conscious acts.

Whether or not city officials would willfully agree to put the lives of their citizens in danger (and most would likely not), they are enabled in their refusal to install the lights by what Titchkosky calls "justification narratives": it is because we lack funds, it is because we plan for a tender, it is because of "*x*, *y*, *z* reason." Such excuses given for the lack of access, Titchkosky argues, make that lack "possible, even expected," and in so doing they "achieve[s] the ordinariness of inaccessibility."[31] The weary tone with which Jérôme recounts these justification narratives suggests that he recognizes this effect. Thanks to such rhetoric, not only is the need to install audible traffic signals or tactile indicators *not* perceived as urgent, but the deferral of action on this pressing problem is made "understandable," "acceptable," and palatable. Each reason, in other words, helps to achieve "the ordinariness of not being alarmed."[32]

The habitus of ableism is what prevents city officials, store managers, or any other agent from noticing the lack of access or even from being able to identify this lack as a problem in the first place. There is no perceived *need* to even think about blind people's presence in the streets, which would in turn require building the affordances (such as that of an adaptive traffic light) that would keep those pedestrians out of harm's way. The *need* cannot even be perceived as the need it is. "The most improbable practices" or affordances, I would say, can be "excluded, as unthinkable, by a kind of immediate submission to order that inclines agents to make a virtue of necessity, that is, to refuse what is anyway denied."[33] Store workers, city officials, bureaucrats, or a layperson can monotonously list "*x*, *y*, *z* reasons," give justification narratives for the access that fails to be provided, and nonchalantly continue to "refuse what is anyway denied." In the meantime, each time blind pedestrians cross streets, they continue to put their lives in danger, without any alarm on the part of city officials.

"Architects Do Nice Doors but They Do Not Think about Disabled Persons"

Jacques and I were in his kitchen, where I was filming him as he did a few chores. Jacques is a tall, well-built man in his early sixties, who lives with his wife in their beautiful house by the riverside somewhere in Quebec. Jacques has had rheumatoid arthritis for about twenty-five years. As he was about to open a jar—a task I requested him to perform—he recalled a story:

> [*Mother tongue French, speaking in English*] Opening these jars. Even if I'm a big guy, I fail. One thing about big guys—I've not been raised, I am not used to ask[ing] for help and this is a message I wanna pass [on], this is why I am telling it right now. I am not used to ask for help. I've not been raised asking for help. I've been raised [*performs a sweeping hand gesture*] "Organize yourself, do it!" . . . I'm a big guy, I am not used to ask for help. I had to learn, it's difficult [*emphasizing*] to learn to ask for help. But you have no choice. I remember that morning. I was at Bell Canada where I used to work in Montreal . . . that tall building . . . with Bell on it. Aluminum-sided building. Next time you go, look at the doors! And University Street [where the building is] is windy! I was coming with my briefcase. I had a meeting at that morning there. I tried to open the door [*mimics the pull of the handle with his right arm*], couldn't open the door, because of . . . the wind. So I put my briefcase down [*mimics putting it down*], I tried with two hands [*mimics pulling with two hands*], and I was in a flare-up, couldn't open the door with two hands. I'm six feet two. I weigh over two hundred pounds. I'm a big guy, couldn't open a simple door. So I said to myself, "I am gonna go to the other door, a revolving door. Might be easier." And a woman came, about, you know, a mid-size woman. Not a big woman. Not a tall woman. And she looked at me standing beside the door asking herself, "What is that guy doing there? Does he have good intention? What is he?" . . . You know, and I could see the lady coming by me and just looking at me, just like this [*mimics suspicious look*], "What does he want?" And she opened the door [*mimics pulling*], and I said, "Thanks ma'am! I couldn't do it."

I asked Jacques in which year this had happened. He answered, "I would say around 1995." I then asked whether the building still had heavy doors that were hard to open. He nodded repeatedly, with an expression of disapproval on his face: "They still have the same. Architects are wild guys. They do nice doors but they do not think about disabled persons."

The Habitus of Ableism in Architecture

What would it mean for architects to think about disabled persons? While doors are not equivalent to the architecture of a building, they are a foundational part because they enable and control entrance and egress. So too, as members of an ableist society, architects are subject to the habitus of ableism,[34] as Jacques observes when he identifies their failure to think about people with disabilities. In *Doing Disability Differently: An Alternative Handbook on Architecture, Dis/ability and Designing*, architect and community-based practitioner Jos Boys makes the following observation that confirms Jacques's: "Architects as a profession, and architecture as a practice and product, act to justify and perpetuate certain norms through unthinking, unnoticed and continuous acts of both living and designing for particular social and spatial practices rather than others."[35]

The history of architecture in North America and Europe, as traced by Boys, Rob Imrie, and others, suggests the formation of a habitus of ableism through its differing ways of treating the body in space.[36] Initially, architectural practice ignored the body altogether, and when it did address the body the able body was taken as given in the form of an "ideal social body," or what Hamraie calls "the normate template," which is featureless and unmarked.[37] But while appearing to be neutral and all-embracing, the template actually represents a very "particular white, European, nondisabled, youthful, and often masculine figure" that, in its claim to universality, erases others.[38] This conflation of a presumed "whomsoever" with "except some," or in Boys's phrasing, the slippage from "the commonsense 'anyone' to 'not anyone,'" has automatically generated a series of architectural exclusions, of which "being disabled" is one.[39]

In the aftermath of the disability rights movements, the disabled body entered the architectural imagination, but in a form devoid of all the complexity and diversity that would make evident the actual range of disabled embodiments requiring consideration.[40] Instead of "starting *from* dis/ability," Boys argues, architects have often adhered to a compliance discourse that "keeps disability in place."[41] Accordingly, disability in architecture has been treated either as an issue of "special needs," "additive design," or "inclusive design" to be addressed only after "the 'normal' design processes" is complete, and only with regard to codes, guidelines, and regulations.[42] This has resulted in what Imrie and Kumar call "design reductionist" approaches and, at times, "obligations to care" on the part of architects and design professionals,[43] rather than actual critical engagement with access.

Overall, disabled embodiment remains largely absent from architecture because the habitus of ableism continues to exert its force in the sense that, while it no longer ignores disability (at best), architecture considers disability only within ableist terms. This is evident as well in the training and practice of architects.[44] In an analysis of interviews he conducted with architects and tutors, Rob Imrie notices that "no one mentioned diseased, impaired, or ill bodies as core to bodily identity, experience, and performance."[45] Again, the perception needed to recognize the absence of disabled bodies was missing. But this omission is hardly surprising considering that architecture itself has traditionally been taught in the ableist spaces of higher education, whose signature "steep steps," as Jay Dolmage notes, materially disavow disability.[46] Exclusionary spaces of architectural education and internships, according to disabled architect David Gissen, further contribute to "the ways we imagine the production of architectural knowledge."[47] The lack of perception needed to recognize the absence of disabled users goes hand in hand with what architects have been taught to see (and not see) in educational spaces.

In a critique of Western design pedagogies and practices, which applies equally well to architecture, design theorist Tony Fry asks: "How can a designer be designed to be a provider of care via the designing of things that ontologically care?" In other words, care and the absence of care (or in this case "thinking about disability," as Jacques put it) are not just human dispositions but inhere in objects as well. Fry is asking what would need to be included in the training of designers for them to design objects (including buildings or built environments) that care. His answer suggests that this would require a radical transformation of the designer's *entire habitus*, or in Fry's words, of "the assumed and taken-for-granted thinking that underscores what a designer believes they are, what they are doing, and how."[48] The central question here again is not what constitutes accessibility in architecture but how architectural design can care about the presence and absence of people with disabilities.

In *Architecture from the Outside*, Elizabeth Grosz takes issue with the virtual presence of the body in architecture. She writes: "To merely say that there is a body is not yet to deal with it. Bodies are there in a way that architects don't want, or can't afford, to recognize."[49] We may adapt Grosz's insights into disability in architecture as well. "To merely say that there is a [disabled] body is not yet to deal with it. [Disabled] bodies are there in a way that architects don't want, or can't afford, to recognize." The environment and its space for action continue to shrink for disabled people as a result of this failure, despite the (virtual) presence of disability in architecture—in its blueprints, building codes, and accessibility standards. For disabled users' spaces of action not to shrink, and for these users to become an *actual presence* in the designers' habitus, architecture needs to face not what or who it keeps in, but what or who it leaves "outside."[50]

In September 2017 Hurricane Maria struck Puerto Rico, devastating the entire island and its already frail infrastructure. On the average, households lost
electricity for eighty-four days and water for more than sixty. Islanders lacked
access to medical care. Elderly people using oxygen machines were reported
traveling long distances to plug them in.[1] The number of "excess deaths" that
the posthurricane period and its infrastructural collapse incurred was found
to be "70 times the official estimate."[2] In consideration of these excess deaths,
environmental activist Katia Avilés-Vázquez reported: "We have not only sui-
cide rates that are increasing but stoplights literally falling on people and killing them; power plants blowing up and catching fire and killing people, and
then people that have continued to die because of the lack of the necessary
and appropriate resources."[3] As I was listening to Avilés-Vázquez, I was struck
by a strange tension. At the time, I was writing about Jérôme's comments
about how the lack of audio cues in the cities of Longueil and Montreal was
putting the lives of blind pedestrians in danger. In disaster-stricken Puerto
Rico, it was the lack of care for traffic lights that was turning them into deadly
weapons. What counts as "disabled" here? Who or what was doing the work

of impairing, injuring, and killing? Who is accountable, who is responsible? Where did death-making for traffic lights begin and where did death-making for those killed by traffic lights end? How can we separate the act of letting power plants explode from the act of making the lands where they were located unlivable for their inhabitants? How can we draw a line between the damage done to the planet by colonial capitalist violence and the damage done by environmental disasters whose number, frequency, and calamitous effects have been multiplied by that violence? What, in other words, are we to make of disability in the destructive times of the Anthropocene?

Events like those that took place in Puerto Rico give rise to experiences that may not obviously count as disability or impairment but that—from the ecological framework of shrinkage—can be understood as "a disability story nonetheless."[4] As in the lives of disaster-stricken Puerto Ricans, these events may entail the gradual incapacitation, or debilitation in Puar's terms,[5] of communities through the withdrawal of subsistence and essential life support systems. They may entail, as in the case of collapsing traffic lights, the denial of maintenance for things and infrastructures. They may also entail, as in the case of our shrinking planet, the impairing of multispecies entanglements, the erasure of organisms' niches, and the erosion of the planet's very livability.

In her article "Moving Together: Side by Side," disability scholar Elizabeth Wheeler asks, "How can the vulnerability of disabled people be perceived as part of our shared vulnerability on the planet, and the vulnerability of the planet itself, rather than a unique and separate kind of weakness?"[6] Up until now, I conceptualized shrinkage in terms of the disabled body and its immediate vicinities, in which the environment of chronically ill, painful, and disabled bodies contracts and affords fewer and fewer possibilities of action. As I conclude part 1, I ask: Can shrinkage be a way to open up the expanded perceptions of shared—if *disproportionately* so—vulnerability that Wheeler calls for?

Rethinking Disability

The efforts to trouble (read: de-essentialize) the category of disability have for a while been underway in disability scholarship and politics. Scholars and activists have called for thinking disability beyond (literally) impaired bodies, expanding disability beyond individuals to populations, from humans to other species and even to landscapes and ecologies.[7] The concept of shrinkage draws on and builds upon these ongoing efforts to rethink disability in broader, multiple, and nuanced terms. In order to better situate how shrinkage enters this conversation and what it contributes, I now turn to some recent epistemological developments in critical disability studies.

Following the establishment of disability as a category of analysis (and of identity, social construction, and oppression), disability has come under criticism as an implicitly universalized concept. On a transnational and transcultural scale, anthropologists of disability long ago identified that "in many cultures, one cannot be 'disabled' for the simple reason that 'disability' as a recognized category does not exist."[8] Further, as a concept that was forged through the imperatives of Western capitalist societies, disability is fraught with colonial and imperial relations of unequal power.[9] Scholars of the Global South point out the serious "question of applicability" at the level of politics and of the models, theories, and vocabularies with which disability has been studied and reclaimed in the Global North.[10] These may not easily translate into, and can in fact remain in tension with, the Global South's local realities.[11] Anita Ghai, for instance, asks: What is the value of "the fight for 'disability rights'" or "the imported packages of 'nothing for us without us'"—discourses that presume an autonomous subject that can fight for rights—for an Indian context, where 75 percent of the population lives in rural areas in poverty, and where there are many aspects to the marginalization of disability, including caste, gender, linguistic, and class divides?[12]

In the Global North, disability activists and scholars have variously adopted disability as a political identity, celebrated it as a pride and a culture, and generalized it as a condition of all human life. While such strategies may powerfully contravene the histories of stigmatization, infantilization, and institutionalization of disabled people in the Global North, they may also fail to address differences among people with different impairments or social conditions, and they certainly overlook such differences across the globe. "How can acquiring disability be celebrated as 'the most universal of human conditions,'" Nirmala Erevelles asks of one key assumption in disability studies, "if it is acquired under the oppressive conditions of poverty, economic exploitation, police brutality, neocolonial violence, and lack of access to adequate healthcare and education?"[13] Instead of taking disability for granted as "the condition of being," Erevelles argues, we need to consider its conditions of "becoming"—conditions that cannot be isolated from "becoming black," "becoming poor," "becoming un-gendered," and other kinds of marginalized becomings.[14] In keeping with Erevelles's intervention, Jasbir Puar asks rhetorically: "Is a young black man without a diagnosed disability living in the United States who is statistically much more likely than most to be imprisoned, shot at by police, or killed by the time of adulthood actually a referent for what it means to be able-bodied?"[15] When the histories of racialization, colonialism, imperialism, capitalist expansion, heteropatriarchy, and sexism are taken into account, "able-bodied," as Puar argues, can hardly stand as a synonym for nondisabled.[16]

Local and global power relations, social differences, and inequalities between bodies—notably racialization—not only blur the boundaries between the categories "able-bodied," "nondisabled," and "disabled" but also contest the separation of environment from the body that some approaches to disability such as the social and misfit models take for granted. When impairment is induced and sustained within deeply rooted historical/material conditions of "becoming," the environment may not be easily identifiable as its cause. As Stephen Knadler writes in his historical analysis of antiblack US necropolitics, "The slow and chronic attritional and accumulative effects and debilitations of Black life within racialized environments . . . cannot be changed simply with curb cuts or the removal of lead paint."[17] There is no outright disablement of the body by its environment, Knadler argues, because the body and the environment do not exist as two separate entities. Instead, there is "a constitutive transcorporeality unfolding within the constant interchange between the body and its racist environments."[18]

With such points in mind, disability critical race theorists and scholars of the Global South have criticized disability studies' parochial Euro-American scope, calling for its "decolonization" through a "global Disability studies project" that can "move beyond the boundaries of the Gulf Stream."[19] Among other shifts, these scholars have analyzed how impairment can be actively "produced" by colonial violence, wars, imperialist projects, militarization, environmental racism, nuclear testing and other atrocities, structural inequality, and injustice.[20] Drawing on the specific ways in which impairments materialize and are valued in local contexts, they have also proposed new lexicons, using terms such as "debility" and "debilitation" to name "disability from the South."[21]

The first wave of disability studies maintained distinctions between categories (disabled/able-bodied, disability/impairment) as well as between the body and the environment (see also chapter 1). The significance accorded to multiple and intersecting systems of oppression by many of the first wave's critics question how such distinctions are drawn: What bodies under what conditions will count as nondisabled rather than disabled, and, ultimately, can these terms carry any stable meaning at all? Without a stable meaning, furthermore, can "disability" support a political identity or even an academic discipline? Advocates of critical disability studies argue that instead of constituting *any* particular relation between body and environment that will count as disability, it is necessary to "disorient" the field away from any essentialized category altogether.[22] In place of a category or a field, critical disability studies proposes an intersectional methodology that, according to Julie Avril Minich, offers ways to apply the theories and frameworks of disability studies to "contexts that extend well beyond what is immediately recognized as disability."[23]

As the field of disability studies has shifted, disability activism has recognized—has been forced to recognize—that the US disability rights–based movement has largely comprised white disabled Americans (often with visible physical impairments) and reflected their particular experience, and that it needs to incorporate bodies that are subject to multiple forms of oppression. Patty Berne of the performance group Sins Invalid articulates the intersectionality of race, ability, and various other vectors of inequality:

> The histories of white supremacy and ableism are inextricably entwined, both forged in the crucible of colonial conquest and capitalist domination. . . . 500+ years of violence against black and brown communities includes 500+ years of bodies and minds deemed dangerous by being non-normative—again, not simply within able-bodied normativity, but within the violence of heteronormativity, white supremacy, gender normativity, within which our various bodies and multiple communities have been deemed *"deviant," "unproductive," "invalid."*[24]

In concert with this expansion of its remit, disability politics has shifted from being rights-based to advocating for justice. Disability justice articulates its politics according to the historical conditions of inequality that function through normativity to exclude body/minds and communities. This transformative epistemological grounding in the workings of normativity, rather than in particular kinds of bodies named "disabled," has grown out of disability justice activism as it overlaps with efforts to rethink disability in the Global North and South through feminist, critical race, and queer approaches, as well as through analyses of colonialism and imperialism. This has given rise to a multi-issue movement—anti-ableist, anti-racist, anti-sexist, anti-colonial, anti-capitalist, anti-war—whose commitment is that "no body/mind" will be "left behind."[25]

The concept of shrinkage enters this conversation with a similar commitment to radical inclusion, articulating a nonlinear process (of *disablement*) rather than categorizing bodies (as able, disabled, etc.) for analysis or identification. In what follows, I suggest that shrinkage responds to the call for radical inclusion by justice-based disability movements and research. It does so by *cutting across* established dualisms such as human/nonhuman, and *traversing* scales, from single bodies in their homes to the planet as a whole.

The Shrinkage of One Niche Is the Expansion of Another

"Technologies," Annemarie Mol, Ingunn Moser, and Jeannette Pols write, "do not work or fail in and of themselves. Rather, they depend on care work."[26] At the beginning of this chapter, I offered Avilés-Vázquez's summary of the situation in Puerto Rico, in which, through the very denial of care, the infrastructures in desperate need of maintenance and care have been weaponized against the populations whose lives that they are supposed to sustain. A traffic light no longer affords safe passage. Left in a state of despair, it affords killing instead. "We must take care of things," María Puig de la Bellacasa writes, "in order to remain responsible for their becomings,"[27] including becomings that can be, as in the case of the traffic lights, murderous.

This particular murderous becoming, enabled by the lack of care, is part and parcel of "disaster capitalism," which Naomi Klein describes as an opportunistic, market-driven reconstruction of the world that is predicated upon the *deliberate destruction* of what already exists. When a large-scale disaster happens (whether it is military, ecological, or financial), disaster capitalism additionally "eras[es] what was left of the public sphere and rooted communities" in order to replace them with profitable investments (luxury hotels, superhighways, tourist havens, gated zones, etc.).[28] Disaster capitalism's accumulation of wealth is built upon this *systemic destruction* of existing lifeworlds.[29]

As deteriorating public infrastructures, decaying buildings, and murderous becomings of things and people in these disaster-stricken places are uncovered, disaster capitalists deny responsibility for taking care of existing structures that, like the traffic lights, fall into potentially injurious and even murderous disrepair. This refusal of care for what has been damaged and the abandonment of an already destroyed place completes the process, as Klein lays out, of clearing the space for free-market occupation and exploitation. In these situations, the shrinkage of an existing niche entails, and in fact enables, the expansion of another characterized by a set of profitable and exploitative affordances.

Klein's work meticulously reveals how this pattern holds for disaster after disaster, crisis after crisis. The 2004 tsunami that hit Sri Lanka, for instance, did the very job that the tourism industry and global creditors had long wished for but had been blocked from accomplishing by the local villagers' resistance. After the tsunami cleared local fishing huts and boats from the oceanfront, international aid money was used to finance a multimillion dollar redevelopment project that promised the construction of luxury hotels, industrial fishing, and mega highways.[30] In the lands grabbed by disaster capitalists, Klein writes, "entire ways of life were being extinguished."[31] Local families, promised state aid in return for their departure, were relocated to militarized inland camps that over time became completely impoverished.[32]

In this case of shrinkage, an existing space did not get smaller compared to what it once used to be. Rather, fishing families were forced out of one (larger) space (the coastal areas which once were their home) and moved into another smaller space (temporary inland camps with dire conditions). The beaches did not decrease in size; they simply were rendered "off limits."[33] What shrank was the entire niche inhabited by fishing people, who were expelled from the lands and waters on which their subsistence depended.

Ontological Shrinkage

In *Designs for the Pluriverse*, postdevelopment theorist and anthropologist Arturo Escobar writes that colonial occupation is first and foremost "an ontological occupation." Territorial occupation "implies economic, technological, cultural, ecological and often military aspects, but its most fundamental dimension is ontological. From this perspective, what occupies territories is a particular ontology, that of individuals, expert knowledge, markets, and the economy."[34] John Law defines the occupying ontology of (European) colonization as the "one-world world" (oww). The oww erases multiplicities and sanctions that there is "a single reality," "a single container universe," and "that we are all inside it."[35]

If we use affordance theory to detail the process of ontological occupation, we may have a better understanding of how this occupation occurs or, rather, an understanding that works through material bodies as they live in material worlds rather than through more abstract entities such as ideology or even politics. Remember that this is the foundation of affordance theory: to describe perception without introducing abstractions such as thought or consciousness. So, too, affordance theory accounts for multiple ontologies, because different versions of the world come into being for organisms according to their perceptive orientation and capacities. The environment and its surfaces, substances, and mediums literally *become* different *things* in relation to its countless different organisms and their corresponding perceptual systems.

Affordance theory can also account for these different ontologies at the scale of individual organisms, groups with shared perceptual systems, or species; and from very local environments like a home or a pond to much more global environments, including the planet itself. To understand how the oww's ontology works requires exactly these capacities: the ability to account for the existence of ontologies other than the oww's, likely at different scales (towns, schools, nations, borders, diasporas, etc.), in order to detail how one ontology, the oww, accomplishes the occupation of another.

According to the fundamental nature/culture divide on which modernity is built,[36] and which persists today, there is only a single Nature (with a capital N) to be studied, examined, and represented by Science (with a capital S), and there are many cultural interpretations of that singular reality/Nature. For the oww, cultures may make sense of the world and interpret it in different ways, but "what the world *is*" is not up for debate.[37] In fact, the concept of culture itself functions to uphold this separation, so that the nature of reality as defined by Western metaphysics remains in the hands of the colonizer. The colonized remain lesser interpreters of the real reality, as their "nondominant reals" are effectively "evacuate[d]," and their ways of dwelling and enacting worlds are made into absences.[38] "Nonscientific relations with other-than-humans [are] reduced to belief" and robbed of any "right to define reality."[39] The oww does not just colonize reality; it sanctions "the coloniality of reality."[40] It dismisses the reciprocal relations that Indigenous peoples have historically established with their land, refutes the affordances and meanings that they have long found in the land,[41] and replaces them with whichever meanings and opportunities that the colonizers have chosen to be of benefit to themselves. It justifies the invasion and subsequent exploitation of nonhuman species' habitats. The oww leaves no environment, no substance, no surface, no affordance unoccupied by its own ontology. The expansion of oww means the shrinkage of the "pluriverse," namely, "*a world where many worlds fit.*"[42]

At the time of Law's writing, oww referred to the Western ontology of rationality and modernism, which refuses any ways of knowing or being other than its own. In the current era that some call the Capitalocene there remains a one-worldedness; but given the scale of climate urgencies and the magnitude of losses, oww will be less and less likely to self-seal as firmly as it once used to. Breaches and fractures are, for better or worse, everywhere. In a planet held together by multispecies assemblages, when one thing starts going down the "death road," as Deborah Bird Rose writes, "other things start going too." When reciprocal relations get undone and "mutualities falter," the result is that "dependence becomes a peril rather than a blessing," leading to "extinction cascades" and bringing on what Rose calls "worlds of loss."[43] In a web of connectivity, shrinking niches become sinking niches that take other niches down with them. Shrinking turns into sinking collectively, deeper and deeper.[44] As the oww's practices physically deplete the earth's environments, clearing habitats and devastating the land, sea, and air, all other affordances also begin to sink. Its practices obliterate—sink—the material sustenance of life, as well as entire cosmologies and ways of being. And this type of shrinkage comes at a cosmic cost.

Shrinking → Sinking

In the precarious Capitalocenic times we are in, marked by the ongoing shrinkage of livable worlds in the pluriverse, the urgency for disability studies is to move beyond the oww's human/nonhuman dualism and its human exceptionalism,[45] beginning with tracing disability's becomings—not all of which are positive, and some of which can indeed be murderous. The urgency is to track the "negative" dimensions of disability, including loss, reduction, pain, and suffering, within the nonsterile, noninnocent, materially and historically situated entanglements of life that transgress and dissolve any dualist boundary that we can think of (human/nonhuman, animate/inanimate, nature/culture). In this part, I mobilized the concept of shrinkage as one way of responding to these urgencies.

What contracts in shrinkage is the space for action, which is ultimately the space for livability afforded by the planet. This shrinkage concerns all species and differentiations among them, including disabled, racialized, gendered, and colonized bodies, threatened organisms, and disappearing species. As a nonanthropocentric account of changing environmental conditions that affect different kinds of bodies within and across species, shrinkage can allow us to trace resonances among and across species-bodies that live and are made to live in a world of shrinking affordances. As a term that emerges from affordance theory and that with its ecological roots situates humans in the larger world of interconnected species, "shrinkage" affects both a nonanthropocentric intervention in disability studies and a disability studies intervention in the ongoing debates about the implications of "Anthropocene" as a name for the current era.

The question then is: What happens in those shrunken worlds of possibilities?

PART II.   PERFORMANCE

A THEORY OF ACTIVIST AFFORDANCES

Disability is an art—an ingenious way to live.
—Neil Marcus, *Storm Reading*

Story 1

Rheumatoid arthritis–related disabilities are quite particular in the way they can fluctuate. You may be feeling well one day, and the next be in a flare-up with painful and swollen joints. Periods of flare-ups may be followed by periods of the disease's inactivity. No matter how long you have lived with the disease, you still may not know which joint may be affected on which day and to what degree. The participants in my fieldwork had vivid memories of highly disabling periods, even if I happened to visit them on "a good day," as they put it. Yasemin told me, almost with a tone of regret:

I wish you were able to see what I go through on a bad day. For example, I cannot sit down or stand up. I drag my feet when I go down the stairs. When brushing my hair, I hold my hair like this [*bends her head down toward her shoulder and holds it with her arm at that level*]. That is why I had my hair cut like this. It used to be long before.

I asked Yasemin if she could show how she combed her hair during flare-ups. She explained, reenacting the movements:

When I had a flare-up, I held my hair [figure 5.1] and bent my head down toward the comb [figure 5.2] and I used my arm as support like this [figure 5.3]. I used to comb it like this.

In part I, I proposed that in ecological terms, disability is constituted as the shrinkage of the environment, its existing affordances, and the actions they make available (and not). In this part, I turn to what follows from that shrinkage. While the environment may become smaller, and while not all of its affordances may be at hand for a particular body or may not exist in a given moment, it is in precisely this situation that something else happens. When the environment AS IS shrinks and previously available affordances disappear, it is the improvisatory space of performance that opens up, and it is in this performative space that bodies can perceive nearly imperceptible affordances they might not have otherwise apprehended, finding ways to survive in the shrunken environment AS IF it were more amenable, as if it were something or someplace else. The two following analytics of site-specific and theatrical performance offer an entry point for describing this improvisatory response more precisely.

Analytic 1

In site-specific performance . . . extended conditions of *surface, climate* and *architectural enclosure* may actually occasion dynamic engagements from the performers, beyond the routine demands of functionality. . . . But the very engagement itself may form the substance of performance: ergonomics *as* performance. In the dynamic interplay of body and environment, both strategically planned and tactically improvised, performers encounter—and counter—the immediate effects of site.[1]

In this quote, performance studies scholar and theater artist Mike Pearson is comparing the relatively well-modulated conditions of traditional theater spaces to the spatial arrangements and the unpredictable and at times even inhospitable conditions of spaces in site-specific performances. He argues that not only may these features—uneven terrain, changeable weather, and built structures—require performers to adapt to them spontaneously, but that

FIGURES 5.1–5.3 IN THE THREE IMAGES ABOVE, YASEMIN DEMONSTRATES HOW
SHE COMBS HER HAIR WITHOUT HAVING TO LIFT UP HER ARMS, WHICH IS
DIFFICULT WHEN RA FLARES UP. IN FIGURE 5.1 (*TOP*), YASEMIN BENDS HER HEAD
TOWARD HER RIGHT SHOULDER. IN FIGURE 5.2 (*MIDDLE*), SHE BRINGS HER LEFT
HAND TOWARD HER BENT HEAD TO HOLD HER HAIR IN PLACE. IN FIGURE 5.3
(*BOTTOM*), SHE USES HER RIGHT HAND TO PULL THE COMB THROUGH HER HAIR.

this "ergonomic" activity may itself become an artistic aspect of the performance. Those who enact performances in everyday sites may not have the conditions to inhabit the spaces that those who use them regularly do. For example, a performance may call for actors to be "in street clothes underwater in a swimming pool," struggling to move while encumbered by billowing garments, or "semi-naked without overalls and goggles in a factory," unprotected from harmful vapors and substances. Performers may, in other words, encounter challenges and even barriers as they enact a performance under its specific conditions, some of which may be purposeful and others, more unexpected. For Pearson, this is precisely the artistic value of site-specific performance. It is "the tension between [performers'] readiness" and the built-in "lack of preparation" that "generates [the performance's] substance and meaning."[2] Unfamiliar or unpredictable environmental properties and conditions require actors to continually improvise and experiment. As performers are "literally battling with the elements," they create new body-environment relations and make the performance "a work of invention."[3]

Analytic 2

In 2018 I attended *Let Me Play the Lion Too*, "an improvisational experiment," in the words of the theater company Told by an Idiot, whose twelve actors with and without disabilities work together to "devise new improvised evenings of *anarchic spontaneity*."[4] At the beginning of the performance, the director spoke directly to us/the audience and described the company's working method, which is based not on scripts but on *improvisation*. It is when you put restrictions on their space for action, the director said, that the actors begin to improvise and act inventively within those constraints.

The play begins. First, the director tells the performers what each act is about and gives them instructions as to, for example, the space in which they can act, and what words, language, facial expressions, or body parts they can use. What follows is, in the theater company's terms, an "anarchic spontaneity." According to the director's explanations, these constraints *generate* creative engagement rather than impede it. As a spectator, I saw that obeying the limits imposed on the actors' performance allowed for a more profound sense of how the performers' bodily singularities, subjectivities, and desires shaped the flow of their creative actions. The constraints that allowed for these actions, carefully chosen for their effect, gave each of these bodies a full presence that defied ableist perceptions of them individually and collectively.

Whether improvisation is employed in theater, jazz, or any other type of art, this simultaneously *unscripted* and *constrained* method can generate creative or "anarchic" spontaneities that turn it into a form of defiance.[5] In improvisation there is no script, no score, no notation in the traditional sense. Improvisation is creativity unrestrained,[6] paradoxically, *due to* constraints or limits. It is a matter of *making do* with what you have, on the spot, with utmost ingenuity. In fact, we can think of the relationship between the environmental *constraints* on improvisation, and the creativity that improvisation generates, as a reverse correlation: the more restrained the space and the means are, the more unrestrained the creativity must become.

Shrinkage → Performance

The two examples of aesthetic performances that I present here explicitly deal with *constraints*—the constraints imposed by the site, the rules of improvisation, or both. Even when the performance in question is a traditional form of theater, it still has to deal with constraints. Think of the theater stage. It is neither physically possible nor desirable for the stage to contain all the material elements of the world in which a story takes place. What renders that imagined world real is not whatever world is already visible and tangible on the stage (the stage can have only so many props!) but the actions of the performers. In moving and behaving in the artful ways they do, performers imagine another possible reality and render it real in the here and now by enacting it.

The same imaginative-performative work, as I shall unpack in this part, takes place in the shrinking environments of disability. The environments disabled people live in are also staged, by the habitus of ableism, and they have "props" in the form of everyday objects (such as combs) that are similarly designed. AS IS, these environments do not contain the shape of disabled peoples' pain, their sickness, and their access needs in a fully available and distinct material form, nor do they easily give rise to the imagination that would do so. It is through their creative engagements with whatever happens to be around them, and through the enormous labor these enactments require, that disabled people come to imagine more livable, more accessible worlds and to render those worlds real to the degree that is possible in the here and now. In other words, a shrunken environment does not readily afford what people with a given disability need. Recall that an affordance "is always there [in the environment] to be perceived" whether the observers perceive it or not.[7] By the same token, activist affordances exist in the environment to be perceived, but they are the most remote and the most unlikely ones to be perceived, because the ableist habitus has pushed them to the extremities of the possible and the plausible. Because these affordances are simply not there—or to be more precise, they are there, but not evident in an overt material/social form, or worse yet, not even within the realm of the feasible in an ableist habitus—it takes a great deal of *effort, creativity,* and *activist* labor to generate these affordances. When my participants perceive the affordances they need and wish for in the shrunken environments they inhabit, they exert precisely this effort, creativity, and activist labor. Within the AS IF framework of performance, they seek out and make do with what is available AS IF it were someplace else, more accessible, welcoming, and habitable, AS IF already furnished with those otherwise distant and almost imperceptible affordances.

In the following chapters, I trace how these more habitable worlds and their imagined affordances are brought into being in and through *performance* and out of the material *constraints* of the present. Weaving together theories of performance and affordance, I argue that the imperatives of a shrunken environment—whether narrowed literally to a theater stage, or to disabled people's everyday orbits—prompts the imaginative work of performance in and through which other affordances are *made up* and *made real,* despite their remoteness from habitual perception, and despite the absence of artifacts and their placement in built spaces that would materialize those affordances. Because the perception of affordances and the behavior that gives rise to them are not separate, and not even simultaneous, but actually one action, I call this bringing into being a *performance of world-building,* and the world it brings into being, "activist affordances." I define activist affordances as the micro, ephemeral, and performative acts/arts of world-making with which disabled people must literally *make up,* and at the same time *make up for,* whatever affordances fail to readily materialize in their environments and their remoteness to perception. Activist affordances are also "micro" in the sense that they are tiny, modest, and humble. They are "ephemeral" in the sense that they are fleeting, nondiscursive, and not materializable in final enduring forms. They are "performative" in the sense that they do not already exist in the environment, like standard affordances, but *come into being as* they give rise to absent but necessary or desirable actions that enact worlds. Finally, activist affordances are activist in the sense that an activist perception/action produces them. The "activism" of activist affordances accounts precisely for this performativity of perception/action that unearths these otherwise submerged or subjugated affordances.

The theory of activist affordances joins the literature on disability that calls attention to what disabled people do to inhabit unfriendly environments. Disability artists, activists, and scholars have long argued that disability is a form of ingenuity, resourcefulness, and flourishing.[8] They have proposed that disabled people be considered problem-solvers, engineers, tinkerers, experts, knowers, and makers in their own right.[9] More recently "crip" has been extensively reclaimed, and corresponding analytics have been elaborated.[10] "Crips are not merely formed or acted on by the world," Aimi Hamraie and Kelly Fritsch write in their *Crip Technoscience Manifesto*; "we are engaged agents of remaking." An extension of feminist technoscience studies, "crip technoscience" describes "disabled peoples' world-dismantling and world-building labors [that] stem from situated experiences of 'misfitting.'"[11] The theory of activist affordances builds on and expands this literature. In turning to everyday choreographies and microimprovisations of disabled and sick bodies, my theory becomes accountable to ways of inhabiting unfriendly environments that, unlike do-it-yourself (DIY) access or even technoscience in its "cripped" forms, are not based on the making of artifacts. The theory of activist affordances adapts affordance theory to disability for a variety of purposes, in this case to articulate aspects of world-making that are always in-the-making and whose capacity to make the world more inhabitable lies in the *performance* itself. In other words, if activist affordances make more habitable worlds, as I claim, then they *world* those worlds in and through the ephemerality of performance.

The performance of affordances, like the performances of actors, necessarily involves bodies in particular sites or in relation to particular artifacts, substances, and surfaces. The actors contend with the vagaries of changing weather, with their unwieldy clothing underwater, and with the lack of protective clothing in a factory. My participants, as I chart in the next chapters, also create activist affordances through their bodily actions (or the bodies of others) rather than (with the exception of some cases) through the alteration of their environments or the artifacts within them. In the face of constraining environments, their bodies "become" affordances in order to accommodate those constraints and *enact* the affordances that until then are only a potential—a potential that is otherwise too remote and too unlikely to be perceived. They enact affordances that without work and ingenuity are too Other to be available, bringing into being an imagined habitability that artifact-based approaches may not account for, perceiving affordances that may exist either in the absence of made artifacts or alongside them. This is where, as I shall explore in the following section (through an intervention to be made in Elaine Scarry's account of making), the significance of activist affordances lies: disabled people *dance* the affordances of accessible worlds in their physical absence.[12]

While full access for some impairments may be a distant dream, full access for all impairments of all organisms is more likely a full-blown fantasy. The value of activist affordances lies in recognizing this limit while accounting for the ways that these ephemeral affordances allow us to make do—to dance—under limiting conditions.

Dancing Pain Away

In *The Body in Pain*, aptly subtitled *The Making and Unmaking of the World*, Scarry discusses two consequences of pain. On the one hand, extreme pain of war and torture can be deliberately inflicted to unmake the made-world. On the other hand, excruciating bodily pain can be the very catalyst for world-making that will redistribute, share, and diminish the pain. For Scarry, world-making involves the creation of an artifact,[13] where the artifact is the projection of human sentience out onto the world.

"The naturally existing external world," Scarry writes, "is wholly ignorant of the 'hurtability' of human beings."[14] Its floods, hurricanes, landslides, and droughts; its uneven terrains, injurious surfaces, and harmful substances; and the bacteria and viruses that it harbors demonstrate that the environment has no "idea" about the vulnerability of human bodies. It is precisely in *making* things, Scarry argues, that we transform the environment's ignorance into a form of cognizance and imbue an otherwise insensitive world with an "awareness of aliveness."[15] In using the materials available in our environment from which to make coats, blankets, and shoes, we transform them into made things that, in a sense, recognize our need for warmth and protection.[16] Scarry suggests that artifacts externalize in the world a *recognition* of and a *response* to what lies beneath our skin, namely, our pains, vulnerabilities, needs, desires, and wishes. The medications we invent offset illnesses our immune systems cannot protect us from. Even when we are able to withstand the temperatures and textures of our environment without protections such as a coat or blanket, we desire to be more comfortable, or decorative, or healthy, and the things we create out of the environment—furnaces, jewelry, paths for walking and riding—meet those desires. In short, in making, we project ourselves out into the world and transform otherwise "oblivious" surfaces and substances into a "compassionate" world of things. In making, Scarry argues, we strip the world "of its immunity and irresponsibility" and render it *"as knowledgeable about human pain as if it were itself animate and in pain."*[17]

In order to illustrate how this *projection of aliveness* occurs, Scarry gives the example of a man making a chair. Perhaps the man embarks on the act of making, Scarry speculates, because he is inconvenienced by his own body weight or perhaps because he perceives the discomfort of his pregnant wife bearing her body weight.[18] While Scarry takes these as equivalent examples, I want to focus on the man's perception of his wife in the chair. At the moment of perceiving his wife's discomfort in having to carry such body weight, Scarry tells us, the man wishes for it to disappear. (Remember Scarry writes that due to its aversive nature, pain "cannot be felt without being wished unfelt."[19]) This wish—the wish that pain were gone—initiates the process of making.

But this "counterfactual wish,"[20] no matter how compassionate, is still confined to the man's consciousness. Making requires two more steps in which compassion manifests in the external world. In the second step, compassion moves out of the man's consciousness. This involves a translation of "what was originally an invisible aspect of consciousness (compassion)" into "the realm of visible but disappearing action." In this process of translation, the body's "willed series of successive actions" externalize "the interior moment of perceiving," "body weight begone." Scarry names this series of actions "the dance of labor." By itself, the dance does not remain in the external world, and it is different in that sense from the chair it produces. To understand this, Scarry asks us to imagine the man in the act of making a chair with the materials erased from the scene. We would then have before us the maker's body moving in all directions, his arms reaching and extending; his legs kneeling down and standing up; his hands grabbing, pushing, and pulling; his fingers gripping and twisting; his neck and wrists turning. As the dance emerges, the man's compassionate "weight begone" enters the social world, now not just as an internal wish but in a tangible and expressive form.[21]

The dance is the expressed recognition of the other's pain, and in this regard, it is more externalized than the counterfactual wish of the first phase. But the dance and its movements are *ephemeral*; they do not remain as an externalized form of the wish for the pain to disappear. It is only when the man's dance of labor leaves its enduring material effects—using the tools, nails, and wood to make a chair, Scarry argues—that the third and final step of transformation occurs: first a wish, second a series of actions, and third an enduring and shareable reality in the form of an artifact, a chair. Through the dance of labor, the perception of pain as something to get rid of is "danced," and the "danced-perception is sculpted" in the form of a chair. The chair diminishes the pregnant wife's pain not because its shape is "the shape of the skeleton, the shape of body weight, not even the shape of pain-perceived," but because its shape is "the shape of perceived-pain-wished gone."[22] Put differently, the chair knows and responds to the pain not by becoming like the body or the perception of pain but by embodying the "counterfactual wish" that *pain be gone*. Thus, while the chair itself is obviously not animate or conscious of a living being's pain, the counterfactual wish has crystallized into the form of that chair, and as a result the chair acts *"as if it were itself animate and in pain."* The chair is the physical manifestation of the wish for pain to be gone. Its shapes, texture, and overall form enunciate "compassionate speech":[23] the chair's very form and substance says, "I too know you are burdened with your body weight. Sit upon me, and let me carry it on your behalf instead."

This is how, Scarry claims, makers translate an otherwise "ignorant" and hostile environment into one that is aware of, is responsive to, and cares about their pains: first by wishing the pain away, even if it is unrealistic to do so; second by transforming that invisible feeling of compassion into a "visible but disappearing" dance of labor;[24] and third by using the tools and substances of the world that expresses the wish in a material form, which otherwise remains as the internal wish and the dance of labor cannot. While this is a beautiful and poetic account of making, there is a critical moment that remains missing in it. For that, I turn to another story.

Dancing Affordances in Their Absence

In 2010, I attended the annual congress of the European League against Rheumatism in Rome, where I presented a poster with the initial findings of the fieldwork I had done in İstanbul. The poster included one of the images of Yasemin (figure 5.4) demonstrating her unique combing practice. A conference attendee, who I later on learned was a member of a patient organization in Sweden, approached the poster with bewilderment. Her gaze fixed on the image, she turned to me and said, in a perplexed tone: "I don't get why she doesn't use an adaptive comb [like the comb in figure 5.5] instead!" Coming from Sweden, where income levels are high, and where there is a well-developed welfare state that obviously has more resources to offer to its citizens than Turkey, the attendee could not understand why the person in the image could not just get an adaptive tool instead of going to all the trouble of performing the action this way. Not for a moment did it occur to her that this adaptive tool might not have been accessible and available to, or known by, the person in the image. In this moment, it dawned on me that Yasemin had not owned,

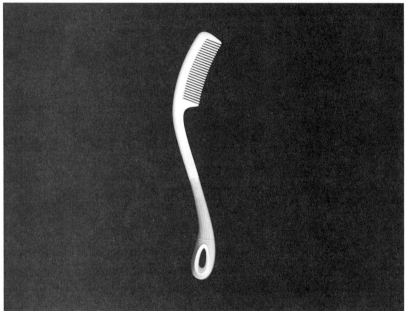

FIGURES 5.4 AND 5.5 YASEMIN, ALONG WITH MILLIONS OF OTHER DISABLED
PEOPLE IN RESOURCE-POOR ENVIRONMENTS, PERFORMS A "DANCE OF LABOR"
IN ORDER TO COMB HER HAIR AND PERFORM OTHER DAILY TASKS. SUCH ACTIVIST
AFFORDANCES STAND IN FOR THE ELONGATED COMB AND OTHER ADAPTIVE TOOLS
FREELY AVAILABLE IN DEVELOPED COUNTRIES.

had access to, or even heard of the elongated comb, and yet she was able to imagine and actualize its very affordance in and through her movements. Yasemin may not have had an adaptive comb, but in her "dance of labor" with bent head, curved body, and crooked movements lay the very affordance of a comb that would make combing possible for her. Yasemin performed this dance in order to minimize her pain, bypassing the movements of her impaired joints that the straight shape of her existing comb demanded. In the absence of an actual assistive tool to alleviate her pains, Yasemin's body became a tool, *making up* and *making real* the very affordance missing in Yasemin's current environment. This was the moment when I first had the idea of activist affordances.

Within the environments that disabled people inhabit, they may not have access to the tools, technologies, and infrastructures that would meet their access needs. They may not even be aware of the existence of such things. But precisely at such instances of lack and constraint—of shrinkage—it is the improvisatory space of performance that may open up, allowing them to reconceive that same environment as something other than itself and what it currently affords. Just like actors improvising on stage, disabled people may move, sense, behave, and communicate in ways that *enact* the affordances that their environments otherwise lack in a substantiated form. In the imagined space of performance they may bring into being the very affordances of otherwise absent access artifacts—whether it is an elongated comb, a chair, or a ramp—in and through their actions. In short, required to live in environments that do not materially provide them with the affordances that they need, disabled people may literally *dance* (as in Scarry's "dance of labor") these affordances.

Going back to Scarry's example of the man making a chair, there is a crucial but missing moment in her account of making: the "original percipient event" of making the chair is not the man perceiving his pregnant wife's body weight and wishing it gone,[25] I would argue, but the pregnant wife dancing away her bodily weight and pain through her own movements. Perhaps she walked by holding her knees. Perhaps she leaned on a wall for support while standing. Perhaps she held her belly with her arms underneath. The point is, whichever action possibility she *choreographed* in order to render the surfaces of the environment inhabitable by her body in its pain and weight, she performed an affordance that did not (yet) exist as an artifact within her niche. And if the man was able to wish his wife's pain away and make that wish real in the shape of an artifact, it was because the pregnant woman had already discovered the affordance of a chair and had already given it an expressive form in and through her movements in the first place. Put differently, long before it was performed by the man making a chair, the dance of labor had been performed by the pregnant woman. Her dance was not the dance of producing an artifact that would endure and be visible and shared beyond the ephemeral moment of its creation. Her dance, in other words, remained within the temporality of performance, as an *anticipation* of a more hospitable and more inhabitable environment that had yet to arrive.

This is exactly what I mean by the term "activist affordances": activist affordances are *danced* affordances, or afford-dances.[26] And what do those dances do? Whether they are danced in solo, in a duo, or in an ensemble, activist affordances bring into being what does not yet exist in durable, socially shareable, and normalized forms in the current order of things but what, in an "accessible future," might. The pregnant woman's dance is an activist affordance, foreseeing the affordance of a chair that will later be made. So are the ingenious choreographies of my participants. In moving her arms and head in combinations very different from those associated with the standard comb and combing, Yasemin literally embodies the layout of an elongated comb, which she has not accessed or known. In bringing his elbow to the same level as the table, Henri enacts an otherwise remote affordance that is a precursor to the potential affordance of an "arthritic mug" that has yet to be designed (see the introduction). In enacting an affordance as they pull, twist, and squeeze the fabric of a shirt and its buttons and buttonholes, my participants perceive the affordance they are enacting and *imagine* and *foresee* the exact affordance of perhaps shirts with magnetic closures, or a buttonhook designed to work with their particular hands, or another assistive tool that is yet to be thought of (figures 5.6–5.9).

If you think about it, the imaginative framework of performance that is at work in these instances is not that different from the imaginative frameworks employed in speculative and critical design.[27] The hypothetical conditions of "what if (I try this action or shape)?" and AS IF are central to both. Activist affordances and speculative design pursue a multitude of alternatives and speculations, as Anthony Dunne and Fiona Raby write, that can "loosen the ties reality has on our ability to dream."[28] The two share a concern with how things *could be* rather than how things currently *are* or *ought to* be. The difference is that performance does not depend on pencils, studios, stylos, and sketches in order to engage in design (or the nails, wood, and hammer that the man in Scarry's work uses to make a chair). In performance, our everyday lives are our studios; our bodies are our pencils; our improvised affordances are our sketches of a world habitable otherwise. To actualize activist affordances in and through performance is not to design alternate worlds, but

FIGURES 5.6–5.9 THESE TWO PAIRS OF FIGURES CONTRAST ACTIVIST AFFORDANCES WITH ADAPTIVE-TOOL ALTERNATIVES. FOR NURHAYAT (FIGURE 5.6, *ABOVE*), A SERIES OF SPECIALIZED MOVEMENTS OF HER OWN DEVISING MAKES IT POSSIBLE TO BUTTON A DRESS SHIRT. AN ADAPTIVE BUTTONER (FIGURE 5.7, *BELOW*) TO MAKE THIS TASK SIMPLER FOR A PERSON WITH RA IS UNAVAILABLE TO HER. ANOTHER PARTICIPANT, SEVIM, USES HER ARMS TO LOWER HERSELF ONTO A SETTEE THAT IS PAINFULLY LOW (FIGURE 5.8, *OPPOSITE TOP*). AN ADJUSTABLE-HEIGHT CHAIR (FIGURE 5.9, *OPPOSITE BOTTOM*) WOULD ALLOW HER TO PERFORM THE SAME ACTION IN LESS TIME AND IN MORE COMFORT.

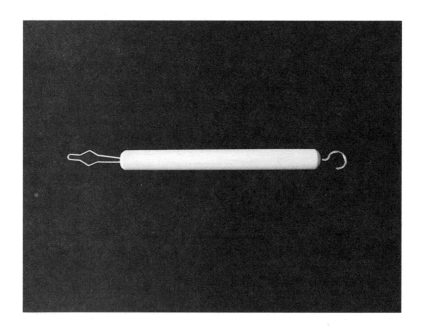

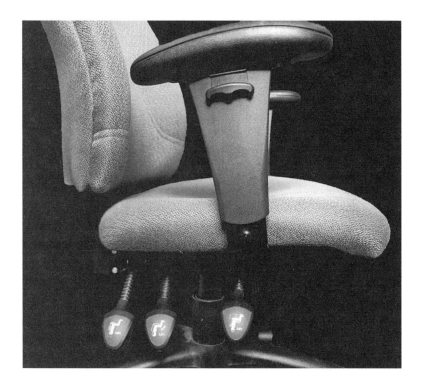

rather to engage in a more radical transformation, or to use Escobar's phrasing, "to design [alternate worlds] otherwise."[29]

Performing World-Making

It matters what thoughts think thoughts. It matters what knowledges know knowledges. It matters what relations relate relations. It matters what worlds world worlds.[30]

Based on the premise of "danced affordances" or afford-dances, we can imagine how any prior activist affordance could be translated into a made artifact, where the artifact would take the form of the prior dance in the same way that the chair "owes" its existence to a prior bodily performance. We can even think of existing access artifacts as the crystallizations of prior repeated danced affordances. But this is not necessarily the point I wish to make. The translation from performance to artifact may or may not happen. A danced affordance may simply disappear without anyone "taking hold" of it by capturing it in a material form. Translations may happen as mistranslations, appropriations, or failed translations in which activist affordances end up being co-opted and normalized or used for other ends than for disabled people's sake. What I wish to claim and emphasize is the existence and intrinsic value of activist affordances. Most importantly, they have a political significance that we, as disability scholars, need to name, recognize, and map out.

First, the historical/local "disability worlds" we inhabit may not provide access to technologies, tools, products, and stuff to *make things with*.[31] World-making requires resources—physical, economic, temporal, and more—that may or may not be available to us. Terms such as "crip technoscience," "DIY," and "maker-cultures" that describe how people with disabilities create access for themselves assume that such resources are simply available. Though it is certainly very important to identify these creative material activities, technologies cannot be "cripped" in all times and places and likely obscure the enactment of activist affordances.

The point is, we may literally not have the *means* to build worlds, and we may not be able to *afford* (monetarily) world-building if it is defined in terms of things that we build. The activist affordances' making, however, only asks for our bodies and our imagination, which at certain times or in certain places may be all that we have. Activist affordances, as I have been describing them, are danced, and they also are literally *choreographed* impromptu, a series of movements designed on the spot with whatever we happen to have in our surroundings. As long as life goes on, we can still afford a dance—an afford-dance—even if that dance entails the most miniscule of movements, such as the blinking of an eye or inhalations and exhalations. Activist affordances multiply the possibilities of world-making by reducing its conditions of possibility to a bare minimum: being able to afford a dance, no matter how tiny and imperceptible that dance may be.

Second, the nuanced variations among disabled bodies and the particularities of impairments—evident in but certainly not exclusive to rheumatoid arthritis—suggest that there can be no fully accessible environment, though it is certainly worthwhile to increase access wherever possible. Again, as the following chapters demonstrate, we may still create more livable worlds in and through our performances. Born from within performance, activist affordances make the act of world-making itself accessible, and this is where their value and significance lie.

Third, as an accessible form of world-making, activist affordances can speak to the realities of the Global South (where resources are scarce) and therefore allow us to respond to Helen Meekosha's call for a "global Disability studies project" that I lifted up in part 1.[32] As a nonexploitative form of world-making, activist affordances also relate strongly to the precarious climate catastrophic conditions of our times and bring in a valuable disability studies contribution to the ongoing debates on the Anthropocene (see chapter 10).

Rethinking Activism in a Shrinking World of Possibilities

I have elaborated the theory of activist affordances specifically to provide a vocabulary for the acts of world-making that can take place in the most adverse, reduced, and constrained of circumstances, and I offer this vocabulary for conversation in the literature on creativity in disability studies and to theories of design and making in general. I also join disability scholars and activists, among others, who have long challenged the exclusions and the taken-for-granted body/mind dualism of activism as conventionally understood. From Susan Wendell's identification of the tension between what activism typically asks for—"a consistently energetic, high-functioning body and mind"—and what the realities of "unhealthy disabled" people are, to the criticisms of the barriers within major political formations, such as the Occupy movement, Quebec student protests, and more recently the climate march, these interventions have questioned which body/minds are presumed to *be able* to do activism and have invented new ways, modalities, and concepts of activism.[33] Activist affordances draw on and contribute to this critical literature that has pushed the limits of what activism can be, and what it may involve. Before elaborating this further, let me first bring in a defining world-making moment from US disability rights movement's history, known as "the Capitol crawl."

In March 1990, about sixty disability activists gathered in front of Capitol Hill in the United States to demand the passage of the Americans with Disabilities Act (ADA), which was about to become a law but was then stalled in the House. In protest, activists left their wheelchairs, crutches, and other mobility aids aside, and in accordance with a preplanned scenario, they "began a 'crawl-up' of the eighty-three marble steps to the Capitol," performing what the failure of the ADA would cost them.[34] A few months after the protest, the version of the ADA signed into law ensured that built environments to come would have ramps. In slowly crawling up the stairs, disability activists actualized the very affordance of a ramp that, were it to be given a material form, would save them from having to do this agonizing "dance of labor."[35]

As the Capitol crawl demonstrates, disability activism has long been occupied with world-making (which in this case was explicit, scripted, and preplanned). In taking to the streets; in occupying spaces and buildings; in chaining themselves to buses, bridges, and fences; and in engaging various other forms of civil disobedience, direct actions, and sit-ins, self-identified disabled people and their allies have demanded access, asked for civil rights, fought for legislative and policy change, and condemned discrimination, barriers, and exclusion in the hopes of creating a more accessible world. Indeed, many accessible spaces and services exist today because of such monumental past work of disability activism. But this does not, and should not, mean that disability activism as traditionally understood is the only way for accessible worlds to come into being. Many actions *world worlds*, and not all of them are disruptively "crip,"[36] or activist, in that narrower, traditional sense.

In fact, not all people with impairments self-identify as disabled, much less as crip. They may not even be recognized as disabled or as having an impairment to begin with. And yet without necessarily adopting any anti-assimilationist position, they may be creating more livable worlds in and through their activist affordances. The theory of activist affordances seeks to draw attention to these possibilities, and to make evident sites, acts, and agents that a narrower definition of activism cannot account for. We cannot understand what could possibly be activist about buttoning a shirt differently if we limit our understanding of activism to the hypervisible, public, intentional, and collectively engaged political actions pursued by self-identified minority groups. We cannot understand what could possibly be activist about brushing your hair differently if we reduce activism to freedom from barriers and the fight for civil rights.[37] But if we define activism by what activism *does* and what it *affords*—the creation of more livable worlds—and by where and how rather than who engages in it, then disorienting brushes, twisting bottles, and transforming shirts into pullovers can also count as activism.

Because the theory of activist affordances points to actions rather than to political or ethical commitments, it does not assume or require that my participants identify their actions as activist or identify themselves as activists—far from it, because most of them do not even identify as disabled. I admit that there are risks involved in naming their actions as activist. Even if I am not making claims about my participants' identities or politics, I still worry about how my participants might feel about having their actions named activism, and I worry about whether I am, in this act of naming, burdening my participants with political or ethical responsibilities. And yet, as an "unhealthy disabled" person living with nonapparent impairments who manages her days through micro acts/arts of survival that are very similar to those of her research participants, I have a strong and persistent desire and longing for my/our micro acts/arts of everyday survival to be *named* and *recognized* alongside more visible and valued forms of activism. Thus, the term "activist affordances" is not meant to overburden their creators with a label that they may not wish for in the first place. Instead, it is meant to name, appreciate, and acknowledge all the labor, effort, and ingenuity that it takes to perceive and actualize barely perceptible and nearly unthinkable affordances that have been pushed to the margins of collective imagination within an ableist habitus. I mobilize activist affordances to open up new ways of thinking about activism—ways that do not limit its world-making capacity to the voluntarily engaged, disruptive, loud, combative, conspicuous, and celebrated actions.

In the next five chapters I track down these actions, these acts of world-making that need to be unearthed. Mundane, elusive, ephemeral, nonvocal, and nondiscursive, they are difficult to grasp and even easier to ignore. I elaborate on the theory of activist affordances by tracing the enactments of more livable worlds. Drawing on my visual ethnographic materials that include images and dialogue, I document and describe how people with various forms of disabilities dance the affordances of the accessible worlds they imagine but as yet lack in material form. As I demonstrate in chapter 6, my participants often engage in this dance by themselves; and in chapter 8, I discuss how at other times, especially at times of extreme bodily and environmental constraints under which the solo dance is no longer possible, they dance those affordances with an other or with multiple others. I also argue that through their repetition, sustained revision, and experimentation, these otherwise ephemeral choreographies leave their residues on the bodies that create them and on the substances and surfaces that are part of their creation. Chapter 9, on disability repertoires, traces these residues. In comparing the testimonies of "newly" and "seasoned" disabled participants, I discuss how disabled people, throughout the course of a life lived with disability, carve out a livable niche for themselves bit by bit, through impromptu acts/arts of everyday survival that I call activist affordances.

6

AN ARCHIVE OF ACTIVIST AFFORDANCES

This chapter is exactly what its title says: an archive of activist affordances. There is no overarching narrative or logic to it (or to the ethnographic materials it presents). It is a list, an inventory. The set of actions documented in the following could look like any other actions to the untrained or unknowing eye, but they are not. These seemingly insignificant everyday moments, in fact, make worlds. Activist affordances make more livable, more accessible worlds—worlds that are not yet and perhaps could never be (fully) materialized, but worlds that are rendered possible and habitable *in this moment* nonetheless. This chapter tells the story of how those worlds are brought into being by offering a description, or rather a redescription, of this "insignificant" set of actions.

In the following, I focus on the creation of a series of activist affordances where the body itself acts as a tool in the absence or scarcity of accessible and hospitable objects, spaces, or infrastructures.[1] The ethnographic descriptions, most of which are provided by my participants, specify why they moved their bodies and engaged with objects and spaces in this or that way, thereby identifying the turning points in their affordances. It is in these descriptions that the reader may find the contours of another possible world that is being designed, drawn, and *danced*. Whether it is an existing adaptive tool that is unavailable in the localities they inhabit (like the elongated comb in Yasemin's story) or a future accessible object that is yet to be designed (like the arthritic mug in Henri's story), these activist affordances choreograph the layouts and features of more livable niches that are yet to arrive. In other words, as readers move from one activist affordance to another, they have the opportunity to encounter, through the very documentations and descriptions provided, many imagined accessible worlds that once were.

How to Read the Archive

The world of things has its normative, or in Alan Costall's phrasing, "canonical" affordances,[2] steering us into certain actions rather than others. Designed stuff, by way of its form and layout, tells us what to do and what not to do. It invites us to use certain parts of our bodies and not others. In fact, according to Tim Ingold, design is based on the deception that designed objects solve problems when designed objects created those problems in the first place. We are *deceived* into believing that the table, for instance, "is the solution of providing support for box, jug, bowl and spoon, when it is only because of the table that we are expected to place things at such a height, rather than at a ground level."[3] In short, designed stuff not only has its canonical affordances; it also creates its own raison d'être, justifying the *need* for the very affordance that it provides.

As will become evident in the following, activist affordances defy, resist, and counter such normativity. Whatever problem designed things pretend to solve, my participants do not buy into that deception. Things are not used for what they are meant to be. Whichever choreography was crystallized in the shape and layout of an artifact does not unfold during its use. Canonized affordances are not abided by. But then, of course, not much of that is exceptional to disability. Whether disabled or not, people may still ignore what things ask them to do. They may hack existing uses of things and, in Sara Ahmed's wording, put them to "queer uses."[4] Countering the normativity of a designed world is therefore not specific to activist affordances. Their defining characteristic lies instead in what *necessitates* creative disobedience.

When my participants come up with activist affordances they do so not at will, or out of some curiosity, or for the mere sake of rebellion. They create these affordances because they *have to*.[5] It is not that things would still be (comfortably) usable for them had they not put them to unusual uses. It is not that the world would still be accessible to them had they not choreographed access in and through their bodies. My point is that activist affordances are not one option among many. They are, instead, the least painful, discomforting, and irritating way—and sometimes the *only* way—of undertaking an action with an impaired body. Activist affordances are *matters of urgency* (a point I return to in chapter 10), and the descriptions provided in this chapter are meant to render those urgencies perceivable and shareable.

I have listed each activist affordance with its corresponding daily task in order to signify the everydayness and unspectacularity of these affordances. I have decided to include as many activist affordances as possible, because each one is shaped by and reflects its creators' unique embodiment and situatedness. I hope that this collection and the thick descriptions it provides can be a resource for professionals, such as designers and occupational therapists, as well as for disabled people who might find a bit of themselves in these moments and recognize their microactivist companions.

Activist Affordance: How to (Un)button a Shirt

When we find readily available counterparts for our bodily attributes in the world of things that surround us, when we follow the lines that are given to us, we are "oriented." Orientations, as Ahmed describes them, are established lines that we reinforce as we follow or trace them.[6] But these lines necessarily also generate the absence of orientation for those who cannot (or do not wish to) follow them. For example, it takes a certain bodily capacity to be oriented to a shirt with buttons—to follow the lines of buttoning the shirt (see figure 6.1). But when one's fingers are in pain and inflamed, when they do not easily bend, when their shapes are reformed by a disease, there is no straight line to follow to put the button through its hole (see figure 6.2). The manipulation of a tiny button and buttonhole requires pain-free hands with fine motor skills, which my participants with RA-related disabilities do not necessarily have.

But they were able to button a shirt. Instead of following the line of orientation, they pulled the fabric around the buttonhole toward the button; bent, twisted, and squeezed it, or wrapped it around their fingers, and found some way of making the button pass through the hole without having to grab the button and the hole directly with their fingers. The unbending of fingers of one hand was, for instance, compensated for by the grabbing of the button

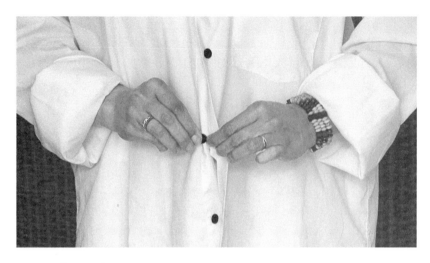

FIGURES 6.1 AND 6.2 IN THE CREATION OF AN ACTIVIST AFFORDANCE, THE
RESTRICTION OF FINE MOTOR SKILLS STEMMING FROM RA GIVES RISE TO A
REORIENTATION OF BODIES TO SHIRTS, BUTTONS, AND FABRICS. IN FIGURE 6.1
(*ABOVE*), A HEALTHY, ABLE-BODIED PERSON USES THE FINGERS OF HER LEFT HAND
TO PINCH A BUTTON ON HER DRESS SHIRT WHILE THE FINGERS OF HER RIGHT
GRASP THE FABRIC. ALTERNATIVELY, A PERSON LIVING WITH RA (IN THIS CASE,
NURHAYAT) MAY USE THE FINGERS OF HER LEFT HAND TO GRASP THE FABRIC AND
LEVER THE BUTTON IN PLACE WITH HER THUMB WHILE USING HER RIGHT HAND
TO PULL THE FABRIC TAUT FROM ABOVE (FIGURE 6.2, *BELOW*).

by the other hand (figure 6.3). Through odd angles, bent positionings, and unlikely entanglements of the fabric, button, and hands, the affordances that lay beyond the coordinates of the existing orientation's lines came into being (figure 6.4). These possibilities arose from the restriction of fine motor skills and from pain, which required a different set of relations in order to be oriented to the shirt with buttons.[7]

My participants came up with improvised affordances within the shrinkage of their environments, transforming actions that were as micro and as mundane as buttoning a shirt into acts of "anarchic spontaneity" akin to those performed in *Let Me Play the Lion Too.* A form of *microdefiance* can be considered a defiance against the normative orientation of bodies to shirts, buttons, and fabrics that ignore our pains, preclude our crooked fingers, and assume that we all have arms and hands to begin with.

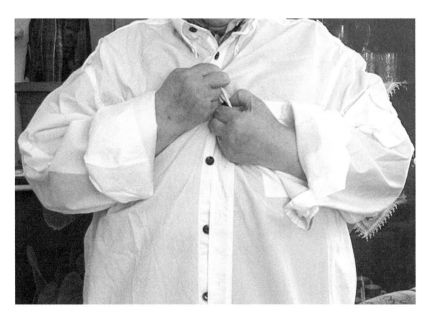

FIGURES 6.3–6.5 MORE OF NURHAYAT'S AFFORDANCES FOR BUTTONING A DRESS SHIRT (*ABOVE AND OVERLEAF*). IN FIGURE 6.3 (*ABOVE*), SHE HOLDS THE FABRIC WITH HER RIGHT FIST WHILE HER LEFT THUMB AND INDEX FINGER MANEUVER THE BUTTON.

FIGURES 6.4 AND 6.5 IN THE AFFORDANCE CAPTURED IN FIGURE 6.4 (*ABOVE*),
NURHAYAT USES THE THUMBS OF BOTH HANDS TO PINCH THE FABRIC AROUND
A BUTTON. IN FIGURE 6.5 (*BELOW*), NURHAYAT'S RIGHT INDEX FINGER COAXES
THE BUTTON THROUGH THE HOLE AS HER LEFT HAND HOLDS THE FABRIC TAUT.

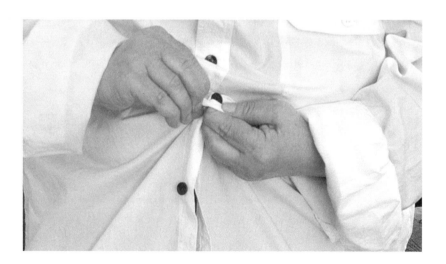

Activist Affordance: How to Wear a Shirt

What one does with a shirt button may also relate to the sleeves or vice versa,
such that putting on a button-up shirt involves affordances that are not self-
contained units of action but are instead part of a seamless continuity of actions that fit together. In fact, my participants did not put on a shirt and then
button it, or unbutton it in order to take it off, as one oriented to a button-up

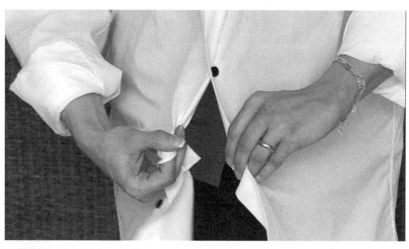

shirt might assume. Indeed, after we finished filming the buttoning, Valerie and Ahmet both told me that they often do not button or unbutton their shirts entirely but leave them partly buttoned (figures 6.11–6.14):

> *Valerie*: Usually, I just take the top [button] and take it off. But then it's . . .
> *Arseli*: You do it that way [*mimics taking off a shirt like a pullover*]?
> *Valerie*: Well, I took one arm at a . . .
> *Arseli*: Like a shirt?
> *Valerie*: Um, no. Yeah. Like this [figure 6.11] if I can, like this [figure 6.12]. . . . If I can, I would do it like that. This one is a big shirt so it would work. So, I wouldn't undo the whole thing. I would do like this [figure 6.13] and pass over my head. So, I don't have to do them.

Ahmet said: "I mean, I do for example, I do them [daily tasks] in a practical way. I undo two or three buttons and take it over as if it were a pullover." Ahmet smiled and pointed to his head, indicating that he looked for solutions. I asked if he could say a bit more about this. He said:

> I do three-four or two-three buttons before wearing the shirt, and the last one with one hand once it is worn. I wear the shirt as if it were a pullover [figure 6.14]. I use it this way [*smiles and winks at the camera*]. That last button is hidden anyway when you wear a tie. This way, I have to do one button only [once I have the shirt on]. This, I do only to save time otherwise if I am free . . . I can do it. I can do each button one by one. But logically speaking, why should I?

Pointing to another benefit of wearing the shirt as if it were a pullover, Ahmet added that this shortcut, when taking off the shirt, also allowed him to undo the buttons using both hands and quickly, facing the shirt instead of while wearing it: "Because the other way around [when the shirt is already on you], only one hand can be at work. But this way, when you wear it as if it were a pullover, I can use my both hands, four or ten fingers at the same time . . . I mean I don't bother undoing it when I come back from work . . . as long as there is enough space to pull it over my head, as if it were a pullover."

Ahmet's activist affordance *countered* and *negated* "the normate template,"[8] sewn into the very form of the garment. But not only did he do so, he also explicitly articulated that microdefiance, saying: "I can do each button one

FIGURES 6.11–6.13 (*ABOVE*) VALERIE'S AFFORDANCE IS RELATED TO HER CHOICE
OF AN OVERSIZE SHIRT. IN A SMOOTH SEQUENCE OF MOVEMENTS, SHE TUGS ONE
ARM OUT OF ITS SLEEVE WITH THE HELP OF HER OTHER ARM AND SLIPS THE SHIRT
OFF HER BODY.

FIGURE 6.14 AHMET'S AFFORDANCE INVOLVES EXTENDING HIS RIGHT ARM AND TUGGING THE COLLAR OF HIS SHIRT WITH HIS LEFT HAND TO PULL THE SHIRT OVER HIS HEAD.

by one. . . . But . . . why should I?" It was almost as if the button said "unbutton me," but Ahmet refused to follow that "demand," fulfill that "request," or respond to that "encouragement."[9] One may as well, as Ahmet did, leave the button as is and transform the shirt into something it was not originally meant to be: a pullover.

Activist Affordance: Self-Care

Just as the two participants used their shirts as if they were pullovers, Ahmet used his bathrobe *as if* it were a cloak. This came out when I asked him how he performed his daily chores, assuming that they must be difficult to undertake. Ahmet shyly urged me to face my own ableist assumptions as he told me, with a tone of confidence in his voice, that he managed to do every chore one could think of:

Arseli: What about self-care, like taking a shower?
Ahmet: Yes, I can.
Arseli: Shaving?
Ahmet: Yeah. I can do all that. I do not depend on anyone in that regard.
Arseli: Washing and drying, for instance?

Ahmet: Sure thing. I got a bathrobe. When you wear it . . . [*smiles*], it does the job of drying anyway. I mean when you wear it as if it were a cloak, it absorbs the water.

Perhaps a bathrobe, given its design, already looks like a cloak, but it is not called a cloak or marketed as such. To Ahmet, however, a bathrobe does what a cloak does. It covers and envelops his entire body, absorbs the water, and saves him from having to use his arms to dry himself with his own movements. To Ahmet, a bathrobe *is* a cloak.

Activist Affordance: How to Wear a Tie

Sometimes wearing a tie can be a bit of a problem, Ahmet said. But he had a solution for that too. Here is his performance of an activist affordance (figure 6.15):

That, I do it first like this. I pull it like this, in this way, with my hand underneath. I fasten it like this by pulling [*pulls the part of the tie under his thumb until both ends are of equal length*]. Then once it arrives at the length it should be, I mean, once it is long enough for me to hold it with my left hand [*smiles*], then I hold it [*holds the tie straight with his left hand*] and adjust it more easily.

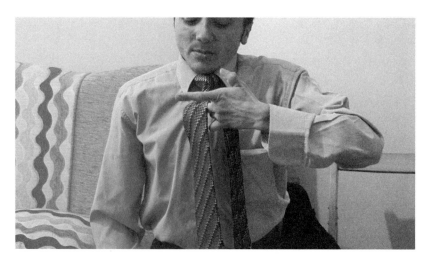

FIGURE 6.15 THE AFFORDANCE AHMET HAS DEVELOPED FOR ADJUSTING HIS TIE INVOLVES A ONE-HANDED TECHNIQUE. WITH HIS MIDDLE FINGER SUPPORTING THE FABRIC FROM BELOW, HE EXTENDS HIS INDEX FINGER ACROSS THE WIDTH OF THE TIE IN ORDER TO ADJUST IT.

As I was doing my fieldwork, I found out that two of my participants have come up with the same affordance for putting on a bra, an affordance I use from time to time as well. The movements that this affordance entails, as another participant noted, also works for wearing a necklace. The affordance goes as follows: you take the bra to the level of your torso, and put it on with its hooks facing your front, not your back. Reversing the bra's intended orientation allows you to use your hands as they face you, bypassing the movements (the extension of shoulders and arms backward) that the intended orientation demands. And once hooked, you twist the bra backward and lift it up and put your arms in.

While ties, zippers, and buttons are often placed at the front of clothing, bra hooks, necklace clasps, and hook-and-eye closures are often placed at the back of the body. These pieces of clothing and accessories, in other words, come with an orientation that asks us to act in certain directions—namely reaching behind the body—rather than others. But my participants' activist affordances reversed and overruled this very orientation, finding ways to use less inflamed and/or impaired joints that the item did not orient toward, and making room for alternative movements that the item's orientation precluded.

The microdefiances of activist affordances can, at times, take a more radical edge. Instead of reorienting the garment by putting it on/taking it off and wearing it in different ways, an activist affordance may materialize as an utter refusal to wear these mis-oriented clothes in the first place. If designed things, to recall Ingold, deceive us by laying a problem in our path that they then purport to solve,[10] then these activist affordances reveal the deception by showing how the refusal to use these artifacts eradicates the problem and its solutions.

The Transformation of Activist Affordances over Time

The bare rehearsal of my progressive disability conceals an increasingly intricate set of exercises in problem-solving that have kept me on my toes . . . for nearly a quarter of a century. What to do when sacks of groceries become too heavy to carry? Ask the clerk to pack more of them with fewer items. What to do when I got too weak to carry them at all? Buy a little four-wheeled wire cart. What to do when I could no longer push the cart? Request someone else carry them to the car?[11]

This is the sequential list of "solutions"—activist affordances—that late feminist author Nancy Mairs comes up with as she anticipates the increasingly shrinking world she will experience due to the progressive nature of her disability. She describes a continual renegotiation and recalibration of the activist affordances that emerge as the environment progressively contracts. My participants' creative affordances, and their gradual transformation over time, followed the same pattern Mairs describes. Consider Louise's observations:

> [*Translated from French*] I think that the more disabilities we have, the more methods we find to have fewer difficulties and still be able to do tasks. We develop new abilities that we wouldn't otherwise have. Sometimes it might take more time [*gestures with her hands, buttoning*], but I will, let's say, turn my hand differently to be able to do something. . . . When you're cleaning, for example, you are doing it with something big. . . . I'm using, like, bigger things, like bigger pens. Everything bigger and larger. . . . There are other things like shoelaces. I cannot use round shoelaces, I need to use flat ones, so I can grab them easily [*gestures with her fingers*]. Otherwise the laces slip through my fingers. It's the same, let's say, when I'm buying clothes. If I cannot handle the buttons, I will buy a shirt with a zipper. *C'est ça la!* [That's it!] [*makes a sweeping gesture with her hand and laughs out loud*].

As Louise cheerfully observed, there is a certain sequence to the creation of activist affordances—a sequence that clearly resonates with Mairs's vivid account of how her improvisatory rehearsals will evolve in accordance with the progression of disability. "The more disabilities we have," as Louise aptly said, "the more abilities we develop"—the more affordances we invent.

I have suggested that when the layout, texture, and form of an object (such as a shirt with zippers or buttons) require movements that our impaired joints cannot perform, we may come up with a counterset of movements that bypass these functional requirements. But what happens when it becomes difficult to enact such affordances—no matter how creatively we seek to do them? It may become necessary to dispense with that particular environment altogether and find another one. That is, when buttoned shirts or zippered pants become more difficult or entirely impossible to put on or take off, we may look to wearing different clothes.

Consider Sevim's account. A "housewife," as she called herself (in Turkish, *ev hanımı*), Sevim mostly spent her time at home. She said, "There are days where I cannot pull my zipper up. That's why I always prefer to wear clothes like this [pointing to the shiny sweatpants she is wearing] with elastic. You know, like sweatpants, sporty clothing within the everyday." Or take Ahmet's relationship with footwear. "My biggest problem," he said with a cheeky smile on his face, "is shoes and socks," which required the help of his sister or brother to put on and take off. He added: "I have a long shoehorn. It does the job. . . . I also try not to buy shoes with laces. I look for Velcro shoes with elastic inserts on the side." For Ahmet, the creation of activist affordances was enabled by multiple agencies, including his siblings and an elongated shoehorn. But the ableist design of shoes with laces assumes that users have the manual dexterity and the hand-eye coordination to manipulate laces, have hands and arms to begin with, or have assistance close at hand. Resisting these requirements, Ahmet chose shoes designed with Velcro closures. With its hook-and-loop strap design, Velcro does the work of fastening shoes with minimal dexterity required of the wearer. Many of my participants with RA-related disabilities echoed Ahmet's preference for shoes with Velcro closures, silently resisting with him the ableism of standard shoe design.

Many of my participants with RA-related disabilities also told me that they made sure that they bought shoes one or two sizes bigger than what they would wear according to standardized ableist measurements, something that I do too. Yasemin, for instance, told me, "The shoes I buy are soft and comfortable and almost two sizes bigger than my feet so I walk like a duck [imitating the movement of a duck with her hands and laughing out loud]." My participants and I buy shoes that allow enough space for our bumpy foot nodules, bunions, and crooked toes. A larger size also allows for the changes in each foot's volume as it undergoes the swelling and deflation common to the fluctuation of inflammatory disease symptoms. We might walk like ducks or look like clowns in our shoes, but underneath that appearance lies an affordance that *expands, explodes*, and *subverts* the standard shoe shapes and sizes based on feet that are fixed, never changing in their volume or size over time.

Garments, shoes, and accessories may also be specifically designed and created to suit bodies that are subject to disability. Here I am reminded particularly of the works of artists Chun-Shan (Sandie) Yi and Freddie Robins and of Frida Kahlo's wardrobe. In her work *Crip Couture*, Yi creates wearable art and adornments that include asymmetrical onesies for babies with limb differences and colorful and delicate gloves highlighting (not hiding) differently numbered and shaped fingers, thereby creating what Alison Kafer calls "crip kin."[12] Robins's *At One* sweater, part of a knitwear series, "acknowledges" and "adorns" the left shoulder of its wearer, Catherine Long, who has one arm.[13] Frida Kahlo, as revealed in the aptly titled exhibit *Frida Kahlo: Making Her Self Up*, designed blouses without fastenings and wore exuberantly colorful dresses of a length that allowed her to move easily, making her disability less noticeable.[14] Such creations, with their particular materials, textures, shapes, and layouts, bear the literal imprint of their owners' crooked, painful, unusual, and deformed bodies. They are not merely functional but embody distinctive aesthetic choices and, of course, their designers' unique tastes and desires, as can be observed in Kahlo's clothing and Sevim's sporty and very shiny sweatpants.

In the Long Run

Our bodies, needs, and impairments are not static. Nor are the activist affordances that we create in order to make room for them in otherwise shrunken environments. We may come up with activist affordances by dancing with an existing world of things in ingenious ways. But for various reasons (such as the progression of disability or aging), there may come a time when these dances are no longer possible. Then our activist affordances, as the previous accounts tell, may take the form of actual material transformation of our environments (including our wardrobes) through the conscious design choices we make in order to match our new bodily needs and impairments with the material properties of *unexpected* newcomers, like Velcro, oversized shoes, and oddly shaped, weirdly textured, irregularly scaled garments. The unusual characteristics of these newcomers materialize the pains and the nonnormative bodily shapes and sizes of their wearers and thereby afford them a less painful and more welcoming way of moving in the everyday.

Activist affordances are, in short, *performatively* repeated and negotiated, always in transformation. We may dance with a shrunken world of things in highly inventive ways, but in time we will need to gradually transform the dance floor itself, because shrinking will inevitably continue (albeit at different degrees) as we age with, and age into, disability.

Activist Affordance: How to Brush Your Teeth

In the video footage from which figure 6.16 has been captured, Mariana brushes her teeth with extremely slow, calculated, and gentle movements. The transitions between her movements are not smooth but rather abrupt, as if they were cut and interrupted by pain and the limits of how much Mariana can move her impaired joints. Mariana's head is slightly tilted to the right. I imagine that the tilted angle saves her from having to lift her right shoulder, which is probably impaired and in pain, to the level of her head. Further, Mariana manipulates the toothbrush with two hands, which (from my own experience)

FIGURE 6.16 MARIANA'S TWO-HANDED TECHNIQUE FOR BRUSHING HER TEETH
IS AN AFFORDANCE THAT ACCOMMODATES THE PAIN FROM RA VIA HER ANGLED
HEAD AND EXTRA SUPPORT FROM HER LEFT HAND.

makes me think that her hands are in pain so that one alone is not enough to
do the job.

Mariana uses two fingers of her left hand to gently hold her right hand,
which grasps the brush. Her left hand enables the movements of the brush
as if the brush and her hand were one object, pushing her right hand back
and forth, tilting it up and down, maximizing the effect of each stroke while
minimizing her pain.

Activist Affordance: How to Squeeze a Toothpaste Tube

At times, activist affordances may involve the creative uses of available surfaces too. To squeeze a toothpaste tube, Henri placed the tube on the edge of
his kitchen sink, instead of holding it with one hand up in the air without any
support, which would be the toothpaste tube's canonical affordance (figure
6.17). Henri said: "It's hard for me [to squeeze the paste], because of those

FIGURE 6.17 HENRI'S AFFORDANCE FOR EXTRACTING TOOTHPASTE INVOLVES BAL-
ANCING THE TUBE OVER THE EDGE OF THE SINK AND PUSHING DOWN ON IT WITH
A FIST RATHER THAN SQUEEZING.

two fingers [*showing his thumb and index finger*]. I don't have a good grip
there." Then he pressed the tube from the top with his hand made into a fist
and said, "It's my trick. To make it easier to get it out, I simply put my hand
on it, and"—he pushed on it with his fist—"press the toothpaste on the brush."

Activist Affordance: How to Lift a Full Mug

A mug can afford containment and transport of a liquid—provided that it
meets the body it expects. To do so, the mug's opening must be leveled
parallel to the ground. This requires an arm with an elbow and wrist that can
bend to a certain degree, and fingers that can grasp the handle with the necessary strength. When Henri's wrists did not bend (enough) to level the cup,
he crouched slightly, bent his elbow, and brought the cup to the same level
as the table instead (see the introduction). In so doing, Henri played around
with the design properties of the object and rearranged them completely in
a somewhat anarchic way. The gravity that pulled, the shape of a mug that
contained liquid, the liquid that was contained, and the position and angle
in which the mug's handle was placed were all reshuffled, reordered, and put
into an eccentric and odd pairing with *what was (meant) to be bent* (that is,
the elbow and wrist) in Henri's activist affordance.

Such odd pairings between the properties of the user and those of the object may also condense into concrete forms, as seen in the "Dyslexic Objects"

series created by UK-based designer Henri Franks. In this project, Franks lets his dyslexic perception find a material form in a series of "seemingly inanimate" everyday objects, including mugs. His "Muglexia Mugs" (figure 6.18) literally embody the inversion experienced by dyslexic people in their flipped shape and reversed handle positions. But these inversions are not merely symbolic. The mugs' inverted design allows them to be "more stable and less likely to be knocked over along with being better balanced in the hand because of the center of gravity and the handle being lower down."[15] They embody the "disability gain," which Jos Boys considers as a benefit of "starting from disability" in all design.[16]

If there can be "muglexic" mugs, then why not arthritic mugs that would crystallize Henri's ingenious affordance in a material form? And what would be their disability gain? Drawing on Boys's proposal for starting with dis/ability

FIGURE 6.18 UK-BASED PRODUCT DESIGNER HENRY FRANKS'S MUGLEXIA MUGS ARE PART OF HIS DYSLEXIC OBJECTS PROJECT. FRANKS DESIGNED A RANGE OF HOUSEHOLD ITEMS IN RESPONSE TO HIS OWN DYSLEXIC CONDITION. "THE AIM," HE SAYS, "WAS TO IMPROVE A SELECTION OF EVERYDAY OBJECTS THROUGH THE ADDITION OF DYSLEXIA, ENCOURAGING PEOPLE TO REENGAGE WITH SEEMINGLY INANIMATE OBJECTS. EACH PRODUCT POSSESSES A DIFFERENT CHARACTERISTIC OF THE CONDITION." HTTPS:// WWW.HENRYFRANKS.NET /DYSLEXIC-OBJECTS.

in design, we need only imagine how disabled people's necessary affordances can be the basis for a radical approach to all design.[17]

Activist Affordance: How to Open Bottles

Almost in a pedagogical tone, Jacques explained his trick for opening bottles with arthritic hands (figures 6.19–6.21):

> Now the trick! Because when you have rheumatoid arthritis, your fingers tend to bend outward like this [*shows fingers that are bent to the side*]. If I would use my right hand to open, I would put strength again to increase that deviation [or curvature], right? So, instead of using my right hand to open . . . if I use my left hand, I put strength against my deviation, right? So, it avoids increasing the deviation, by using my left hand to open. And then I should use my right hand to close it (but I'm stronger with my left hand because my right hand is more affected and I'm naturally right-handed). But if I use my right hand to close it, then again, I put strength against the deviation. . . . I don't push the fingers in the same side [that is, direction] of the natural deviation because of arthritis.

I asked Marielle, who has cancer and rheumatoid arthritis and lives by herself in the city, whether she is able to open bottles easily. She right away

FIGURE 6.19 IN THIS AND THE NEXT TWO FIGURES, JACQUES EXPLAINS HIS AFFORDANCE FOR OPENING A SODA BOTTLE. IN THIS FIGURE, JACQUES DEMONSTRATES HOW THE FINGERS OF HIS RIGHT HAND ARE BENT OUTWARD.

FIGURE 6.20 IF JACQUES MAKES A FIST OF HIS RIGHT HAND TO PINCH THE BOTTLE CAP, THE RA-RELATED DEVIATION WEAKENS HIS GRIP.

FIGURE 6.21 BY USING HIS LEFT HAND IN A FIST WITH HIS THUMB AND INDEX FINGER PINCHING THE BOTTLE CAP WHILE BRACING THE BOTTLE WITH HIS RIGHT HAND, JACQUES'S AFFORDANCE WORKS *WITH* THE RESTRICTIONS RA PLACES UPON HIS BODY.

took out an old pair of gloves from her kitchen drawer, and said, "So, I use *caoutchouc* [rubber]," and smiled. She added: (translated from French) "It's because my hand cannot close [*trying at the same time to make her hand into a fist and demonstrating that her fingers do not fully close*]. I had hand surgery. . . . It [the glove] enlarges [*pointing at the cap made larger by the glove*] and it grips. It is easier to open with the glove." As Marielle finished explaining her movements, her expression changed with a gentle smile on her face, as if to say, "I don't know if it's good, but this is my way."

Marielle later provided a detailed account of what gripping and twisting of the cap demanded from her fingers, and how she avoided those prescribed movements by using the base of her palm and the glove instead (figures 6.22 and 6.23).

FIGURES 6.22–6.24 IN THESE FIGURES (*ABOVE AND OPPOSITE*), MARIELLE DEMONSTRATES HOW SHE ENLARGES A SODA BOTTLE'S CAP WITH A RUBBER GLOVE SO SHE CAN GRASP IT WITH STIFF FINGERS THAT RA OFTEN DOES NOT ALLOW HER TO FULLY CLOSE.

"Sometimes, I can't," she said (speaking in English). In order to demonstrate the movement she was describing, she raised her hand and brought her thumb and index finger tips close to each other, opening and closing them (figure 6.24). Noticing that her two fingers were able to get closer to each other much more easily than she expected, she added: (translated from French) "Oh, today, I can. But sometimes it goes like this [*widens the space between her fingers*]. So, how can you [*brings her hand to the top of the cap and mimics gripping and twisting it*]? I have no strength."

At times, activist affordances were brought into being by putting body parts, organs, and limbs to unorthodox uses. I was in the kitchen filming Henri as he undertook a series of manual tasks. I asked him if it hurt when he did such things, or if his hands got stuck in certain positions. He tried bending his wrist, straining his hand to move it up and down, left and right, and the limited range of motion became apparent as he said, "Like I say, my mobility—that is all I got, you know. So, if I'm doing stuff, it's coming from shoulders, coming from the elbow. My hands, there is very little mobility." He tried opening the cap of a bottle. First he held the cap from the top with one hand and the side of the bottle with his other hand, twisting (figure 6.25). He was able to open the cap in a single go. Upon hearing the hissing sound as the bottle opened, he said, "Oh, I got it." He kept turning the bottle slowly and pointed at the nodules on his fingers (figure 6.26), smiled, and said, "It's [the bottle is] stuck right here [between the nodule and his palm]." Chuckling, he said: "See, all the nodules have a . . . They serve for that. Not pretty, but it works."

For many of my participants, teeth functioned as if they were another limb, and like Henri's nodules, they became central in creating their activist affordances. As Nurhayat told me how she used various methods to open bottles and jars (figures 6.27 and 6.28), I remembered that she once told me about another affordance she created:

FIGURE 6.25 HENRI DEMONSTRATES HIS METHOD OF OPENING A SODA BOTTLE, POWERED BY HIS SHOULDERS AND ELBOW SINCE THE MOBILITY OF HIS HANDS IS RESTRICTED.

FIGURE 6.26 HENRI HAS INCORPORATED HIS ARTHRITIS NODULES INTO THE AFFORDANCE HE HAS CREATED IN ORDER TO GRIP THE BOTTLE WITH RA-STIFFENED HANDS.

Arseli: You mentioned that at times you open Coke bottle caps with your teeth.

Nurhayat: Yes, it happens. I open the water and Coke bottles with my teeth.

FIGURE 6.27 NURHAYAT, ANOTHER PARTICIPANT WITH RA, DEMONSTRATES HER SODA-BOTTLE AFFORDANCE, WHICH DIFFERS FROM HENRI'S. STEP ONE IS TO GRIP THE BOTTLE CAP WITH HER LEFT FIST THUMB DOWN, STEADYING THE BOTTLE WITH HER RIGHT HAND.

FIGURE 6.28 STEP TWO OF NURHAYAT'S AFFORDANCE INVOLVES TILTING THE BOTTLE AWAY FROM HER BODY WHILE TWISTING THE CAP WITH HER FIST.

An Archive of Activist Affordances · 143

Arseli: You do?

Nurhayat: Yes, let's say if I don't have the time to go down [to the shop owners for help], then at home I twist them with my teeth.

Similarly, as Mariana and I were in her kitchen talking about the difficulties of grasping things, she took a tiny bottle out of her fridge and started giggling (figure 6.29). She tried to pull up the tiny lid with her hand and said, "To open this is difficult, very difficult. Because [the lid] is not big enough for me to pull." Then she brought the bottle to her mouth and pulled the lid off with her teeth easily. She smiled and said, "[See, I do it] with my teeth."

Teeth, which are *meant* to bite and chew, can be given entirely different *meanings* and attributed different functions in the creation of activist affordances. For Nurhayat, teeth gained the function of grasping and twisting; for Mariana, the function of grasping and lifting. For Ed Roberts, a pioneering activist in the US disability rights movement, teeth gained yet another function: as Roberts was pursuing his political science degree at the University of California, Berkeley (paving the way for his famous "Rolling Quads"), he used "a stick that he clenched between his teeth" to turn the pages of his books.[18]

More examples: a colleague, after having seen my videos, joyfully shared with me the activist affordance of her disabled friend who turns light switches on and off from her wheelchair with her head. In her video series *Stump Kitchen*, Edmonton-based artist Alexis Hillyard uses her stump on her left

FIGURE 6.29 MARIANA USES HER TEETH, MEANT FOR BITING AND CHEWING, IN THE AFFORDANCE THAT ENABLES HER TO PEEL THE CAP FROM A SMALL BOTTLE.

hand, in her own words, in "'Stumptastic' ways" to "expand the vocabulary of what's possible in the kitchen." In Hillyard's stumptastic affordances, her stump becomes a juicer to squeeze an orange, or a spatula to scrape the meat of an avocado from its skin.[19]

Throughout the creation of an activist affordance, any part of our bodies—stumps, crooked limbs, and deformed fingers—can be put to innovative uses and *made* to afford action possibilities that they do not initially seem to offer. At times they may also prove more effective than or have uses not available to their "normal" counterparts.

Activist Affordances: How to Open Milk Bottles, Hold Spoons, Seal Bags, and Do a Few Other Things

Knowing beforehand that I wanted to film her as she went about her everyday life and performed her daily chores, Anna, in line with our participatory methodology, asked me if I wanted to come over to her place and accompany her as she baked muffins, which she loves to do. I accepted her generous invitation and filmed her baking process throughout. To my surprise, Anna's baking turned out to be a seamless choreography of activist affordances, danced with grace and eloquence. Let me bring in some of them, at the risk of reducing their complexity to mere notations.

Anna noted that she used a heavy ceramic bowl because she liked it, though it was hard to turn, hold, and manipulate. In a gentle movement, she almost hugged the weighty bowl, distributing the power needed to mix the sticky dough inside it to her overall upper body rather than concentrating it solely in her hands (figure 6.30).

In order to mix the dough, whose stickiness made it harder to manipulate, Anna turned not just the plastic spatula but also the ceramic bowl, hooking her thumb on the lip and pushing outward. Two countermovements (hand holding the spatula pulling, and hand turning the bowl pushing) offset the dough's sticky resistance and distributed the pressure across her two hands (figures 6.31–6.33).

As Anna's right hand held the ceramic measuring cup and poured the sugar it contained, her left hand literally *lent a helping hand*. One hand carefully held the other from beneath, supporting its wrist under strain. An activist affordance came about through this gentle moment of care between her hands (figure 6.34).

Anna placed a sealable bag flat on the counter. As she held it from one side with her hand, she pressed her other hand, made into a fist, all over the

FIGURE 6.30 ANNA HAS DEVELOPED AN ELEGANT CHOREOGRAPHY OF AFFORDANCES THAT ENABLE HER TO BAKE WITH HER IMPAIRMENTS. HERE SHE HUGS THE MIXING BOWL TO HER BODY WITH HER LEFT ARM WHILE STIRRING BATTER WITH HER RIGHT.

FIGURE 6.31 ANNA'S AFFORDANCE WITH THE SPATULA INVOLVES WRAPPING HER RIGHT FIST AROUND THE HANDLE WITH HER THUMB RESTING BEHIND IT.

seal (figure 6.35). Just as in Henri's activist affordance for squeezing toothpaste, the rigid countertop was brought into the creation of an affordance, providing the solid support needed to seal the bag firmly as opposed to using only the hands.

Instead of placing the handle of a spoon between her left thumb and index finger, Anna encircled it with her index finger as she pressed on it with her

FIGURE 6.32 HOOKING HER LEFT THUMB OVER THE RIM OF THE BOWL IS AN AFFORDANCE ANNA HAS DEVELOPED THAT ENABLES HER TO HOLD IT STEADY WHILE SHE MIXES WITH HER RIGHT HAND.

FIGURE 6.33 USING HER THUMB-HOOK AFFORDANCE, ANNA IS ABLE TO ROTATE THE MIXING BOWL AS SHE STIRS.

knuckles and thumb, providing support underneath (figure 6.36). With her right hand (figure 6.37) she choreographed an entirely different affordance, placing the spoon in between her index and middle finger. This activist affordance reappeared in other moments in which an object required effort from Anna's thumb and index finger (figure 6.38).

Anna came up with these activist affordances on the spur of the moment, as she danced with spoons, bowls, cups, bottles, and baking materials in

FIGURE 6.34 WITH ANOTHER AFFORDANCE, ANNA AVOIDS SPILLAGE WHEN POURING SUGAR INTO THE BOWL: HOOKING HER RIGHT THUMB INTO THE SCOOP WHILE HOLDING HER HAND STEADY BY GRIPPING HER RIGHT WRIST WITH HER LEFT HAND.

FIGURE 6.35 ANNA'S AFFORDANCE FOR SEALING A ZIP TOP BAG IS TO SECURE THE BAG ON THE EDGE OF THE COUNTER WITH HER LEFT FINGERS WHILE USING THE KNUCKLE OF HER RIGHT INDEX FINGER TO PRESS THE ZIPPER CLOSED.

FIGURE 6.36 THE AFFORDANCE ANNA HAS DEVELOPED FOR SCOOPING BATTER INTO A MUFFIN TIN USES THE INDEX FINGER OF HER LEFT HAND TO WRAP AROUND THE HANDLE OF A METAL SPOON AND THE KNUCKLES OF HER THUMB AND PINKY FINGER TO STEADY HER GRIP.

FIGURE 6.37 A SECOND AFFORDANCE—GRIPPING ANOTHER SPOON BETWEEN THE INDEX AND MIDDLE FINGERS OF HER RIGHT HAND—ENABLES ANNA TO SCRAPE MUFFIN MIX INTO THE TIN FROM THE SPOON IN HER LEFT HAND.

ways that complemented the shape, strength, and form of her fingers, hands, and arms (figure 6.39). Anna did not comment on (and perhaps did not even notice) the range of activist affordances she skillfully choreographed. She just did them as she went along.

FIGURE 6.38 HOLDING A SPOON BETWEEN THE KNUCKLES OF HER MIDDLE AND INDEX FINGERS IS ANNA'S AFFORDANCE FOR MEASURING INGREDIENTS SUCH AS BAKING POWDER IN SMALL AMOUNTS.

FIGURE 6.39 TO REMOVE THE CAP FROM A CARTON OF MILK, ANNA'S AFFORDANCE CALLS FOR HER TO HOLD THE CARTON WITH HER RIGHT HAND WHILE TWISTING THE CAP WITH THE KNUCKLES OF HER LEFT MIDDLE AND INDEX FINGERS.

To reiterate, during my fieldwork on RA-related disabilities I asked my participants to perform single tasks (such as peeling a potato, not the entire event of cooking). This framing around a single task brought to my participants a particular awareness of their own ingenuity, especially to Jacques, who was actively involved in patient advocacy and had participated in an arthritis self-management program. In almost all of the daily chores I asked Jacques to do, he noted his activist affordances with a heightened self-awareness. He identified each turning point of the action, explaining why he moved his body and the objects involved in particular ways. For instance, when I asked Jacques whether he had any preferences for peeling potatoes (which he confessed he did not do often), he demonstrated (figures 6.40–6.43):

> Well, you can tell that it is difficult working with a small thing like this [the peeler]. I had difficulties. This is why I use the other way of going down like this [*starts peeling from the top and goes toward the bottom*]. Instead of trying to [*mimics pushing the peeler upward*] . . . It's hard, because . . . you do two or three combination of movements at the same time. So, it's complicated, it is hard to do. Especially, I am using a small handle. This is not the perfect tool to do this. For me, at least. Um, and left-handed, I would have probably less difficulty, but I am not used to work[ing] left-handed so, this is why I went like this [figure 6.43].

FIGURE 6.40 JACQUES HAS DEVELOPED AN AFFORDANCE FOR PEELING POTATOES, WHICH IS DIFFICULT WITH HIS RA-AFFECTED HANDS.

The vegetable peeler that Jacques used had a small handle,[20] which is hard to grip with arthritic hands. Further, its layout, the way its blade and handle are placed both in relation to each other and to the user's body, requires the user's elbows and hands to be placed in particular ways. In order to be able to operate this peeler, one has to grip the handle that is aligned with the blade and twist it, pulling the blade up while holding it against the

FIGURE 6.41 JACQUES'S STIFFENED RIGHT HAND CANNOT GRIP THE PEELER'S SMALL HANDLE EFFECTIVELY.

FIGURE 6.42 JACQUES DEMONSTRATES THE DIFFICULT UPWARD TWISTING AND PULLING TECHNIQUE FOR REMOVING POTATO SKINS DICTATED BY THE PEELING TOOL'S DESIGN.

FIGURE 6.43 JACQUES'S AFFORDANCE SHIFTS THE PEELER TO HIS RIGHT HAND WHILE HIS LEFT HAND HOLDS THE POTATO STEADY. THREE FINGERS OF HIS RIGHT HAND GRIP THE HANDLE WHILE HIS INDEX FINGER STEADIES THE BLADE, EN-ABLING HIM TO PEEL POTATOES WITH A 45-DEGREE DOWNWARD STROKE.

hard texture and tough skin of the potato—all of which, as Jacques tellingly noted, are "complicated" and "hard" movements for arthritic hands (particu-larly for an inflamed thumb). Instead of pulling the blade up, Jacques held the potato slanted at 45 degrees to the counter and pushed the peeler's blade down while holding it against the potato. He was using the end of the peeler rather than the blade edge to do the peeling, because in this way he did not have to grip as hard. This also diminished the work otherwise expected of his thumb. With the affordance he created, Jacques almost foresaw the af-fordance of *another peeler* that you could pull along the direction of the handle—exactly like the peeler in the following ethnographic encounter.

Sylvie said she prefers the peeler she holds in figure 6.45 over the one in figure 6.44. "This one [figure 6.44], that's for my visitors, when they have to do that because you see it's not [*exerting force as she is peeling*] . . . It's more difficult for me." I asked if it was difficult because the peeler was small. She answered: "No. It's because I have to go this way [*she pushes the peeler upward, perpendicular to the handle*; figure 6.44]. You know [*pointing at her index finger and implying that is hard for her to use it*] . . . But this way [figure 6.45], I can really have it in my hands."

Given their round, rigid, and often palm-size shape, potatoes afford grasp-ing, which Yasemin deftly integrated into her affordance for peeling (figures 6.46 and 6.47). After giving a slight exclamation, "Argh," upon finishing

An Archive of Activist Affordances · 153

FIGURE 6.44 SYLVIE FINDS USING A THIN-BLADED POTATO PEELER IN TWISTING UPWARD STROKES AS UNCOMFORTABLE AS JACQUES DOES.

FIGURE 6.45 FOR PEELING POTATOES, SYLVIE PREFERS USING A Y-SHAPED PEELER WITH A THICK HANDLE USING DOWNWARD STROKES, AN AFFORDANCE SIMILAR TO JACQUES'S THAT PROVIDES A MORE SECURE GRIP.

peeling the potato, Yasemin said as she smiled, "My husband, thankfully, peels and slices the potatoes for me."

> *Yasemin*: If you noticed, I put it [the potato] here [in her palm] when cutting it.
> *Arseli*: Are you getting support from your palm?
> *Yasemin*: Yes, I'm getting support from here [*pointing at her palm*].

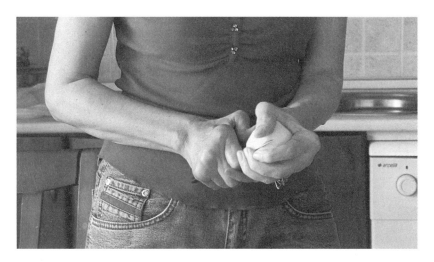

FIGURE 6.46 YASEMIN'S HUSBAND USUALLY PEELS POTATOES FOR HER (A TYPE OF
AFFORDANCE DISCUSSED IN CHAPTER 8). GRIPPING A PEELED POTATO IN HER LEFT
PALM, YASEMIN USES A KNIFE IN HER RIGHT HAND TO SLICE IT IN TWO.

FIGURE 6.47 YASEMIN EXPLAINS THAT HER POTATO-SLICING AFFORDANCE
PROVIDES SUPPORT TO HER RIGHT HAND FROM THE POTATO GRIPPED IN HER LEFT
PALM.

As he opened a jam jar, Jacques said:

> Again the trick! Instead of trying like this with your fingers [figure 6.48], you see I have difficulty even if it has been opened. . . . Try with the palm of your hand, it is stronger [figure 6.49]. And if you have a problem, you can use one of these grip aids [*points to a round flexible grip aid he took from the drawer*]. So, it's anti-slippery. It's just a piece of rubber. This one was made by/for the arthritis society. And of course, with some pharma industry ad on it [*reverses the aid so the ad will not show*], but whatever. Use kind of an aid, just an aid to give you some grip, and use the palm of your hand, instead of the small joints again. It's always a matter of using the strongest part of your body instead of the weakest part of your body.

What a specialized grip aid afforded Jacques was already imagined and discovered by Marielle within the materiality of a pair of old gloves (and a few prior procedures), as we have seen. She turned to the same gloves after having failed to open a jar using a number of other options, from twisting the jar to holding it under hot water and repeatedly hitting the lid's metal edges with the plastic handle of a knife. She grabbed the old pair of rubber gloves and put one on top of the jar's lid. She tried twice pushing hard, and as she heard the lid make a popping sound, she said, confidently, "Voilà!" With this

FIGURE 6.48 JACQUES DEMONSTRATES THE DIFFICULTY OF USING FINGERTIPS TO TWIST OFF THE LID OF A PREVIOUSLY OPENED JAM JAR.

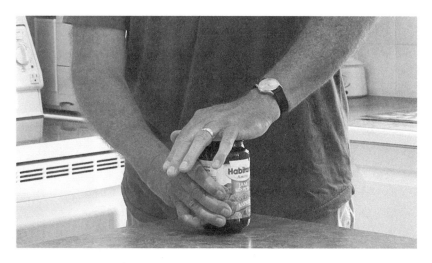

FIGURE 6.49 JACQUES'S AFFORDANCE IS TO USE THE FLAT OF HIS PALM TO TWIST
OPEN THE JAM JAR'S LID. HE SOMETIMES PLACES A PURPOSE-DESIGNED RUBBER
SHEET ON TOP OF THE LID IN A MOVE SIMILAR TO MARIELLE'S IMPROVISED USE OF
A RUBBER GLOVE TO IMPROVE HER GRIP (SEE FIGURES 6.22–6.24).

activist affordance, Marielle created her own rubber-based solution to the
task of opening a jar with arthritic hands.

Curiously enough, the DIY grip aid that Marielle invented turned out to
work better than some tools specifically designed for this purpose. Susanne
had a grip aid (figures 6.50 and 6.51) with a circular plastic part to be put around
the lid, adjusted so it was tight, and then pulled sideways by the handle. But the
thin strap of plastic was much narrower than the glove's surface, which fully
enclosed the top and sides of the lid. As Susanne tried popping the lid with
the grip aid, the plastic strap repeatedly slid out of place, and it took a while
for Susanne to place it around the lid again. She tried and tried but was not
able to open the jar with the aid. At some point my husband, François, who
was there with me filming, intervened to adjust the strap's tightness around
the lid. Susanne then tried once more. As soon as the plastic moved out
of place again, she said, with a sense of annoyance: "Not today!" A grip aid
might be seamless in design and its plastic part might be perfectly cut—but
an old pair of gloves with dirt stains on them proved to have more of the exact
properties that an arthritic hand needed. A worn-out glove not only foresaw
the affordance of Jacques's purposely designed grip aid but also worked in a
much more effective way than the badly designed one that Susanne had.

Susanne mentioned that at times she also used a knife that she inserted
under the lid to pop it open (figure 6.52)—an affordance that was taken up by
another participant too (figure 6.53).

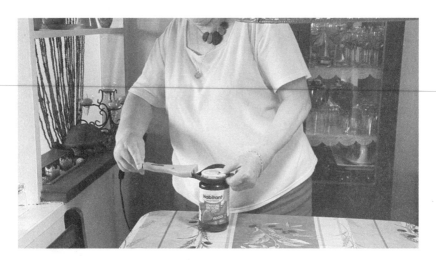

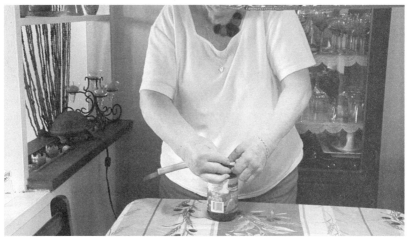

FIGURE 6.50–6.51 SUSANNE STRUGGLES TO USE A COMMERCIAL ADAPTIVE AID FOR OPENING JARS; THE RUBBER LOOP KEEPS SLIPPING OFF THE LID BEFORE SHE CAN GAIN TRACTION USING THE TOOL'S HANDLE.

But what affords an action possibility for one person and her bodily properties may be an obstacle or a (potential) danger to another. As Mariana inserted a spoon under the lid (figure 6.54), she said that she might cut herself if she were to use a knife, and that was why, she added, she preferred to use a spoon instead.

As I observed Valerie opening a lid by grasping the jar with her left hand and the lid with her right, and bringing the jar to the level of her torso, I asked whether she would use a knife to pop it open. She answered, "I wouldn't do it.

FIGURE 6.52 SUZANNE'S AFFORDANCE, USING A DINNER KNIFE TO POP THE JAM JAR'S LID OFF, IS ONE THAT SEVERAL STUDY PARTICIPANTS DEVISED.

FIGURE 6.53 LIKE SUZANNE'S, ANOTHER PARTICIPANT'S AFFORDANCE ALSO UTILIZES A KNIFE BUT INCORPORATES A DIFFERENT CONFIGURATION OF HANDS TO REMOVE THE LID FROM A JAM JAR.

FIGURE 6.54 FOR MARIANA'S JAM-JAR AFFORDANCE, SHE BRACES THE JAR AGAINST HER CHEST AND USES A SPOON TO POP OPEN THE LID SINCE SHE FEARS CUTTING HERSELF WITH A KNIFE.

I would ask Patrick [her husband] to do it or I would put hot water on it and a towel and try to open it." François, who was again there with me filming, commented that we had seen other participants using a spoon to give some air and pop the lid. Valerie immediately said, "I would not try the spoon thing because it will hurt my fingers." Gloves, knives, spoons, towels: to reiterate, activist affordances do not provide a single universal solution that works for all but are instead fluid and constantly negotiated in situ, and in relation to one's body and its changing needs.

I asked Sylvie if she had any special tools to open jars. She answered, "When it is really hard, usually I have this here [*taking pliers from her kitchen drawer and laughing out loud*]. Very useful because you can have large [*enlarging the pliers*] or small [*closing the pliers*]." (See figures 6.55 and 6.56.) She tells me that she keeps the pair of pliers in her kitchen drawer, "where it belongs, along with some cookbooks."

This particular series of activist affordances shows how aware my participants are of the ecological laws of surfaces that James Gibson outlines. The rigidity of a metal cap, its resistance to deformation, and its round shape necessitate an effort that my participants' swollen hands could not exert, but they knew very well that metal expands when exposed to hot water, that the handles of a pincer multiply the effort exerted on the cap, or that the elasticity of rubber prevents hands from sliding off of that metal

FIGURE 6.55 SYLVIE TURNS TO A PAIR OF PLIERS FOR HER JAM-JAR AFFORDANCE.

FIGURE 6.56 PLIERS ARE SYLVIE'S TOOL OF CHOICE SINCE THIS AFFORDANCE AL-
LOWS HER TO HANDLE JARS IN A RANGE OF SIZES.

shape. The affordances they invented are imbued with a "tacit knowledge" of surfaces and substances, and what they can be made to afford when the existing material and shape of objects do not reciprocate the participants' bodily properties a knowledge that also manifests itself, as I shall discuss in chapter 7, when my participants literally *make* affordances in the form of actual things.

Knives are meant to be held by their handles, not by their flat, thin metal blades. But when the object is rigid in its substance, such as a potato, and requires more force to be exerted for it to be cut, and when the hands to cut it are not that powerful, their fingers and wrists not flexible enough to exert the force needed, one may use the top part of the knife's blade to complete the cut. This is exactly what Henri did in his activist affordance for cutting potatoes. In addition to holding the knife handle and pushing it downward with one hand, he placed his other hand on top of the blade, exerting enough extra pressure for it to slide through the hard texture of a potato (figure 6.57). The other hand's extra support minimized the pain he experienced when he used his impaired joints.

Indeed, knives can be made to afford cutting in many different ways, depending on the solidity, shape, and size of the substance to be cut and which part of the body is impaired and in pain. In a joyful moment of confession, one of my participants told me that she sliced cabbages (a pretty big vegetable to manipulate) into small pieces by grasping the knife by the blunt end of the handle to push the blade down into the cabbage multiple times. As she mimicked stabbing an imaginary cabbage, almost evoking a horror movie scene, she laughed and added: "It's not very elegant, but it is only my kitchen that sees me!" What mattered to my participant, in her brilliant affordance,

FIGURE 6.57 APPLYING PRESSURE USING HIS OTHER HAND TO PUSH DOWN ON THE HAND HOLDING THE KNIFE IS AN AFFORDANCE THAT LETS HENRI MINIMIZE THE PAIN HE EXPERIENCES WHEN CUTTING A POTATO.

was the additional pain that she was saved from experiencing through her "inelegant" affordance of cutting *as if* stabbing.

Again, the creativity of activist affordances as a dance (done with existing things) has its own limits, and when that limit is reached, the dance "stage" and its "props" might have to be changed. Consider this moment. The participant who showed me how she had to forcibly open her arthritic fingers from the locked position they were in after peeling a potato also said: "I hate to peel potato!" and laughed out loud. Holding the potato in her hand, and talking to it in a highly theatrical manner, she said in a frustrated tone: "That's! . . . I hate [it] so much that I don't even eat potato!" She laughed and almost threw the potato onto the counter—a move that implied that whatever gave her pain, she could do away with.

My participants also employed affordances when they were not preparing food but eating out. One of my participants singled out *börek* (a baked, filled pastry popular in Turkey and the Balkans) as an example: "You need to cut *börek* [*holding a knife at the same time, imitating the action*]. But I cannot use the knife." She asked whether I could. "I cannot really," I answered. "But then if you don't use it, you may kind of look rude. That's why I eat the *börek* as if it were a slice of pizza," I added. She told me that she often did the same: "Or I just stab my knife into it. They can call me rude if they wish, I don't care. It's not that we lack manners or anything. It's just that we cannot eat that way."

In a similar tone, another participant told me that when eating at a restaurant, she would first ask her partner if he would be willing to cut the food for her. "If he is okay with it and if there is nobody around," she said, "then I order the food." But if there were people around, she would refrain from asking for help, indicating the role of social pressures on the use of affordances. And when she was at home without her partner, she said: "I just take the whole thing and go like that [*mimics the action of eating a whole chicken directly with her hands*]." We both laughed out loud and started exchanging our messy affordances of eating. She said: "Can I take the whole chicken, is it okay [*laughing*]? Okay! All right!" She then mimicked eating the whole chicken with her bare hands in a theatrical manner. I confessed to her that when I ate soup, I spilled it everywhere. Nodding her head in agreement, she said, "Yeah, or take the bowl like that [*holding it from the bottom, drinking directly from it*] and then the soup is everywhere."

Every design object, Max Rolfstam and Jacob Buur write, comes with an "institutional package," with its own "should's" and "should not's."[21] Or, to go back to Ingold, "every object of design sets a trap by presenting a problem in the form of what appears to be its solution"—the should's. The spoon, for instance, appears to be a solution "to the problem of how to transport food from bowl to mouth, when in fact, it is the spoon that determines that we should do so rather than say holding the bowl directly to our lips."[22] But when the solutions that design provides are not taken as solutions, as is the case with my participants, then the problems that they purport to be the solution to are not taken as problems either. Soup can be sipped from the bowl. *Börek* and cabbage can be stabbed. A whole chicken can be torn and eaten with mouth and hands. There is no "problem" that the spoon or knife can pretend to solve. Our activist affordances open up possibilities of eating the food we want to eat, in the way we feel comfortable eating it.

Activist Affordance: How to Cook (or Not)

Consider Jérôme's story. Jérôme was blind from birth, and at the time of our interview he was living with his parents, one of whom was blind and the other partially sighted, and his other siblings, one of whom was also blind. A care worker came regularly to help with the family's daily chores. I asked Jérôme how they managed cooking.

> *Jérôme*: [*mother tongue French, speaking in English*] It's longer, it's more difficult because, um, there is some things that we cannot do, um, easily or that we cannot really do safely as I can say. Like, to be sure that meat is well-cooked, it's a challenge . . . because you cannot use the color of the meat so we have to use other methods.
>
> *Arseli*: Like what?
>
> *Jérôme*: I am not a specialist in cooking, honestly [*smiles*]. But yes, it's possible, if you have the time one day, you can check on the internet, a blind person won the most powerful international cooking competition, so it's possible [*smiles*]. . . . It's possible but it's more complicated.

I asked if it was riskier to manipulate things such as knives and cutting. Jérôme answered:

> [*Mother tongue French, speaking in English*] Um, we have to pay more attention. Yes, we have to pay more attention and we have to think about some, um, some strategies. Yes, for the using of knives . . . but also, er, for some really basic, er, daily activities like putting milk in a coffee. . . . If you have to put a liquid in a, um, in a bottle or in any content like that, you have to, um, use a liquid detector that is a device that rings when . . . it touches the detector. Or, if it's just for me, I can

use . . . the hand and check if it's okay. But it's less precise to do that. . . . For example, if you have to give a cup of water to someone, you have to pay attention and, um, use this sort of [detector] device . . . um, with microwave or with . . . stove, with these kitchen appliances, you have to be sure that it's really well-adapted. You have to verify. . . . And I prefer microwave, it's more previsible [*sic*] I can say . . . because you know that if you put the . . . recipe at the good time, and, um, you're sure of the reaction. With a stove, it's not always, um, clearer or . . . a lot of time, you have to check, and "Oh it's not okay. I'll put it longer time." Normally microwave is more easy. . . . And with stove you have to be sure that you can touch it.

Later on, Jérôme gave me a tour of the kitchen, explaining, in quite exquisite detail, which appliances he used and how. He then walked toward a microwave, which was carefully placed in the corner that divided the kitchen from the dining room (most likely in order for it to not clutter the space). The microwave was rather old and was placed closer to the back of the dining table, making the path from it to the table easier. Jérôme told me that he was surprised that the microwave was not originally adaptive when they received it. His family had to adapt it themselves by adding stickers:

[*Mother tongue French, speaking in English*] It can be just stickers with no information but the place that they are positioned, we know the signification of that. Or it can be a sticker for each number for one out of two numbers for . . . the function. Or it can be a sticker for "stop," a sticker for "start," and some others. Yes, normally we adapt our microwave this way. . . . So when I use it, I just have to tap and I know where I have to [do that].

In *Beasts of Burden*, Sunaura Taylor writes about "the joys of being a crip with a microwave."[23] Jérôme's family's kitchen evokes a similar joy. Standard ableist kitchen appliances (such as stoves), utensil design, and the time it can take for a disabled person to prepare food (including the time it takes to shop for, carry, and cook food in a world full of barriers) can make "conveniences" such as microwaves a *necessity*, not a preference. As Eli Clare writes, "A food processor is not a yuppie kitchen luxury in my house, but an adaptive device."[24] Many "efficiencies such as microwaves, fast-food restaurants, and precooked meals help disabled, elderly, and low-income individuals who are pressed for time get by."[25] These may be the only efficiencies (if any) at their disposal to be able to eat.

In the documentary film *Vital Signs*, the late disability scholar and activist Harlan Hahn offers an anecdote about a disability community meeting held in Los Angeles. An attendee challenged the idea of disability culture by saying, "If there is such a thing as disability culture then there's got to be a disability food. You know, every other culture has a food." Hahn replies: "'No, we do have a food.' And we went around the room and we discovered that everybody went primarily to drive-thru restaurants. Fast food places. Because it was too hard to get in and out of the car to go to a regular restaurant."[26]

I would expand Hahn's point further and add that there are other variables that lead to the creation of disability food, including what type of food is financially affordable, physically manipulatable, easily chewable, and digestible; what kinds of appliances and utensils such foods require to cook and eat them; and with what material and sensory properties appliances are equipped. The active negotiation of these variables means that not all food makes it to being disability food. For example, when the substantial properties of food, or the tools and devices my participants cooked with, warranted the use of body parts and organs that may have been impaired, my participants came up with affordances that counterpoised those demands and requests. But when such counteraction became difficult or impossible—that is, when the limits of affordance-creation emerged again—they dispensed with the food altogether. Most of my participants mentioned that they avoided cooking vegetables that were hard in texture and larger than their hands, such as potatoes, squash, and cabbage. Several participants told me that whenever they went to a restaurant, they ordered dishes that would be easier for them to slice, manipulate, and chew (which is also what I do). Our activist affordances shape the kinds of foods we eat and how we eat it, and they eventually transform our diets in the form of disability food.

The *Afford*ability of Food

Mariana has RA-related disabilities, and at the time of our interview she was in quite a bit of pain. She and her husband, who is also disabled and uses a wheelchair, were living in a half-basement, barely lit, sparsely furnished apartment in a low-income neighborhood of Montreal. Neither of them was able to work, and it was clear that life was not easy for them, financially or physically. At some point during our interview, Mariana was telling me about (and simultaneously demonstrating) what she usually cooked and how. First, she opened the pantry to show all the canned food they had stored. She then turned to the fridge and took out the eggs, bacon, potato, and onion they often ate and started peeling and cutting the onion. Once she finished cutting the bacon and putting it in a pan, Mariana suddenly remembered something that she definitely wanted to explain to me. She grabbed a wooden spatula with one hand and a plastic scoop with the other. Pointing at the former, she said, "This one [figure 6.58] is strong and rigid" whereas the other one (figure 6.59), which she simultaneously pressed against the table to show its flexibility, "is soft. It's a problem with the material. It's not good [for me]." Using the wooden spatula, she then started stirring the bacon cooking in the pan by grasping the spatula's handle with a fist, holding it vertically at a 90-degree angle to the pan, and regularly pounding it in order to separate and stir the sticky bacon (figure 6.60). During Mariana's affordance-creation of cooking bacon many variables coalesced, including the pain and inflammation of arthritic hands, the sturdiness of the wooden spatula, the plasticity of bacon, and its affordability for a disabled couple with little means to get by. In other words, Mariana's activist affordance emerged not from the physical properties of the food, which were the most easily manipulable for her, but from the constraining properties of the food that she and her husband could afford.

As demonstrated by Mariana's story, the most basic determinant of disability food was the financial *afford*-ability of food itself, because disability is tied to income generation. I did visit affluent middle- and upper-class families that were exceptions to this pattern, but in many cases, my participants were not able to work due to disability. Some retired early, some relied on their partners' incomes, some were dependent on social assistance, some received help from care workers. In these cases, financial affordability served as the baseline determinant and limit on affordance-creation. Disability food, in short, emerged at the intersections of multiple marginalizations and out of the constraints that they intensified.

Activist Affordance: How to Stand Up from a Chair

> *Sevim:* For instance, this couch feels too low for me nowadays. I have difficulties standing up from this couch when my knees are in pain. Something a little bit higher, the couch in the living room is a bit higher, I can stand up more easily from that one. But my knees . . .
>
> *Güven* [Sevim's husband]: But here at least you have the chance to hold onto the edges and all.
>
> *Sevim*: Still! When my knees are in pain, like that day, both my knees were in pain. I tried holding onto the armrest like this [figure 6.61].

An Archive of Activist Affordances · 167

FIGURES 6.58–6.60 MARIANA TESTS THE PROPERTIES OF HER COOKING TOOLS.
FOR ARTHRITIC HANDS. THE STIFFNESS OF THE WOODEN SPATULA IS PREFERABLE
TO THE FLEXIBILITY OF THE LARGE PLASTIC COOKING SPOON. GRASPING THE
WOODEN SPATULA'S HANDLE VERTICALLY WITH A FIST, MARIANA CREATES THE
AFFORDANCE OF STAB-STIRRING HER BACON AS IT COOKS.

FIGURE 6.61 SEVIM'S COUCH IS TOO LOW FOR KNEES IN PAIN. AFTER TESTING OUT THE COFFEE TABLE, SHE SETTLED ON THE AFFORDANCE OF USING THE COUCH'S ARMREST AS A MOBILITY AID.

First, I tried to put these [her knees] here [on the corner of the sofa]. And somehow, it was still not . . . I tried holding onto this [the coffee table in front of the sofa]. No, it didn't work. . . . Then I turned to this [*puts both her hands on the armrest*]. Nope. In this position [figure 6.62], this time, it was my wrist that was in pain and I was supposed to exert force with it.

FIGURE 6.62 SEVIM EXTENDS HER LEFT HAND ACROSS HER BODY; IT COMES TO REST BESIDE HER RIGHT HAND ON THE ARMREST.

FIGURE 6.63 SEVIM REACHES ACROSS THE ARMREST AND, CLUTCHING IT WITH BOTH HANDS, GENTLY PULLS HER BODY TOWARD IT AND PUTS HER WEIGHT ON HER RIGHT KNEE.

> *Güven:* What if you brought this coffee table here [*moves the table in front of Sevim*]?
>
> *Sevim:* No. I'm telling you, I couldn't do it, while you guys were watching the game in the other room.
>
> *Güven*: [*still moving the coffee table*] Like this!
>
> *Sevim:* Cık [interjection meaning "no"]. Like that, no way! It was impossible, I couldn't stand up. . . . The most . . . was like this [*going on to demonstrate*]. Of course, I can do it now. . . . I did it like this that day [figure 6.63]. . . . First like this [*puts her bent right knee on the sofa*]. I just couldn't manage to turn my knee around, and then I took force from my other knee [her right knee, which is, as seen in figure 6.64, bent and on the sofa], and only then I was able to stand up.

The shrinking environments that my participants experienced at times of flare-ups and extreme pain, and the activist affordances that they had to create out of them, had often left a vivid trace in their memories. For instance, Henri recalled that in 1994, when he "was in a bad shape," he could stand up from the sofa only in a particular way. He explains:

> I would always sit on the end of the couch, over here [figure 6.65], 'cause when the time came to stand up, I *couldn't* use my knees then, they were

FIGURE 6.64 WITH WEIGHT ON HER PAINFUL RIGHT KNEE AND ARMS, SEVIM PUSHES HERSELF UP WITH BOTH ARMS EXTENDED AND BRACED AGAINST THE ARMREST. WITH PAIN IN BOTH KNEES AND WRISTS, SEVIM'S AFFORDANCE IS IMPERFECT FROM A PAIN STANDPOINT, BUT IT ENABLES HER TO STAND ON HER OWN WHEN HER FAMILY IS IN ANOTHER ROOM.

too, um, they were too painful. So when it was time to get up, what I [did] was put my arm on the armrest over here, and my knees would be straight [figure 6.66]. . . . Then I turn my body around to push with my arms [figure 6.67]. . . . Keep my knees straight [*with a lot of effort, he mimics the straight knee*], push with the arms. [*in a joyful manner*] Here we are, not using the knees, I am standing up!

While an activist affordance created in the distant past can be recalled evocatively in the present and broken down into its constituent acts with a high degree of self-awareness, another affordance invented on the go in this very moment might not even be noticed. As Henri and I were in his kitchen, I noticed his affordance for standing from a chair (see figure 6.68). When I brought his affordance-creation to his attention, Henri was taken by surprise: "Tricks come naturally," he said. "But," he added while laughing, "now that you mentioned [it], it won't be natural anymore." Then he went on to actively reflect on his affordance for sitting:

I got a hand in here [*makes his left hand a fist and puts its knuckles and their sturdy surface on the table*] and a hand on the chair [*makes his right hand a fist and puts its knuckles on the chair*]. There you go [*sits down*]. You got half or, um, fourth of my weight on my hands instead of my knees [*smiles proudly*].

An Archive of Activist Affordances · 171

FIGURE 6.65 HENRI, LIKE SEVIM, HAS AN AFFORDANCE FOR RISING FROM THE
COUCH. FIRST, HE EXTENDS HIS ARM TO THE ARMREST AT HIS SIDE.

FIGURE 6.66 NEXT, HENRI LEANS TOWARD THE ARMREST AND PLACES BOTH OF
HIS FOREARMS ON IT.

During our interview, I told Henri how keenly aware the participants
of this project were about the methods and tricks they had developed.
He said:

> Well, I don't think about those. Like I said, it just comes naturally after
> a while. It's easier, you know you do things the way [that is] easier
> for you. Nobody showed me to press the toothpaste like that. I just

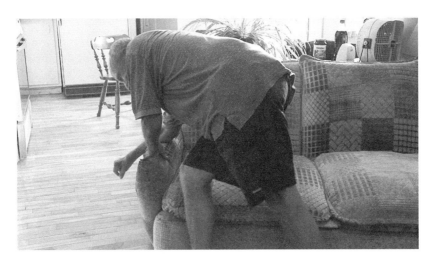

FIGURE 6.67 BRACING HIS LEFT ELBOW ON THE ARMREST WITH HIS RIGHT FORE-ARM STILL ON THE ARMREST, HENRI PIVOTS ON HIS RIGHT HIP AND PUSHES UP WITH HIS RIGHT ARM TO STAND.

FIGURE 6.68 SEATED AT HIS KITCHEN TABLE, HENRI DEMONSTRATES HOW HE RISES FROM A CHAIR, A TRICK—AS HE REFERS TO HIS AFFORDANCES—THAT COMES NATURALLY UNTIL HIS ATTENTION IS DIRECTED TOWARD IT.

learned it on my own. It's easier, you know [*mimics his technique of pressing toothpaste*].... You know, one day you do it a certain way it works, well, keep on doing that way. But you don't think of it as a trick actually, you just [do it].... [It is a] way of doing things [*shrugs*], it's just natural after a while.

Contrary to the naturalized flow of action Henri mentioned, Jacques described his affordance for getting in and out of a car in minute detail and in an almost pedagogical way:

> The main thing is: instead of trying to use one leg and jump in your car, you know like a "normal" [*mimics scare quotes*]—we are normal, but a person without arthritis would go like this [*extends his right leg into*

FIGURE 6.69 IN THIS AND THE NEXT FIVE IMAGES, JACQUES DISPLAYS HIS SERIES OF AFFORDANCES FOR GETTING IN AND OUT OF HIS CAR. HERE, HE DEMONSTRATES THE "NORMAL" WAY OF INITIATING THIS MOVEMENT, RIGHT FOOT FIRST.

FIGURE 6.70 TO SIT WHILE ACCOMMODATING RA-RELATED IMPAIRMENTS, JACQUES BACKS INTO THE CAR'S FRONT SEAT WHILE BENDING AT THE WAIST AND KNEES.

the car; figure 6.69] and sit down and bring [the other leg]. [But] then you are . . . in an unbalanced kind of situation. It may be dangerous. And also, you may hurt [*points at the top of the car*]. You know, you are only standing on one leg! So, instead of doing this, watch your head, go down like this [*turns his body parallel to the door, his back facing the side of the seat*]. Like you would sit in a chair [figure 6.70] . . . And then

FIGURE 6.71 ONCE SEATED, JACQUES CAN PIVOT ON HIS BUTTOCKS TO FACE THE STEERING WHEEL.

FIGURE 6.72 TO STAND, JACQUES REVERSES THE PIVOT, SWINGS HIS LEGS OUT OF THE CAR, AND PLACES HIS FEET ON THE GROUND.

FIGURE 6.73 JACQUES USES AN ELBOW ON THE DASHBOARD TO HELP HIMSELF RISE
TO A STANDING POSITION.

FIGURE 6.74 ALTERNATIVELY, JACQUES MIGHT USE THE DOOR'S ARM TO HOIST
HIMSELF FROM THE CAR SEAT. "HELP YOURSELF!" HE SAYS.

rotate, and bring both your feet in. And again, when you go out of the
car, instead of trying to go out only on one leg ... Bring both legs out
[*reverses the rotating movement he did earlier*; figure 6.71] Then help
yourself. . . . Help yourself [grab the dashboard or the door frame] to
get out of the car [figure 6.72]! If you have [a] problem with your knees,
help yourself!

FIGURES 6.75–6.77 WHEN ENTERING HER CAR, ANNA DEMONSTRATES A SET OF AFFORDANCES QUITE DISTINCT FROM JACQUES'S. LIKE JACQUES'S "NORMALS," SHE STARTS BY PUTTING HER LEG INTO THE FOOTWELL BUT BACKS INTO THE POSITION. TO BEGIN SITTING, SHE BRACES HER RIGHT KNEE WITH HER RIGHT ARM AND HAND AND THEN PIVOTS TO A SITTING POSITION ON HER BENT LEFT KNEE.

Grab! Grab the door [figure 6.73]! Grab something! Help yourself! You got the dashboard [figure 6.74]! [*stands up with ease*]. . . . So, the main thing is rotate, and bring both your feet down! You have more strength!

But then the activist affordance that works for one (in this case, Jacques) might not for another (in the following case, Anna). In her own affordance, seen in the series of figures (6.75–6.77), Anna used the movement of standing up on one leg that in Jacques's case qualified as "dangerous." As she did so, Anna grabbed onto the door, held onto its frame, and almost threw her body inside the car. She then very carefully carried her legs inside the car with her arms. What was for Jacques a risky movement became central for Anna, together with ways of bracing herself against the car, as she created her unique activist affordance.

Activist Affordance: How to Navigate Public Places

In what he calls a "blind style of perception," STS scholar Siegfried Saerberg compares blind people's "crisis of navigation" to how scientific perception operates in high-energy physics.[27] "Crises of navigation" are situations where blind people cannot readily implement their habitual perceptions of places. When confronted with such crises, blind travelers, Saerberg argues, try to make the unknown knowable in the way a scientist does in an experiment. They theorize what the right paths could be, they test that theory, they collect sensory data, they make mistakes, they take wrong paths, they backtrack, and they theorize again in accordance with the data they have so far collected. In short, blind travelers, Saerberg concludes, relate to the variables of their environment with the "self-observation," "self-description," and *self-care* of a high-energy physicist.[28]

Most of the activist affordances I have so far documented take place in the flow of action, without much conscious thinking, almost automatically or "naturally," as Henri puts it. It is only in retrospective description that such thinking comes into play. When an activist affordance emerges as, say, Yasemin moves her arms and her head in ways that avoid the pain of combing her hair, it emerges not out of preplanned calculation but through spontaneous movements that may have been learned over time. And even if there may be thinking of a kind, it happens so quickly that it appears not to exist. There are, however, other situations in which activist affordances come into being by way of deliberate planning, step-by-step calculation, and continuous experimentation. We can think of these activist affordances along the lines of the scientific ordering that Saerberg identifies as the "blind style of perception." As Jérôme navigated the public places of Montreal, for instance, I realized that a spate of variables factored into the making of his activist affordances. These variables included the affordances and failures of people, their mobilities, and habits; those of infrastructure and technologies; and hourly, daily, and seasonal changes and events. Jérôme recounted these multiple interferences and enablements in his environment in the precise manner of a scientist conducting an experiment while we were standing with my cameraperson at one of the busiest intersections in Montreal on a winter weekday around lunchtime. On our left side was a four-lane street, which intersected with the two-way street in front of us. As we were waiting at the traffic lights, which were not adaptive for blind pedestrians, we asked Jérôme what he did in this situation:

> [*Translated from French*] I need to rely on the traffic to cross. But what's complicated in intersections like this is that there is not a lot of parallel traffic, and I need to rely on parallel traffic to be able to cross [parallel traffic refers to the cars passing on our left side; the fact that they are moving indicates that the light in front of us is green]. At a spot such as this one [where there are multiple lanes], however, the parallel traffic is not obvious, because almost all the traffic flows toward the same direction. When that happens, you have to make a wild guess. . . . But the street needs to be straight. If the street is straight, you can still cross it. As long as you're sure of what you're doing and when to start. Because you have to start walking as soon as the light turns green. But if there is no traffic either, then it becomes a nightmare to try to cross the street! We have many traffic lights like that mostly at night, or late at night, or during the weekend, when the streets become all too quiet. Like a nightmare! Too much traffic is a problem but too little traffic is a problem too!

The operation of traffic "lights," as its single sense–based name reveals, relies on the very entity—light—that Jérôme hardly ever perceives. But then, as he aptly explained, Jérôme concentrates on perceiving the acoustic (and perhaps even haptic) consequences of what the visual perception of the lights prompts other travelers to do. That is, the sound (and perhaps even the waft) of cars passing on his side signals to Jérôme that the light must be green in the direction he faces. Jérôme's highly intricate affordance obviously *made up* and at the same time *made up for* what the current traffic lights lacked—that is, audio cues. But his affordance-creation worked only on certain days of the week, only at certain times of the day, and only under certain conditions. This is because dis/ability, as John Law and Ingunn Moser put it, "is about specific passages between equally specific arrays of heterogeneous materials."[29] When there are "good passages" between bodily, material, and social contingents, there is ability. (At a crossroad with easily distinguishable parallel traffic, Jérôme could invent the very affordance that the current traffic lights lacked by listening to the sound of the traffic flowing in the direction he was supposed to cross.) Conversely, when there are "awkward displacements, movements that are difficult or impossible"—that is, when there are "bad passages"—then there is disability.[30] (At complex intersections with more than one parallel traffic, and late at night and on weekends, when the sound of parallel line of traffic was minimized, the complex pairing of the technological object and the behaviors of other actors that underlay Jérôme's activist affordance no longer applied.) In short, whether Jérôme's activist affordance would be realized or not depended on the contingency of these passages because there was no adaptive traffic light that would readily ensure a good passage on behalf of Jérôme's activist affordance.

During his daily commute to the university from his home on the south side of Montreal, Jérôme had to travel in public buses without audio announcements— a journey that involved yet another complex negotiation of multiple variables. To begin with, Jérôme made up for the lack of audio announcements by using his mobile phone, its location-aware app, and a voice-over that alerted him to the stops ahead. But his activist affordance for making an otherwise inaccessible bus accessible did not end here. In anticipation of the possibility that his phone might die or fail to work properly, Jérôme also carried a GPS device as a backup in his backpack. In the event that both devices had lags and failures, Jérôme still asked the bus driver to alert him to his stop, as he used to do in the days when no such technologies existed or were unavailable to him. And in the event that all these safety measures foundered (both devices lagged and the driver forgot) and Jérôme ended up in an unfamiliar location, he then resorted to the experimental "blind style of perception," as described by Saerberg. Jérôme told me that he tried and tested paths, building his activist affordances through the scientific methodologies of trial and error. More broadly, in his daily navigations Jérôme calculated many variables in a stream of affordance-creation that involved the "corrections, errors and uncertainties" of (scientific) experimentation.[31]

In Turkey, toilets have retained their historical squat design and lack of accessibility. More recent constructions such as shopping malls, condos, airports, and government buildings do have "Western" water closet toilets as part of their "modernized" architecture. But squat toilets remain prevalent, especially in rural areas and in buildings of older construction. I remember many hospital visits from my early teenage years for the treatment of rheumatoid arthritis that gave me swollen legs, where—ironically, given that my legs prevented me from doing so comfortably—I had to use a squat toilet to provide a urine sample. Having experienced this firsthand (and somewhat naively assuming that modern toilets would be ideal for everyone), I asked Ahmet what kind of toilet he preferred. To my surprise, he answered:

> I mean it doesn't matter really, as long as the toilet is narrow. I mean if the walls are close enough so that I can hold onto them in case I lose my balance, or close enough so that I can hold onto them and take support. As long as the toilet space is not too wide, it is fine. Otherwise it doesn't matter if it is a water closet or squat.

To Ahmet, it was not *the type* but *the space* of the toilet that mattered. It was not the Western-style seated WC that made a toilet accessible for him, as I had expected, but the proximity of its walls. It was their narrowness that gave him the necessary support—the very support that grab bars would have afforded in an "accessible" toilet.

Arif Amca shared Ahmet's requirements. Standing in front of the bathroom sink that was quite close to the wall it faced, he made the following observation:

> Now, for example, the narrower the bathroom space is, the more comfortable I am using [the sink], performing ablutions and all. But if it isn't narrow, and if I can't lean my back like this [*leans against the wall*]—because this back of mine doesn't hold up by itself—it is more difficult for me [to use the sink].

I asked Arif Amca about what type of toilets he preferred. He told me that his home had both a seated toilet and a squat toilet, but:

> *Arif Amca:* I try to avoid seated toilets at all costs. Always by squatting and standing up, by clutching the doorknobs and all. Sometimes my knees would make it impossible for me to squat. But I always try to use that one [the squat] so that . . .

Arseli: Do you have a place to hold onto in the squat toilet?

Arif Amca: For sure, for sure. There are faucets. . . . There is the door-knob, there is the water tap. So, I stand up.

"Tightness," in its dictionary definition, "leaves little room for maneuver." It seemed to me, until I talked with Ahmet and Arif Amca, that that tightness would be a barrier in a toilet. But in their experiences of toilet space, tight-ness functioned as an aid to action. As they squatted, stood up, and extended their hands or feet toward the sink, they held onto, took support from, and leaned against the walls and clutched faucets and doorknobs. Thanks to the narrowness of the space, the walls, water taps, and doorknobs became sup-ports for their hands, arms, and backs, partaking in their affordances as if they were extensions of their bodies. In a culture where squatting remained the common toileting habit, and in the absence of accessible toilets with grab bars, it was the proximity of walls, water taps, and doorknobs that was made to afford action possibilities that in an accessible toilet would have been af-forded by grab bars and seated toilets.

In contrast to Ahmet, however, Arif Amca had a water closet in his house. He simply preferred not to use it, in order "not to let go of myself all at once" and instead to "try to do everything as long as I can." What does that "as long as" mean? It means up until the time when the body no longer *can.* But why push the limits of the body? Why wait until that point before letting an already available seated toilet carry your body weight and save your painful knees from having to bend?

As Arif Amca's fervent attitude demonstrated, activist affordances are created not just due to the physical constraints of a shrunken environment but also due to the feelings, emotions, and desires that come with having to live a life within those limits. Not surprisingly, such feelings are not always positive or celebratory. Frustration, anger, resentment, and fear (about the future, about becoming more disabled) may seem to *force* one into seeking some affordance for standing up from a squat toilet when a seated toilet already exists, and even at the expense of increased pain and potential in-jury. *Forcibly* creating an activist affordance at the cost of pain means that activist affordances do not always benefit their creators. As I shall discuss in the following section, activist affordances can at times be at the service of "compulsory-ablebodiedness"—the cultural assumption that able-bodied identity is the default position that we all prefer to occupy.[32] And when they are, they can be more injurious than gentle and more destructive than favor-able to their inventors.

Namaz is the Muslim daily prayer performed five times a day, according to a particular ritual and rules, and preceded by another mandatory ablution ritual (*abdest*). The choreographies of these rituals require the movements of the hands, arms, knees, neck, and so on. But in cases where this is not possible, as in sickness and disability, the Koran provides different "degrees of alleviation." When one cannot do these movements, for instance, "then one may reduce them to gestures, or even to intentions in heart when doing gestures is also impossible."[33] Raised as a Muslim, I knew of these alternatives beforehand, and from our conversations I also knew that Arif Amca was in a great deal of pain. I asked:

Arseli: Can you perform *namaz*, Arif Amca?

Arif Amca: Of course. If God allows [*Nasib olursa*].

Arseli: Are you doing it sitting, or in a chair or standing?

Arif Amca: No, no. I don't perform *namaz* in a chair.

Arseli: Are you able to prostrate [*secdeye yatmak*] and things like that?

Arif Amca: To prostrate, and all these things, I try to do all so that . . .

Arseli: You can do that with even your knee [which he previously mentioned was in pain and impaired]?

Arif Amca: Of course, of course. If you want [*he stands up from the sofa where he has been sitting with an expression of deep pain*

FIGURE 6.78 ARIF AMCA DEMONSTRATES HOW HE LOWERS HIMSELF ONTO THE CARPET WHILE RESTING HIS WEIGHT ON THE KNUCKLES OF HIS CLOSED FIST, AN AFFORDANCE THAT ENABLES HIM TO PERFORM *NAMAZ*.

on his face and takes support from the sofa by pushing with his hands].

Like this [figure 6.78], when going down, I do like this [*puts his right hand as a fist on the ground, takes support from its knuckles placed against the hard surface of the floor, and then moves into "prostrate" position*] so that I would move my body. Everybody gets angry at me, saying, "You dear [*Efendim*] are torturing yourself!" If I am to do this movement, how do I not torture myself? And when standing up, like this, my hand is like this [with his hand in a fist, its knuckles pushed against the ground].

I do not do it like this [with his thumb and index finger facing the ground and clumsily carrying his body's weight; see figure 6.79]. I do it like this [referring to his previous movement in figure 6.78, where his hand is in fist]. But I press on this [*pointing at his left knee*]. Look, I keep it steady by pressing on it [figure 6.80]! This [knee], the impaired one, remains in my palm.

Arseli: So, you stand up like this?

Arif Amca: Of course.

Arseli: Do you perform *namaz* five times a day like this?

Arif Amca: Of course.

Arseli: Why do you not perform it sitting? You could!

FIGURE 6.79 LOWERING HIS BODY ONTO THE CARPET SUPPORTED BY HIS THUMB AND INDEX FINGER IS AN UNSTABLE PROPOSITION, ACCORDING TO ARIF AMCA.

FIGURE 6.80 PRESSING ON HIS LEFT KNEE WITH HIS PALM IS AN AFFORDANCE
THAT ENABLES ARIF AMCA TO REMAIN STABLE WHEN RETURNING TO A STANDING
POSITION AFTER PRAYERS.

Arif Amca: When I do it sitting, then I would cut down on this movement. What would I do when the mobility is gone? [*after a bit of
silence*] I need the future, not the now.

Arseli: [*with surprise*] You don't have morning stiffness, in your hands
or . . . ?

Arif Amca: Yeah, so what? Movement in the morning is *namaz* [mean-
ing that *namaz* is what he does to move]!

Arseli: How long does it [the stiffness] last?

Arif Amca: Ten to fifteen minutes.

Arseli: You perform *namaz* even in that state?!

Arif Amca: Sure! Sure! Sure! *Namaz* is a different matter.

Özcan [the cameraman]: Can you perform *abdest*?

Arif Amca: [*nodding yes*] I hold this foot like this [figure 6.81]. It [his
foot] was not moving the other day. So, I held it from the sweatpants and lifted it up. I tried to wash it [passively] in this movement
[figure 6.82; *all giggling*].

Arseli: [*with surprise*] You washed it like that?

Arif Amca: Yes, I washed it like this, yeah. Nobody would believe that!

Arseli: In the house, all by yourself?

Arif Amca: Sure. I literally held my feet like this, with the sweatpants. . . . It wasn't lifting up by itself. I lifted it up. So I brought it up and
down [passively] with force, bit by bit. After two times of washing, it

An Archive of Activist Affordances · 185

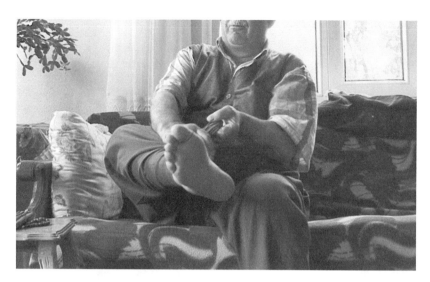

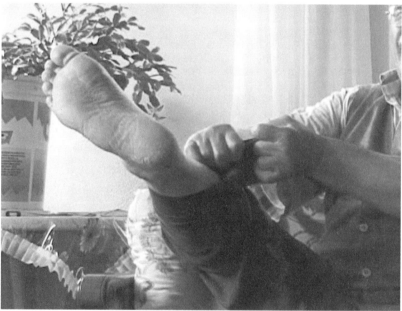

FIGURES 6.81 AND 6.82 IN ANOTHER AFFORDANCE, ARIF AMCA RAISES AND
LOWERS HIS FOOT WITH AN ASSIST FROM PULLING ON HIS TROUSERS' LEG WITH
BOTH HANDS.

started to move [on its own]. It [the foot] said: "I won't let you bend down for *secde*." But I put my hand like this [like a fist, as shown earlier] and I bent it down with force [*zoru zoruna indirdim*].

At a later point during the same interview, I asked Arif Amca whether he got help for tasks such as putting on shoes. He made a very sharp gesture, indicating a definitive no, and added:

There is no help at the moment. Thank God! God forbid that from happening! What if that day comes? That's what I am thinking. That's why I try to perform *namaz* with my hand [*enacts his movement of making his hand a fist to push against the ground*]. . . . Even my family doesn't know how I lifted my foot [*repeats his satisfaction with his ingenious affordance*].

I repeated to Arif Amca that he somehow found a way of doing things and he agreed with full certainty, "For sure." After explaining me how he used his sink to wash his feet during ablution, he almost exclaimed, "Who are you gonna ask for help? Are you gonna say, 'Come, son, wash my feet?'"

Consider this other testimony attesting to the forced creation of activist affordances and the complex emotional process that led to it:

Valerie: [*mother tongue French, speaking in English*] I am still in that emotional phase where I don't know how I'm supposed to be. I don't know if I'm supposed to, like you said, am I supposed to push myself beyond what I feel I am capable to do to show that I [make] an effort? Or I should use something to help me, and I get very angry also. So, I do a lot of things out of rage. Angry, you know. If I get really angry, I can pick up the bag.

Arseli: I can understand that.

Valerie: I don't have to tell anybody that I have a hard time. I get really angry and I pick up the bag, you know. So, nobody has to listen to me saying [*in a tone that mimics seeking pity*], "Can you help me do this?"

Arif Amca and Valerie are not exceptions in negotiating their bodily capacity and independence. I too often (and regrettably) push my body beyond what it is capable of tolerating without additional pain. All of my participants with rheumatoid arthritis except Ahmet told me that they tended to do the same. Sometimes this happens because we simply lose ourselves in the joy of doing an activity (as I do when I walk kilometers for leisure), not realizing that we will be in pain the next day. At these times our "anticipatory scheduling" skills simply falter, or we choose to enjoy the pleasure despite future pain.[34] At other times, however, we may compel ourselves to do things because of compulsory able-bodiedness, because of how much we internalize what Tobin Siebers calls the "ideology of ability."[35] "We are all in thrall" to this ideology, Therí Pickens writes, "because we are all wedded to a desire to be healthy or well or able," and this desire strongly shapes our understandings of both our past and our future selves.[36] In these fictitious reflections of ourselves there is no place for disability, so we push our bodies to behave as if they were able, or as close to that as we can. So too, in collective imaginaries shaped by compulsory able-bodiedness, Kafer writes, "disability too often serves as the agreed-upon limit of our projected future selves."[37] The fear of "losing" one's abilities and the thought of "becoming disabled" can haunt people to such a degree that they force their bodies beyond a healthy capacity in order to *not* look, feel, or function anything like that.

Conversely, in the case of acquired disabilities such as those related to RA, the past can also be shaped by what Kafer calls "compulsory nostalgia,"[38] which splits the self into a pre- and postdisability where the preself's abilities come to define the self such that the postself must remain entirely severed from it. That is, the postself can never become a self to be lived in the present or future.

Compulsory able-bodiedness turns toward the future, fed by the fears of becoming disabled, while compulsory nostalgia turns toward the past, longing for all that it had and that has now been lost. As previous testimonies affirm, these emotion-driven compulsions can all *turn* the creation of affordances in their own direction. When Arif Amca grabbed one leg of his trousers and carried his feet up to wash them at the sink, he was not so much creating a new physical match between his painful leg and the sink as he was fulfilling an able-bodied desire not to ask for help (a point that I will return to at the end of chapter 8). When Valerie found a way to pick the bag up from the floor, her invention had less to do with accommodating her pain than inhabiting a "compulsory nostalgia"—a longing for a time when she was not impaired and could simply do so without consequences. In these affordances, internalized ableism overrode feelings of pain, soreness, limitation. It took precedence over what the physical properties of the body and the environment could actually afford for each other. It led less to the alleviation of pain and accommodation of impairment than to the apparent realization of an ideal (read: normative) able-bodied self.

The point is, not all activist affordances have a positive value. Some may, in fact, bring us more pain instead of saving us from it. As much as they allow us to carve out a niche for ourselves in which our pain is minimized and our impairments are somewhat reciprocated, activist affordances can be abusive to their very own creators. They can end up being our futile attempts at belonging to a society that has left us no other option than to do so at the price of pain, irritation, and compulsion.

7

ALWAYS IN-THE-MAKING

Writing about "The Temporality of Landscape," Tim Ingold argues that the entire landscape is "a pattern of activities 'collapsed' into an array of features" of the world.[1] In the previous chapter, I demonstrated how activist affordances materialize in the ephemerality of performance, disappearing as they are being made. I also suggested that activist affordances can "collapse" into the form of actual objects—such as a garment with one sleeve, or a glove with three fingers. But even when they crystallize in the form of an artifact, *their making does not necessarily end with the existence of an artifact.* Their collapse amounts neither to a finalization nor to a termination. Rather, as the following testimonies reveal, activist affordances remain in-the-making within the temporality of performance, where no form, layout, or shape—no matter how solidified it looks—is equivalent to their closure. In this chapter I explore this *ongoingness* by focusing on three stories of making that concern DIY insoles, a DIY-adaptive bike, and a concrete-block pedal. In these stories, activist affordances begin with hacking existing uses of things (such as cheap flip-flops, gel cushions, or a concrete block), followed by a prolonged time of a disabled person's body dancing with the relevant materials. The materials afford ease of movement for their users, and these users' movements, in turn, leave their traces on the materials, just as dancers leave their movements on a stage. In this continual exchange, the user and the material keep transforming and remaking each other, so that activist affordances remain always in-the-making.

Activist Affordance: DIY Insoles

Henri generously shared with me a series of his brilliant activist affordances. In one instance, he explained how he forged a pair of DIY insoles through a complex make-use process:

> Like I said, I used to have a lot of problems walking, with the bones wanting to come out of my feet so, um, being barefoot, was a, was a real pain. It was really bad. So I, I . . . at a certain point, I didn't like going and take my shower because your feet are directly on the ceramic in the bath. That was quite painful. So, I tried to find a trick for making it better for the shower. So I started by putting a bath towel in the bottom of the bath, so that worked out but there was a lot of drying up to do and stuff like that. So, I tried to find a better trick for the shower, and finally I did. Simple, very simple, give me second? I will get my [*smiling as he says this, he goes to another room and brings back a pair of rubber flip-flops*; figure 7.1] . . . So, this is my trick for the shower. I've simply bought a pair of sandals, cheap sandals, two-to-three-dollar sandals, and I put them on and got used to those sandals. Afterward there was no problem for me taking showers and standing in the bath. Um, of course, walking was a big problem also for me . . . um . . . because of my bones that are all crooked in the feet. So, I thought to myself, "If it, if those sandals work for the bath, maybe they can also work for my shoes." So, what I did is: I went to the store, I bought a pair of shoes that is one size bigger than what I usually put on and . . . I took out the sandals [meaning insoles] that were in them and I made sure that the bottom of the shoe was flat. That was very important! So, I took the sandals that I used for the bath and I drew my feet and I drew the sandals that was in the shoe, afterward I cut the shape that I needed, and I simply put the sandal in my shoe! And it took some adjustments afterward, you know, sometimes I had to take out at the bottom, um, . . . some of the rubber just so that it feels good.

Henri explained to me in great detail how he made his DIY insoles:

> The first phase of those sandals for me is when . . . I use them in the shower. The . . . second phase is . . . Like, this one [figure 7.1] is fairly new [*pointing at the new flip-flops he is holding*] so you don't see the . . . shape of my foot in it. It's, it's a "beginner." The second phase of those sandals is: I'm wearing one pair right now in my feet, and . . . I will be wearing them for months . . . until the, the shape is perfect. And the third phase [figures 7.2 and 7.3] is to cut them up and put them in shoes [*smiles proudly and mimics putting the sandal in the shoe*].

As a virtuoso affordance-creator, Henri knew all the details of how his feet, his act of standing, walking, and the surface of the material work together. But most importantly, he was well aware that the making process did not end with the "end" product but was coterminous with the use-process:

> I guess from 1996 to, um, at least 2006, I used to modify the sandals that were in my shoe. So, I would have to add on different kinds of materials, you know, to lift up places and to cut off some places [*mimics the act*] just to try to get that sole to fit my feet. It was a lot of work. But having a sole made like this is a lot less work, and once you got it, probably it's just that they are perfect for me [*smiles and shrugs his shoulders*].

After witnessing Henri's ingenuity, I told him that I had thought that the inserts were bought from a specialized store and modified along the way. He answered:

> Actually, I bought some sandals from orthopedics, and I simply hated them. I didn't like them, they didn't work for me. So, I had to figure out some other way to be able to walk properly. Um . . . as you can see, this [figure 7.2] is pretty old. See where I draw the shape of my foot [figure 7.4]? Of course I didn't cut the top. And unfortunately, I cut the bottom so I shouldn't have done that, so I just added a piece there [*pointing at the black tape*] so it fits perfectly in my shoe. And there you go, it's a miracle on ice!

What Henri's activist affordance reveals is that "adaptive" objects, "assistive" technologies, and "specialized" tools (such as insoles and other devices) that

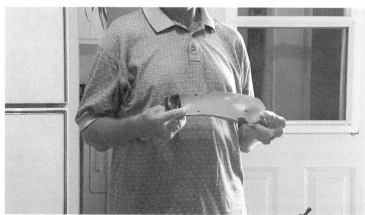

FIGURES 7.1–7.3 HENRI DEMONSTRATES HIS AFFORDANCES FOR PAIN IN HIS FEET, BOTH INVOLVING FLIP-FLOPS. TO STAND MORE COMFORTABLY IN THE SHOWER, HENRI SIMPLY DONS HIS FAVORITE CHEETAH-PRINT FLIP-FLOPS (*TOP*). HE ALSO TRIMS DECONSTRUCTED FLIP-FLOPS TO CREATE DIY INSOLES (*MIDDLE*) THAT HE WEARS INSIDE HIS RUNNING SHOES (*BOTTOM*).

are designed by others in the name of making (in this case) the consumer's feet more comfortable do not necessarily fulfill their marketed promise. Rather, it is Henri's self-engineered insoles made from two-dollar flip-flops, which have been showered in, walked on, drawn upon, and cut and patched along the way, and which may not be as shiny and seamless as the purchased orthotics, that provide an affordance for walking with less pain. As if he were an orthotist himself, Henri was very aware of what specific substances (rubber, tape) afforded for his nodules and painful feet and what his feet needed in order to feel less pain.

We can consider Henri's DIY insoles as samples of what Sara Hendren and Caitrin Lynch describe as "engineering at home," or what Williamson calls "homemade access."[2] Henri's insoles are not a commercialized product, a rehabilitative tool, or an assistive device that is provided by some expert or professional. They are instead built by making do with whatever he has within reach. They are ad hoc designs that emerge from exigency. Torn, worn-out, and patched, they may not look as smooth and sleek as their marketed counterparts (self-aid tools or assistive devices). But they are equally, if not more, effective. Recall Henri's words: "I bought some sandals from orthopedics . . . and I simply hated them. So . . . I had to figure out some other way." "Figuring out" a way on one's own and using one's experiences create a unique expertise (rather than the "expertise" of others) that makes Henri's DIY insoles a case of "crip technoscience" too.[3] As a form of knowing-making, crip technoscience centers disabled people "as designers and world-builders, as knowing what will work best":[4]

> See the shape of my toe here [figure 7.4], how thick it is here [*points at the midpart of the sole and then at the toe*]? This big toe of mine needs a lot of space and also the heel is, um, the bone is quite sticking out [*makes a fist to illustrate the bone sticking out*], so see the hole from my heel also. And you see some of the holes here that are from my bones. This sandal fits perfectly in my shoe and now I'm walking much better [*smiles*]. That's the trick for my sandals!

Henri has been making his DIY insoles for the past three years, and he says that his practice has matured over time. So far, he has engineered two insoles that are ready for use, and he is currently wearing a newly purchased pair of flip-flops that will be ready in a couple of months to be transformed into new insoles for his winter boots.

FIGURE 7.4 HENRI HAS DISCOVERED THAT BREAKING HIS FLIP-FLOPS IN BY WEAR-ING THEM FOR A FEW MONTHS BEFORE TRIMMING THEM TO FIT HIS SHOES MAKES FOR AN AFFORDANCE THAT PROVIDES BETTER FIT AND COMFORT.

Activist Affordance: A DIY-Adaptive Bike

In another one of his activist affordances, Henri cobbled together a mish-mash of affordances in order to be able to ride his bike with the least amount of pain and discomfort possible. Again, as in the case of DIY insoles, his DIY-adaptive bike emerged through a process of careful reflection, calculation, and experimentation. Henri first observed, with great precision, which parts of his body he could use for how long and for which action. He then gave a material form to the very surfaces and substances that would comple-ment these observations: a DIY seat with gel cushions that allowed him to sit with ease and for longer periods, and a bike handle with a modular shape that allowed him to alternate among three different ways of holding the handle (in order to avoid demanding too much effort from the same joint for too long). The shape of the modular handles also fit to the shape of the nodules on his elbows and allowed him to use them as support, and thus he invented the affordance for, in Henri's own words, "wheel-driving" his bike:

> Like I said, for a long long time, I . . . didn't enjoy walking. Not at all.
> So, for the past three years, what I did, um, just to try to get back in
> shape is . . . I got back on my bicycle. At first it was very hard. . . . Being
> that the knees aren't too strong and hips and stuff like that. So . . . most
> of the weight is gonna be on your buns, and not on your feet. So, um,

FIGURES 7.5–7.7 HENRI'S "WHEEL-DRIVEN" BIKE IS AN AFFORDANCE BUILT FROM CAREFUL OBSERVATION OF HIS BODILY CIRCUMSTANCES AND HIS RA-AFFECTED PHYSICAL CHARACTERISTICS. HE ADAPTED THE SEAT AND THICK, C-SHAPED HANDLEBARS SO THAT HE CAN SHIFT POSITIONS WHILE RIDING TO AVOID OVER-STRESSING HIS JOINTS.

that's why . . . I've bought an extra-wide seat and I've added a cushion made of gel, um, just, just to make it easier on my buns. That was the first problem I've had. The second problem I had with the bicycle was my hands and especially wrists. Um, I won't be able to ride my bicycle for a long time holding the handle bars like this [figure 7.5]. . . . The wrists are gonna hurt too much, and the hands, uh . . . It's too, too painful. So, I bought these handlebars that I put on and . . . the nice thing about these handlebars is that you have three different positions for your hands. I have over here [*demonstrates*; figure 7.5]; over here, I can put my hands [*demonstrates*; figure 7.6]; and I also have over here that I can put my hands [*demonstrates*; figure 7.7]. So, just the fact of switching places helps to reduce some of the pain. But not all of it. The only way I can drive this bicycle without, um, having, um, so much is by driving with my elbows [*smiles, having a moment of epiphany*]. So, this is the way that I do it: I simply put my elbows in the corner here like this [figure 7.8], I join my two hands [*places his other elbow on the opposite side*], and . . . I'll wheel-drive my bicycle with my elbows [*proudly smiles*; figure 7.9]. And my hands are free [*shows his freed hands*]. . . . I plan to buy, um, the extension over here [*points at the middle part of the bike*] so that my hands would be . . . more secure [*points at his hands holding the post*] and less dangerous to drive only with the elbows.

Just like insoles, adaptive "special needs" bicycles (and tricycles) as well as bike seats with gel cushions exist as commercial products or as devices made by professionals. But again, just as in the case of the DIY insole, it was not those premade items but Henri's DIY-adaptive bike that afforded him the possibility of biking in ways that made room for and even welcomed his impairments.

Activist Affordance: Concrete-Block Gas Pedal

Anna explained to me the affordance she had invented for being able to press the gas pedal more easily when driving, which she did two-footed. "Because I have, like, really small feet," she explained, "this pushing motion [pushing the gas pedal] is kind of, like, difficult for me." In order to prop her foot up and push more directly from her knee, Anna found a concrete block (figure 7.10) and placed it on the car's floor, slightly in front of the gas pedal (with some space in between). Pointing at the block, she said:

FIGURES 7.8 AND 7.9 HENRI DEMONSTRATES HOW HE "WHEEL-DRIVES" HIS
MODIFIED BIKE. AS HE LEANS FORWARD FROM THE SEAT, HE RESTS HIS ELBOWS
ON EACH HANDLEBAR AND JOINS HIS HANDS. THE ARTHRITIS NODULES ON HIS
ELBOWS PROVIDE SUPPORT.

It kind of helps me to keep my foot up a little higher because I cannot
really push, like, with my toes. I push, like, with my heel. So, it helps me
hold my foot up higher so I have, like, more of my whole foot on the
pedal. If that makes sense! And you can see I've worn holes through the
carpet. . . . So, like, instead of pushing like this [with her toes] I can
push, like, with my whole foot. And then I drive with both feet [placed
on the block].

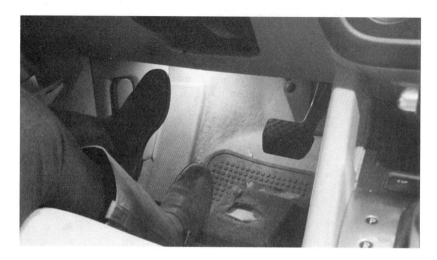

FIGURE 7.10 SINCE HER FEET ARE VERY SMALL, ANNA'S AFFORDANCE, A CONCRETE BLOCK IN THE FOOTWELL OF HER CAR, ALLOWS HER TO PUSH ON THE GAS USING HER KNEES AND BOTH FEET RATHER THAN THE TOES OF JUST ONE FOOT.

An old concrete block. Gel cushions. A pair of inexpensive sandals. This was the "stuff" that Anna and Henri found, cobbled together, and hacked for their own use. They matched and repurposed these objects' physical properties in ways that corresponded to their bodily requirements, took some weight off of their impaired body parts, and relieved the burden of pain from having to (over)use their (currently) inflamed or (previously) damaged joints. The gel cushions patched onto an extra-wide seat took the edge off the weight on Henri's buttocks. The concrete block counteracted the force required of Anna's toes to push the gas pedal. In each of these affordance hacks, the existing affordances of objects were overridden by what their substance, surface, and layout could potentially offer had their materiality not been locked into their "canonical affordances."[5]

Ultimately, Anna's and Henri's ingenious hacks demonstrate that even when activist affordances take a (seemingly) more solid and enduring form than an improvised performance, they still remain in-the-making within the temporality of performance, throughout which the relevant use process becomes inextricable from the making.[6] Recall the complex process through which Henri made his DIY insoles. He bought a pair of cheap flip-flops and wore them in the shower over a sustained period of time. The "shower phase," as Henri called it, allowed the spongy texture of the flip-flops to absorb water, rendering the rubber more responsive and reciprocal to Henri's feet and the arthritic nodules underneath. In a second phase, Henri wore the flip-flops (the layout and texture of which have now been partially changed by way of the shower phase) in his house for another period of time, until he felt they reached a desired shape that dovetailed with the shape of the bottom of his feet. Henri then drew the blueprint of his feet on the flip-flops and then cut them so as to make them fit into his shoes. But Henri's making of his insoles did not end here. As he used his DIY insoles and as their shape and texture changed day by day, he modified them by making further cuts and adding patches of tape here and there. In Henri's ongoing activist affordance, *making emerged from use process,* because he made his insoles by literally wearing a pair of cheap flip-flops long enough to let them take the shape of his feet and carry the residue of their ongoing use. Conversely, *use process became a process of making in itself,* because Henri continually altered his insoles so as to accommodate and counterbalance the effects of their use. The same can be said for Henri's makeshift bike, for Anna's concrete block–supported pedal, or, in fact, for any other artifact made.

This is exactly why activist affordances do not equate to the artifacts that may be made. Instead, *affordances* refers to perpetual *making* and *remaking* through performance. Whether they disappear as they are being made, as in danced affordances, or whether they lead to the creation of a new artifact without the concretization of its "ultimate" shape, activist affordances remain in a perpetual state of creation.

Activist Affordances Make Matter Give Birth

The environment, with its concrete contours, substantial matter, and firm surfaces, may seem to be cast out of time, inert, unresponsive, and lacking the very qualities that we associate with temporality, livelihood, and animacy—it is this very dichotomy that Ingold targets and undoes in his work on "The Temporality of Landscape."[7] But when activist affordances emerge, as they do in these ethnographic examples, the seeming "fixity" of the materiality of the world cannot remain static. "The world itself," as Ingold puts it, "begins to breathe."[8]

As an activist affordance is being improvised and the world is perceived not AS IS but AS IF, previously recalcitrant surfaces and substances become fluid. The firmly drawn contours of objects, things, and places begin to dissolve. It could be that my participants choreograph the affordances of an accessible object that is yet to be designed (such as Henri's arthritic mugs), or it could be that their dancing with a world of materials (as in Henri's DIY insoles) turns into a prolonged performance, during which use-process becomes a process of making in and of itself. But in whichever modality activist affordances take place, my participants do not take for granted that the environment is recalcitrant and unchanging, as the currently occupied niches of the environment make them appear to be. They instead circumvent the limited sphere of opportunities through which the environment presents itself to them, and they imagine the very same environment otherwise. As they do so, the environment multiplies in its meanings and proliferates in its possibilities as whatever has been locked up behind the fixity of its surfaces begins to flow. Potentialities unfold.

Throughout the creation of activist affordances, it becomes apparent that behind the limits of an already occupied niche and its stultifying AS IS, there is actually plenty of room to for bodies and the environment to maneuver, reciprocate. As my participants come up with activist affordances—distinguished by their difference from those that have thus far been used—*matter* appears for what it inherently is, that is, pregnant with possibilities for action.[9]

The etymological origin of the word "matter," as marked by Judith Butler and others, goes back to *mater, mother, matrix* (the womb).[10] According to Butler, it is in this lineage that we can find how matter was once imbued with "a certain capacity to originate"[11] and understand how matter comes to matter. Ingold's and Donna Haraway's considerations of matter resonate with Butler's. "Far from being the inanimate stuff typically envisioned by modern thought materials (or matter) in this original sense," Ingold writes, "are the active constituents of a world-in-formation."[12] "*Matter* is a powerful, mindfully bodied word," Haraway reminds us, "the matrix and generatrix of things."[13] Activist affordances make matter matter precisely in this sense of the term.

The material world may appear inert, unchanging, and lifeless. It may seem to materialize particular uses only. What matter *is* may appear to be defined by (and as such identified with), in Sara Ahmed's phrase, what matter is *for*.[14] But if we take into account the origin of the word "matter" in the matrix (the womb), then it follows that matter must be available for alternative affordances; it must "contain" that capacity to afford otherwise to begin with. This very capacity (of matter) to generate is what activist affordances unveil and bring into focus. If normative affordances "deaden" matter by calcifying and ossifying particular uses of it only, then activist affordances make matter give birth, laying bare its potential to afford otherwise. During the creation of activist affordances, matter becomes alive, so to speak, offering many other possibilities of action than the affordances that have been canonized by way of reiteration and those that have been concretized by their design in specific forms and layouts. These activist affordances are, in a way, *excess affordances,* by which I mean that they are (and will always be) in excess of the *decided* affordance that has been solidified or the *chosen* act that has collapsed into the concrete features of the environment. In this regard, activist affordances are not about *what is* or *what ought to be*, but always about *what could be.*

Performance: Making without Closure

According to theater scholar Alan Read, the impossibility of closure for the imaginative possibilities of performance is exactly where an ethics of performance lies. "Ethics . . . defines a distance between what is and what ought to be,"[15] and it is in this very space—between "what is" and "what ought to be"— Read argues, that theater takes place:

> Both ethics and theatre are concerned with possibility. On the contrary representation is the reflection of an "existing" proposition as though it were fact, and this is never what theater achieves. The theatre image unlike any other is always a possibility without closure, like the ethical relation which awaits creation.[16]

Theater offers openings into other ways of being in this world, but it does so by way of performing. Precisely because it brings other possible worlds into being by way of *doing*, these other possible worlds are never presented as though they were facts, as though they were *the* reality. Instead, they always remain a potentiality. So are the "inhabitable worlds" that activist affordances bring into being by way of performance.[17]

Activist affordances are concerned less with what is given durable forms than with the dissolution of that fixity that allows for new horizons of possibility. These affordances point to how action-possibilities can be exponentially multiplied rather than how they get to be ossified in the seeming concreteness of things. Whether performance refers to the fleeting gestures of a hand buttoning a shirt or to the use-process of wearing and (deliberately) tearing a flip-flop over the course of months, performance is what allows us to *make up* and *make real* activist affordances. Therefore, activist affordances never culminate in a final form. Instead, they remain in movement toward the forms that they are yet to take. So do the accessible futures whose contours they draw.

As activist affordances bring "accessible futures" to life, they do so without a solid claim on what those futures "should" be or what those inhabitable worlds "ought to" look like. Just as the "the theatre image . . . is always a possibility without closure,"[18] these futures oscillate between *what is, what could be*, and *what ought to be*, without ever settling in any one. Because they are brought into being in and through performance, these accessible futures do not calcify into yet another stultifying present. Emerging from and staying within performance, activist affordances remain *a continual search for accessible futures* that are yet to arrive, for livable niches that are yet to be occupied.

"Access," Margaret Price reminds us, "is not going to happen overnight." "We must [therefore] try, think, query, flex, observe, listen, and try again."[19] As performances, activist affordances can allow us to experiment, improvise, try, fail, try again, and chase access precisely in its inexhaustibility.

PEOPLE AS AFFORDANCES

Performance is a doing to, a thing done to and with the spectator.
—Diana Taylor, *Performance*

I first met Ahmet at his workplace, a public library in a municipality center that offers educational activities, arts and crafts courses, and other services for people with disabilities. After explaining to Ahmet the purpose of my research and what we would be doing, I asked about how his experience of rheumatoid arthritis started:

> *Ahmet:* When I was six, in my feet and then my wrists . . . I couldn't
> stand on my feet. I was holding onto the walls. At first, they thought
> I was playing around, I mean, when it started in my feet. But I
> couldn't walk. I mean, I could walk but I was tired right away, and
> then I asked my dad to carry me— and then my dad thought, this kid
> is just playing around. You know sometimes kids are like that. They
> don't want to walk. So my dad thought that's what I was doing. Then
> gradually my feet started to swell. Then my back and neck [*pauses*

and tries to remember] . . . I remember a time—in the 1990s—we were going to the city. . . . Whenever the car and the wheels shook [*mimics shaking*], I was dying from the pain. . . . I mean, I could move my head but it was so painful, you know, when the car was bumping along the road.

Arseli: Like the vibrations in a minibus [*dolmuş, a common method of intercity travel in Turkey*] . . . ?

Ahmet: Of course. Imagine, even with those minimal movements, I was in immense pain.

When Ahmet was about ten years old, he was hospitalized for a time.

Ahmet: The disease, of course, progressed a bit. . . . You know, like when I was going to primary school, I walked by holding onto things, like walls [*his eyes gaze into the distance as he recalls the past*]. That was it. I was holding onto things.

Arseli: Did you have any support while you were going to primary school?

Ahmet [*smiling*]: Well, I could walk, but only by hanging on to things.

Arseli: Were you able to attend classes?

Ahmet: Of course. But my dad helped me. He carried me in his arms. Because it was a village road, and the school was a bit far, about one and a half country bus stops (*durak*) away. They call it a footpath (*patika*), but it was a rough country road. Because it was rough, my dad would carry me to school in his arms and then go back. At the end of the day, he would come back to pick me up.

Arseli: Every single day, your dad carried you?

Ahmet: [*smiling emotionally*] Sure, he did—almost until middle school . . .

During his middle school years, Ahmet had to take a five-year break due to illness. He continued, "My dad, of course, told me to get an education (*oku*). So I went back to school. In the meantime, he started to work somewhere else. My father's an imam, a hodja (*hoca*). I went back to school. And again, my father brought me back and forth to school in his arms."

Consider a second story. Maya was born without legs due to a congenital disorder. Having escaped the debilitating conditions of war, and living in an extreme state of deprivation in a resource-deprived Syrian refugee camp in Turkey, with scarce daily sustenance and no medical care or very limited access to it, Maya had no way to move around other than by crawling. Her father, Mohammad, who has the same condition, engineered a "homemade prosthetic made from tubes and tuna cans," rendering navigable for her the otherwise hostile materiality of the hot, dusty campground.[1]

Up until now I have discussed activist affordances as the creations of a single person, which emerge as a single disabled person finds inventive ways of making an otherwise shrinking environment inhabitable. But in Ahmet's story, his father also became an affordance for him, especially when no affordance existed that would enable him to access education. So did Maya's father, who invented a prosthesis from tuna cans that enabled his disabled daughter to move around the uneven and dusty ground of the camp. While his body did not itself function as an affordance, he engaged in the act of making for the benefit of another—specifically his daughter—rather than for himself, as, for example, Henri did with his bicycle (see chapter 7).

These stories provoke the question: What if the making of activist affordances is not—and perhaps has never been—one person's individual affair?

People as Affordances: When It Takes More Than One

Affordances, according to James Gibson, are environmental properties "taken with reference to the observer": "If a terrestrial surface is nearly horizontal . . . nearly flat . . . and sufficiently extended (relative to the size of the animal) and if its substance is rigid (relative to the weight of the animal), then the surface *affords support.*"[2] This was obviously not the case with the footpath for Ahmet. The physical properties of the cluttered path in reference to his body were a *barrier* to affordance. So what made school nevertheless attend-able for him? How did an un-walk-on-able path become walk-able?

The answer is: Ahmet's father. In the absence of a wheelchair, accessible roads, or public transport, *Ahmet's father became his affordance.* This is exactly what I mean by "people as affordances." Building on the analysis of Ahmet's and Maya's stories, I propose the concept of people as affordances to name how people can enable the emergence of affordances or directly become affordances for one another, including the very situations in which the affordances that their coming-together creates do not otherwise exist within the niche they share.

People as affordances is an important subset of activist affordances because of the addition of *people* to the properties that are part of the environment.[3] It names the improvised relationalities between the world and one's own body as well as between multiple bodies. If activist affordances emerge through a dance—a dance that brings into being an otherwise absent affordance—then when people become affordances, it means that an activist affordance is danced in a duo or an ensemble. Let us rethink Ahmet's story in these terms. Ahmet grew up in a small Turkish village in the early 1990s. In addition to the problem of getting to school, accessing hospital care and medications required a trip over a long distance to the nearest town. His parents could get medication for Ahmet only when they drove into town. Add to this that Ahmet's medications worked only if taken regularly; otherwise, the disease could suddenly flare up. And it did flare up. Ahmet's primary school was far from his home, with neither a proper road nor a transportation system between them. Connecting the two was a rough country road (a *patika*—literally, "a path to be walked upon"). Ahmet's feet were inflamed and swollen. He could not walk without support. While many people with disabilities can *make do* by putting their bodies and surrounding materials in noncanonical combinations (as I have thus far documented), there was no way for Ahmet to negotiate the footpath, to make it afford him slantwise. Its uneven surface, cluttered with pebbles and weeds, and the lack of a railing were hostile to his disabled body in pain—unless, of course, another body came in between Ahmet and the path, as did Ahmet's father, who lent his arms for Ahmet to be carried within and his feet to walk for Ahmet, becoming the affordance of what in ideal circumstances would have been a wheelchair, an adaptive public transportation system, or a smooth-surfaced road.

The affordance of support comes about in Ahmet's story because his body relates with his father's as it constitutes part of the environment involved in this affordance. But it is not the father's body's properties alone that are responsible for the possibility of this affordance. In addition to arms and feet, the father's love and *care*, and his strong belief in the value of education, also walk *with* and *for* his child. Similarly, in Maya's story, it is ostensibly the father's devotion to his daughter that moves him to make a prosthesis, providing her with mobility under extremely challenging conditions, including few resources.

Mutual Affordances

To be clear, Gibson does not restrict the definition of "environment" to the landscape, because he considers other animals as *part* of the environment. In fact, he writes: "The richest and most elaborate affordances of the environment are provided by . . . other people."[4] Our bodies, materially speaking, are substances with surfaces whose layouts change as we move, do things, and make gestures. These changes emit perceptual information about us, what we are, and what we ask, demand, promise, encourage, and so forth:

> What the infant affords the mother is reciprocal to what the mother affords the infant; what the prey affords the predator goes along with what the predator affords the prey; what the buyer affords the seller cannot be separated from what the seller affords the buyer, and so on.[5]

Such reciprocal behaviors give rise to what Gibson terms "mutual affordances." It is important to keep in mind that Gibson is operating within evolutionary scientific discourse, in which the goal of all life ultimately is to reproduce. Accordingly, mutual affordances refer to evolutionary reciprocal behaviors (such as the one between the infant and mother) and socially conditioned behaviors (such as the one between the seller and buyer), all of which are learned in an evolutionary socio-ecological niche that requires and actively enables their development. In other words, the term mutual affordances refers to and assumes a certain normativity in the relevant behaviors.

However, my use of the concept of people as affordances troubles, complicates, and at times entirely undoes this normativity. As I demonstrate in the second half of this chapter, people may become affordances for each other precisely by *not* engaging in the kind of behaviors expected of mutual affordances—such as a mother *not* hugging her kids, or a couple *not* engaging in any sexual behavior.

Further, there are multiple factors at play in the creation of people as affordances. Just as with any other activist affordance, the concept of people as affordances foregrounds the historical/material conditions that necessitate their making, whereas this is not the case for normative mutual affordances. Recall how Yasemin danced the affordance of an elongated comb in its material absence. Similarly, when people create or directly become affordances for one another, they collectively dance and dwell in a more habitable and welcoming, accessible world in the very absence of those features that would otherwise make it so. Thus, we cannot understand how the footpath becomes walk-on-able for Ahmet apart from the relationship between him and his father, nor apart from their specific living conditions and access to resources. Rural Turkey in the 1990s lacked basic infrastructure and services (well-tended roads, hospitals, schools, public transportation), never mind more "luxurious" devices or services that are routine in a well-functioning social-welfare state, such as automated wheelchairs and social workers. The refugee camp where Maya lived offered even fewer resources, providing only the most meager existence. In the two stories we witness complementarities emerging *between people—within a social environment.* In Ahmet's story, the complementarity arises between a disabled school-age child, his ambulatory father who loves him and values education, *and* a rudimentary footpath between school and home in a system where basic infrastructure and support for the disabled child and his family fail to materialize. In Maya's story, complementarity emerges from a disabled child, her father who devotes himself to her mobility, and a subsistence-level environment with only the most basic resources, where attention to disability seems almost beyond imagination. It is in these important aspects that the concept of people as affordances builds upon and complicates the idea of mutual affordances.

In the following, I flesh out the concept of people as affordances by laying out its various dimensions. People as affordances, for instance, entail the "leakiness" of pain.[6] They enact "access intimacy."[7] They remake mutual affordances. I name and articulate these dimensions through the guidance of ethnographic materials[8] and break them down further into additional elements, such as their distribution or functioning as role reversals. The concept, in other words, comes into being in the form of a collage as I add, expand, and break down its differing dimensions and aspects. In the framing of this collage lies its boundaries. People may enable and facilitate, but also interfere with and entirely *disable*, the emergence of affordances for one another. In the final section of the chapter, I turn to situations in which people do *not* become affordances but in fact may come to be *barriers* to affordance. I focus particularly on the stigma of "help" and reflect on how people as affordances can allow us to offset it by offering an alternative imaginary to help.

People as Affordances Entail the Leakiness of Pain

I visited Valerie and her husband, Patrick, at their country cottage in Canada. They lived in a stone-built house—the house of their dreams—amid vast open lands, far from neighbors. They had a farm, and Valerie had a huge vegetable garden where she spent most of her time when she was still mobile. Patrick had installed an irrigation pipe so that Valerie could water the garden by just opening the tap without having to manipulate the hose, which was now difficult for her given her painful joints. When I met her, Valerie had been living with rheumatoid arthritis and its related disabilities for only a few years. The flare-ups, health complications, and pain that arose during our interview, as well as throughout her days, were difficult for her. I asked Patrick how the illness has affected their life as a couple:

> Well, it started showing up very shortly after we were together. So, it's not like we have, you know, ten years before and ten years after. Um, but yeah, I can see that she is in pain and I think we have just developed a way of, you know for some things, just doing stuff, day-to-day life. . . . I don't think about it very much anymore . . . um, but there are times when it's not always easy to understand and you know, "Just, just pick it up!" Like, it's, you know, there is stuff lying around and [*mimics the gesture of saying so*] "Just pick it up!" and you don't always think about, "Ah, you know, maybe that day she is not feeling, you know, well enough to pick whatever it is, um, on the ground up." Yeah . . . sometimes. It's not always easy [*turning to Valerie*], but I think we manage.

I ask Patrick whether he could give some examples of the routine he mentioned, and whether they did anything differently now than before the onset of Valerie's illness:

> *Patrick:* Yeah . . . just trying to pay attention. Yeah, like when you put the cap back on something . . . not to put it, not to tighten it, right?
>
> *Valerie:* Let's say we are at a place outside and people come with a, I don't know, a water bottle. Brand-new water bottle. You always crack the seal and then you give it to me.
>
> *Patrick:* Hmm [*nods his head slightly, showing agreement*].
>
> *Valerie:* Always, always, always. Or open a pop can, you know the little lid [*mimics opening a can*]. You always do it.
>
> *Patrick:* Yeah, it's true.
>
> *Valerie:* I don't think you notice it anymore.
>
> *Patrick:* Yeah, no.

Drawing on Margrit Shildrick's idea of "leaky bodies," Alyson Patsavas writes of her own experience of pain as "leak[ing] onto those around me in a way that cannot be contained by the boundary of my body or experience."[9] Accordingly, she proposes in her "cripistemology of pain" that pain "flows through, across, and between always-already connected bodies."[10] Patsavas goes so far as to suggest that one person's experience of pain and another's experience of living with that person's pain "bleed and leak onto one another," making it impossible to talk exclusively of "one's" individual pain.[11] I sometimes imagine a similar kind of sharing, my pain flowing through the pores of my skin like my sweat, touching my partner, François, and those around me in invisible yet visceral ways. I know this is not only my own sense but that it is also shared by François, because when I get up in the morning, I find bread that François has sliced and a kettle on the counter that he has half filled. He shares my pain in this way, offering me this anticipatory care with limbs that do not experience pain, so as to prevent me from experiencing the pain of my morning-stiff limbs. François has become the affordance that allows me to eat breakfast every morning without undue pain.

Let me put it this way: if the bread becomes edible to me, this is not because I have come up with an ingenious affordance for slicing the loaf but because François has it sliced on my/our stiff hands' behalf. Here is then another subdimension of people as affordances: shared pain may translate into a shared body (or body parts) so that the body in pain is saved from the pain of doing things. Valerie's and Patrick's account of living with Valerie's pain also echoes the notion of pain as leaking between bodies, and the notion of shared body parts. When he cracks the seal on a water bottle and leaves it for Valerie, Patrick is not responding to an explicit request but to the pain he anticipates she will otherwise feel. He is aware of Valerie's pain; he is with it, and it is with him.

People as Affordances Enact Access Intimacy

There is a further affective dimension, or a dimension of care, that also marks these instances of people as affordances. Mia Mingus's concept of "access intimacy" names this dimension. Access intimacy refers to the "elusive, hard to describe feeling when someone else 'gets' your access needs" without your having to make it explicit.[12] When Patrick acts as an affordance, he does so not only as a practical matter but as an enactment of access intimacy. That is, the idea of people as affordances provides the mechanism—the material and embodied enactment—that creates access intimacy. Patrick becomes an affordance through his sensing that the pain is there in Valerie's swollen fingers and knowing that he has the capacity to care for the pain, to alleviate or at least diminish it. He not only "gets it" but also engages in a highly specific, material enactment of "getting it"—of care. In this process, Valerie and Patrick enact an otherwise world in which pain can be communicated at least to the degree that the transmission—the leaking—inspires not just care, but care that anticipates Valerie's need for care out of a shared sense of "her" pain.

People as Affordances May Be Distributed

Valerie's testimony reveals that their household tasks do not have to be performed in the moments they are "expected" to be (such as dishes that need to be put into the dishwasher); they may instead be postponed for later in order for Patrick to do them. People as affordances may, in short, be distributed.

Another aspect of this kind of affordance and its distribution is that tasks involving multiple actions can be broken down into their constituent actions, which are then taken up by Valerie and Patrick through a careful consideration of who can do what and when. Grocery shopping is one such task. When I asked Valerie about this activity, she told me:

> Usually, I do it by myself because Patrick works a lot of hours and he works outside of town sometimes. So I do. . . . Every time I have to drive [to the grocery], I pick up what we need for the next few days so I don't have a big grocery [load] and it's not very heavy and it's easier for me. Especially if I am by myself to take it out of the bags. 'Cause most of the time, I do it, and then when Patrick comes home, he puts it away.

For Patrick and Valerie, getting and storing groceries entail an extended dance for two, in which one (Patrick) becomes an affordance for the other (Valerie). Affordance-creation becomes multiple, as bodies come into and leave the environment in which those affordances are needed, according to the timing of their lives and their bodily capacities. "Distribution" names this additional element of people as affordances, which takes the form of an ongoing dance, with multiple scenes.

Valerie, Patrick, and the objects in between them come together to invent an affordance that reduces Valerie's pain. Only when a person—Patrick—becomes part of Valerie's environment can these "people" (person in this case) "as affordances" arise. These intermittent affordances are not "problematic" or "disordered"; rather they enable Valerie and Patrick to take care of their household needs together *in their own time*, while caring for Valerie's pain.

People as Affordances Leave Traces

The vital affordances of Valerie's and Patrick's common environment begin to have traces of pain and impairment that are shared as they live together. Things lie on the ground; groceries and dirty dishes wait on the counter until the environment includes a second person who can become available as an affordance. Patrick cracks bottles' seals, acting as an affordance for Valerie to make use of at a later point. A full grocery bag stays on a lowered counter until Patrick gets home and introduces the affordance necessary to lift and store its contents; dishes lie on the counter until he becomes the affordance that allows for them to be washed in the dishwasher.

In his concept of "dwelling perspective," Tim Ingold writes: "The landscape is constituted as an enduring record of—and testimony to—the lives and works of past generations who have dwelt within it, and in so doing, have left there something of themselves."[13] Drawing on Patrick and Valerie's story, I argue that disabled dwellers of the environment and their allies *leave* there something of themselves *through* their cooperatively shouldered affordances. As much as they do something *with* the environment at this moment in time, people as affordances, through their distribution and cocreation, do something *to* the environment over time as well.

People as Affordances Remake Mutual Affordances

Sevim and Güven, a long-married couple whom I interviewed at their home in İstanbul, reflected on how illness and disability complicated their relations with their children and grandchildren:

> *Sevim*: [*proudly pointing at a photo*] This is my granddaughter, that's our daughter. When she started walking—let's say we're going to the park or something—poor kid, she tugs my hand [*mimics her hand being pulled*], and I go, "Ow, ouch!" [*mimics expression of pain*]. I say, "Don't do that!" She got scared and let my hand go. But then she got used to it. She started asking, "Which one of your hands was it, grandma? Should I hold this one, or the other one?" I mean the kid is . . .
>
> *Güven*: I mean, it [illness] does not just affect the person who's sick. It affects the people around her.
>
> *Sevim*: [*interjecting*] Like I say to her, "Ouch! Don't pull me, my dear."
>
> *Arseli*: How does it affect the people around her, for example?
>
> *Güven*: Look, here you go. Even if her granddaughter is young . . .
>
> *Sevim*: [*speaking at the same time*] I mean, it does hurt of course . . .
>
> *Güven*: . . . subconsciously at least . . .
>
> *Sevim*: . . . then she asks, "Which one hurt, Grandma?"
>
> *Güven*: . . . she thinks it could hurt her grandma if she holds her hand.
>
> *Sevim*: But what can the kid do? From the moment she opened her eyes, that's how she saw me. Even then I couldn't hold her in my arms.

In Sevim's case, neither she nor her grandchild could become affordances for each other. The child worried about hurting her grandmother, and the grandmother could not hold the child as she wished.

Marielle, now an elderly grandmother, has spent almost thirty years of her adult life with rheumatoid arthritis and its related disabilities. This brought "turmoil" (*drame* in French) into her family's life, she said, because she had three kids when she fell ill. She was not able to do daily chores, cooked as little as possible, and got help from her mom and sister. At a certain point she was hospitalized for a month, and her children had to stay with their grandmother. "My life changed completely," Marielle said. In a teary and regretful tone, she recalled how, like Sevim, she was not even able to hug her kids because her entire body was in pain:

> [*Mother tongue French, speaking in English*] Oh, it [hugging] was difficult. I had to choose the right moment. I was sitting and after, they were coming on me and then I opened my [*mimics opening her arms*]. Because my shoulders, my neck [*points and gestures pain*], the white of my eyes was, um, . . . and the jaw, and all. . . . All my joints were affected.

Melanie, her husband, Antoine, and I sat at their dining table as François helped me film the interview. Perhaps because I was the ethnographer with a similar illness to Melanie's and was there with my partner, or perhaps because she simply wanted to talk about it, Melanie reflected on the difficulties of engaging in sexual activity when living with a highly disabling illness:

> *Melanie*: [*mother tongue French, speaking in English*] And it affects too . . . our sex life! I was so much tired. So much pain. [*mimics a hand touching her arm*] "Don't!" You can't touch me. Do this [*extends her arm, touches me very gently, and then screams*], "Argh! [*mimics pain*]. No [*recoils in pain*] touch. Don't touch me! I have pain, you know." So it affects this part too. Because it's important to know that we want to but we can't. It's not because I don't love you, it's not because I don't feel like. I can't. . . . I am tired.
> *Arseli*: It hurts.
> *Melanie*: It hurts! It hurts a lot and I am tired and after that it's "Argh," double pain you know [*mimics aching, with her tongue out*]. It's "Argh! Argh! Argh!" [*Each "argh" is preceded by one of her arms touching the other. She lets go of her hands.*] It's important in this way too. It may not be easy for him because we were so young. At the age of thirty, you know, you want it, eh! It's good. But, um [*makes a face so as to signal, What can I do?*], "I'm sorry!"

Thus far, my discussion of people as affordances has focused on how affordances are collectively brought into being as one person dwells in another's experience of disability, including chronic disease and pain. But what of situations where the *non*performance of an (expected) action becomes an affordance in and of itself? Philosophers of action note that not-doing or negative actions can be as important as positive ones and, in some cases, withdrawals or intentional omissions may also become acts of resistance.[14] In what follows I want to briefly consider how mutual *avoidance* can become an activist affordance in its own right, and how it can bring a "new kinship imaginary" into being.[15] But first I must ask: What affordance is being mutually given *up* here?

If we follow Gibson's logic (explained earlier), we must assume that in Sevim's and Melanie's stories "mutual affordances" are simply being given up, as sexual activity is not engaged in and a hand is not held. But Rayna Rapp and Faye Ginsburg's notion of "new kinship imaginaries" leads me to ask, Is it really thus? *Must* it be?

Perhaps not. In their longtime work on the experiences of families with disabled children in the United States, Rapp and Ginsburg trace how families, in the face of such experiences, "find themselves recognizing and reorganizing tacit norms about familial relations."[16] Living lives in which "the temporalities and expectations of conventional kinship narratives" such as "college, job, marriage, children" will not necessarily materialize, families begin to rewrite the normative social and cultural scripts of the middle-class American nuclear family.[17] "From household budgets to school careers to sibling relations to models of humanity," these families remake everything "in ways that take into account life with a difference," opening up meaningful spaces for what normative expectations preclude.[18] This is how they bring into being "new kinship imaginaries."

This seems directly applicable to Sevim's, Marielle's, and Melanie's stories: a granddaughter's hand is *not* held; a mother is *not* hugged; a lover's body is *not* touched.[19] But this absence of action does not necessarily mean the absence of mutual affordance. Rather, within a new kinship imaginary, it may mean only that the mutual affordance does not materialize according to traditional *normative expectations* that presume that a grandchild's hands should automatically be held by his/her grandparent, that mothers should hug their children, and that couples should make love. People as affordances can, indeed, *rewrite* the social scripts of mutual affordances.[20] They can undo the canonized mutual affordances and build new ones in their place instead.

Nonperformance as Affordance: Loving Nonetheless

Mutual affordances are not like other affordances, however. When they fail to actualize in expected ways, they elicit a response from the person in need of affordance, such as acceptance, refusal, indifference, or encouragement (none of which one may expect, say, from a water bottle that one may or may not be able to open). The mutual forgoing of an action can be an activist affordance in itself—one that brings into being a new kinship imaginary—not because an otherwise unimaginable action possibility is cocreated, but because an already established and socialized action possibility is, through mutual consent, *not* undertaken. Thus "Please don't" and "Don't touch me" are the terms of the (non)engagement of a grandmother and her grandchild, or of a couple. A mutual affordance emerges not because the action in question is performed, but because it is mutually *let go of*.[21] Here, people become affordances for each other not by way of enabling the emergence of, or by directly undertaking, an affordance, but by way of agreeing to let go of an affordance that could have been of benefit to them. It is the *nonperformance* of a canonical mutual affordance that becomes an affordance in and of itself, as Sevim's grandchild enacted by asking, "Which one [of your hands] hurts, Grandma?" The grandchild can be seen as "sharing pain" with her grandmother and acting accordingly to avoid hurting the "wrong" hand, while still wanting to hold a hand.

Not touching, not holding, not caressing, and loving nonetheless. This is how people as affordances may come to forge new kinship imaginaries—imaginaries where there literally is *room* for impairment and pain.

Family Members as the Affordances of Infrastructures

Yasemin recalled the time when she fell ill. Her entire body flared up with pain and inflammation, making her unable to move:

> *Yasemin:* My biggest son was four years old when I was diagnosed with rheumatoid arthritis. It was as if I had [had] a stroke back then. I couldn't eat my food. I was not able to go to the toilet. I was not able to do anything at all. I wasn't able to get dressed. When he was only four, my son supported me a lot. He used to feed me, bringing the spoon to my mouth [*pauses in silence, slowly getting teary and biting her lips*]. I do not even want to remember those days.

Melanie, whose home is in Canada, is in her mid-forties and has been living with disability and a chronic illness similar to rheumatoid arthritis for the last fifteen years. Her husband, Antoine, and I were standing with Melanie in Antoine's garage, where he said he spent most of his time when Melanie was not well or busy with her dancing exercises. I asked how the illness affected their lives in terms of looking after kids, the house, and hospital visits. Their native tongue is French, but they spoke in English for my sake:

> *Antoine:* Now, I have to make my life with that. . . . But at the beginning, I talk about fourteen, fifteen years ago, I start a company here, and she had the . . . very little child. And sometimes she call me . . . I was in the rush . . .
>
> *Melanie:* Yes, I remember I was calling him at the office, and tell him, "Oh come, I need you, I need you. I can't move." It was not easy [*making a tense face*]. He comes but he goes back after and, uh . . . [*pauses, remembering the past in silence and with emotion*]. I was alone. I was really alone. I needed help. Today, I will never do this. With my experience . . . I will never do this but . . . it was not easy for him.
>
> *Arseli:* What about neighbors? Friends?
>
> *Melanie:* No, I don't have anybody in this city [in the past]. I just arrived. We just arrived . . . I found a doctor and that's it. And the CLSC [Centre local de services communautaires][22] helped me a lot. Because my mother was coming here for help me for one week . . . and one time, she look at me and she said: "I can't go home and leave you like this. I have to do something." So she called the CLSC to explain my case. And they come home, um, to see how well I am. And when they see myself and my three kids, "Oh, my God! We have to help you!" So they, they gave me a person. She comes three hours per day to help me every morning. . . . For five year, I get her. She come at seven until ten, and she's doing my potatoes [*smiles*], my bad potatoes, my [*points at the deformities of her hands*], home cleaning, everything. . . . My son was one year, two year, and, in the morning, he is going around [*mimics walking in full diapers*] with his "la couche la" [diaper] is full of urine. And I can't do. I can't change it. So, she was there for that. And she became my best friend. I don't need her anymore, but she gave me so much in my life, in our life. She's my best friend. So that was . . . a nice period because I know [*in a tone of relief*] I can count on somebody for the first time to help me.

Melanie's story of searching for care tells us once again that how, where, and under which conditions people become affordances for each other is inextricable from the conditions of their living. Melanie lives in Quebec, which offers the CLSC, a public health system with extended services including social and care workers for home visits. At the time, Melanie recounted, this infrastructure had offset the need for Antoine or her mother to become affordances for Melanie and her children.[23] In fact, Melanie's social worker took care of Melanie and her children for five years, eventually becoming her best friend.

Now let us return to Yasemin's story. In the early 1990s, when Yasemin fell ill, no extended health infrastructure with social services like the CLSC existed in Turkey. As I know from my own experience, care work was (and is still) largely left to family members, especially women, or, if the person is wealthy enough to afford it, to workers who do not happen to be women but who are literally named as such, *kadın* (and the act of hiring them is called "to hire women," *kadın tutmak*). In Yasemin's case the caretaker was her four-year-old child, who fed her, enacting the very affordances of a care professional that would have otherwise been provided by the operational infrastructures of a welfare state.

In comparing Yasemin's story to Melanie's, I do not mean to draw a crude dichotomy between a "developed" and a "developing" state. I am also not suggesting people do not need to become affordances for one another in Canada, while in Turkey that is the rule. Instead, I suggest that the emergence of people as affordances and the specific circumstances that give rise to them cannot be predicted. Consider the story of Guylaine, who is in her fifties and has lived all her life in Quebec. She had experienced episodic pain since she was very young, but after the birth of her second child the pain became chronic and debilitating, and she was diagnosed with rheumatoid arthritis. Guylaine was talking with my husband, François, who was helping with the filming and translation during my interviews:

> *Guylaine*: [*translated from French*] The situation got serious. My hands, my feet were very swollen and reddish. I wasn't able to lift my baby or change his diapers. This was when the problem occurred. . . . I went to the emergency room. . . . My back was crooked. I had difficulties to stand up. I was looking like an eighty-year-old. I had to put my back on the wall to get my back straight. . . . I can say that I was not functioning at all. For the younger one [her baby], I had to grab him under his arm. I had difficulties shopping and to lift the bags, open the bags, everything was going bad. My hip was bad. My back was bad. The arms. The pain. I had no strength in my hands. I can say it was like hell for many years.

François: Did you have anybody help you at that time?

Guylaine: In fact, I had my older child. He was able to lift his younger brother, change his diapers. Most of the time, it was he who would do things on my behalf. Since my partner wasn't much around.

In a later part of our conversation, I asked Guylaine whether she sought help from the services of CLSC. She replied, "I managed on my own. Because I had family close by. For sure, if I lived far [away], I would have asked someone for help from CLSC."

As Guylaine's story suggests, an existing system of extended healthcare and social workers does not mean that they are always used. Nor does it mean that these services are unquestioningly and indiscriminately provided to those in need. For example, Valerie, one of my participants living in Quebec, desperately needed professional help given the extent of her disability and access needs. When I asked her whether she sought help from CLSC, she replied that she was not eligible according to CLSC criteria because she did not have children under her care (as Melanie did), and she had a family member (her husband) who could function as her caretaker. Even when a universal health and social care infrastructure exists, as in Quebec, care workers are available only to those who meet its criteria. The system requires that the family members present become affordances for one another first, and only in the absence of that possibility does it bestow people as affordances in the form of a care worker.

People as Affordances Remake Family Roles

Melanie, her husband, Antoine, and I were seated around their dining table talking about how their lives, as a family, were affected by the onset of illness. Antoine recounted a memory. "At five years old, I saw my . . . older daughter, she washed her mother." Melanie interrupted in an emotional tone:

> She helped me to get back and get in the bath. And I was not crying. When I want to cry, I go alone in my bedroom, and I cry because it is pain for me and what my child saw, I don't like that. So, I come back [*mimics herself acting as if she were fine*], "Oh, thank you, sweetheart! You're sweet!" You see, I have to protect them [her children] from that.

Melanie and her five-year-old daughter. Yasemin and her four-year-old son. Guylaine and her older child. Three different stories of how people, in this case children, become affordances for others, in this case their mothers. The affordances that children become for their family members go against canonical mutual affordances, reversing traditional kinship roles of parent or older relative as caregiver and child as cared-for. Children become mothers to their sick moms, feeding and bathing them. An older brother becomes a parent to the younger one, changing his diapers.

But these role reversals do not happen in the form of the much-critiqued process of "parentification," where adults abdicate their parental roles, leaving their children few options but to take them on.[24] Instead, these reversals emerge from the child's love and *care*. As children become affordances for their mothers, they afford the nurturing and caring behaviors traditionally expected of mothers according to the logic of mutual affordances. Emotional responses to the perceived failure to meet behavioral expectations, like Yasemin's not wanting to remember those days or Melanie's crying in secret, are expressions of heteronormative ableism, which holds that mothers should be able to take care of a child's every need and that children have no capacity to care for others. As children take on the behavioral affordances of a mother, they not only reverse and redefine parent-child roles but also unknowingly subvert and unsettle this ableism. Mothers can indeed be sick, vulnerable, disabled, and on the *receiving* end, rather than the giving end, of care in relation to their children; and children can be fully capable and on the *giving* end of care in relation to their mothers.

When People as Affordances Fail to Materialize

In this chapter I have added "people" to affordances following Gibson's theory of affordance, where it accounts for other beings in the environment. I have proposed the term "people as affordances" as a specific subset of *activist* affordances (people as activist affordance, in other words) in which people enable the emergence of affordances or become affordances for one another. But let me be clear: this does not always happen. There can be many situations in which people as affordances do not emerge from the relationship between a person and the other people who form part of that person's environment.

In one story, a grandchild may, over time, learn to ask which one of her grandmother's hands is in pain and *not* hold it. But in another, one's own child may fail to perceive or "misperceive" the call for an affordance.[25] Jacques, now in his sixties, reflected on his younger years of living with a debilitating and disabling illness:

> I was the only one working, my wife was taking care of the kids. The kids! . . . Our children were born in '68, '70, and '74. So . . . if you go back

to 1982, when it all started, the oldest one was fourteen, right? And the youngest one was eight. So, at fourteen, when you cannot do something, and you ask your son, "Could you cut the grass for me please, I cannot do it?" or "Can you clean the snow with a snowblower? I cannot do it." What he thinks is "Ah, here is another way that Dad has found me to get me to work!" Right? He doesn't realize that you have arthritis and you cannot do things like this.

Jacques's son misperceived his father's request as a call for him to work rather than for affordance.

People as affordances may also fail, or be slow to materialize, because "sometimes we all need care, simultaneously."[26] There can be situations where disabled people simply cannot provide care. But as disability justice activist Leah Lakshmi Piepzna-Samarasinha aptly observes, just because "I am chronically ill and don't have the energy/strength to lift you onto the toilet doesn't mean that I am a bad ally."[27] It means that the access intimacy that people as affordances entails can still be in place even in the absence of its actualization.

Finally, pain may not always leak. Patrick's careful, self-critical reflection that "there are times when it's not always easy to understand [another's pain]" reminds us of this. Further, pain may fail to reach and "contaminate" the other because the person in pain may deliberately contain it. Recall Valerie's remarks about getting angry and pushing herself to do things instead of having to ask in the "pitiful" tone she mimicked, "Can you help me do this?" But Valerie's testimony is not simply a matter of living up to the "fetishized" ideals of independence and autonomy characteristic of Euro-American cultures.[28] Recall how Arif Amca, living in Turkey, also forced himself to wash his feet on his own rather than asking for help from his sons. No one knows, he asserted, the bodily cost of managing to wash his feet that day. He tried, and will keep trying, he insisted in an assertive tone, to do everything on his own until the very end. "I tell you I am cruel," he said, and "If that cruelty hadn't been there, I would have been more affected [by the disease]." Jacques's reflections resonated with Arif Amca's conviction:

Especially men . . . men of my age were not raised, you know, to ask for help. Ask for something. No! Organize yourself! Do it by yourself! Don't bother me! That's the way I was raised. So, when you are raised like this . . . not to ask for any help, you're not used to ask for help. Especially a man, a big guy like me asking for help to open the door [referring to the door he could not open back then]. Can you imagine?

My participants' confessions also strongly resonate with me, as I too often contain my pain, not just trying to pass but *sur*pass as able-bodied. I do this rather instinctively, out of habit, only later wondering why I did so. Why did the words "Oh I'm fine" automatically come out of my mouth that day, when my guest asked me if I needed any help in the kitchen? Why did I reply "No, no. It's fine" when a fellow passenger offered his seat to me, when I desperately needed to sit? Why did I refuse a helping hand to carry my bags, when my arms and hands were in so much pain?

People as Affordances as an Antidote to the Stigma of Help

Undoubtedly there is a deeply entrenched stigma around help, and as I discussed in chapter 7, compulsory able-bodiedness feeds into it mightily. The compulsion and urge to enact and conform to an able-bodied self can triumph over the chance to save ourselves from pain—the most averse of all bodily states. For reasons we may not even understand (as in my confession), we might prefer to undergo the physical pain and discomfort of doing things rather than failing to perform a completely self-sufficient able body.

When letting others become your affordances does not present itself even as one option among others, we know that compulsory able-bodiedness is at work. We also know that, as Robert McRuer argues, compulsory able-bodiedness never acts alone.[29] The compulsion to perform social identities such as masculinity and motherhood, as these testimonies attest, strengthen the compulsion to be "able" according to able-bodied terms. In a habitus where cisheteropatriarchy and ableism are deeply entangled, any sign that evokes the weakness of the male body, including the very human need for help and care, is foreclosed. The idea that elderly fathers might ask their sons to wash their feet becomes simply *inconceivable* for Arif Amca under notions of appropriate masculinity and fatherhood. Similarly, as Jacques's question "Can you imagine?" reveals, "big guys" like him are simply prevented from asking for help according to similar masculine norms that in fact make the entire thought of seeking help *unthinkable*. The powerful fiction of gender, as shown by Carrie Noland, Eli Clare, and others, is contingent on the performance not just of gender but of an abled body as well.[30] A man cannot risk appearing to need help if he is to effectively enact his gender. He has to "man up." This is why Jacques makes the following appeal: "This is a message I want to pass, this is why I am telling it right now . . . I'm a big guy, I am not used to ask for help. I had to learn, it's difficult to learn to ask for help. But you have no choice!"

But what if there actually is a choice? What if there is an alternative? And what if people as affordances were that alternative?

People as affordances may appear to constitute help in a way that creating an affordance with a button-up shirt does not. This is because help carries with it the notion of two mutually exclusive positions, one of "being able" and the other of "being in need." But what if people as affordances actually allow us to challenge these positions and therefore the very notion of help? What if the inherent *mutuality* of the concept can trouble and even cancel out the mutual *exclusion* at the root of help? Think of this: when a dancer extends his arm to his fellow dancer on stage, we do not consider this as a gesture of help or charity. Rather, we perceive it as an activity of mutual engagement that continuously unfolds before us. Why not think the same of people as affordances, that they are mutually or collectively engaged affordances that emerge and unfold in everyday life? In leaving two slices of bread and a half-full kettle on the counter, François is not helping me per se. Rather, François and I are engaging in a choreography—a choreography that I have called people as affordances—in order to make our lives more habitable for each other.

With its subset of people as affordances, understood in terms of mutuality rather than one-directional aid, the theory of activist affordances may provide a liberating alternative to the stigma of help, which confines us to a world that can only imagine individual undertakings, and where help comes into the picture only as an indication of their failures.

In Hindsight

As I have discussed, people as affordances may not materialize for a variety of reasons. Sometimes, pain does not leak. Sometimes, people may not have the active tentacles to sense and respond to another's impairment. But as Arif Amca's, Valerie's, Jacques's, and my own self-observations show, people as affordances fail to emerge most miserably because ableism is so deeply embedded and so powerfully *compels* us to perform able-bodiedness. This is especially the case when disabilities are acquired rather than congenital, and especially when it takes time for us to *become, accept* ourselves as, and *come out* as disabled. "She is getting better," Patrick said about Valerie, but, he added, "It's a very slow process. For years, she didn't have anybody helping her." When I asked Marielle (who is now in her late sixties) how her children responded to seeing their mother ill, she replied in a moving, regretful tone that was reminiscent of Valerie's:

[*Mother tongue French, speaking in English*] Well, you know, something happened [in the past] and today, I'm so sorry for that. But, I wasn't able to accept the sickness. I wasn't able. . . . So, I was trying all the time to do . . . more than that I can do. And the kids tell me today, we knew that you were suffering but I didn't want them to see me suffering. So, I was hiding myself, and, um, I was not coping a lot with the sickness, [*shaking her head sadly*] no. . . . But now today, I, I tell to myself, it would have been the best solution to say, "Mom is sick and, um, we have to care, um, about her" and explain. . . . But for many years, there was a lie in the family situation.

Ellen Samuels writes that "crip time means listening to the broken languages of our bodies, translating them, honoring their words."[31] But as so many of my disabled interlocutors' stories reveal, this time comes in its own time, not necessarily determined by our desire to inhabit it. In other words, depending on the specificities of the impairment in question, it *may take time* to bend one's time to crip time. We need to account for this time that it takes to occupy crip time, if we want to address, in Emma Sheppard's phrasing, the "messy and untidy" ways in which crip time moves,[32] and to nuance the term accordingly so that it can speak to the differing temporalities of becoming disabled.

The truth is that no matter how hard we may force ourselves to enact the movements and gestures of an able body, there comes a point when our own body resists us. No matter how deeply ingrained the habitus of ableism may be in its materiality, the body not only "speaks back,"[33] as Noland reminds us, but *forces us* to listen. At that tipping point, the compulsion to conform to able-bodiedness fails,[34] simply because the body *can no longer* obey us. But this moment of failure, so to speak, is an opening into another way of being embodied. What previously was unthinkable (and hence was not even a choice) now begins to become thinkable and possible. When our bodies call for our full attention in their pain and suffering, we have "no choice" but to recognize and respect their limits, our inherent vulnerability, and our need to become affordances for one another for our collective survival. Of course, as Samuels's description of crip time suggests, we do not, and likely *should* not, have to wait as *long* as Jacques and Marielle did. In the next chapter, I tell the story of what could potentially save us from that *long wait*.

DISABILITY REPERTOIRES

Performance, or actions, or acts remain—but remain *differently*.
—Rebecca Schneider, "Performance Remains"

The question of whether performance disappears or remains, and, more broadly, the relation between performance and the archive, has been one of the key debates in the history of performance studies. Peggy Phelan has famously argued that "performance's only life is in the present." Performance "becomes itself through disappearance."[1] According to Phelan's approach, performance matters insofar as it escapes saving, documenting, and preserving and thus resists entering into a political economy of reproduction and circulation.[2]

At the same time, other scholars have argued that although performance is ephemeral, it can also remain.[3] Performance, in fact, very much *remains*— but, as Schneider writes, it "remains *differently*."[4] It remains not in the sense of an archive in which, through a colonial, discursive, and logocentric lens, what remains is the document as a physical record.[5] Performance, instead, remains in the body as "a kind of archive and host to a collective memory."[6] Contrary to the normative archive's discursivity, Diana Taylor names this remaining "the repertoire," which is a "kind of archive" that is not an archive at all. It is instead "a nonarchival system of transfer" that includes expressive movements, rituals, stories, rehearsals, and other modes of embodied knowing and remembering.[7]

In this chapter I argue that as performances, activist affordances also remain. Traditional modes of activism remain by leaving their effects in legislative and policy changes, accessibility codes, guidelines, and the like. In contrast, activist affordances remain in what endures of them *in the long run*, or in what I term, after Taylor, "disability repertoires." If activist affordances are about the ephemeral, then disability repertoires avoid or prohibit their vanishing. Rehearsal after rehearsal, stage after stage, dance after dance, "disability repertoire" is the embodied, nondiscursive, and nonverbal knowledge and memory that activist affordances generate.

Just as a group of choreographies that a dancer's body or a dance troupe gets trained in and remembers creates a repertoire, so too does a set of activist affordances that a disabled body has mastered and remembers generate a disability repertoire. There is, however, more than that to disability repertoires. A disability repertoire is not only made up of what stays in the body as a kind of archive; it is also made up of what stays in the environment as the imprint of activist affordances. Throughout the emergence of disability repertoires, both the body and the environment function as memory pads.

We can appreciate what a disability repertoire allows us to do by focusing on its three key aspects. First, a disability repertoire refers to the persistence of activist affordances over time. Second, a disability repertoire makes a disabled life livable. Third, it makes its livability transferable to others. I unpack these three central aspects by moving from the micro level of daily tasks to the macro level of the life course, including roles, events, and ongoing activities.

Shrinkage of Space → Expansion of Time

> *Valerie*: You know, I really have to choose what I do. I can't get up, take a shower, get dressed, make breakfast, clean up, take the car, go to the grocery, come back, put it away or go to an appointment or go shopping. No, no. . . . It is one thing. One thing and then I have to lie down.

As Valerie's observations unveil, in the experience of disability, time cannot afford to host actions and events in close sequence. As the environment and its existing set of affordances shrink, time expands, conversely. As the spatiality of the environment becomes less and less welcoming, and as its affordances transform into constraints that must be sorted out, things begin to *take time*. This is not the time that is typically expected of a task or movement, but the time that the disabled person needs to take in order to continue to achieve them under the conditions of a shrunken world.

In disability studies, this expansion or, rather, "explosion" of time is known as "crip time" (see chapter 8).[8] Crip time, in Alison Kafer's definition, "requires reimagining our notions of what can and should happen in time, or recognizing how expectations of 'how long things take' are based on very particular minds and bodies."[9] As a form of crip time, the temporality of inhabiting a shrunken and a shrinking environment *blows up* ableist notions of time and lets time expand (or shrink) exponentially, as needed. We can think of crip time as a subversion not just of what "on time" is but also of what is supposed to happen "over time." When time stretches and expands in shrunken worlds (as is the case in Valerie's testimony) there is "less" that can be done over time. When "less" is done in a day, then there is "more" left to be done in a week, and when "less" is done in a week, "more" is left to be done in a month, and so on. The "delays" in the micro has its cumulative repercussions on the macro. Consider the following testimonies about living a disabled life from three interlocutors we have already met. The first testimony belongs to Valerie, who has relatively recently fallen ill and begun to acquire a disability. She reflects on the transformations that have taken place in her life and the prospects of a life to be lived with a gradually disabling disease. The latter two testimonies belong to Henri and Jacques, two elderly men who have been living with rheumatoid arthritis and its related disabilities for a long while. How do these three testimonies present the "less" and "more" that can be done as time stretches in everyday lives lived with rheumatoid arthritis? How do they describe disability repertoires in relation to the "less" and "more" of stretched time, and living an imaginable life with disability?

Valerie's Story

Valerie, her husband, and I were sitting around a dining table, talking about how the disease has affected our lives. Valerie described the loss of her life as she had lived and imagined it, following the onset of her experience of rheumatoid arthritis:

Another big part that was hard for me . . . especially the first five years, I would say, was seeing everybody getting out of the university, um, starting their job. You know, it's kind of a very big time in your life. You start a job, you meet somebody, you start living with somebody and you're . . . you know, you are going up in work, you get bigger responsibilities, you become, you know, a higher, um, job title or, and then people were getting . . . they were having kids. . . . I was looking at them and everything was going so fast, and me, I felt like I was standing still . . . I couldn't, I couldn't. . . . Everything was standing still. It was very, very hard. . . . They have a fast pace in life that I would love to have, you know, I really wanted to do that before. So, every time I see them, I am super happy for them and all that but it always brings me back facing the fact that I can't do that. I can't. I see my limits a lot, I see them and it makes me angry [*imitates anger in her voice*].

After a pause, Valerie continued: "I wanted to have a career, I wanted to be efficient. I wanted to provide, I wanted to be a provider also, moneywise, for the family. That was very important for me. So, I had to let go of my career, all the sports I was doing, all the activities," she said, and then asked in a frustrated tone:

How do you come from life A to life B [*draws an imaginary line with her hands and mimics crossing*]? How do you do this? 'Cause there is not many things . . . in life B that touches what you wanted in life A or what you were in life A.

If crip time *explodes* ableist notions of time, temporality, and futurity, then what we witness in Valerie's account is the disappointment in the aftermath of that explosion. For Valerie, disability slowed down time so that she could not move at the same pace as others or as the future self she had previously imagined. She had to do less with her time, which from her perspective meant that she was frustrated in imagining a livable life with disability. Compare Valerie's mourning for a loss of life as known and imagined for the future with Henri's.

Henri's Story

Henri and I were talking about the pasts and futures of living with a chronic, debilitating disease. Henri has lived a large portion of his adult life with rheumatoid arthritis. In a moment of recollection he went back to the beginning of the 1990s, when he was working close to sixty hours a week as a store manager, overseeing close to twenty employees:

Henri: Now looking at it today, um, for somebody with polyarthritis rheumatoid, it's not a good idea, for so many years, to be putting all this time and all that pressure and stress from work. . . . A person in our situation need to be more careful about the time and how they use it. Um, rest is a priority, working sixty hours a week is not . . . [*fixing his eyes in the distance and smiling*]. Knowing what I know today, I never would have done that.

Arseli: Is it because you were young?

Henri: Well, when you are young, you want to succeed, you want to . . . have promotions, you want to, you know, it's the same as everybody. You wanna improve your life, you want to improve your work, and I was in the same line of thinking then. But today, I know priority is not money or work, but is the way I feel and that's where I have to concentrate my thoughts.

It *took time* for Henri to arrive at this way of thinking, from when crip time "detonated" the ableist assumptions of time and its "normative life course."[10] In the intervening time, Henri was able to go beyond Valerie in terms of knowing how to migrate from life A to life B.[11] In fact, not only has Henri had time to "heal" from the explosion, but he has also found meaning and healing in becoming disabled, because for him this bodily change enabled a process of liberation from the shackles of a normative life course and its limited values.

Jacques's Story

Jacques's story offers a similar narrative of living a disabled life with joy after the initial disappointment of losing the life he knew. Now in his sixties, Jacques is highly informed about rheumatoid arthritis and also a committed patient activist. As I sat with Jacques and his wife, Suzanne, they generously shared with me their life journey with a chronic, disabling illness. When I asked how their lives were affected overall, Jacques offered these responses:

It changes a lot about your goals in life, right? Um, not only your goals but also your projects in life. For example, I was working in engineering, in telecommunications, more working with the pen, the computer and my brain than putting up bricks or being a carpenter or being I don't know, um, a mechanic. This would have been completely different. . . . It changes your vacation projects, it changes your sports. . . . But there is always two ways of seeing things in life: Is the glass half full or half empty? For me it's half full. All the time! Still half full [*mimics a glass*].... It's easy to say but it's not that easy to do, however. Because at the beginning you have to live your disease, you have to learn to live with your disease, you have to admit that you have some limitations, your family has to cope with the disease also and . . . all of these, once this is done, and it may take time. [*In an assured tone*] It's not bad!

Jacques and Henri are able to envision and enact their lives after disability in a way that Valerie, who has experienced disability for a much shorter time, cannot (yet). I suggest that the primary difference is not that Valerie is missing some capacity but that what has happened over time for Jacques and Henri is not yet perceivable or even imaginable to her and others who have not yet gone through that extended temporality.

As crip time *blows up* the presumptions about how long it *should* take to complete daily tasks, the roles, event categories, and ongoing activity to which such tasks belong also *explode*. One thing at a time during the day becomes one thing at a time over longer periods of time. In the long run, the micro gradually transforms the macro. Eventually "disability disrupts normative understandings of time and the life course."[12] This time lived with disability allows Jacques and Henri to live and imagine their lives as disabled people, while Valerie's lack of that time does not yet allow the same.

In the Long Run

It is not surprising that time, temporality, life course, and futurity have been recurrent themes in queer and crip theory.[13] Under ableist standards, the "long run" that seems required to achieve a livable life with disability is *too* long. Inefficient. Impatience-provoking. Similarly, the "longer" time it takes to complete "simple" tasks is problematic. Given these ableist relations to time, early death due to disability is necessarily the ultimate "tragedy" of a disabled life. In resistance to ableism, queer and crip theorists have questioned the normativity of ableist and straight time, including the presumed time required for completing tasks, future-orientation, and normative expectations about the life course and what the future holds—or should hold.[14]

"Straight time," together with ableist time, orders the future for us through norms of productivity and reproductivity that have already been agreed upon as the common "good."[15] The heterosexual (reproductive) family functions as the normative unit through which such lives are lived and requires normatively embodied members to carry out the ableist (productive) future. The normative future is clearly "deployed in the service of compulsory able-bodiedness and able-mindedness,"[16] together with compulsory hetero-sexuality. Valerie's mourning of the future life she had imagined for herself demonstrates her initial acceptance of such a normatively predetermined future—starting a job, meeting a partner, living with a partner, moving up in rank at work, having children, and so on. At the same time, however, Valerie perceives this form of time as "fast." It has no tolerance for "slow" movements through time and cannot perceive their potential value. It is a future that does not allow you to do "one thing at a time." It is a future in which people like Valerie are bound to feel always "behind" (some predetermined goal).

Normative time impairs Valerie's ability to imagine a different time in both the present and the future; it sets expectations that preempt more creative ways of living in time. But, as Kafer puts it, there are ways of "imagining futures and futurity otherwise."[17] Futures that are not so fast. Futures where you can concentrate on, in Henri's words, "the way you feel" instead of how you have progressed. Futures in which we are allowed to "stand still," if need be, and live a life in recognition of and with respect for our bodily limits, pains, and vulnerabilities. And futures in which we take one thing at a time, including whatever new or different limits, pains, and vulnerabilities may come. I suggest that Henri and Jacques are living such futures because of their disability repertoires—the ways both their bodies and environments know and remember—and thus these repertoires enable them to live disabled lives as "good" lives.

Disability Repertoires Endure over Time

As I document in this book, disabled people may improvise all sorts of activist affordances as they go about their everyday lives, at times in passing, at times by making and remaking things, at times by allowing others to become their affordances. Across many of these examples of activist affordances, and over the long run, these activist affordances, no matter how tiny and fleeting, quite literally slowly leave their sedimentary effects on bodies and environments.[18]

That the body becomes a record of activist affordances is already implicated by the word "repertoire." How the environment remembers is perhaps less obvious. Here I turn to the much larger scope in which disability repertoires mark their environments. The continuous repetition of activist affordances, their renegotiations and fine-tuning along the way, imprint them on the environment. The environment—its substances, surfaces, and textures as well as its mutual and social affordances—literally takes on the shape of the impairments, pains, fatigue, access needs, and desires that disabled people project out into the world, in and through their activist affordances. Shirts remain partially buttoned; food is left on lower shelves to be stored by another; furniture shapes can be deliberately misaligned or their edges softened with makeshift padding. Wardrobes may become transformed by loose and soft clothes without zippers or buttons and flat, Velcro-closed, larger-than-measured-size shoes. Indeed, the meaning of each room in a house can be rewritten with bedrooms-cum-offices, bedside dining tables, and unusual sleeping arrangements. Kitchens are *bent*, furniture gets contorted, wardrobes are twisted. Further, it is not only the solidity of the material world that is transformed through disability repertoires but also the conventions of social and kinship relations. Mothers become the ones in need of care, children become their mothers' affordances, and pain leaks into partners who become affordances. Each of these gradually (trans)formed environments literally embodies the very forms, layouts, and textures that would correspond to and reciprocate nonstandard bodily shapes, sizes, and scales, as well as the pains, vulnerabilities, needs, and desires of their creators.

Remembering Tim Ingold's "dwelling perspective," or the way that the environment records the living of every generation that has dwelt there, I have argued that disabled dwellers not only *leave* something of themselves in the environment, as Ingold suggests, but do so *through* their activist affordances (see chapters 6 and 8). Disability repertoires are precisely the bits and pieces of ourselves that we, as disabled people, use to mark the very environments we dwell in as we dance our activist affordances *again*, and *again*, and *again*.

Disability Repertoires Make a Disabled Life Livable

A disability repertoire is slowly and patiently erected in the space left after crip/queer time explodes ableist/straight presumptions of the future and what it should hold. Disability repertoires are the *pasts* we build over the long run as we live with disability, and the *futures* we imagine.

In the way a foot leaves its imprint on sand, the gradual accumulation of a disability repertoire in a life lived with disability slowly molds a corresponding shape, form, and texture for itself from the very environment that previously failed to recognize or register its pains, diseases, and atypical bodily forms. Disability repertoires carve out livable niches that distribute and diminish disabled people's pains, environmentally reciprocate their odd bodily shapes and forms, and allow their sick bodies to make do with whatever they can tolerate and not more, against all of the odds that work against the creation of livable lives.

All told, a disability repertoire makes living a disabled life possible through its staying power. It is exactly this possibility that Jacques brings to the fore when he goes over the transformations of a life lived with a chronic disabling illness and says, "It's not bad." Lacking such a disability repertoire, Valerie is driven to ask, "How do you come from life A to life B?" With various ways of accessing such a repertoire, Jacques and Henri can offer: "Here is how you create a new life with rheumatoid arthritis that is much more than mere survival." They can not only say but also know that it is possible to live a livable—even a satisfying and thriving—life with disability.

It is exactly these repertoires that people like Valerie need to be acquainted with in order to learn that an ableist/straight future is not their only option and that there are other possible futures in which they would not have to feel "behind." Understanding and communicating disabled people's disability repertoires, their precision and value, can enable us, especially those of us (like Valerie) who are newly becoming disabled, to dream of these futures that we were never allowed to dream of, and to pass on our new knowledge in turn. For disability repertoires to unsettle and upend the hegemony of ableist/straight futures in our collective imaginaries, they need a vocabulary to identify them, and venues where they can be shared. This is exactly what I have tried to do in theorizing activist affordances.

Disability Repertoires Are Transmissible

In almost all the academic and community settings where I have presented my ethnographic materials and have shown videos of my participants' creative affordances, several audience members who have experienced some form of disability have rushed to see me afterward. They have excitedly told me how much they recognized and related to what they witnessed my participants doing and what I was talking about. With a sparkle in their eyes, they shared with me their own activist affordances, giving the exact details of why they move their bodies in particular ways, explaining their own hacks and tricks, describing their own ephemeral dances for avoiding pain. It has felt to me as if these were moments that they had long been waiting for. Their previously hidden, unknown, and harder-to-articulate ingenuity and perseverance were now suddenly named, recognized, and given value.

Activist affordances will not ignite a revolution any time soon. Nor are they likely to mobilize hundreds in the way a rally might. But the fact that so many audience members were *moved* by seeing other people's activist affordances and were eager to share theirs tells me that there is something deeply transmissible and communal about them. "Disability repertoire" describes precisely this transferability and the potential to forge a community. Naming a disability repertoire further valorizes these otherwise seemingly insignificant ways of moving, sensing, and behaving in the world and gives it value among a group of people who are rarely, if ever, valorized, and who may not be otherwise connected or related. To name and identify something previously unnamed brings it into social existence, giving it value and making it possible to identify with, share, and transmit it.

Ten years after I interviewed Valerie, I keep watching footage of that moment when she asks how to go from life A to life B. I wish that I could somehow, magically, bring Jacques and Henri and so many other disabled people I know into the conversation. I wish Henri could share his life's revised priorities. I wish Jacques could assure Valerie that "it's not bad." Even more, I wish that whoever was born disabled or has passed through the "life stages and rites of passage of becoming disabled" could be with Valerie, me, Henri, and Jacques,[19] so we could tell one another about the possibility of living a disabled life that at one time we were not allowed to imagine. This book is born from that wish. It is an archival transfer of the disability repertoire—a repertoire that refuses to accept the unlivable futures that an ableist world order offers us, in favor of "disability futures" that we can imagine as a glass half full, that is not bad, and that we still have yet to imagine.[20]

10 SPECULATIONS FOR A SHRINKING PLANET

What if, as I'm suggesting, precarity *is* the condition of our time—or, to put it another way, what if our time is ripe for sensing precarity? What if precarity, indeterminacy, and what we imagine as trivial are the center of the systematicity we seek?
—Anna Lowenhaupt Tsing, *The Mushroom at the End of the World*

Back in 1979, James Gibson wrote: "There is only one environment, although it contains many observers with limitless opportunities for them to live in."[1] In 2021, there is plenty of evidence that these opportunities are *not* limitless. The environment is, quite literally, shrinking. Even as I write this, glaciers are melting. Coastal areas are sinking inch by inch. The ozone layer is becoming more and more depleted. Swaths of ocean are running out of oxygen. There are so many dead lands, dead waters, and dead ocean zones around the planet.[2] Many habitats are shrinking, melting, disappearing, and entirely *dematerializing*. Times are indeed precarious.

In a poem by Somali-British poet Warsan Shire, the earth's response to the question "Where does it hurt?" is as follows:

everywhere
everywhere
everywhere.[3]

The earth is vulnerable, sick, injured, and dying. The question of disability that I have addressed throughout this book extends from human beings to the earth itself. It is time that we extend the referents of disability and its cognate terms such as vulnerability, pain, sickness, and suffering beyond the limits of human exceptionalism, which is itself a cause of the earth's debilitation.[4] To be clear, the typical disability studies impulse has been to distance disability from such sentient terms in order to reject any negativity that they may bring to disability. "To be disabled" (as the social model goes) is to be disabled by a discriminatory society. "To be disabled" (as the cultural and minority models go) is a matter of identity, a cause for celebration and pride. It is time that we resist that impulse in order to acknowledge the loss, reduction, pain, and negativity that those who "are disabled" may experience—as feminist scholars of disability have long argued (see chapter 1). It is also time that we refuse to deny those who are suffering, vulnerable, and in pain because nonhumans, other-than-humans, and the entire planet itself are at risk. In the climate catastrophic era, losses, reductions, and shrinkage are happening at a mass scale and in highly entangled ways (see chapter 4). What, then, can activist affordance theory, a theory born of shrinkage, offer to this shrinking planet? What would it mean for activist affordance to make a quantum leap from the micro level of bodies to the macro level of the universe, where we see the earth *as* disabled?

A Final Twist: Micro → Macro

Think of the looming catastrophe of climate change, the recent devastating COVID-19 pandemic, and the increasing rate of infectious diseases in the past decades. Most of these phenomena are zoonotic—meaning they jump from animals to humans, which itself has to do with deforestation, losses of habitats, and other climate-chaos-driven causes.[5] In response to these events and emergencies, many stakeholders, from epidemiologists to scholars of the Anthropocene and climate justice activists, began to look for ideas, insights, knowledge, and alternatives in all sorts of directions. In the meantime, disabled people have repeatedly said, "Why not just ask us?"[6] In the podcast "Coronavirus: Wisdom from a Social Justice Lens," host Kate Werning comments that chronically ill and disabled people are "at the forefront of wisdom and expertise on how to deal with health crisis moments like the one [COVID-19] we're collectively facing right now."[7] Similarly, in their article "To Survive Climate Catastrophe, Look to Queer and Disabled Folks," Patty Berne and Vanessa Raditz argue that the history of these marginalized groups "has continually been one of creative problem-solving within a society that refuses to center our needs."[8] Sunaura Taylor echoes Berne and Raditz in writing: "Turning to the critical and generative understandings of health, limitation, wound-edness, loss, adaptation, and care that have emerged from disabled and ill people and communities can help us as we navigate and salvage a changing, imperiled world."[9] In this chapter, I build on these important claims. The prior chapters document how disabled people have mastered the arts of having to live in shrunken and shrinking environments that afford fewer and fewer possibilities for action. To conclude the discussion, I take that final leap from the micro of the prior chapters to the macro of global environmental degradation by asking: Can the micro "arts" of disabled survival be among the "arts of living on a damaged planet" that Tsing and her colleagues illuminate?[10] In these precarious times of rapid planetary decline, with the "on-goingness" of life in peril,[11] can disabled people's activist affordances under conditions of shrinkage be a way to think about *how to make things work with whatever is within our limits*, and *how to keep life going against all odds*?

Shrinkage → Activist Affordances

One of activist affordance theory's foundational claims is the indispensable link between shrinkage and the creation of affordances. Consider again Yasemin's account, from chapter 5, of how her living environment considerably shrank during times of rheumatoid flare-ups and how she dealt with these reduced circumstances. No matter how much pain and suffering Yasemin was in, the thing-world couldn't have cared less. Chairs and sofas did not afford sitting on or standing-up-from without inducing pain. Stairs became surfaces over which Yasemin had to laboriously drag her swollen feet. The comb's particular design proved hostile to her inflamed arms and shoulders. But then what did Yasemin do? She danced an activist affordance in order to still be able to comb her hair.

And what did Yasemin's dance entail? The short handle and straight shape of the comb may have called for arm flexion. But counter to that canonical directive, Yasemin bent her head, brought her left hand toward it, and pulled her hair down to comb it. Irrespective of what the design of the comb solicited from her body, Yasemin moved the parts of her body that could still move with relative ease in ways that made up for the parts that were less able to do so. As she positioned the comb, her head, her arms, and her hair in particular ways, she moved them together in unthought-of directions, making them complement one another in atypical combinations. As Yasemin externalized what otherwise remained under her skin—the inflammation in her joints, their pain and limited range of motion—an entirely new action possibility emerged from what otherwise was a seemingly indifferent and hostile materiality. In and through her danced affordance, Yasemin *bent* the solidity of the comb's canonical directive, as it were, dissolving and remolding it in ways that gave it a new, imagined form—a form that knew of, responded to, and *cared for* her impairments. How might we *care for* the earth in similar ways?

Just as Yasemin invented a new choreography of combing her hair that saved her arms from having to be lifted up, Valerie invented an affordance that, in this case, altogether avoided the hairbrush: "I put my fingers in when I am in the shower like this with the conditioner [*gently sliding her fingers through her hair*] and then that's it! I don't brush my hair." To Valerie, the conditioner and her fingers afford the same action possibility that a brush affords, without her having to perform the painful movements that the layout of a brush requires to actualize brushing. Valerie delegated the brush's affordance to the combination of fingers and conditioner. Fingers slide through her hair AS IF they were the brush bristles and the liquid, lubricant substance makes the hair slippery enough for her fingers to slide easily through it. "Brushing" without brushes is the activist affordance that Valerie invented. What activist affordances might we invent to altogether avoid the materials whose "canonical" substances and layouts cause the earth pain?

I have argued that activist affordances are like no other affordance in the sense that shrinkage necessitates them (see chapter 6). Shrinkage is the imperative for the creation of activist affordances, as the many accounts offered in this book suggest. Had the environment not shrunk, had its existing set of affordances not proven inaccessible, insufficient, unreciprocating, constraining, or simply hostile, there would have been no need to search for, discover, or actualize such affordances. A shrinking world is the condition of possibility—of necessity—for the emergence of what I distinguish as "*activist* affordances."

Urgency, Not Luxury

To unpack this indispensable link, I turn to Georges Canguilhem's conceptualization of disease and vitality. To be clear, Canguilhem writes about disease, not disability. This might raise problems for a field that has long worked to decouple disability from pathology.[12] However, Canguilhem's approach provides a useful parallel to the idea of ecological shrinkage and, in particular, to the question of how affordances emerging from that shrinkage could be specific rather than generic to all such inventions.

Canguilhem discusses disease as a narrowing down of patients' environments—exactly what I call "shrinkage" with regard to people with disability. Drawing on neurologist Kurt Goldstein's work, Canguilhem describes disease as a "mode of life" that is "narrowed" in the sense that the body has a reduced capacity to manage risks and unpredictability effectively, in the way the healthy body does.[13] A sick person has fewer bodily assets available to reciprocate "the demands of the normal, that is, previous environment."[14] More precisely, "the patient is sick," Canguilhem writes, "because he can admit of only one norm."[15] That is, disease has its own, but very limited, "normal" as compared to the multiple normalities under which the healthy body can remain well. Disease is defined by this limitation to a single norm (rather than by the absence of a norm). The resulting "precariousness of the normal established by disease" requires that the patient inhabit an environment that is not only narrowed but also "rigidly protected" to disallow exposure to conditions that the body is unable to manage.[16] Similarly, a person is disabled because she can live the everyday only in certain ways, not in a broader range of possibilities available to the able-bodied normate. A person in a wheelchair can go up or down using only elevators or ramps, not by climbing stairs, taking escalators, and using elevators or ramps at her whim. In other words, activist affordances arise out of *limited* environmental conditions that may even offer just *one* possible action, rather than arising out of an *abundance* of possibilities.

I argue that finding activist affordances is a *need*, rather than just the choice or option to act otherwise, and that this necessity separates them from other affordances. When my participants move, sense, and behave in the particular ways they do, they do so not because they choose to but because they *have to*. The able-bodied may even enact the same affordance—like combing one's hair as Yasemin does—but in that case the affordance will exist alongside possible others, whereas the creation of activist affordances is not a matter of choosing between alternatives. The precariousness of disease finds its parallel in disability in that they share limited available norm(s). Just as the diseased body has only one norm, the disabled body has very limited environmental conditions—and perhaps only one—from which affordances can emerge, as we remember that affordances arise out of the mutuality between an organism and some aspect of its environment. Activist affordances are consequently *precarious*: each one provides a single way of engaging in a given environment that is already narrowed. Narrowed environments enable narrowed affordances. This is the *precarity* of disability.

The creation of activist affordances is a response to a necessity for everyday survival. Activist affordances enable their creators to survive within constraints that any other affordance would not. The ingenious affordances that my participants come up with spare them the pain and discomfort that they would otherwise experience. Their affordances save them from having to use impaired body parts that they would otherwise have to employ. These affordances counterbalance the remoteness or lack of a world-counterpart that they would otherwise be forced to contend with, unsuccessfully. They provide *the* (sometimes only) affordance that the constrained environments they inhabit can actualize.

Because activist affordances are, in short, matters of *urgency*, I resist subsuming them in the general term "affordances." If *having to* create affordances where none exist were one and the same thing as having *the option* to create affordances, why would one wish to create them? The matter of distinguishing between affordances in general and activist affordances is a political need. It is political because, at the end of the day, there is only one environment to which we all have to relate. How its diverse inhabitants come to relate to and survive in our shared environment, and through what amount of *painstaking* labor and *precarity*, matters.

Creation at the Extremities

> Beyond the expansive ground of ordinary, naturally occurring objects is the narrow extra ground of imagined objects, and beyond this ground, there is no other. Imagining is, in effect, the ground of last resort. That is, should it happen that the world fails to provide an object, the imagination is there, almost on an emergency stand-by basis, as a last resource for the generation of objects.[17]

To reiterate, activist affordances emerge when that reciprocity between the environment's properties and those of the perceiver cannot be easily and readily found within the given order of things and instead has to be effortfully searched for within the world of potential but nearly imperceptible affordances. Activist affordances become necessary precisely at those extremities (which Elaine Scarry also refers to in the preceding passage) where the world AS IS shrinks and becomes just-inhabitable-enough.

When I summarized how Scarry conceptualizes "making" in chapter 5, I noted that she considers artifacts as the projection of human sentience onto the world. The most extreme form of this projection occurs, according to Scarry, in the making of an artifact that responds to "the most *contracted* of spaces,"[18] that is, *the body in pain*. In all other acts of making, a bodily state, or its sentience, is projected onto the world outside, and the projection constitutes merely an "alteration in degree" of its already-existing counterpart, meaning the aspect of the body that is being projected. In contrast, the projections that emerge from pain together with imagination are much more radical than any other, for Scarry, because they entail the wholesale replacement or elimination of the "original given . . . by something wholly other than itself."[19] They are a kind of world-making that is different from all other kinds, particularly in that bodily pain is their foundation: projections of this pain actually constitute the "framing events" within which "all other perceptual, somatic and emotional events occur."[20] This is because pain and imagination are constituted by a lack, or absence; the two are "each other's missing intentional counterpart."[21] Pain is an intense bodily state without an object or worldly counterpart; imagination is made up of objects without any experience, or "experienceable sentience" whatsoever.[22] Without these original givens, the world-making that comes about through their merging is the moment of creation itself, that is, the creation of something from nothing.

In the act of making in which pain and imagination coalesce, it is precisely these original givens that the act offsets. Pain becomes an object—precisely what it originally lacked—by working with the imagination. Neither pain nor imagination replaces or eliminates the other, but instead the two undergo an alchemical transformation. As pain is "brought into relation with the objectifying power of imagination," what was once a wholly unresponsive materiality gains the "'awareness of aliveness.'"[23] Correspondingly, what was once an utterly objectless and passively suffered state is transformed into "a self-modifying and, when most successful, self-eliminating one."[24] This is how pain and imagination, according to Scarry, become the framing events of all intentional states.

For these exact reasons, I consider activist affordances to be the framing condition of all affordances and distinguish the act of making that they entail from all other types of affordance-making. For Scarry, the act of world-making takes place in and as the object that is made. I proposed instead that world-making lies in performance, not in the objects made (see chapter 5). With activist affordances, I am concerned with where *making* remains *in-the-making*, where it is *performative,* rather than focusing on the objects that world-making makes.

Performance: A Making and a Thing Made

Even though Scarry is talking about physical pain, the very characteristic she ascribes to pain—the lack of a world-counterpart—can be taken as a general condition of disability as put forth in my ecological definition. According to this definition, disability occurs when the environment contracts and becomes affordance-less, no matter where that absence comes from—whether it is due to a barrier, an ableist habitus, or the experience of chronic pain, disease, or debilitation. Precisely at the moment when the environment narrows down in its readily available affordances, as I have argued, the improvisatory space of performance opens up and allows us to imagine the environment otherwise—that is, other than what it currently affords. Both in *everyday life lived with a disability,* and in *aesthetic performance improvised within the disorienting conditions of stage or site,* the affordances being created emerge not from a pregiven body-environment complementarity but from *the remoteness* and the *lack* of a materialized presence of that affordance instead. In fact, it is this distance and lack, as I previously argued, that prompts the imaginative work and subjunctive (AS IF) mood of performance.

Upon not finding a world-counterpart for the pains and diseases that they experience, and for all the corporeal differences that their bodies come with, disabled people may relate to the environment in ways that circumvent the limited affordances it presents to them. They can be highly attentive to the substances and surfaces that surround them and to their material properties. They may *not* take for granted whatever formal qualities have been attributed to those surfaces, whatever the uses to which they have been put, and whatever the function has so far been affixed to them. They may instead move, sense, or act in ways that uncover the possibilities of an imagined ecologically richer environment. As they do so, hitherto unknown properties of the environment and its latent potentialities reciprocate and welcome disabled people's otherwise unreciprocated bodily pains, needs, and unwelcome corporeal particularities. An initially hostile and shrinking environment becomes a compassionate, welcoming, and even accessible one—no matter how momentarily, ephemerally, and counterfactually. This is how performance enables us to *make livable worlds* out of considerable constraints.

Elin Diamond defines performance as *"always a doing and a thing done."*[25] Drawing on Diamond, I consider performance as both the *doing* of an activist affordance (an affordance that does not yet exist in the present in a material form) and an activist affordance *done* (an affordance that is *materialized* in the present through the performance of an action nonetheless). Just as the actions, words, and behaviors of performers on stage or at a site bring into being the very worlds that they imagine, so do disabled people's actions create the affordances and, thereby, the inhabitable worlds that were not readily given. For the same reason that we do not call the performances of actors on stage "just another way of doing things differently," we cannot so label the improvisations of my participants. Nor are their affordances created as an *addition* to, or as an *expansion* of, those that already exist. These affordances are created because of an *absence* and the distance of their perceivability. They are created because the environment AS IS *lacks* something—that is, more livable worlds.

Activist Affordances: AS IF Accessible Futures Have Already Arrived

"The here and now," José Esteban Muñoz writes, "is a prison house. We must strive, in the face of the here and now's totalizing rendering of reality, to think and feel a *then and there*."[26] Written about aesthetic performance cultures and the subversive performativity of queer identities, Muñoz's work offers a vision of transformative change based in a critical relation to the present time and place in which the current reality contains all that is possible. Through this understanding, discontent with the present can become feeling into an alternative reality in a future time ("then") and space ("there").[27]

In her proposal and desire for "crip futures," Alison Kafer argues that Muñoz's vision of futurity is precisely the kind we need for disability because it does not reject but instead embraces futures.[28] Drawing on how Muñoz is speaking against the positing of queer (in some queer theory) as always antinormative, and without a foreseeable future, Kafer demonstrates how Muñoz's reclaiming of futures can also be productive for disability.

Along with Muñoz and Kafer, I suggest we think of activist affordances' futurity as a queer utopia not because the two are analogous but because of what the queer, as Muñoz shows, can contain. Activist affordances, I argue, are a precursor to accessible futures that will never take a final material form but will nonetheless arise from constant searching, improvisation, and dreaming.

The thing-world of today's reality is the "prison house" for disabled people. The world that the normates have come to create for themselves appears to be the only one possible, and it is hostile to what does not look, act, or behave in those terms. Curved backs, missing limbs, signing hands, crablike fingers, stumps, stutters, disorderly minds, and short-statured, shaky, limping bodies are not meant to find anything in the niches occupied by normates. They are situated out of place and out of time. At the same time, the here and now is sealed off from fleshly vulnerability, weakening, and death. Its ordering of reality has no room for aching, sore, sick, slow, or dying bodies.

These refused bodies, if they are to survive and thrive, have to choreograph activist affordances that materialize an accessible world that does not yet exist. With their activist affordances, they can invent and inhabit a *then and there*. Even if this *then and there* is only an imagined reality, even if it is not tangible and widely shareable, it can nonetheless provide a refuge from the constraints that the world AS IS imposes on their body/minds and actions. Even if activist affordances allow their creators to occupy made-up realities only *momentarily* and *quietly*, they can still allow them to cut loose from the constraints of the present.

Recall the ethnographic moments that demonstrate these claims. Tiny buttons and bottlecaps ignore my participants' loss of fine motor skills. My participants then bend, contort, stretch, and release the fabric of garments, manipulating buttons and buttonholes without having to use only their fingers. Twist-off caps prove hostile to their painful and damaged joints. My participants resist that hostility by using an old pair of rubber gloves, or by squeezing the caps between arthritic nodules, or by biting and tearing them off. Necklaces, bras, buttons, or whatever piece of clothing or accessory that comes with a prescribed orientation asks them to move parts of their body in ways that they cannot move with ease. My participants go against that orientation and create pullovers out of shirts, cloaks out of bathrobes. The rigidity of a metal cap, its resistance to deformation, and its round shape necessitate an effort that their swollen hands cannot exert. My participants then multiply the effort exerted on the cap with the handles of a pincer, or they expose that recalcitrant metal to hot water, expanding and softening it. These affordances defy the circumscribing demands and constraining solicitations of the thing-world. No matter how brief, tiny, and transient it may be, they bring into being a world—*a then and there*—designed otherwise.

If disability (understood as shrinkage) is "that thing that lets us feel that this world is not enough, that indeed something is missing" (for Muñoz it is queerness);[29] if we must, against all odds, strive, survive, and dream of an environment livable otherwise, then activist affordances are a form of queer utopia. They, too, are born *of the constraints of the here and now*. They, too, are born of a *need* and a *desire* to go beyond the limits of a narrowed environment and a stultifying present in which our sick, impaired, injured, painful, hurting, dying, and nonstandard bodies/minds are not recognized or welcomed as they are, made to feel *out of place* and *out of time,* bereft of an environment in which they can see a semblance of themselves. Activist affordances emerge from an insatiable need to look beyond the boundaries of what the AS IS environment presumably affords. They, too, actualize a counterfactual wish; imagine *a then and there*; make up "'an elsewhere'" and "'elsewhen'" in which the world becomes habitable otherwise.[30] They, too, actualize the "counterfactual wish" to break free from a limiting environment and suffocating present, to imagine the world otherwise.[31]

Following C. L. R. James, Muñoz proposes that we consider embodied queer performances as "a future in the present," and as "outposts of an actually existing queer future existing in the present."[32] Following Muñoz, I propose that we consider activist affordances as the outposts of actually existing accessible futures. Think of how my participants, in moving their arms, fingers, and legs in odd ways, in positioning their bodies and their world of substances and surfaces at crooked angles, and in squeezing, biting, releasing, twisting, and bending things anticipate the affordances of self-help aids and assistive tools (such as elongated combs and buttonhooks) that they never owned or had access to. Think of how disabled users and their allies, as documented by Bess Williamson, were already constructing "homemade access" in their individual households long before designers or architects would become aware of their access needs.[33] Think of how disability activists, in taking up sledgehammers to dismantle the corners of sidewalks, which remained utterly ignorant of wheeled bodies' needs, carved out the affordance of curb cuts, anticipating their later standardized and institutionalized creation en masse in the form of what Hamraie calls "liberal curb cuts."[34] All of these affordances-to-come were first imagined and enacted within the hypothetical—AS IF—framework of improvisation.

Within the environment AS IS where we, as disabled people, eke out activist affordances, we may not have "adaptive" tools, "assistive" devices, and technologies at our disposal; we may not be readily provided with accessibility infrastructures or services that would sustain our movements and activities; we may not live in an accessible world, and perhaps we never will. But when an activist affordance is created, it is AS IF such "inhabitable worlds" were already built;[35] it is AS IF such accessible futures already arrived except that they exist in our doings, actions, performances, and unfinished makings. In brief, activist affordances bring accessible futures to life, AS IF those futures had already arrived, AS IF they had already materialized.

Chasing Accessible Futures

In the same way that "we are not yet queer,"[36] as Muñoz writes, accessible futures are not yet here and will, in fact, never arrive. An environment that is simultaneously and fully accessible for all of its inhabitants (human or otherwise) is a sheer impossibility: not only because of the diversity of its inhabitants and their access needs, not only because of the "conflicts of access" that would inevitably emerge along the way,[37] but also because the inhabitants and their environments are alive. This means that their access needs change. A living environment's access is itself alive and cannot be exhausted or petrified in an artifact. As long as life continues on the earth, accessible futures will always slip out of the present's stifling grasp.

This is exactly why we *must* keep chasing accessible futures. We must strive for accessible futures: because in the very impossibility of their arrival lies the possibility of imagining the environment—wherever and whenever the need arises—otherwise. It is this possibility, as I have documented throughout this book, that activist affordances offer us.

I Would Rather Live in an Accessible World
Than Have to Continually Invent It

And yet wouldn't it be preferable to live in an already accessible world? Of course it would, for a variety of reasons.

First, forging affordances where none exist is no easy task. "For bodies to inhabit spaces that don't extend their shapes," as Sara Ahmed writes, entails "hard work."[38] The body has to dance the activist affordance each and every time it finds itself bereft of things that would have done that dance on its behalf.[39] This taxing labor would not be required in a properly functioning and well-maintained accessible environment.

Second, to argue that people can create necessary activist affordances that are not enabled by the existing environment is prone to co-optation by a neoliberal agenda.[40] In a political and economic system that uses individualism to refuse structural solutions to what are actually social and structural problems, to emphasize what appears to be "individual" agency and creativity can seem to support its individualist agenda. In the current context of similarly individualist global austerity cuts that offload the duties of the state and its institutions to individuals, the idea of "individually" created affordances may promote individual over social responsibility. That is, if disabled people are so resilient and can make access and manage on their own, then why bother building costly systems and providing expensive services?

Let me be clear: when I say that the affordances of "accessible futures" can be anticipated in and through performance, I do not mean to undermine the significance of an "accessible present." Nor by any means do I mean to take attention away from indispensable services and infrastructures that must be provided in the name of access and equity. To claim that the affordances of accessible but nonexistent technologies, infrastructures, objects, and services can be actualized in and through performance is not to claim that their existence would be redundant; definitely not. What I want to point out is something else entirely.

Activist Affordances: A Nonexploitative Form of Making

What does performance afford to lives that have to be lived in a shrinking world of possibilities? As Diana Taylor argues, we need to look not at what performance *is* but at "what it allows us to do."[41] What does performance allow us to do that other mediums of creation do not?

When the environment AS IS narrows down and constrains actions, when it lacks an already existing material world of things for a particular body, performance alone can take hold and, through its AS IF conditionality, let us transform the very same environment into someplace else—an accessible but not yet materialized reality. When existing affordances of the world leave no room for disabled people's atypical bodies and minds, when the world becomes most unresponsive to the impairments and pains we live with, and when the world's offerings become unreachable in states of deprivation and debilitation, again, it is the improvisatory space of performance that lets them imagine an alternative reality out of the very same materiality. In fact, when all other venues and materials of creation become unavailable (such as when we have no tools, no materials, no stuff to make an artifact), and when all other possibilities for articulation shrink to zero, performance is still there to provide a possible place of articulation that can resist the mandates of the everyday in order to survive and even thrive, and to live a life against all odds. This is exactly what performance allows us to do that other mediums of making do not. Performance enables us to make, even when resources are extremely scarce, and when making becomes less and less, and at times least, likely.

Admittedly, a danced affordance will not alleviate our pains or reciprocate our nonnormative bodies as effectively as an artifact would, whether that artifact goes by the name of "assistive" technology, "adaptive" tool, or "accessibility."

Neither are activist affordances as durable, as easily shareable, and as smooth as the world of materialized things. But activist affordances do offer one advantage over a world of materialized artifacts: they need no nails, no tools, no materials. They are surely not waiting for someone else to make any *thing*, for that matter. Because they emerge from within performance, it takes (at a bare minimum) just the body and imagination to choreograph an activist affordance. Think of actors on stage and disabled people in everyday life. When they *make up* and *make real* other possible worlds, they do not necessarily do so by making (more) things, constructing (more) stuff, building (more) artifacts. They do it by improvising, dancing, playing, experimenting—in short, *performing* with what already exists.

What I am theorizing as activist affordances are thus not just a form of world-making but, crucially, *an accessible* and a *nonexploitative* form of world-making. Because they take place within performance; because they can sometimes be enacted solely in and through our bodies; because they are *an art of making do with what we have*, activist affordances are the arts/acts of survival that can still take place in the least hospitable, the least welcoming, and the least permitting of circumstances.

How Do We Build Built Worlds?

In his concept of "defuturing," which refers to "the negation of world futures for us, and many of our unknowing nonhuman others," design theorist Tony Fry argues that "creation," by which he means the creations of Western civilization, "is indivisible from destruction."[42] To build something somewhere is to destroy something else in another place: "Everything created requires the transformative force that both takes away and brings into being."[43] Defuturing names this "taking-away" that making/creation of modernist Western tradition entails.[44] Defuturing—destroying world futures while building something—lies at the core of a capitalist economic system whose survival is predicated on endless growth or, in Livingston's phrasing, "self-devouring growth."[45]

For capital to accumulate, Jason Moore writes, "cheap food," "cheap energy," "cheap raw materials," "cheap labour," and in fact "the whole [of] nature had to be put to work."[46] "Cheap Nature as an accumulation strategy" has treated the earth as if it were an endless resource.[47] Centuries of colonialist, capitalist expansionism and unlimited economic growth have plundered, overused, and otherwise depleted the earth's natural resources. Earthly exploitative violence has come from many different but linked directions, including colonial land grabs, fossil fuel extraction, the plantation system, agroindustrialism, deforestation, overfishing, uncontrolled poaching, open pit mining, pollution havens, chemical contamination, imperialist wars, militarization, and nuclearization, among many others. All of these forms of Capitologenic violence have destroyed the earth at such "scale, rate/speed, synchronicity, and complexity" that "changes in degree [have] become changes in kind."[48] The damage done to the planet is beyond what the planet itself can repair. In these climate catastrophic times it is not just the life of a single species that is at stake but the entire "livability of the earth" or, in Haraway's wording, the earth's "ongoingness."[49]

The urgent question of our times is how to negotiate a world of shrinking possibilities, and how to keep life *going on* within the constraints of finite resources and in recognition of and in respect for those limits. At a time when the careless occupation of the earth's niches and the misuses and abuses of its offerings have brought the earth to the brink of catastrophe, we need everyday techniques of survival that are born from within constraints—techniques that "act futurally," with responsibility and "response-ability."[50]

A Theory of Affordances for a Shrinking Planet

In his book *Design, When Everybody Designs*, Ezio Manzini traces local design cultures emerging worldwide, as community members work together in ways that bring production and consumption into closer proximity and that encourage resilient systems. These design practices, Manzini writes, are "beautiful islands of applied cultural and socioeconomic wisdom" emerging "in a sea of unsustainable ways of being and doing. . . . The good news is that the number of these islands is growing and generating a wide archipelago."[51] Along with Manzini, we can think of activist affordances as "beautiful islands" of disability survival wisdom emerging in a sea of ableist, consumptionist, defuturing, self-devouring, and drowning liberal capitalist world order.

The creation of activist affordances, as I have been arguing, does not require having access to maker's tools, materials, and spaces, which may or may not be available in the localities we live in. Nor do they necessitate "having" the training of a technician or "possessing" the professional knowledge of a designer or an expert of some kind. The creation of an activist affordance asks only for our bodies and whatever happens to be around us, or even just our bodies, which at times, especially at times of extreme deprivation, may be all that we have.[52] This leaves *performance* as the only medium of making we can access.

When disabled people speculate "accessible futures" in and through their activist affordances, they do so with a cautious negotiation of their bodily and environmental resources. When they bring into being, through their activist affordances, what does not yet exist in a material form, they do so by *making do with* whatever is at hand. After all, what prompts the creation of activist affordances is *shrinkage*, not abundance and repletion. It is the lack, loss, reduction, and scantness of corporeal and environmental resources that necessitate the *art* of how to make things work within those limits. The *virtuosity* of these seemingly trivial survival techniques is their making do with whatever energy, effort, and functioning parts that disabled people have (left) in their sick, painful, and nonstandard bodies, and with whichever entities happen to be in their surroundings. These tiny acts/arts of world-making are born from the imperatives of shrinkage and the *need* to respond to and bear response-ability for limits.

Precisely for these reasons, ecological survival under the macro, massive, and overarching scale of planetary shrinkage perhaps lies in these seemingly insignificant and transitory but deeply important moments of making and surviving; in the tiny, momentary, and earthly scale of affordance-creating. The activist affordances that disabled people have long mastered can perhaps be a way of addressing the pressing question of how to negotiate a shrinking planet with diminishing resources, or provide a starting point for doing so. It is high time that the rest of the world turns to, recognizes, and learns from them. Hence the proposal for a new theory of affordances—a theory, a conceptual toolkit, and a critical vocabulary with which we can give a name to, identify, and trace these otherwise unrecognized micro acts/arts of everyday survival that are born from the urgencies of a shrinking world of affordances.

NOTES

1 Along with disability communities and scholarship, I have moved from naming disabilities "visible" and "invisible" to "apparent" and "nonapparent." "The concept of visibility itself," Carrie Sandahl notes, "relies on a metaphor that assumes able-bodiedness" and therefore bolsters ocularcentrism (Sandahl, "Queering the Crip," 54). Appearance, in contrast, is a multisensorial phenomenon. Moreover, the idea of apparency, as Schalk writes, "shifts the onus for noticing or not-noticing disability onto the perceiving person rather than onto the visibility of disability via a person's bodymind, accoutrements, or behaviors" (Schalk, *Bodyminds Reimagined*, 124).

2 Throughout the book, I will be using both "disabled people" and "people with disabilities" as a way to acknowledge the situated and nonstatic nature of language. The former phrase, which, after the social model, highlights the disablement of the people by the society and its barriers, and the latter phrase, which is known as people-first language, are valuable in their own right as their effectiveness varies, depending on who uses them, in which context, and how.

3 Gibson, *The Ecological Approach*, 127.

4 Activism is traditionally associated with collective and intentionally engaged activities (such as sit-ins, protests, rallies, occupations) that have a disruptive potential, are explicitly visible, and often involve confrontation and demands for change. As disability scholars and activists have already noted, there is a certain ableism and normativity to this understanding (Wendell, "Unhealthy Disabled"; Wong, "Valuing Activism of All Kinds."; Genest, "The Body as Resistance Art/ifact"). Who else can do the work of such activism but an able-bodied/minded subject capable of acting, of moving around, and of having intentions and determinations? In bringing in the idea of performance *as* activism, I want to challenge these ableist presumptions and demonstrate that activism can take many other forms, such as activist affordances, that may fall through the cracks of recognition. I discuss activism in more detail in chapter 5.

5 Austin, *How to Do Things with Words*. Judith Butler and Jacques Derrida have
   used Austin's speech act theory as a foundation for their theorizations of
   performativity.

6 Performer and author Neil Marcus has famously described disability as "an
   art" and "an ingenious way to live" (Marcus, *Storm Reading*). Siebers talks
   of the "artfulness" of disability (Levin and Siebers, "The Art of Disability").
   Belser conceptualizes the relationality between wheelers and their wheelchairs
   as "vibrant artistry of life with disability" (Belser, "Vital Wheels," 7). Various
   scholars and activists argue that disability can be considered as a "gain" rather
   than a loss (Bauman and Murray, *Deaf Gain*); as "benefits rather than deficits"
   (Garland-Thomson, "The Case for Conserving Disability," 339); and as the
   equivalent of biodiversity rather than abnormality (Bauman and Murray, *Deaf
   Gain*, xviii; Clare, "Notes on Natural Worlds," 258). Some claim that disability
   generates its own standpoint knowledge and "cripistemologies" (McRuer and
   Johnson, "Proliferating Cripistemologies"). Scully, for instance, writes about
   "the epistemology of the disabled experience" (Scully, *Disability Bioethics*, 13).
   Wendell argues that the sphere of experiences that disabled people have access
   to generates a particular form of knowledge, and were it to be taken seriously
   (rather than being silenced or dismissed), "an explosion of knowledge of the
   human body and psyche would take place" (Wendell, "Toward a Feminist
   Theory of Disability," 120). Garland-Thomson considers disability as a generative, narrative, ethical, and "epistemic resource" (Garland-Thomson, "The
   Case for Conserving Disability," 349). With respect to design and disability,
   various concepts and approaches have been proposed, such as "DEAFSPACE"
   (Bauman), "starting with dis/ability" (Boys, *Doing Disability Differently*), "crip
   technoscience" (Hamraie, *Building Access*), and "crip design" (Williamson,
   Accessible America), in order to foreground how disability embodiments
   and standpoint knowledges can be at the center (rather than at the margins)
   of design practices. In this emergent body of work, the traditional deficit
   perspective of disability has been turned upside down: disabled people not
   only have been compared to artists and scientists alike (Saerberg, "The Sensorification of the Invisible") but have also been called "original life hackers,"
   self-taught experts, and "unrecognized" and "unlikely engineers" (Jackson,
   "We Are the Original Lifehackers"; Williamson, *Accessible America*; Hartblay,
   "Disability Expertise"; Hamraie and Fritsch, "Crip Technoscience Manifesto";
   Hendren and Lynch, "This Counts Too"; Hamraie, *Building Access*, 106, 113).
   For a broader emphasis on design and making, see Gunn, Otto, and Smith,
   Design Anthropology; Murphy, "Design and Anthropology"; Escobar, *Designs
   for a Pluriverse*; Costanza-Chock, *Design Justice*. See also Hartblay, Hankins,
   and Caldwell, "Keywords for Ethnography and Design."

7 Within recent literature, a few works have looked at disability and affordances,
   but their engagement with the terms has been rather preliminary in that either
   disability or affordances appear in passing. Disability, in particular autism,
   has attracted the attention of some ecological psychologists (see Loveland,

"Social Affordances and Interaction II"), but their work has largely been less ecological and more psychological, or rather infused with psychologizing overtones. In "Bodies, Technologies and Action Possibilities," Bloomfield et al. present one of the most interesting studies to date on disability and affordances. Drawing on research designed to "combat social isolation among housebound disabled individuals," the authors examine how objects, people, and situations interact in the creation of affordances (422). While their study is well-informed on affordances, it lacks a critical disability perspective and the experiences and viewpoints of disabled people themselves. Burns et al. ("An Inclusive Outdoors?") and Clapham ("The Embodied Use of the Material Home"), on the other hand, integrate a critical disability perspective into the deployment of affordances, but their mention of affordances remains rather cursory, without any substantial exploration of the term or any engagement with Gibson's ecological approach.

8 Gibson, *The Ecological Approach*, 127.

9 Kafer, *Feminist, Queer, Crip*, 141.

10 D. Taylor, *Performance*, 6.

11 Turner, *From Ritual to Theatre*, 84.

12 Turner, *From Ritual to Theatre*, 83. Following Taylor's style in her definition of performance, and in order to further emphasize the difference between the indicative "as is" and the subjunctive "as if," I will use AS IS and AS IF in their capitalized forms throughout the rest of the book.

13 These approaches shift the traditional consumerist, market-centered, and industry-centered focus of design to "the realm of the unreal, the fictional." They are concerned not with finding solutions to the needs of the industry but with posing questions, prompting debates, and proposing speculation about alternative futures, possibilities, and how things *could be* (Dunne and Raby, *Speculative Everything*, 11).

14 Charles Eames cited in Pullin, *Design Meets Disability*, xiii. Pullin's research shows that "it was the particular constraints of the U.S. Navy brief that led the Eameses to develop their own technology" with plywood curves and create a leg splint for injured personnel in the Navy—the plywood technology which then became "an iconic mainstream furniture" (xiii).

15 Throughout the book, I will be using the word "resource" in order to refer to bodily and environmental resources (understood as capabilities) while keeping in mind that "resource" is far from being an innocent word. As feminist environmental scientist and activist Max Liboiron writes, resource is "a colonial, settler, and imperial concept" (Liboiron, *Pollution Is Colonialism*, 63); "resources refer to unidirectional relations where aspects of land are useful to particular (here, settler and colonial) ends" (62). Further, it is not only the land that is a resource in the colonial mindset; as Indigenous scholar and activist Leanne Betasamosake Simpson points out: "My culture and knowledge is a resource. My body is a resource and my children are a resource because they are the potential to grow, maintain, and uphold the extraction-assimilation

system" (Simpson, "Dancing the World into Being"). I use the word "resource" partly because of its noninnocent genealogy rooted in colonialism and capitalist voraciousness.

16 Haraway, *Staying with the Trouble*, 2.

17 Chapman and Sawchuk, "Research-Creation," 6. See also Nelson, *Practice as Research in the Arts*; Loveless, *How to Make Art at the End of the World*.

18 Dokumacı, "Disability as Method."

19 Garland-Thomson, *Staring*, 193.

20 Mingus, "Access Intimacy."

21 Clarke and Haraway, *Making Kin*.

22 Susan Wendell writes that in the public conception, "the paradigmatic person with a disability is healthy disabled and permanently and predictably impaired" ("Unhealthy Disabled," 21).

23 Kafer, *Feminist, Queer, Crip*, 16; emphasis added.

24 Friedner and Weingarten, "Introduction."

25 Kafer, *Feminist, Queer, Crip*, 11.

26 Minich, "Enabling Whom?"; Kafer, *Feminist, Queer, Crip*, 11.

27 Nixon, *Slow Violence and the Environmentalism of the Poor*.

28 Sobchack, "Choreography for One, Two, and Three Legs," 62.

29 Names of participants from my first fieldwork have been anonymized. Translations from interviews in Turkish are my own.

30 For further projects on inaccessibility in Montreal, please consult Montreal in/accessible Collective (m.i.a.) Collective, 2013. https://cjds.uwaterloo.ca/index.php/cjds/article/view/113.

31 Megafone is a project initiated by media artist Antoni Abad in collaboration with local marginalized communities worldwide. For further details, visit https://megafone.net/site/index.

32 Saerberg, "'Just Go Straight Ahead,'" 9.

33 Reed, *James J. Gibson and the Psychology of Perception*, 54.

34 Gibson, *The Ecological Approach*, 253.

35 "Let us consider the possibility," Gibson writes, "that the stimulus input contains within it everything that the percept has. What if the flux of stimulation at receptors does yield all the info anyone needs about the environment?" (Gibson, *Reasons for Realism*, 319).

36 Gibson, *The Ecological Approach*, 253.

37 Gibson, *The Ecological Approach*, 139.

38 Gibson, *The Ecological Approach*, 138.

39 Costall, "The Meaning of Things," 79.

40 Gibson, *The Ecological Approach*, 129.

41 I use "shrinkage" to signify the contraction of space for action. This contraction may be caused by an increase in environmental stimulants, as well. For example, when a person living with multiple chemical sensitivity passes through a busy street with shops and is bombarded with fragrances of all sorts, that body's space for action collapses on itself. That is, actual increases in density

or size can *also* lead to shrinkage or contraction in the freedom to move, act, and sense. I would like to thank Jonathan Sterne for bringing this important point to my attention.

42 Garland-Thompson, *Extraordinary Bodies*, 24.

43 Garland-Thomson, "Misfits."

44 Siebers, "Disability in Theory," 177; Siebers, *Disability Theory*, 25; Kafer, *Feminist, Queer, Crip*, 12; Puar, *The Right to Maim*, xix.

45 Scarry, *The Body in Pain*, 162.

46 Gibson writes that the affordances can be "of injury or benefit" (Gibson, *Reasons for Realism*, 405).

47 Canguilhem, *The Normal and the Pathological*, 199.

48 The idea of "spooning out" comes from disability justice communities. The spoon theory was first developed by writer and patient advocate Christine Miserandino in order to illustrate the immense effort it takes to strategize one's energy when living with a debilitating chronic disease like lupus (Miserandino, "The Spoon Theory").

49 Leder, *The Absent Body*, 81.

50 Bourdieu, *Logic of Practice*, 56.

51 Ingold, *Perception of the Environment*, 375.

52 Ingold, *Perception of the Environment*, 36.

53 Laurence Parent defines "walkism" as "the normative expectation that someone can walk and climb stairs" (Parent, "Je Me Souviens," 211). For earlier uses of the term and its conceptual underpinnings see Michael Oliver, *Understanding Disability*, 108–9; Freund, "Bodies, Disability and Spaces," 695.

54 Bourdieu, *Logic of Practice*, 57, 56.

55 Titchkosky, *Question of Access*, 77.

56 Nixon, *Slow Violence and the Environmentalism of the Poor*.

57 In occupied Palestine, for instance, checkpoints, in Puar's vivid description, function as "choke points," and the space is shrunken further and further by the Israeli state with the exact aim of producing "an entire population with mobility disabilities" (Puar, *The Right to Maim*, 135–36).

58 Popularized by chemist Paul Crutzen, the term "Anthropocene" refers to the proposed geologic epoch in which human activity has become the central and most profound force shaping the earth (Crutzen, "Geology of Mankind"). The Anthropocene is a contested term widely criticized for a variety of reasons, including its underlying assumptions of a homogeneous Anthropos/human; its dismissal of the unequal ways in which different populations contribute to planetary damage, and the disproportionate ways in which they bear the burden of its consequences; and finally, its centering of the Anthropos/Man-the-maker and perpetuation of human exceptionalism (see Malm and Hornborg, "Geology of Mankind?"; Haraway, *Staying with the Trouble*; Haraway et al., "Anthropologists Are Talking"; Moore, "Capitalocene"). Since then, other critical terms (e.g., the "Capitalocene," "Plantationocene," "Chthulucene") have been proposed to enrich the debate and to foreground the omissions of the

term "Anthropocene." In this book, I use the term "Anthropocene" but also bring in other terms, such as "Capitalocene," in order to acknowledge the contested nature of the term and to recognize the critical work done by feminist, postcolonial, and STS scholars on the issue of naming the current epoch.

59 Vidal, "Tip of the Iceberg."

60 The social and the medical/individual models of disability are two binary models that have been conceptualized by British disability grassroots activists and scholars (see UPIAS, "Fundamental Principles of Disability," and Michael Oliver, *Social Work with Disabled People*). According to this conceptualization, the medical model locates disability in the individual's body, its abnormalities, and its pathologies, whereas the social model locates disability in the society and the environment, and their barriers. I address the model and its subsequent criticisms further in chapter 1.

61 Minich, "Enabling Whom?"

62 Meekosha, "Decolonising Disability," 670.

63 Sara Ahmed uses the notion "slantwise" in reference to Maurice Merleau-Ponty's phenomenology, where he describes the effect of seeing a room not straight but obliquely and as "queer" (Ahmed, *Queer Phenomenology*, 65).

64 In fact, the "Design for All Showcase" held by the White House in 2016 featured a series of garments and devices modeled by disabled people, including "shirts with magnet closures to avoid the use of buttons," as well as alternative lacing systems and jeans with side closures for wheelchair users (Williamson, *Accessible America*, 211).

65 Friedner and Cohen, "Inhabitable Worlds."

66 Muñoz, *Cruising Utopia*, 49.

67 See Scarry, *The Body in Pain*, 291.

68 Scarry, *The Body in Pain*.

69 D. Taylor, *Archive and the Repertoire*.

70 Mairs, *Waist-High in the World*.

71 Kafer, *Feminist, Queer, Crip*, 45.

CHAPTER 1. AFFORDANCE ENCOUNTERS DISABILITY

1 Garland-Thomson, "Misfits," 593.

2 In their "Fundamental Principles," the UK-based grassroots organization the Union of the Physically Impaired Against Segregation (UPIAS), whose work was instrumental to the formulation of the model, famously wrote: "In our view, it is society which disables physically impaired people." Therefore, they added, "it is necessary to grasp the distinction between the physical impairment and the social situation, called 'disability,' of people with such impairment. Thus, we define impairment as lacking part of or all of a limb, or having a defective limb, organ or mechanism of the body; and disability as the disadvantage or restriction of activity caused by a contemporary social organisation which takes no or little account of people who have physical

impairments and thus excludes them from participation in the mainstream of social activities" (20).

3 Michael Oliver, "Politics of Disablement," 34.

4 Whether the social model omitted impairment entirely or not was an issue of ongoing debate among social modelists and their critics, but the fact remains that the proponents of the model made a clear separation between impairment and disability, making the latter the project of the model for social change. In response to the critiques directed at the social model, Mike Oliver proposed the potential of a social model of impairment in addition to the social model of disability, but he still retained their distinction. "Pain, medication and ill-health," he wrote, "properly belong within either the individual model of disability or the social model of impairment" but not within the social model of disability (Michael Oliver, "Defining Impairment and Disability," 40).

5 See the table that Mike Oliver prepared to compare and contrast the medical and social models. Oliver quotes the medically oriented questions used in the United Kingdom's Office of Population Censuses and Surveys (1987) and replaces them with socially framed ones (Michael Oliver, "Politics of Disablement," 7–8).

6 For variations of the social model, see Shakespeare, *Disability Rights and Wrongs Revisited*. It is important to recognize that disability activism and scholarship have taken different trajectories, depending on which historical contexts they emerged from and what kinds of political, institutional, and governmental structures they emerged as a response to. The US-based disability rights movement was focused on civil rights and legislative changes, and it was (as were many other liberatory movements of the 1970s and 1980s) identity-based and celebratory of disability pride and cultures. In the United Kingdom, where universal healthcare and a stronger welfare system existed, efforts were directed at social policy change. Disability activists, as exemplified in the history of the formation of the Union of the Physically Impaired Against Segregation (UPIAS), gathered against infantilizing approaches of healthcare professions, segregated residential institutions, and paternalistic policies of the welfare state. Despite their nuanced differences, US and UK disability studies and activism have shared a common discourse and pragmatism (which was later popularized within global disability movements) around access and the social creation of disability. See Shakespeare, *Disability Rights and Wrongs*; see also Meekosha, "Drifting Down the Gulf Stream," and her comparison of "British Materialist vision" and "American non-materialist cultural studies."

7 Hahn cited in D. Mitchell and Snyder, "Talking about Talking Back," 323.

8 For an extensive criticism of the social model, see Shakespeare, *Disability Rights and Wrongs Revisited*. Drawing mainly on feminist critiques and others, Shakespeare unpacks the limits of the model from a variety of angles and emphasizes the need to go beyond "the impasse of 'social creationist' disability studies" (2).

9 Crow, "Including All of Our Lives," 208.

10 See Morris, *Pride against Prejudice*; Crow, "Including All of Our Lives"; Wendell, *Rejected Body*; Linton, *Claiming Disability*; Thomas, *Female Forms*; Wendell, "Unhealthy Disabled."

11 Crow, "Including All of Our Lives," 224. Cara Jones has, in fact, called for "a model of disability that centralizes pain," on the basis that pain can be a defining characteristic of disability as in the experience of endometriosis (Jones, "Pain of Endo Existence," 556).

12 Linton, *Claiming Disability*, 138.

13 Wendell, "Unhealthy Disabled," 18.

14 These are two kinds of being disabled that Wendell proposes in order to highlight the complex relationship of chronic illness and disability while also acknowledging that the two are fluid categories, "with sometimes uncertain membership" (Wendell, "Unhealthy Disabled," 19).

15 Kafer, *Feminist, Queer, Crip*, 27.

16 Wendell, "Unhealthy Disabled," 18.

17 Livingston, "Insights from an African History of Disability," 119.

18 For a genealogy of the transformations of "disability studies" toward what is now called "critical disability studies" see Goodley, "Dis/entangling Critical Disability Studies"; Garland-Thomson, "Disability Studies"; Meekosha and Shuttleworth, "What's So 'Critical' about Critical Disability Studies?"

19 Siebers, *Disability Theory*, 25.

20 Ahmed, *Queer Phenomenology*, 23.

21 Bloomfield, Latham, and Vurdubakis, "Bodies, Technologies and Action Possibilities," 416. See also Davis and Chouinard, "Theorizing Affordances," 2. In media studies, for instance, affordances are largely used as shorthand for the functions of mobile and interactive devices, captured by the ubiquitous use of the term "media affordances." In design, "for many designers," Flach, Stappers, and Voorhorst note, "the term affordance meant a visual icon to express hidden functionality," and it often is just a cue for function (Flach, Stappers, and Voorhorst, "Beyond Affordances," 79). Drawing on such reductive uses, some commentators argue that affordance has "become a buzzword used almost by anybody to describe anything and is in risk of losing contents altogether" (Baerentsen and Trettvik, "Activity Theory Approach to Affordance," 52). Some even assert that the term has outlived its usefulness and should be discarded altogether (Martin Oliver, "Problem with Affordance").

22 Gibson, *The Ecological Approach*, 127. Partly because of Gibson's plain style of theorizing, and partly because of the term's complexity, much debate has taken place since its coinage and even empirical studies have been designed to render affordances measurable (Warren, "Perceiving Affordances"; Warren and Whang, "Visual Guidance of Walking through Apertures"; Cesari, Formenti, and Olivato, "Common Perceptual Parameter"; Cesari, "Invariant Guiding Stair Descent"). In the subsequent redefinitions of the term, some commentators strengthened the link between sociality and affordance (I address these critiques

later in this chapter) and between intentionality and affordance (Heft, "Affordances and the Body"), while others expanded its scope beyond the body to intellectual, conceptual, and symbolic matters. For instance, Sanders wrote that the environment does not have to be "limited to the physical surround." It can, in fact, relate to "anything that the organism 'can do,'" including symbolic and conceptual activity (Sanders, "Ontology of Affordances," 108). Similarly, Holbraad proposes the notion of "conceptual affordances," pointing out how thought processes can have offerings of their own (Holbraad, "Can the Thing Speak?"). Windsor and Bézenac argue for applying affordances to the perception of "complex cultural artefacts," such as music and other types of artwork (Windsor and Bézenac, "Music and Affordances"). Ginsburg explores how language can be "a source of affordances . . . as do other objects and processes" and how it can "create, stipulate and specify affordances," as in speech acts (Ginsburg, "Ecological Perception Debate," 361). Windsor also examines affordances in relation to the perception of semiotic signs (Windsor, "Ecological Approach to Semiotics").

23 Even though Gibson came up with the neologism "affordance" in order to capture the mutuality of the organism and the environment, commentators were divided with regard to where to locate affordances—whether in the environment or in the body or in both. Linking affordances to evolutionary biology, Edward Reed considers affordances as "resources" in the environment (Reed, *Encountering the World*). Similarly, Michael Turvey attributes affordances singly to the environment, redefining them as "dispositions" (i.e., "causal propensities") (Turvey, "Affordances and Prospective Control," 178). Dispositions by definition imply pairs, and given that affordances stand for "the environment" part of the pair, Turvey comes up with another term, "effectivities," to refer to the animal side (Shaw, Turvey, and Mace, "Ecological Psychology," 197). "Whereas an affordance is a disposition of a particular surface layout," Turvey writes, "an effectivity is the complementing disposition of a particular animal" (Turvey, "Affordances and Prospective Control," 179). William Noble and Martin Oliver, on the other hand, claim that Gibson's theory put too much emphasis on the environment side, downplaying the agency of organisms (Noble, "Gibsonian Theory," 76; Oliver, "Problem with Affordance," 412). Some scholars argue against these attempts to attribute affordances in an either/or manner (either to the animal or to the environment). John Sanders claims that the creation of two separate concepts (such as dispositions and effectivities) goes against the very organism-environment complementarity built into the notion of affordances (Sanders, "Ontology of Affordances"). Erik Rietveld and Julian Kiverstein seek to bridge the two different camps on affordances, arguing that "an affordance can be understood as being both relational and a resource" (Rietveld and Kiverstein, "Rich Landscape," 327). Thomas Stoffregen claims that affordances "are properties of the animal–environment system, that is, that they are emergent properties that do not inhere in either the environment or the animal" (Stoffregen, "Affordances as Properties," 115). Anthony Chemero writes that "affordances

are not properties of the environment; indeed, they are not even properties";
instead, they are "relations between particular aspects of animals and particular aspects of situations" (Chemero, "Outline of a Theory of Affordances," 184).
Faraj and Azad note that affordances are "not just a single attribute or property"
but are "multifaceted relational structure[s]" that are actualized through "the
enactment of several mutuality relations between the technology artifact and
the actor" (Faraj and Azad, "Materiality of Technology," 26).

24 Shaw, Mace, and Turvey write that it was James J. Gibson who took up "the term
ecological psychology to emphasize this animal-environment mutuality for the
study of problems of perception" (Shaw, Turvey, and Mace, Foreword, xiii).

25 Reed, *James Gibson and the Psychology of Perception*, 284.

26 Heft, *Ecological Psychology in Context*, xxiv.

27 Gibson, *Reasons for Realism*, 407.

28 Gibson, *Reasons for Realism*, 416.

29 Gibson, *The Ecological Approach*, 18.

30 Because we are defining the environment at an ecological level, what counts
as the medium changes depending on the type of organism in question: for
humans, the medium is air; for aquatic animals, it is water; and for amphibians
and earthworms, it can be both.

31 Gibson, *The Ecological Approach*, 19. "The notion of substances . . . should not
be confused with the physical concept of matter" (Gibson, *Reasons for Realism*, 111). A gas or a liquid is matter but neither is a substance. When a solid
melts into a liquid, or a liquid evaporates into a gas, matter changes its state.
But "when a substance goes into gaseous state, it becomes . . . a component of
the medium." It is not *dematerialized*" but it is "*desubstantialized*" (Gibson,
The Ecological Approach, 99).

32 Gibson, *The Ecological Approach*, 23. Given surfaces' significance to action and
perception, Gibson comes up with what he calls "ecological laws of surfaces."
According to these laws, the list of which is inexhaustive, all surfaces have
layouts. Depending on the underlying substance, its solidity, cohesiveness,
chemical and physical composure, and surfaces resist deformation and disinte-
gration to different degrees. All surfaces have particular textures, and a texture
is significant to perception because it "specifies what the substance is" and what
it affords (28). All surfaces have shapes, which define their layouts, facets, edges,
and vertices, which, in turn, define what a surface affords for manipulation (29).

33 Gibson, *The Ecological Approach*, 94.

34 Gibson, *The Ecological Approach*, 239.

35 Ingold, "Materials against Materiality," 6.

36 Ingold, "Materials against Materiality," 7.

37 Gibson, *Reasons for Realism*, 207.

38 Gibson, *The Ecological Approach*, 100.

39 The medium, Gibson writes, is "filled with illumination (to say nothing of sounds
and odours)" as well as molecules and particles (Gibson, *Reasons for Realism*, 207).

40 Gibson, *The Ecological Approach*, 55.

41 Gibson, *The Ecological Approach*, 17. Gibson further adds: "Gravity, heat, light, sound and volatile substances fill the medium. The chemical and mechanical contacts and vibrations impinge on" the perceiver's body, immersing the perceiver "as it were in a sea of physical energy" (57).

42 Traditional theories explain perception in terms of what came to be known as the "stimulus-response formula." The theories borrow the notion "stimulus" from physiology, where it is used to refer to "whatever application of energy fires a nerve cell or touches off a receptor or excites a reflex response" (Gibson, *The Ecological Approach*, 56). According to the formula, stimuli consist of different forms of energies, including mechanical, electrical, and chemical ones, which hit various receptors in the body. If they surpass a certain threshold, the stimuli then trigger the corresponding receptors, and what then follows is *a series of conversions*. The excited receptors convert the incoming energy into signals, which are, in turn, converted into perception by way of mental operations. The existing theories differ as to what "operation" renders the sensory inputs meaningful, but they all agree on the assumption that the sensations triggered by light or by mechanical or chemical vibrations constitute the core data of perception. According to the stimulus-response formula, "all we ever see directly [in the case of visual perception] is what stimulates the eye," namely light, and in the case of overall perception, all we ever perceive is stimuli. Instead of readily taking up notions such as "stimuli," "energy," and "radiation" from natural sciences, Gibson first questioned the usefulness of such concepts to psychology. He asked: Do we ever perceive stimuli? "Do we ever see light as such?" (54). Perceptual systems of organisms, Gibson argues, can detect things they can see, feel, touch, and taste, not energies, radiations, and atomic particles (9). For these reasons, Gibson turns to the scale of where organisms act and behave in the world, that is, the environment.

43 Reed, *James J. Gibson and the Psychology of Perception*, 26.

44 Gibson, *The Ecological Approach*, 52. Stimulus and stimulus information also differ in the following aspect: stimulus refers to "*anything* that touches off a receptor or causes a response." It is momentary, and as such, it "carries no information about its source in the world." Stimulus information, on the other hand, emerges through extended temporality, and as such, it spells its precipitator, because "only stimulation that comes in a structured array and that changes over time specifies its external source" (56).

45 Gibson, *Reasons for Realism*, 168.

46 Heft, *Ecological Psychology in Context*, xxiv.

47 Gibson, *The Ecological Approach*, 126.

48 Gibson, *The Ecological Approach*, 75. For example, in the case of visual perception, "the optical information to specify the self, including the head, body, arms, and hands *accompanies* the optical information to specify the environment" (116).

49 The medium is dense with energies, and any point that an observer can occupy in it contains perceptual information specific to that and that point only. "For each point of observation there is one and only one arrested perspective" (Gibson,

The Ecological Approach, 73). Accordingly, when observers move or when an object is moved, the "figure" (in the case of visual perception) does not "simply move over the ground" (103). What happens instead is an entire transformation of the way light is positioned—more specifically, of the particles on which light falls. In other words, perceivers, in moving, do not only move themselves but also move other constituents of the environment of which they are a part.

50 When looking around a room, for instance, "the world is revealed and concealed as the head moves, in ways to specify exactly how the head moves" (Gibson, The Ecological Approach, 118).

51 Gibson, The Ecological Approach, 10, 251.

52 Gibson, The Ecological Approach, 73.

53 The invariants refer to all sorts of "relations in the ambient light [and other forms of energies] that owe their existence to the persisting features of the environment" (Gibson, The Ecological Approach, 308). "The invariant structure is whatever optical [acoustic, mechanical, chemical] pattern persists despite the changes of perspective structure" (Reed, James Gibson and the Psychology of Perception, 290). For example, when an observer moves or when an object is moved, what was revealed becomes concealed and vice versa (Gibson, The Ecological Approach, 308), but the fact does not change that "whatever goes out of sight, will come into sight, whatever is lighted will be shaded," whatever is the far side will be the near side (92). Also unchanged is the fact that "all solid angles shrink to zero" at the horizon of the earth (signifying maximum remoteness) and that "the largest possible visual solid angle" occurs at the occluding edge of the nose, signifying maximum proximity (117). Nor do the ratios change of light gradients that lie between the two. None of these change because the substantial surfaces of the environment that structured them do not change.

54 Gibson, The Ecological Approach, 76.

55 Gibson, The Ecological Approach, 123.

56 The notion of "action" should not be limited to the gross bodily locomotion. One does not need to have a mobile body in order to perceive (otherwise this would give rise to the incorrect deduction that only ambulatory animals can perceive). The perceptual systems are made up of organs, such as the eyes, the head, and the limbs which, "being equipped with muscles," can move in their own right (Gibson, The Ecological Approach, 218). Even at the most micro scale, the eyes can never be fully steady because the "muscles that control their posture undergo tremor" making the eyes undergo "a series of miniature movements and microsaccades" and "looking at a tiny thing consists of making tiny movements" (212).

57 Gibson, The Ecological Approach, 239.

58 Gibson, The Ecological Approach, 141.

59 Gibson, Reasons for Realism, 416–17.

60 Gibson, The Ecological Approach, 140. Note, however, "the compound invariant" does not emerge in steps. I do not first perceive the properties of the surface, and then mine, and eventually cross-match them to figure out which

action I can perform in this situation. An infant, Gibson writes, "does not begin by first discriminating the qualities of objects and then learning the combinations of qualities that specify them. The affordance of an object is what the infant begins by noticing" (134).

61 Gibson, *Reasons for Realism*, 408.

62 Heft, "Affordances and the Body," 3.

63 Stoffregen, "Affordances as Properties," 117.

64 Heft, "Affordances and the Body," 11.

65 Gibson, *The Ecological Approach*, 135.

66 Stoffregen, "Affordances as Properties," 124.

67 James, *Essays in Radical Empiricism*, cited in Heft, *Ecological Psychology in Context*, 127.

68 Gibson, *The Ecological Approach*, 129.

69 Gibson, *The Ecological Approach*, 140. When "a surface is horizontal, flat, extended, rigid, and knee-high relative to a perceiver," that is, when its "properties are seen relative to the body surfaces and the self, they constitute a seat and have a meaning" (128). This is why some scholars consider the theory of affordances as "the theory of meaning in ecological psychology" (Michaels, "Affordances," 138). Alan Costall argues that the theory of affordances "addresses one of the most fundamental theoretical issues of modern psychology, the reality of meaning" (Costall, "Socializing Affordances," 468). Ginsburg even claims that affordances are "equivalent to meaning" (Ginsburg, "Ecological Perception Debate," 359).

70 Gibson, *The Ecological Approach*, 127.

71 Sanders writes that the concept "provides us with the most general access to ontology, or perhaps one should say, to ontologizing" (Sanders, "Ontology of Affordances," 111). See also Sanders, "Affordances," 131.

72 Put this way, affordances seem to take on, in Harry Heft's wording, an "apparently contradictory character." "If a property exists relative to a perceiver, then isn't its existence dependent on the perceiver? Conversely, if a property is independent of a perceiver, then how can it be relational with respect to a perceiver?" This contradiction is only on the surface, and it is resolved once one considers that there can be *actual* as well as *potential* affordances (Heft, *Ecological Psychology in Context*, 132).

73 This is where Gibson parts ways with the phenomenologists and Gestalt theorists who have previously offered concepts similar to affordance (see Gibson, *The Ecological Approach*, 138). Kurt Lewin, for instance, proposes the term "Aufforderungscharakter," which has been translated into English as "invitation character" and "valance" (Lewin cited in Gibson, *The Ecological Approach*, 138). Kurt Koffka invents a similar notion, called "demand-character," by which he means how "each thing says what it is," how "the postbox 'invites' the mailing of a letter, the handle 'wants to be grasped,' and things 'tell us what to do with them'" (Koffka, cited in Gibson, *The Ecological Approach*, 138). (Missing from Gibson's brief genealogy of the concept of affordances is Edward Tolman's concept of "manipulanda"; see Heft, *Ecological Psychology in Context*,

128). Like Gibson, Gestalt psychologists argue that meanings and values are present in immediate perception and are directly perceived, but differing from Gibson, they place meanings, "valences," and "demand" or "invitation characters" solely in the phenomenal world (Gibson, *The Ecological Approach*, 138). "Aufforderungscharakter were held by Lewin to be elements of a 'phenomenal field,' rather than in the physical world" (Sanders, "Affordances," 129). It is precisely such an assumption of two worlds that Gibson seeks to avoid with the idea of affordances.

74 Gibson, *The Ecological Approach*, 139.

75 Reed, *James Gibson and the Psychology of Perception*, 294.

76 Chemero, "Outline of a Theory of Affordances," 193.

77 Reed, *James Gibson and the Psychology of Perception*, 294.

78 Gibson, *The Ecological Approach*, 138; emphasis added.

79 Sociologists, anthropologists, and other scholars of psychology and cognitive science have revised the concept since its coinage. These revisions have emphasized the need to "socializ[e]" affordances (Costall, "Socializing Affordances") and to situate them historically and culturally—in contrast to what their authors saw as the original theory's overly individualized psychological premises. See Noble, "Gibsonian Theory"; Heft, "Affordances and the Body"; Costall, "Meaning of Things"; Hutchby, "Technologies, Texts and Affordances"; Dant, *Discourse and Material Culture*; Turner, "Affordance as Context"; Schmidt, "Scaffolds for Social Meaning"; Bloomfield, Latham, and Vurdubakis, "Bodies, Technologies and Action Possibilities"; Faraj and Azad, "Materiality of Technology"; Rietveld and Kiverstein, "Rich Landscape."

80 Scholars such as Noble, Harry Heft, and R. C. Schmidt agree that social and cultural aspects of affordances can still be explained in ecological terms. The information relevant for sociocultural properties, Heft writes, "is embedded within a temporally extended flow of events that includes the perceiver's history of engagements with the environment," going back to their "perceptual learning and development" (Heft, "Affordances, Dynamic Experience, and the Challenge of Reification," 158). Agreeing with Heft, Schmidt argues that events are nested within one another in one's lifetime, and "the context for any given moment of perception is the ongoing event or events in which that moment is nested." For example, in the case of a mug received as a gift from one's child, the perception of the mug's affordance is an event nested within others, including the recipient's birth, their previous engagements with other gift-giving/receiving practices, and the birth of their daughter, who would later give them the mug (Schmidt, "Scaffolds for Social Meaning," 146). Hence, the person is able to directly pick up the gift affordance not because there is "static information in the stimulus array at a given moment," but because their whole past figures into the current perceptual activity (145, 148).

81 Schmidt, "Scaffolds for Social Meaning," 139–40.

82 Schmidt, "Scaffolds for Social Meaning," 142.

83 Heft, "Affordances, Dynamic Experience, and the Challenge of Reification," 172. Some artworks presented in galleries, for instance, exhibit aesthetic properties that derive their meanings precisely from the very way in which they distort our everyday perceptions, "such that one set of affordances is supplanted and contradicts another," as in Marcel Duchamp's making of art out of a urinal (Windsor, "Ecological Approach to Semiotics," 195).

84 Gibson, *Senses Considered as Perceptual Systems*, 6. Gibson explains "perceptual learning" through the notion of "perceptual systems" (instead of stimulus-response theories). "If the senses are perceptual systems," he writes, "the infant does not have sensations at birth but starts at once to pick up information from the world. His detection equipment cannot be exactly oriented at first, and his attention imprecise; nevertheless, he looks at things, and touches and mouths them, and listens to events. As he grows, he learns to use his perceptual systems more skillfully, and his attention becomes educated to the subtleties of stimulus information" (5). William James, whose work had an influence on Gibson, similarly writes: "Every perception is an acquired perception" (James, *Principles of Psychology*, 2:78).

85 Gibson, *The Ecological Approach*, 254.

86 Gibson writes that we "learn to perceive" affordances (Gibson, *Reasons for Realism*, 403).

87 Costall, "Meaning of Things," 79.

88 Heft, "Ecological Approach to Psychology," 165; Rietveld and Kiverstein, "Rich Landscape of Affordances," 332; Noble, "Gibsonian Theory," 73.

89 Costall, "Meaning of Things," 79. Similar concepts have been proposed by other scholars. Loveland uses the notion "preferred affordances" as a way to refer to "participation with other people in a shared cultural milieu that predisposes the individual to use objects, interpret events, and so on, in particular ways" (Loveland, "Social Affordances and Interaction II," 101). Rietveld and Kiverstein appropriate Witgenstein's term "forms of life" in order to describe the "relatively stable and regular ways of doing things" which become "manifest in the normative behaviors and customs of our communities" (Rietveld and Kiverstein, "Rich Landscape of Affordances," 328–29). Heft writes that the environment "is already rich in 'use meanings' constituted by its available affordances, tools and artifacts" (Heft, *Ecological Psychology in Context*, 344).

90 Costall, "Meaning of Things," 79.

91 Heft, "Affordances and the Body," 17.

92 Here it would be important to not limit sociality to humans, even if post-Gibsonian theorists' critiques and extensions of affordances focus on the sociality of affordances vis-à-vis humans. As Actor Network theorists have taught us, it is not only that nonhuman animals, organisms, microbes, bacteria, objects, and the inanimate world have sociality, but also that these socialities can be interlinked (see Latour, *Reassembling the Social*).

93 Gibson, *The Ecological Approach*, 129.

94 Gibson, *The Ecological Approach*, 129.

95 Gibson, *The Ecological Approach*, 141

96 The word *amca* means uncle in Turkish, but it is used to refer not only to kin but also to elderly men in general as a sign of respect. I chose to keep the word *amca*, as this was how I interacted with Arif Amca during our interview.

97 Unless otherwise noted, all other interviews during my second fieldwork were conducted in English.

98 Price, "Bodymind Problem." Price proposes "bodymind" as a single word in order to avoid the distinctions implied by the common usage of conjunctions, hyphens, or slashes between the two words (269).

99 "Fitting and misfitting," Garland-Thomson writes, "denote an encounter in which two things come together in either harmony or disjunction" (Garland-Thomson, "Misfits," 592). I am using the word "hope" here because we cannot take for granted that we know what an affordance is for all organisms and in all situations in order then to be able to identify its absence or presence. Likewise, we cannot concretely and once and for all define what constitutes access in order then to be able to detect its absence/presence. Finally, as Margaret Price points out in her critique of the concept of misfit, there can be "murkier" situations (such as a "psychotic break" that a person with mental disability is having) without easily identifiable targets to blame (such as the stairway standing in front of a wheelchair), and where we cannot readily tell what fits/misfits to what before making a value judgment first (Price, "Bodymind Problem," 27).

100 Minich, "Enabling Whom?"

CHAPTER 2. CHRONIC PAIN, CHRONIC DISEASE

1 Melzack and Wall, *Challenge of Pain*, 161.

2 See Asad, "Agency and Pain," 43.

3 Fannin, "Labour Pain," 43.

4 See Flanagan, *Pain Journal*; Sheppard, "Using Pain, Living with Pain."

5 Shilling and Mellor, "Saved from Pain or Saved through Pain?"

6 Asad, "Agency and Pain," 41; Struhkamp, "Wordless Pain," 702. Talal Asad argues that passive states of suffering and agentive states of suffering are not "either/or" positions and that their boundaries can, in fact, blur. Referring to the rituals of "the Passion of Christ or the Martyrdom of Hussain," during which participants willfully subject themselves to suffering, and in so doing enact a particular form of agency and belonging, he asks: "How helpful is it, therefore, to be always offered a choice between two mutually exclusive options: either an agent (representing only herself) or a victim (a passive object)?" (36). Likewise, in a fascinating ethnography of suffering, Struhkamp unpacks the complexity of suffering and traces how suffering, contrary to its general conception, does not have to be a state that is passively experienced by an individual but can in fact be actively dealt with and collectively tackled.

7 See Bendelow and Williams, "Transcending the Dualisms."

8 Scarry, *The Body in Pain*.

9 Scarry, *The Body in Pain*, 5.

10 Scarry, *The Body in Pain*, 162.

11 Scarry, *The Body in Pain*, 162.

12 Leder, *The Absent Body*, 73.

13 Scarry, *The Body in Pain*, 52. The negativity and suffering associated with pain, and the idea that pain is something to be "gotten rid of," have been heavily criticized within disability studies. Tobin Siebers, for instance, argues that the societal fears of pain as something inherently aversive can lead to tremendous disability oppression. The fear of pain as the ultimate form of suffering and the ableist assumption that painful lives are lives "not worth living," he writes, have historically oppressed disabled people during everyday social interactions and through vital medical and life-and-death decisions (Siebers, "In the Name of Pain," 184). Similarly, Alyson Patsavas criticizes the dominant discourses around chronic pain that frame it as "a devastating tragedy," as "a fate worse than death." Not only do these discourses, Patsavas writes, "prevent us from examining the structural conditions that *make* experiences of chronic pain tragic," they also reject outright the possibility that people in chronic pain may still live "rich, varied, and complex lives" (Patsavas, "Recovering a Cripistemology of Pain," 203–4). For further criticism of cultural and societal assumptions about pain, see Holmes, "Pain"; Sheppard, "Using Pain, Living with Pain." I wholeheartedly agree about the dangers of society's assumptions about pain as something inherently negative and tragic. At the same time, I cannot, nor do I want to, deny the negativity of the pain that I experience on a daily basis, the immense suffering it causes me, or the fact that I *do want to* get rid of pain. I do not believe that the two positions have to be mutually exclusive.

14 Scarry, *The Body in Pain*, 52.

15 Scarry, *The Body in Pain*, 290.

16 Scarry, *The Body in Pain*, 52.

17 Leder, *The Absent Body*, 77. Drawing on the works of neuroscientists and experimental physiologists, such as Claude Bernard, Kurt Goldstein, and Bud Craig, Mark Paterson makes a similar argument about pain's capacity to generate action. Pain, Paterson writes, "involves a set of signals that build up an intra-organismic sequence of responses that have the potential to tip the whole organism from perception to action, from sensation to motility" (Patterson, "On Pain as a Distinct Sensation," 126–27). Pain, he adds, "prompts activity," "eliciting in the whole organism movement, or movement-potential" (128).

18 Gibson, *The Ecological Approach*, 127.

19 Leriche, cited in Canguilhem, *The Normal and the Pathological*, 96. "Chronic pains," Ronald Melzack writes, "are not a warning to prevent physical injury or disease. They are the disease" (Melzack, "Pain and the Neuromatrix in the Brain," 1378).

20 World Health Organization, "ICD-11 for Mortality and Morbidity Statistics."

21 Gibson, *The Ecological Approach*, 127.

22 Leder, *The Absent Body*, 73, 75.

23 Given its medicalized uses, the term "disease" has a contested place in disability studies, and I could have chosen a more humanities- and social sciences–friendly

term such as "illness" (for the distinction between disease and illness, see Klein-mann, *Illness Narratives*). In this book, I do not deploy the concept of disease as a shorthand for diagnostic categories; "diagnosis," as Shakespeare reminds us, "is not the same as disease" (Shakespeare, *Disability Rights and Wrongs*, 58). I instead use "disease" in order to refer strictly to the *experiencing* of a disease. Disease, as deployed in this book, concerns not the level of cells, tissues, or organs but the level of the environment in which the sick person lives and *experiences* the disease. Disease, in other words, is understood ecologically.

24 Ingold, *Perception of the Environment*, 200.

25 Scarry, *The Body in Pain*, 288.

26 Canguilhem, *The Normal and the Pathological*, 197.

27 Canguilhem, *The Normal and the Pathological*, 197.

28 Canguilhem, *The Normal and the Pathological*, 200. What "normative" and "norms of life" refer to in Canguilhem's seminal text is quite different from their connotations in the contemporary humanities today. In philosophy, Canguilhem notes, the concept of "normative" means "every judgment which evaluates or qualifies a fact in relation to a norm." In Canguilhem's use of the term, normative refers to "that which establishes norms," implying change and possibility rather than stability and closure (126–27).

29 Canguilhem, *The Normal and the Pathological*, 198; Canguilhem, "Health," 474.

30 Canguilhem, *The Normal and the Pathological*, 199.

31 "There is an expectant distrust" in the cardiac heart, Leder writes (Leder, *The Absent Body*, 80), and hence a distrust in the environment that one can expand oneself into with such a heart.

32 Canguilhem, *The Normal and the Pathological*, 199.

33 Chen, *Animacies*, 198, 198–99.

34 Leder, *The Absent Body*, 81.

35 Leder, *The Absent Body*, 81.

36 Scarry, *The Body in Pain*, 32–33.

37 Garland-Thomson, "Misfits."

38 This is how Garland-Thomson defines misfit: misfit "describes an incongruent relationship between two things: a square peg in a round hole" (Garland-Thomson, "Misfits," 592–93).

CHAPTER 3. THE HABITUS OF ABLEISM

Earlier versions of some sections in chapter 3 appeared as "Disability as Method: Interventions in the Habitus of Ableism through Media-Creation," in *Disability Studies Quarterly* 38, no. 3 (2018).

1 Since the time of my fieldwork, accessibility has slightly improved for public transportation in Montreal. As of 2016, public buses have automated audio announcements.

2 Hamraie, *Building Access*, 13.

3 See Williamson, *Access*.

4 Williamson, *Accessible America*, 209.

5 Hamraie, *Building Access*, 13. Brendan Gleeson similarly uses the term "'conventional' access studies." But his usage of "conventional" refers to the studies of access by "spatial scientists, including geographers, urban planners and architects" which, while having made contributions to policy development, have lacked social and political theorization of access (Gleeson, "Disability and the Open City," 252).

6 Anthropologists of disability trace meaning-making and valuation processes of access in global contexts. In her ethnography on ramps in Northwestern Russia, Cassandra Hartblay demonstrates the difficulty of tracing the cause of inaccessibility to a single source, because access is not simply created by an object, such as a ramp, but is deeply embedded in local moral fields, social relations, diffuse infrastructures, and responsibilities that bring access into being or not (Hartblay, "Good Ramps, Bad Ramps"). In their fieldwork in the "world class" *accessible* cities of New Delhi and Bangalore in India, Michele Friedner and Jamie Osborne find that governmental access audits do not lead to any actual environmental or policy change (Friedner and Osborne, "New Disability Mobilities," 13). With their term "disability development," the authors argue that the rhetorical work of access has been taken up, marketized, and turned into a commodity by multinational corporations, NGOs, and the state in ways that bring financial and moral benefit to these actors rather than benefiting disabled people themselves (12). The rhetoric of access ends up enabling disabled people only "to claim moral authority," without achieving the creation of actually existing accessible spaces (Friedner and Osborne, "Audit Bodies," 44).

7 Williamson, "Access," 17; Hartblay, "Good Ramps, Bad Ramps," 19; Imrie, "Oppression," 144; Friedner and Osborne, "New Disability Mobilities," 13, 17.

8 Hamraie, *Building Access*, 5.

9 Titchkosky, *The Question of Access*, 64, 16.

10 Titchkosky, *The Question of Access*, 126, 132.

11 Hamraie and Fritsch, "Crip Technoscience"; Titchkosky, *The Question of Access*, 3.

12 As several scholars point out, there also are many problems with the legislative frameworks under which professional codes and regulations fall. Statements such as "where 'reasonable and practical'" (in the building regulations in England and Wales) and "where 'readily achievable'" (in the ADA), for instance, are known to leave too much room for interpretation and allow professionals to get around the legislation (Imrie and Hall, *Inclusive Design*, 48, 54; Imrie and Kumar, "Focusing on Disability and Access," 359). Further, the documented problems in the enforcement of accessibility laws and policies reveal what Gleeson calls "a vacuum of accountability" within which "responsible authorities" are hardly ever held accountable for their ignorance (Gleeson, "Disability and the Open City," 257).

13 Aimi Hamraie writes, for instance, that the "ADA has not resulted in a postdiscrimination World," just as the outlawing of segregation laws did not create a "postracial" United States (Hamraie, *Building Access*, 3). Similarly, Nirmala Erevelles takes to task the limits of formal justice and equality, which antidiscrimination legislation, such as the ADA, is supposed to secure. Drawing on

Crenshaw and Freeman, Erevelles argues that "the ADA ... is formulated from the perspective of ableist society (the perpetrator) and therefore only serves as the watchdog for inappropriate events." These laws treat discriminatory acts as isolated events and exceptions rather than situating them within the deeply ingrained structural material inequalities that they emerge from (Erevelles, *Disability and Difference*, 155). In her book *Beyond Ramps*, disability advocate Marta Russell wrote that the ADA was "a product of 'free market civil rights in a public relations era,' and images of successful, taxpaying wheelchair users zipping up ramps concealed a host of issues when it came to true inclusion of disabled people" (Russell, cited in Williamson, *Accessible America*, 185).

14 Canguilhem, *The Normal and the Pathological*, 175.

15 Bourdieu, *The Logic of Practice*, 54.

16 Bourdieu, *The Logic of Practice*, 69.

17 Ingold, *The Perception of the Environment*, 375.

18 Ingold, *The Perception of the Environment*, 375.

19 Bourdieu, *The Logic of Practice*, 69.

20 Gibson, *The Ecological Approach*, 138.

21 Ingold, *The Perception of the Environment*, 36.

22 Campbell, "Inciting Legal Fictions," 44.

23 Dolmage, *Academic Ableism*, 7.

24 Bourdieu, *The Logic of Practice*, 73. I am here taking my cues from Sara Ahmed, who writes of "whiteness as a bad habit: a series of actions that are repeated, forgotten, and that allow some bodies to take up space by restricting the mobility of others" (Ahmed, *Queer Phenomenology*, 129). Ahmed draws attention to the casualness and ordinariness of how whiteness is done.

25 Bourdieu, *The Logic of Practice*, 73.

26 Titchkosky, *The Question of Access*, 87.

27 Titchkosky, *The Question of Access*, 83.

28 Titchkosky, *The Question of Access*, 34.

29 Bourdieu, *The Logic of Practice*, 55.

30 Bourdieu, *The Logic of Practice*, 56.

31 Titchkosky, *The Question of Access*, 77.

32 Titchkosky, *The Question of Access*, 88.

33 Bourdieu, *The Logic of Practice*, 54.

34 The task here, however, is not so much to "fetishize design" and put the blame on architects for the production of a disablist environment (Dickens, cited in Imrie and Hall, *Inclusive Design*, 94) as to unveil the ableist habitus that permeates all levels of human activity, including the pedagogies and practices of design professions. In this regard, it is important to add that architects do not act in silos but are part of a heterogeneous material/social network that erases and omits disability (94). In an ableist habitus, the architect is but one actor among many. In addition to architects, there are property developers, investors, contractors, planning regulators, building control officers, project managers—a variety of experts, among other actors, constituting what

Michael Ball calls the "structures of building provision" (Ball, cited in Imrie and Hall, *Inclusive Design*, 7; see also Imrie and Kumar, "Focusing on Disability and Access"). In this tightly knit network the actions of architects are mediated, controlled, and at times delimited by the actions of others, as well as by broader economic, political, social, legislative, and technological developments. Within this restructuring, "the most significant design decisions are made before the project ever reaches the architect" (Harvey Rabinowitz, cited in Imrie and Hall, *Inclusive Design*, 94). Further, situational or structural conditions stymie architects' abilities to respond to disabled people's building requirements (111). From this perspective, putting heavy metal doors at the entrance of a private office building on a windy street may well have to do with cost efficiency concerns and heat and energy conservation, while simultaneously disabling users like Jacques.

35 Boys, *Doing Disability Differently*, 46. See also Fry, "Design for/by 'The Global South.'"

36 After having conducted a series of interviews with architects and tutors, and having analyzed illustrations in architectural textbooks, Rob Imrie finds that architectural education "devotes little or no time or instruction to matters concerning the human body" (Imrie, "Architects' Conceptions," 53). Bess Williamson also notes that "architectural drawings and blueprints rarely include images of the humans who will use them" (Williamson, *Accessible America*, 165). And where the body appears, it often appears as a normalized body based on "abstract theories of the self" (Imrie, "The Body, Disability and Le Corbusier's Conception," 26) rather than as "an organic, fleshy entity" (Imrie, "Architects' Conceptions," 57). The body in architectural blueprints is an "archtype," or "an 'identikit' which reduces users to technical categories" (Imrie and Kullman, "Designing with Care," 9; Imrie and Hall, *Inclusive Design*, 4). See also Williamson, *Accessible America*, 150–51.

37 Siebers, *Disability Theory*, 85; Hamraie, *Building Access*, 20.

38 Hamraie, *Building Access*, 20.

39 Boys, *Doing Disability Differently*, 103. For a detailed discussion of architectural exclusions, see Grosz, *Architecture from the Outside*.

40 Since the second half of the twentieth century, much has happened in architecture to address the exclusions based on disability. Thanks to the efforts of disability movements, important changes have been introduced to architectural guidelines in Canada, the United States, the United Kingdom, and other Western countries alike. In the United States, the Architectural Barriers Act was passed in 1968, with American National Standard A117.1 (a previously voluntary accessibility guideline) being adopted as "the basis of barrier-free design" (Hamraie, *Building Access*, 91). In 1990, the Congress passed the landmark ADA with its enforceable standards for accessible design. In Quebec, accessibility standards for new buildings were introduced in the province's building code in 1976, and the Act to Secure Handicapped Persons in the Exercise of Their Rights was adopted in 1978. While these legislative changes

have brought many gains for disabled people, the responses of architecture as a profession, as many disability scholars point out, have been rather limited. "Wheelchairreductive models of disability," Imrie and Hall argue, "dominate professionals' attitudes" as though there were no other disability than mobility impairments; as though disability were a single type (Imrie and Hall, *Inclusive Design*, 43). See also Imrie, "The Body, Disability," 42.

41 Boys, *Doing Disability Differently*, 24, 4.

42 Imrie and Hall, *Inclusive Design*, 14; Boys, *Doing Disability Differently*, 28–33. Alternatively, it is flattened out and erased within a design for "everyone" rubric, where the particularities of disability would no longer matter (see Boys, *Doing Disability Differently*; Hamraie, *Building Access*).

43 Imrie and Kumar, "Focusing on Disability and Access," 367; Imrie and Kullman, "Designing with Care," 8. Aimi Hamraie also notes that when the ADA was introduced, "the frustrating proliferation of codes and standards, and their unpredictable interpretation in the courts" had caused a backlash against ADA from architects (Hamraie, *Building Access*, 230).

44 "The consideration of disability issues," an architect comments in an interview, "is not in the mind of architects as a general rule. It just isn't. It's not part of our culture" (Imrie and Hall, *Inclusive Design*, 96).

45 Imrie, "Architects' Conceptions," 56.

46 Dolmage, "Academic Ableism," 62.

47 Gissen, "Why Are There So Few Disabled Architects?" Gissen's observations are confirmed by statistics about architects that show that "less than 4 per cent in the USA, even fewer in the UK have a disability" (Imrie, "Oppression, Disability and Access," 133).

48 Fry, "Design for/by 'The Global South,'" 28–29.

49 Grosz, *Architecture from the Outside*, 13.

50 Emphasizing "the outside," Grosz writes: "The place of the destitute, the homeless, the sick and the dying, the place of social and cultural outsiders— including women and minorities of all kinds—must also be the concern of the architectural and the urban just as it has been of philosophy and politics" (Grosz, *Architecture from the Outside*, xvi).

CHAPTER 4. PLANETARY SHRINKAGE

1 Katia Avilés-Vázquez, in *Democracy Now!*, "Naomi Klein."

2 Kishore et. al., "Mortality in Puerto Rico after Hurricane Maria."

3 Katia Avilés-Vázquez, in *Democracy Now!*, "Naomi Klein."

4 McRuer, *Crip Theory*, 204.

5 Puar, *The Right to Maim*.

6 Wheeler, "Moving Together Side by Side," 595.

7 Disability justice activists, scholars, and groups such as Sunaura Taylor, Eli Clare, and Sins Invalid have taken to task the speciesism implied in "disability" by writing about the impairment of nonhuman animals, landscapes, and

earthly beings. Disability justice and eco-ability movements emphasize the interconnectedness of earth and disability oppression and liberation (Nocella, Bentley, and Duncan, *Earth, Animal and Disability Liberation*; S. Taylor, *Beasts of Burden*; Sins Invalid, *Skin, Tooth, and Bone*). Stacy Alaimo argues that "posthumanisms, new materialisms, and ecomaterialisms may help crip the environmental humanities and extend disability studies beyond the anthropocentric" (Alaimo, "Foreword," xi.). Nocella draws attention to the foundations of eco-ability theory that considers that "nature, nonhuman animals, and people with disabilities promote collaboration, not competition" (Nocella, "Defining Eco-ability," 150). Sunaura Taylor proposes the concept of "disabled ecologies," which she defines as "the material and cultural ways in which disability is manifested and produced among human and nonhuman entities" (S. Taylor, "Age of Disability").

8 Ingstad and Whyte, *Disability and Culture*, 7.

9 Disability, Snyder and Mitchell write, "is the product of a nineteenth- and early twentieth-century arsenal" in Euro-American societies (Snyder and Mitchell, *Cultural Locations of Disability*, 23). "The United States and parts of Europe," the authors add, "manufactured the need to constitute a class of disabled citizens when individuals came to be increasingly defined by industrial labor practices within a capitalist marketplace" (23). In fact, "the term *disability* was first coined in the mid-1800s to designate those incapable of work due to injury" (D. Mitchell and Snyder, "Disability as Multitude," 184). Early British disability scholars also tie the emergence of disability to the rise of capitalism and the assembly line. The transformation from an agrarian to an industrialized capitalist mode of production, Michael Oliver and Colin Barnes write, resulted in "the creation of the disabled individual," as, in the process, "what was essentially a labour market issue [was turned] into an individualized medical problem" (Michael Oliver and Barnes, *New Politics of Disablement*, 16). In her classic work *The Disabled State*, Deborah Stone traces how disability was created as an "administrative category" in the United Kingdom, the United States, and Germany in order to control labor supplies. Two distributive systems, Stone writes, work-based and need-based, defined how wealth and services should be distributed in capitalist societies. Confronted with the "distributive dilemma" of how to reconcile the two systems, welfare states had to come up with a bureaucratic classification that help distinguish those deserving of social aid from those undeserving of it. In the process, medicine, due to the truth-seeking power attributed to its "clinical gaze," was brought into the picture in order to validate who "truly" needed state aid. Accordingly, disability was produced first as "an administrative category that creates automatic entitlements [to state aid], and second, [as] a clinical concept that defines the nature of those entitlements" (13). The creation of the disability category, as these studies demonstrate, was enabled by an intricate set of historical conditions, events, and practices—some of a discursive order (such as the emergence of modern medicine) and some of a nondiscursive one (such as changes in the economic mode of production)—that had taken place

in Euro-American geographies (see Foucault, *The Archaeology of Knowledge*, 164). Once such medicalized, institutionalized, and governmentalized classifications and understandings of disability had been put in place, they could then be challenged and unmade within newly formed definitions and identifications of disability. Disability was reclaimed and redefined in North American and European settings by scholars, activists, and their allies beginning in the last decades of the twentieth century. Disability was redefined as a form of oppression, systemic discrimination, and social construction; reframed through social, minority, and cultural models; reclaimed as a rights-based issue and an identity category; and celebrated as a form of culture, pride, and transgression. Disability was divorced from its negative connotations, was brought from the peripheries to the center, and shifted from being considered a deficit, an exceptional tragedy, or a calamity to being seen as "perhaps the most universal of human experiences" (Garland-Thomson, "Feminist Disability Studies," 1568). Genealogically speaking, it was through these very developments that a new kind of knowledge, a new way of thinking and talking about disability, emerged "as a counterpoint to the medicalized perspectives," and in opposition to what Linton calls "Not Disability Studies" (Linton, *Reclaiming Disability*, 132–56).

10 Barker and Murray, "Disabling Postcolonialism," 223.

11 See Meekosha, "Decolonising Disability," 668; Grech, "Decolonising Eurocentric Disability Studies"; Grech and Soldatic, "Disability and Colonialism"; Grech and Soldatic, *Disability in the Global South*.

12 Ghai, "Disability in the Indian Context," 93–94.

13 Erevelles, *Disability and Difference*, 130.

14 Erevelles, *Disability and Difference*, 26, 47.

15 Puar, *The Right to Maim*, 74.

16 In their critique of the disability category and disabled/able-bodied binary, Puar questions whether we can consider able-bodied as synonymous with nondisabled (Puar, *The Right to Maim*, xxiii).

17 Knadler, *Vitality Politics*, 29.

18 Knadler, *Vitality Politics*, 113.

19 Barker and Murray, "Disabling Postcolonialism," 227; Meekosha, "Drifting down the Gulf Stream," 731; Meekosha, "Decolonising Disability," 678; Grech, "Decolonising Eurocentric Disability Studies," 18; Grech and Soldatic, "Disability and Colonialism," 2; Meekosha, "Decolonising Disability," 731.

20 Meekosha, "Decolonising Disability," 668.

21 While doing fieldwork and writing a history of disability in Botswana, Julie Livingston realizes that the conceptual apparatus of disability studies does not neatly apply to, and at times remains in conflict with, Tswana understandings of body and impairment. "In a context where the predations of colonialism and capitalism have contributed to rising rates of physical impairment," Livingston writes, "it is hard to think about the suffering induced through the casting of impairments as disability . . . without also considering the potential suffering induced through the generation of such impairments

in the first place" (Livingston, "Insights from an African History of Disability," 117–18). Botswana workers brutally impaired in South African mines, for example, were considered "lucky," and they welcomed the "pity" of others (112). In a local cosmology that understood the body to be permeable through physical contact and social relations, impairment was not secondary, as it was to the rights-based discourses of disability in North America, but was central to Tswana notions of disability. It is in consideration of these local specificities that Livingston proposes the term "debility." The term points at the convergences between "people with disabilities and those whose bodies are debilitated or otherwise impaired by virtue of illness or aging" and histories of colonial attrition (119). Building on Livingston's notion of debility, and drawing from Foucault's notion of biopolitics, Jasbir Puar proposes the notion "debilitation" (Puar, *The Right to Maim*). Debilitation, Puar writes, expands biopolitics "beyond simply the question of 'right of death and power over life,'" as foundationally laid out by Foucault, to what Puar calls "the right to maim" (136). The exercise of maiming entails "slow but simultaneously intensive deathmaking," happening on "both bodily and infrastructural fronts" (139). Puar mobilizes "debility" and "debilitation" as distinct terms from disability and disablement. Debility refers not to an identity or a culture, she writes, but to "a verb," a "doing," "a process" (72), and debilitation "foregrounds slow wearing down of populations instead of the event of becoming disabled" (xiii–xiv). "Disability from the South" is a Somatosphere series edited by Michele Friedner and Tyler Zoanni (2018–2019).

22 Friedner and Weingarten, "Introduction."

23 Minich, "Enabling Whom?"

24 Berne, "Disability Justice."

25 Berne, "Disability Justice."

26 Mol, Moser, and Pols, *Care in Practice*, 14.

27 De la Bellacasa, *Matters of Care*, 43.

28 Klein, *The Shock Doctrine*, 9–10.

29 Disaster capitalists, Klein writes, are unable to "distinguish between destruction and creation, between hurting and healing" (Klein, *The Shock Doctrine*, 54).

30 Klein, *The Shock Doctrine*, 467.

31 Klein, *The Shock Doctrine*, 480.

32 Klein, *The Shock Doctrine*, 466–67.

33 Klein, *The Shock Doctrine*, 466.

34 Escobar, *Designs for the Pluriverse*, 69.

35 Law, "What's Wrong with a One-World World?," 134, 128.

36 See Latour, *We Have Never Been Modern*.

37 Law, "What's Wrong with a One-World World?," 127.

38 Law, "What's Wrong with a One-World World?," 134. Mario Blaser also writes that "the enactment of a modern world . . . actively produces other ontologies or worlds as absences" (Blaser, "Ontological Conflicts," 555).

39 De la Cadena, "Indigenous Cosmopolitics in the Andes," 345–46.

40 This is a term that Anders Burman is using in his commentary on Blaser's work. Burman, cited in Blaser, "Ontological Conflicts," 561.

41 "If our waters are undrinkable, our forests destroyed, our lands rendered toxic," Waziyatawin asks, "how do we practice Indigenous ways of being?" (Waziyatawin, "Indigenous Resurgence at the End of Empire," 79).

42 Pluriverse is credited to William James, although James, to be more precise, used the word "multiverse." "Visible nature is all plasticity and indifference," he writes, "a multiverse, as one might call it, and not a universe" (James, "Is Life Worth Living?," 10). Escobar mobilizes the term by referring to the Zapatista slogan, "a world where many worlds fit" (Escobar, *Designs for the Pluriverse*, xvi).

43 Rose, "Shimmer," G52.

44 Take coral reefs—a telling case of those entangled shrinkages. Coral reefs, also known as "the rainforests of the sea," are the refuge of highest biodiversity in marine habitats. They provide food and shelter to more than a quarter of marine species. Hundreds of millions of people, most of whom live in impoverished coastal regions, rely on coral reefs for livelihood and basic sustenance (Cabral and Geronimo, "How Important Are Coral Reefs?"). Greenhouse gas emissions of climate catastrophic times cause global warming and ocean acidification, which in turn "sicken and bleach coral reefs, killing the photosynthesizing zooanthellae and so ultimately their cnidarian symbionts" (Haraway, *Staying with the Trouble*, 56). The death of coral reefs means that the quarter of marine species that they harbor will also die. It means that the populations whose sustenance relies on coral reefs will face food shortages. It also means that those regions whose protection from disasters is afforded by coral reefs are going to be put at increased risk (it is reported that almost "200 million people depend on coral reefs to protect them from storm surges and waves"; see World Wildlife Fund, "Living Planet Report 2018," 54).

45 Other scholars and activists have already made similar calls (see S. Taylor, *Beasts of Burden*; Sins Invalid, *Skin, Tooth, and Bone*).

CHAPTER 5. A THEORY OF ACTIVIST AFFORDANCES

An earlier version of chapter 5 appeared as "A Theory of Microactivist Affordances: Disability, Disorientations, and Improvisations," in *South Atlantic Quarterly* 118, no. 3 (2019): 491–519. Copyright © 2019 Duke University Press.

Earlier and much condensed versions of some of the material in chapter 5 appeared as "Vital Affordances, Occupying Niches: An Ecological Approach to Disability and Performance," in *Research in Drama Education: The Journal of Applied Theatre and Performance* 22, no. 3 (2017): 393–412; and as "On Falling Ill," in *Performance Research: A Journal of the Performing Arts* 18, no. 4 (2013): 107–15.

1 Pearson, *Site-Specific Performance*, 171–72.

2 Pearson, *Site-Specific Performance*, 171.

3 Pearson, *Site-Specific Performance*, 172.

4 Emphasis added. Told By an Idiot is a UK-based theater company famous for its devised theater and improvised performances that emerge from the collaborative work of actors on stage that is "rooted in the live event & thrives on a sense of spontaneity & risk" (see https://www.toldbyanidiot.org/about/).

5 The defiance can be the defiance of the hierarchies within aesthetic production (such as the hierarchical relations between the director and actors) or the defiance of the dominance of text over play. For further discussions on improvisation see Born, Lewis, and Straw, *Improvisation and Social Aesthetics*.

6 Whether improvisation can be (intentionally) uncreative and useless (as a form of social critique) has also been raised (see Wershler, "Kenneth Goldsmith and Uncreative Improvisation").

7 Gibson, *The Ecological Approach*, 139.

8 Marcus, *Storm Reading*; Siebers and Levin, "The Art of Disability"; Garland-Thomson, "The Case for Conserving Disability."

9 Hendren and Lynch, "This Counts Too"; Jackson, "We Are the Original Lifehackers"; Hartblay, "Disability Expertise."

10 Aimi Hamraie comes up with the term "crip technoscience," as they trace the histories of US postwar disability maker-cultures, independent living movement of the 1970s, and late twentieth-century experiments in universal design. Based on these histories and their contemporary extensions, crip technoscience describes how disabled people have long been tinkering with science and technologies, adapting tools and built environments in nonconformist ways (Hamraie, *Building Access*). In *Accessible America*, Bess Williamson writes about the same historical period in the United States. In the chapter titled "Electric Moms and Quad Drivers: Do-It-Yourself Access at Home in Postwar America," she charts how in accord with the consumer culture of the era, disabled people in the postwar United States appropriated available products and technologies for their needs, thereby creating access by their own means (Williamson, *Accessible America*, 69–72).

11 Hamraie and Fritsch, "Crip Technoscience Manifesto."

12 Here, I am taking my cue from Scarry's notion of "dance of labor" (Scarry, *The Body in Pain*, 316).

13 Scarry has a wide understanding of artifacts. By the word "artifact," she does not just mean concrete objects, such as a chair or a blanket, but all sorts of material, verbal, infrastructural, philosophical, and political phenomena that have been made, ranging from thought categories to justice systems, from "skilled acts of surgery" to "a marketplace, or . . . nation-state" (Scarry, *The Body in Pain*, 302, 308).

14 Scarry, *The Body in Pain*, 288. Scarry's book was written in 1985. In the age of the Anthropocene (see chapter 5), we cannot really think of "natural" disasters in separation from the *disastrous* consequences of human activities. If disasters show the "ignorance" of the environment about human hurtability, disasters today are, in many ways, the reflection of the very ignorance of the human beings of the hurtability of the environment itself.

15 Scarry, *The Body in Pain*, 286.

16 Of course, humans do not make only clothing, shelters, blankets, and medicine. They also make weapons, atom bombs, nuclear plants, pipelines, agroindustries, and many other forms of what Tony Fry terms "designed uncaring" (Fry, "Design for/by 'The Global South,'" 13).

17 Scarry, *The Body in Pain*, 288–89.

18 Scarry, *The Body in Pain*, 290.

19 Scarry, *The Body in Pain*, 290.

20 Scarry, *The Body in Pain*, 315.

21 Scarry, *The Body in Pain*, 290.

22 Scarry, *The Body in Pain*, 290.

23 Scarry, *The Body in Pain*, 289.

24 Scarry, *The Body in Pain*, 290.

25 Scarry, *The Body in Pain*, 290.

26 It is important to not limit dance to its ableist understandings, which take the movements of a bipedal ambulatory body for granted. Movement can be done in many ways and dance can take many forms, as have already been explored by disability and performance scholars (see Albright, *Choreographing Difference*).

27 "What if?" scenarios, props, and make-believe are among the commonly used strategies of critical design (Dunne and Raby, *Speculative Everything*, 90–94).

28 Dunne and Raby, *Speculative Everything*, 189.

29 Escobar, *Designs for the Pluriverse*, 69.

30 Haraway, *Staying with the Trouble*, 35.

31 Ginsburg and Rapp, "Disability Worlds."

32 Meekosha, "Drifting Down the Gulf Stream," 731.

33 Wendell, "Unhealthy Disabled," 24, 26. Disability artist/activist Oriana Bolden, unable to attend a political rally due to her condition, makes a video which, according to Snyder and Mitchell, "becomes her unexpected contribution to a politics that would otherwise march without her" (Snyder and Mitchell, "How Do We Get All These Disabilities Here?," 22). Similarly, disability justice activist Alice Wong argues that disability activism may entail forms of political engagement that allow for the participation of diverse embodiments other than literally "'show[ing] up' in rallies, town halls, marches, or protests"—actions that not all disabled people can afford to undertake (Wong, "Valuing Activism of All Kinds"). In fact, the Disability Visibility Project that Wong has created and the #CripTheVote nonpartisan online movement in which she is actively engaged vividly demonstrate the kinds of activism that she is referring to (see https://disabilityvisibilityproject.com).

  In disability studies, new concepts of activism have been developed. With their concept of "epistemic activism," Aimi Hamraie shows how activism can take place "in the relatively illegible spheres of knowledge-production and dissemination" such as architectural education, design research, various bureaucratic procedures, and code development, where disabled user-experts, architects, and designers may intervene in the process of knowledge-making and subtly reshape *what* is known, by *whom*, and *how* (Hamraie, *Building Access*, 132). In their work on new kinship imaginaries, anthropologists Rapp and Ginsburg discuss how activism can also be done "accidently." In light of the online community that filmmaker Dan Habib created through his film *Including Samuel*, its website, and its promotional materials (which Habib calls the "Including Samuel Effect"), Rapp and Ginsburg discuss how parents of "atypical children" reimagine kinship and extend those new kinship imaginaries beyond their homes to their communities, thereby becoming accidental activists (Rapp and Ginsburg, "Reverberations," 380–81).

34 Shapiro, *No Pity*, 133.

35 The Capitol Crawl protest was instrumental in the passage of the landmark Americans with Disabilities Act—a legal affordance that would enforce the building of elevators and ramps.

36 As indicated by its first constituent "crip," crip technoscience is informed by the transformation of US identity politics where the word "crip" emerged as a fluid category.

37 In her critique of anti-oppression discourses, Elizabeth Grosz argues that it is possible to think of "freedom" in different ways; freedom may concern individual choice and civil rights, implying "liberation from, or removal of, an oppressive or unfair form of constraint" (Grosz, "Feminism, Materialism, and Freedom," 140). But freedom may also concern matter, and the body's "capacity for movement and thus its multiple possibilities of action" (152). The politics embedded in activist affordances follows Grosz, who argues that we move beyond (a limited) "freedom from" a discriminatory world to (a broadened) "freedom to" bring action possibilities into life—possibilities that are otherwise unimaginable.

CHAPTER 6. AN ARCHIVE OF ACTIVIST AFFORDANCES

Earlier and much condensed versions of some of the material in chapter 6 appeared as "Vital Affordances, Occupying Niches: An Ecological Approach to Disability and Performance," in *Research in Drama Education: The Journal of Applied Theatre and Performance* 22, no. 3 (2017): 393–412; and as "On Falling Ill," in *Performance Research: A Journal of the Performing Arts* 18, no. 4 (2013): 107–15.

1 In his seminal essay "Techniques of the Body," Marcel Mauss writes, "Man's first and most natural technical object, and at the same time technical means, is his body" (75).

2 Costall, "The Meaning of Things."

3 Ingold, "Introduction," 20–21.

4 "Queer use," Ahmed writes, "might refer to how things can be used in ways other than how they were intended to be used or by those other than for whom they were intended" (Ahmed, *What's the Use?*, 44).

5 For my earlier formulations of the *necessity* of activist affordances and the politics this *necessity* creates, see Dokumacı, "Vital Affordances," 407.

6 Ahmed, *Queer Phenomenology*.

7 By this I surely do not mean to valorize and exceptionalize what in actuality can be a quite discomforting experience. I instead want to argue that while the world and its currently utilized affordances shrink with the experiencing of pain, disease, and impairment, another field of possibility opens up to make that same world afford otherwise in ways that recognize, respond to, and reciprocate these states.

8 Hamraie, *Building Access*, 20.

9 Such solicitations and invitations are inherent to the term "affordances" and used in its theorizations. For instance, in his theory of affordances, Gibson quotes Kurt Koffka, "Each thing says what it is. . . . A fruit says 'Eat me'; water says 'Drink me'" (Koffka, cited in Gibson, *The Ecological Approach*, 138). Jenny Davis and James Chouinard propose the following mechanisms for what artifacts afford: "request, demand, allow, encourage, discourage, and refuse" (Davis and Chouinard, "Theorizing Affordances," 241).

10 Ingold, "Introduction," 20.

11 Mairs, *Waist-High in the World*, 33.

12 Kafer, "Crip Kin." See Yi's website at https://www.cripcouture.org/about.html.

13 Pullin, *Design Meets Disability*, 116, 119.

14 In 2018, the Victoria and Albert Museum in London held the exhibition of Kahlo's personal artifacts and clothing. *Frida Kahlo: Making Her Self Up* demonstrates how Kahlo was a master affordance-maker. The details of her microactivist affordance-creations can, for instance, be traced in the following description in a *New York Times* review of the exhibit: "The boxy huipil blouses were made without fastenings, and could drop loosely over a back brace or plaster cast. Their short length was well suited to working while seated, whether in a chair, bed or wheelchair. The long flowing skirts covered her wasted leg, and their motion helped conceal her limp" (Judah, "Real Story behind Frida Kahlo's Style"). I am grateful to Faye Ginsburg for bringing this exhibition and Kahlo's affordance-creations to my attention.

15 Franks, "Dyslexic Objects." I found out about Franks's fascinating work in Boys's book *Doing Disability Differently* (138–39).

16 Boys, *Doing Disability Differently*, 191.

17 Such an approach can be part of what Graham Pullin terms "resonant design." Resonant design, Pullin writes, "is intended to address the needs of some people with a particular disability and other people without that disability but perhaps finding themselves in particular circumstances" (Pullin, *Design Meets Disability*, 93). Classic examples would be hearing people at a loud sports bar who watch the TV by reading closed captions, or the case of audiobooks. While audiobooks were initially designed for blind users, nowadays many sighted users also "enjoy the alternative experience of hearing a book read to them" (95).

18 Shapiro, *No Pity*, 46.

19 Hillyard, "Stump Kitchen."

20 It is no coincidence that the famous OXO Good Grips line of products, which emerged in the late 1980s, was developed together by a retired designer and his wife, who had arthritis. As Bess Williamson documents, these kitchen products, ranging from peelers to scissors, characteristically had "thick bar handles [and] oversized curves to protect the hand from sharp blades," which were of particular importance to people experiencing the loss of fine motor skills, although the products were marketed as having a universal design that was good for everyone (Williamson, *Accessible America*, 177). One of the marketing lines for the products read: "Hold the tools the way you want to hold them, not some way you're forced to hold them" (178). This tagline speaks directly to whichever affordance the users are to find in the tool in accordance with their bodily properties and needs rather than a particular action possibility imposed upon them by its designer.

21 Rolfstam and Buur, "An Institutional View," 69.

22 Ingold, "Introduction," 20.

23 S. Taylor, *Beasts of Burden*, 202.

24 Clare, *Exile and Pride*, 6.

25 S. Taylor, *Beasts of Burden*, 173.

26 D. Mitchell and Snyder, *Vital Signs*.

27 Saerberg, "The Sensorification of the Invisible," 17.

28 Saerberg, "The Sensorification of the Invisible," 16.

29 Law and Moser, "Good Passages, Bad Passages," 201.

30 Law and Moser, "Good Passages, Bad Passages," 205.

31 Saerberg, "The Sensorification of the Invisible," 16.

32 McRuer, *Crip Theory*, 9.

33 Glassé and Smith, *The New Encyclopedia of Islam*, 400.

34 Kafer, *Feminist, Queer, Crip*, 39.

35 Siebers, *Disability Theory*, 8–9.

36 Pickens, *Black Madness*, 78.

37 Kafer, *Feminist, Queer, Crip*, 27.

38 Kafer, *Feminist, Queer, Crip*, 42.

CHAPTER 7. ALWAYS IN-THE-MAKING

Earlier and much condensed versions of some of the material in chapter 7 appeared as "A Theory of Micro-activist Affordances: Disability, Improvisation and Disorienting Affordances," in *South Atlantic Quarterly* 118, no. 3 (2019): 491–519; as "Vital Affordances, Occupying Niches: An Ecological Approach to Disability and Performance," in *Research in Drama Education: The Journal of Applied Theatre and Performance* 22, no. 3 (2017): 393–412; and as "On Falling Ill," in *Performance Research: A Journal of the Performing Arts* 18, no. 4 (2013): 107–15.

1 Here, Ingold is building on George Herbert Mead. "If, as Mead argued (1977 [1938]: 97), every object is to be regarded as a 'collapsed act,'" Ingold writes,

"then *the landscape as a whole must likewise be understood as the taskscape in its embodied form*: a pattern of activities 'collapsed' into an array of features" (Ingold, *The Perception of the Environment*, 198).

2 Williamson, *Accessible America*, 68.

3 As I explained in chapter 6, the difference between activist affordances and crip technoscience lies in how they build those worlds, that is, in and through performance. In performance, use and making become inextricable from each other, AS IF an activist affordance were a dance without an end.

4 Hamraie and Fritsch, "Crip Technoscience." Hamraie and Fritsch compare "crip technoscience" with what they call "disability technoscience," that is, the products designed by experts "*for* disabled people rather than with or *by* disabled people." The tension between disability technoscience and crip technoscience goes way back. Bess Williamson notes that from the 1940s to the 1960s, the initiation of disabled people into assistive technologies happened in US hospitals under the direction of medical professionals with little or no input from patients. A patient in the early 1950s, for instance, "recalled that the hospital had 'set ideas' for how patients could feed themselves, but that he learned a different technique on his own" (Williamson, *Accessible America*, 78, 80).

5 Costall, "The Meaning of Things."

6 Scholars of anthropology, design, and architecture have already pointed out that design cannot be understood in isolation from doing, that use process can be a form of making, and that users of architecture are also its makers. See Ingold, "Introduction"; Gunn and Clausen, "Concepts of Innovation and Practice"; Hill, *Occupying Architecture*.

7 Ingold, *The Perception of the Environment*. Here I am drawing mainly upon Ingold's emphasis on "the temporality of landscape" and the "livelihood of the environment." Life, Ingold writes, "is not a principle that is separately installed inside individual organisms, and which sets them in motion upon the stage of the inanimate." Instead, it is "a name for *what is going on* in the generative field within which organic forms are located and 'held in place.'" From this perspective, the world does not just provide sustenance for life; it is itself alive, "a total movement of becoming which builds itself into the forms we see." It is precisely this livelihood of the world that becomes evident in the creation of activist affordances (Ingold, *The Perception of the Environment*, 200).

8 Ingold, *The Perception of the Environment*, 201.

9 Dokumacı, "Vital Affordances," 404.

10 Butler, *Bodies That Matter*, 31.

11 Butler, *Bodies That Matter*, 32.

12 Ingold, "Materials against Materiality," 11.

13 Haraway, *Staying with the Trouble*, 120.

14 Ahmed, "What's the Use?" In this book, Ahmed takes "*forness* as key to why use matters" (7). Accordingly, what something is "for"—through use—comes before (and as such comes to define) what something is. Forness takes us to canonized affordances.

15 Certeau, cited in Read, *Theatre and Everyday Life*, 90.
16 Read, *Theatre and Everyday Life*, 90.
17 Friedner and Cohen, "Inhabitable Worlds."
18 Read, *Theatre and Everyday Life*, 90.
19 Price, *Mad at School*, 101.

CHAPTER 8. PEOPLE AS AFFORDANCES

An earlier version of chapter 8 appeared as "People as Affordances: Building Disability Worlds through Care Intimacy," in *Current Anthropology* 61, no. s21 (2020): s97–108. Copyright © 2019 by The Wenner-Gren Foundation for Anthropological Research. All rights reserved.

1 See Al Jazeera, "Syrian Girl Who Used Tuna Cans for Legs."
2 Gibson, *Ecological Approach*, 143, 127.
3 Although I am adding "people" here to the creation of activist affordances, I could have as easily added "nonhuman animals" or "plants." There are many accounts of how disabled people may form symbiotic, enabling, and, I would add, mutually affordance-making relationships with their service animals. See for instance blind scholar and author Rod Michalko's account of navigating spaces with his guide dog Smokie (Michalko, *The Two in One*). We can imagine, for instance, how plants can also be companions and enable the affordance of relaxation to those perhaps having anxiety issues or facing isolation. My point is: there can be many "companion species," to borrow from Haraway, to add to the making of activist affordances. In this case, I added "people" because that is what my ethnographic materials have directed me to.
4 Gibson, *Ecological Approach*, 135.
5 Gibson, *Ecological Approach*, 135.
6 I borrow the idea of "leakiness" of pain from Alyson Patsavas, who develops this idea by drawing on Margrit Shildrick's concept of "leaky bodies" (Patsavas, "Recovering a Cripistemology of Pain").
7 Mingus, "Access Intimacy."
8 I should note that most, if not all, instances of people as affordances that I discuss in this chapter involve family relations. This is the case not because family relations are essential to people as affordances but because they happen to stand out in the context of the ethnographic materials and the RA-related disabilities that I examined. One could easily imagine that if my focus had been on another kind of disability (perhaps one that involves caretakers) in another locality (perhaps in care homes), then people as affordances would have materialized differently (perhaps through the involvement of caretakers). Because I have not (yet) done such ethnographic work, I can only speculate about potential variations of people as affordances based on the existing ethnographies of others. One such example is Don Kulick and Jens Rydström's fascinating ethnography of the sexual lives of significantly disabled adults in Denmark and Sweden (see Kulick and Rydström, *Loneliness and Its Opposite*). Drawing on a

comparative analysis of the two nations' histories and contemporary practices, Kulick and Rydström demonstrate how sexual lives of severely disabled adults are acknowledged, enabled, and facilitated by others in Denmark, while they are entirely rejected and blocked in Sweden. Kulick and Rydström's work provides a rich resource to speculate about what other forms that people as affordances may take, and how their emergence (or lack thereof) may bring about a complex set of ethical issues, tensions, and frictions.

9 Patsavas, "Recovering a Cripistemology of Pain," 214.

10 Patsavas, "Recovering a Cripistemology of Pain," 213.

11 Patsavas, "Recovering a Cripistemology of Pain," 215.

12 Mingus, "Access Intimacy."

13 Ingold, *The Perception of the Environment*, 189.

14 Kärki, "Not Doings as Resistance," 365.

15 Rapp and Ginsburg, "Reverberations."

16 Ginsburg and Rapp, "Cripping the New Normal," 2.

17 Rapp and Ginsburg, "Reverberations," 385, 400.

18 Rapp and Ginsburg, "Reverberations," 383.

19 While the term "new kinship imaginaries" concerns a more macro temporality (that of life course) in comparison to the rather micro scale of people as affordances, the two concepts are related, precisely because each social role, life event, or activity that the broader temporality of life course entails is itself constituted by microactions of the everyday that the term "people as affordances" refers to. Based on this constitutive link, we can imagine how this kind of affordances constructs "new kinship imaginaries" piece by piece over days, months, and years. I explore the accumulation of activist affordances over time in the next chapter.

20 Consider disability activist Sunaura Taylor's reflections on not being able to hold hands with her partner as they, a wheelchair user and a bipedal, went on strolls together: "How would my notions of how a couple is 'supposed' to interact differ if he and I had grown up in a culture where images of disabled or interabled couples were abundant, if we had seen people strolling together the way we do, with him leaning his elbow or hand on my shoulder and me leaning my head on his arm in return?" (S. Taylor, *Beasts of Burden*, 143).

21 Disability activists, advocates, and scholars have already called attention to the creative possibilities and pleasures to emerge from sexualities of disabled embodiments (see Wendell, "Toward a Feminist Theory of Disability," 119–20; Shildrick, *Dangerous Discourses of Disability*, 128; Erevelles, *Disability and Difference in Global Contexts*, 89). What I want to add is that at times, not engaging in sexual activity, no matter how involuntarily it is done, can open up new ways of imagining sexual relations as well.

22 The CLSCs are local community health services in the province of Quebec, providing free common health and social services, rehabilitation, and reintegration services.

23 This dimension of people as affordances, which captures how family members can take on the affordance of (otherwise unavailable or inaccessible) infrastructures, is in conversation with AbdouMaliq Simone's notion of "people

as infrastructure." With his notion, Simone traces how "limited resources can be put to work in many possible ways" by urban residents of the inner city of Johannesburg, where institutions and infrastructures fail and immiseration prevails (Simone, "People as Infrastructure," 426).

24 For a history of the term "parentification," see Hooper, "Parentification."

25 Gibson, *The Ecological Approach*, 135.

26 Piepzna-Samarasinha, *Care Work*, 65.

27 Piepzna-Samarasinha, *Care Work*, 65.

28 Livingston, "Insights from an African History of Disability," 121.

29 McRuer, *Crip Theory*, 7-9. There is much more to write and consider about how identities affect people as affordances, specifically, and activist affordances, in general, than I could capture in this brief paragraph. Consider, for instance, disability justice activist Leah Lakshmi Piepzna-Samarasinha's candid self-reflections in this regard. Coming from a working-class family and as a disabled femme of color, Piepzna-Samarasinha asks: "What stops us from being able to ask for care when we come from Black and brown communities, for example, who have always been the ones forced to care for others for little or no money?" We feel, they continue, "we could never, ever think about asking someone to do our dishes or clean our toilet or help us dress, because that is the work we or our families have done for little or no money during enslavement, colonial invasion, immigration, and racist poverty" (Piepzna-Samarasinha, *Care Work*, 35–36). These complex relations between intersecting identities and people as affordances are important, but exploring them in detail is out of the scope of this book.

30 Eli Clare, for instance, writes: "The mannerisms that help define gender . . . are all based upon how nondisabled people move. A woman who walks with crutches does not walk like a 'woman'; a man who uses a wheelchair and a ventilator does not move like a 'man'" (Clare, *Exile and Pride*, 130). In her analysis of solo autobiographical performances of Greg Walloch, Robert DeFelice, and Julia Trahan, Carrie Sandahl discusses how queer/crip drag performances can unveil not only the fictitiousness of gender categories but also their reliance on able-bodiedness for that fiction to continue (Sandahl, "Queering the Crip," 45). Though not writing from a disability studies perspective, Carrie Noland also questions, in a fascinating analysis, the relationship between the performance of gender and the body that may not always feel so "well." Reflecting on the enactment of "femininity" through small gestures like a curtsy, she asks: "What if in performing the curtsy the subject felt not only 'feminine' but also sore? What if the socially established meaning of the act were overwhelmed, at least momentarily, by the somatic experiences of pressure, friction, and pain? What if, in other words, the body spoke back?" (Noland, *Agency and Embodiment*, 193–94).

31 Samuels, "Six Ways of Looking at Crip Time."

32 Sheppard, "Performing Normal," 45.

33 Noland, *Agency and Embodiment*, 191.

34 Drawing on Butler's work on the performativity of gender and how heterosexual identities are constituted through repeated performances, which are

bound to fail, McRuer argues that compulsory able-bodiedness too involves its own failure. "If anything, the emphasis on identities that are constituted through repetitive performances is even more central to compulsory able-bodiedness. . . . Moreover, as with heterosexuality, this repetition is bound to fail, as the ideal able-bodied identity can never, once and for all, be achieved" (McRuer, *Crip Theory*, 9).

CHAPTER 9. DISABILITY REPERTOIRES

1 Phelan, *Unmarked*, 146.
2 Phelan, *Unmarked*, 146, 149.
3 Roach, *Cities of the Dead*; Schneider, "Performance Remains"; D. Taylor, *The Archive and the Repertoire*. "What is at risk politically," D. Taylor questions, "in thinking about embodied knowledge and performance as that which disappears? . . . Whose memories, whose trauma, 'disappear' if only archival knowledge is valorized and granted performance?" (D. Taylor, *The Archive and the Repertoire*, 193).
4 Schneider, "Performance Remains," 105.
5 Schneider, "Performance Remains," 100; D. Taylor, *The Archive and the Repertoire*.
6 Schneider, "Performance Remains," 103
7 D. Taylor, *The Archive and the Repertoire*, xvii.
8 I am here referring to Alison Kafer's definition where she writes: "Crip time is flex time not just expanded but exploded" (Kafer, *Feminist, Queer, Crip*, 27).
9 Kafer, *Feminist, Queer, Crip*, 27.
10 Ljuslinder, Ellis, and Vikström, "Cripping Time," 35.
11 This is not to say that the process of coming to terms with one's disability and the realities of a progressive disability are all smooth and easy. As Ellen Samuels observes of her experiences of becoming (further) disabled and sick, there can be less celebratory aspects of crip time, and therefore we may need to "allow ourselves to feel the pain of crip time, its melancholy, its brokenness" (Samuels, "Six Ways of Looking at Crip Time"). Pointing at the "multiple ways of moving through crip time," Emma Sheppard similarly writes: "Crip time includes—must include—time to be unsure, ambivalent about disability, and time to mourn future possibilities that can no longer be. We need the time to be sad, to be frustrated, even as we acknowledge that the reason for our sadness and frustration is ableist structures, norms, and expectations about how our bodyminds work and move through places and times" (Sheppard, "Performing Normal But Becoming Crip," 45).
12 Ljuslinder, Ellis, and Vikström, "Cripping Time," 35
13 See Halberstam and Halberstam, *In a Queer Time and Place*; Muñoz, *Cruising Utopia*; Kafer, *Feminist, Queer, Crip*, 25–46; Kuppers, "Crip Time"; Samuels, "Six Ways of Looking at Crip Time." See also the special collection "Cripping Time: Understanding the Life Course through the Lens of Ableism," edited by

Ljuslinder, Ellis, and Vikström. By naming the heading of this section "In the Long Run," I am drawing on anthropologist Susan Reynolds Whyte's work in Eastern Uganda, where she explores "the long run of lifetimes" lived with disability (Whyte, "In the Long Run," S132).

14 "Disability," Ljuslinder, Ellis, and Vikström write, "disrupts the stages of the life course both in terms of when normative life stages are achieved (if ever) and the time it takes to complete activities" (Ljuslinder, Ellis, and Vikström, "Cripping Time," 36).

15 Muñoz, *Cruising Utopia*, 186; Kafer, *Feminist, Queer, Crip*, 34–35.

16 Kafer, *Feminist, Queer, Crip*, 27.

17 Kafer, *Feminist, Queer, Crip*, 27.

18 Disability does not have to be progressive for the activist affordances to leave their effects on the environment. For example, in Jérôme's home setting, the way its furniture is organized and the way his family members carefully find their way around demonstrate that the experience of disability (whether acquired or congenital, whether progressive or not) always already involves a literal remaking of the materiality of the environment in a way that does not "look," "sound," or "feel" so *straight*.

19 Piepzna-Samarasinha, *Care Work*, 241.

20 Kafer, *Feminist, Queer, Crip*, 3. Here, I am sharing the same wish, or "desire," with Kafer. "I have written this book," Kafer candidly writes, "because I desire crip futures: futures that embrace disabled people, futures that imagine disability differently, futures that support multiple ways of being." And not surprisingly, this "desire is born largely of absence. We lack such futures in this present" (45).

CHAPTER 10. SPECULATIONS FOR A SHRINKING PLANET

1 Gibson, *The Ecological Approach*, 138.

2 In her book *Expulsions*, sociologist Saskia Sassen writes about how mining, manufacturing, and extraction industries have caused about 40 percent of the earth's agricultural land to be severely degraded and eventually die (Sassen, *Expulsions*, 152). The fertilizer that drains away from industrialized agricultural lands to the ocean has deprived at least four hundred ocean zones of oxygen, gradually killing marine life (187–88). Further, the gyres of the world's oceans, which have become colossal plastic dumps, literally asphyxiate marine life (150). These cascading deaths of lands, waters, and marine life, in turn, translate into food insecurity and ongoing precarity for already resource-deprived populations of the world.

3 Shire, "What They Did Yesterday Afternoon," cited in A. Mitchell and Todd, "Earth Violence."

4 As I discussed in chapter 5, disability justice activists and some critical disability studies scholars have already pointed out the need to think about disability justice and liberation beyond the human. San Francisco–based performance

project Sins Invalid has written (Sins Invalid, *Skin, Tooth, and Bone*), talked (https://www.sinsinvalid.org/podcast), and performed about (Sins Invalid, *We Love Like Barnacles*) the inextricability of disability justice and climate justice. Disability scholar, activist, and artist Sunaura Taylor has extensively written about the disablement of animals through exploitative human activities and depicted shared vulnerability and disability among species in her artwork (see S. Taylor, *Beasts of Burden*). See also Kafer, *Feminist, Queer, Crip*; Clare, *Brilliant Imperfection*; Wheeler, "Moving Together Side by Side"; Belser, "Disabled People Cannot Be 'Expected Losses.'"

5   See Center for Climate, Health, and the Global Environment, "Coronavirus and Climate Change"; United Nations Environment Programme and International Livestock Research Institute, "Preventing the Next Pandemic."

6   Since the outbreak of the pandemic, many have pointed out how the realities of disability have suddenly become the realities of many, albeit in highly disproportionate ways. From being denied access to public spaces, to restricted movement, confinement, and dependency on basic support systems (like food delivery); from online education to working from home or dealing with unemployment; from managing sanitary rituals and equipment to feelings of loneliness, isolation, and precarity, COVID-19 has introduced to the broader public many of the issues that disabled people have long been facing. Disabled people have emphasized how relevant their knowledge and wisdom are to our times and have argued that their creativity, resourcefulness, and expertise can provide highly practical models that can be mobilized to respond to the conditions of the pandemic (see Davids et al., "Coronavirus Wisdom"; Ignagni et al., "Crips and COVID in Canada"; Kukla, "Disability during a Pandemic"; Loner and Rosenau, "Crip Currencies"; Shew, "Let COVID-19 Expand Awareness"; Wong, "I'm Disabled and Need a Ventilator").

7   Davids et al., "Coronavirus Wisdom from a Social Justice Lens."

8   Berne and Raditz, "To Survive Climate Catastrophe."

9   S. Taylor, "Age of Disability."

10 Tsing et al., *Arts of Living on a Damaged Planet.*

11 Haraway, *Staying with the Trouble*, 101.

12 It is important to keep in mind that Canguilhem's "word of choice," as Kevin Gotkin points out, is "disease," not "disability." This initial check aside, I concur with Gotkin that there is much we can import from Canguilhem's philosophy to disability scholarship, and that his take on disease is "helpfully aligned with disability scholars' activist and epistemological goals" (Gotkin, "The Norm___ and the Pathological").

13 Canguilhem, *The Normal and the Pathological*, 188.

14 Canguilhem, *The Normal and the Pathological*, 185.

15 Canguilhem, *The Normal and the Pathological*, 186.

16 Canguilhem, *The Normal and the Pathological*, 228, 185.

17 Scarry, *The Body in Pain*, 166.

18 Scarry, *The Body in Pain*, 22; emphasis added.

19 Scarry, *The Body in Pain*, 285.

20 Scarry, *The Body in Pain*, 165.

21 Scarry, *The Body in Pain*, 169.

22 Scarry, *The Body in Pain*, 162.

23 Scarry, *The Body in Pain*, 164, 289.

24 Scarry, *The Body in Pain*, 164.

25 Diamond, *Performance and Cultural Politics*, 1.

26 Muñoz, *Cruising Utopia*, 1.

27 Muñoz, *Cruising Utopia*, 26.

28 Kafer, *Feminist, Queer, Crip*, 32. "The task, then," Kafer writes, "is not so much to refuse the future as to imagine disability and disability futures otherwise" (34).

29 Muñoz, *Cruising Utopia*, 1.

30 Kafer, *Feminist, Queer, Crip*, 3.

31 Scarry, *The Body in Pain*, 315.

32 Muñoz, *Cruising Utopia*, 49, 56.

33 Williamson, *Accessible America*, 127.

34 Hamraie, *Building Access*, 97. In a demonstration that took place in Denver in 1978, wheelchair users protested the lack of curb cuts at street corners and intersections by bringing hammers and picks and carving out their own curb cuts (Guffey, *Designing Disability*, 151). There are unfounded rumors that disability activists in the 1960s had done the same in Berkeley, California, but as a covert protest in the middle of the night (see Hamraie, *Building Access*, 95; Williamson, *Accessible America*, 127). Such "guerrilla curb-cutting," which essentially was against the status quo, Hamraie argues, was then followed by the materialization of assiminalist "liberal curb cuts" instituted en masse by the city of Berkeley (Hamraie, *Building Access*, 97).

35 Friedner and Cohen, "Inhabitable Worlds."

36 Muñoz, *Cruising Utopia*, 1.

37 Margaret Price, cited in Dolmage, "Universal Design."

38 Ahmed, *Queer Phenomenology*, 62.

39 Scarry, *The Body in Pain*, 291.

40 McRuer (*Crip Theory*; *Crip Times*), Dolmage (*Academic Ableism*), and D. Mitchell and Snyder (*The Biopolitics of Disability*), among others, have powerfully called attention to the detrimental effects of neoliberalism on disabled people, including austerity measures, privatization of infrastructures, the offloading of the provision of welfare services from the state onto individuals, and ongoing cuts to social services and benefits that continue to harm most marginalized populations. In the context of design cultures, Ezio Manzini also cautions against misinterpretations and appropriations of social innovation projects by a neoliberal agenda. Social innovation projects, he writes, "could [inadvertently] become the acceptable face of a program of cuts in public social budgets (supporting this program with the assumption that civil society should step in and deliver services previously delivered by the welfare state)" (Manzini, *Design, When Everybody Designs*, 15).

41 D. Taylor, *The Archive and the Repertoire*, 16.

42 Fry, *Defuturing*, 10; Fry, "Design for/by 'The Global South,'" 30.

43 Fry, *Defuturing*, 45.

44 Dilnot, "Tony Fry's Defuturing," xi. Interestingly, Dilnot is defining Fry's concept of "defuturing" in contrast to Elaine Scarry's conceptualization of making in relation to Western civilization.

45 Self-devouring growth is a form of growth that is "predicated on uninhibited consumption." Its dictum of "grow" is "so powerful that it obscures the destruction it portends" (Livingston, *Self-Devouring Growth*, 5). "Within this telos of [unrestrained] growth," Livingston asks, "what kind of bios is possible?" (34).

46 Moore, "The Capitalocene," 613.

47 Moore, "The Capitalocene," 611.

48 Haraway, *Staying with Trouble*, 99.

49 Tsing et al., *Arts of Living on a Damaged Planet*, 176; Haraway, *Staying with the Trouble*, 101.

50 Escobar, *Designs for the Pluriverse*, 40. With the phrase "act futurally," Escobar is referring to Tony Fry's conceptualizations of "defuturing" and "futuring." For the concept "response-ability," see Haraway, *Staying with the Trouble*, 2.

51 Manzini, *Design, When Everybody Designs*, 26.

52 Think of durational performances and extreme cases of deprivation. Hunger strikes, Diana Taylor writes, are "an excruciating example of 'durational' performance of noncompliance by those who have lost control of everything except their bodies" (D. Taylor, *Performance*, 24). Slave suicides found in archives and folk tales are the enactments, according to Paul Gilroy, of "death *as* agency" by those who are made to live with the death of their own agency (Gilroy, *The Black Atlantic*, 63; emphasis added). The Tunisian street vendor Tarek al-Tayeb Mohamed Bouazizi's self-immolation which instigated the Arab Spring, Mark LeVine and Bryan Reynolds suggest, can be considered as "an act of radical anti-government performance activism" by someone who had been dispossessed of any means to make a living within a debilitating necropolitics (LeVine and Reynolds, "Theatre of Immediacy," 201). In bringing these particular situations and histories, I surely do not mean to simplify the complexity of their situatedness, locality, and historicity. Nor do I mean to romanticize and embed these acts with "intrinsic morality or meanings" (Makley, "The Political Life of Dead Bodies") that may or may not be intended by their agents. Rather, I wish to point out the different forms that agency may take, including the agency of those who had entirely been deprived of affordances, except those that can be done on, in, and through their bodies. (For further discussions on the agency of dead bodies, see Kim, "Continuing Presence of Discarded Bodies." In this article Kim introduces the notion of "necro-activism," with which she names the political significance that dead bodies may take in their afterlife through their incorporation into activism.)

BIBLIOGRAPHY

Abad, Antoni. "Communities + Mobile Phones = Collaborative Webcasts." Megafone .net, 2004. https://megafone.net/site/index.

Ahmed, Sara. *Queer Phenomenology: Orientations, Objects, Others*. Durham, NC: Duke University Press, 2006.

Ahmed, Sara. *What's the Use? On the Uses of Use*. Durham, NC: Duke University Press, 2019.

Alaimo, Stacy. "Foreword." In *Disability Studies and the Environmental Humanities*, edited by Sarah Jaquette Ray and Jay Sibara, ix–xvi. Lincoln: University of Nebraska Press, 2017.

Albright, Ann Cooper. *Choreographing Difference: The Body and Identity in Contemporary Dance*. Middletown, CT: Wesleyan University Press, 1997.

Al Jazeera. "Syrian Girl Who Used Tuna Cans for Legs Receives Prosthetic Limbs." July 7, 2018. https://www.aljazeera.com/news/2018/7/7/syrian-girl-who-used -tuna-cans-for-legs-receives-prosthetic-limbs.

Asad, Talal. "Agency and Pain: An Exploration." *Culture and Religion* 1, no. 1 (2000): 29–60.

Austin, John Langshaw. *How to Do Things with Words*, 2nd ed. Cambridge, MA: Harvard University Press, 1975.

Baerentsen, Klaus B., and Johan Trettvik. "An Activity Theory Approach to Affordance." In *Proceedings of the Second Nordic Conference on Human-Computer Interaction*, 51–60. New York: Association for Computing Machinery, 2002.

Barker, Clare, and Stuart Murray. "Disabling Postcolonialism: Global Disability Cultures and Democratic Criticism." *Journal of Literary and Cultural Disability Studies* 4, no. 3 (2010): 219–36.

Bauman, Hansel. "DEAFSPACE." In *Deaf Gain: Raising the Stakes for Human Diversity*, edited by H-Dirksen L. Bauman and Joseph J. Murray, 375–401. Minneapolis: University of Minnesota Press, 2014.

Bauman, H-Dirksen L., and Joseph J. Murray, eds. *Deaf Gain: Raising the Stakes for Human Diversity*. Minneapolis: University of Minnesota Press, 2014.

Bellacasa, María Puig de la. *Matters of Care: Speculative Ethics in More Than Human Worlds*. Minneapolis: University of Minnesota Press, 2017.

Belser, Julia. "Vital Wheels: Disability, Relationality, and the Queer Animacy of Vibrant Things." *Hypatia* 31, no. 1 (2016): 5–21.

Belser, Julia Watts. "Disabled People Cannot Be 'Expected Losses' in the Climate Crisis." Truthout, September 20, 2019. https://truthout.org/articles/disabled -people-cannot-be-expected-losses-in-the-climate-crisis/.

Bendelow, Gillian A., and Simon J. Williams. "Transcending the Dualisms: Towards a Sociology of Pain." *Sociology of Health and Illness* 17, no. 2 (1995): 139–65.

Berne, Patty. "Disability Justice—a Working Draft by Patty Berne." *Sins Invalid* (blog), June 10, 2015. https://www.sinsinvalid.org/blog/disability-justice-a -working-draft-by-patty-berne.

Berne, Patty, and Vanessa Raditz. "To Survive Climate Catastrophe, Look to Queer and Disabled Folks." *YES! Magazine*, July 31, 2019. https://www.yesmagazine.org /opinion/2019/07/31/climate-change-queer-disabled-organizers.

Blaser, Mario. "Ontological Conflicts and the Stories of Peoples in Spite of Europe: Toward a Conversation on Political Ontology." *Current Anthropology* 54, no. 5 (2013): 547–68.

Bloomfield, Brian P., Yvonne Latham, and Theo Vurdubakis. "Bodies, Technologies and Action Possibilities: When Is an Affordance?" *Sociology* 44, no. 3 (2010): 415–33.

Born, Georgina, Eric Lewis, and Bill Straw, eds. *Improvisation and Social Aesthetics*. Durham, NC: Duke University Press, 2017.

Bourdieu, Pierre. *The Logic of Practice*. Stanford, CA: Stanford University Press, 1990.

Boys, Jos. *Doing Disability Differently: An Alternative Handbook on Architecture, Dis/ability and Designing for Everyday Life*. London: Routledge, 2014.

Burns, Nicola, Kevin Paterson, and Nick Watson. "An Inclusive Outdoors? Disabled People's Experiences of Countryside Leisure Services." *Leisure Studies* 28, no. 4 (2009): 403–17.

Butler, Judith. *Bodies That Matter: On the Discursive Limits of "Sex."* New York: Routledge, 1993.

Cabral, Reniel B., and Rollan C. Geronimo. "How Important Are Coral Reefs to Food Security in the Philippines? Diving Deeper Than National Aggregates and Averages." *Marine Policy* 91 (2018): 136–41.

Cadena, Marisol de la. "Indigenous Cosmopolitics in the Andes: Conceptual Reflections Beyond 'Politics.'" *Cultural Anthropology* 25, no. 2 (2010): 334–70.

Campbell, Fiona Kumari. "Inciting Legal Fictions: 'Disability's' Date with Ontology and the Ableist Body of Law." *Griffith Law Review* 10, no. 1 (2001): 42–62.

Canguilhem, Georges. "Health: Crude Concept and Philosophical Question." *Public Culture* 20, no. 3 (2008): 467–77.

Canguilhem, Georges. *The Normal and the Pathological*. New York: Zone Books, 1989.

Center for Climate, Health, and the Global Environment. "Coronavirus and Climate Change." C-CHANGE, Harvard T. H. Chan School of Public Health, May 19, 2020. https://www.hsph.harvard.edu/c-change/subtopics/coronavirus -and-climate-change/.

Cesari, P., F. Formenti, and P. Olivato. "A Common Perceptual Parameter for Stair Climbing for Children, Young and Old Adults." *Human Movement Science* 22, no. 1 (2003): 111–24.

Cesari, Paola. "An Invariant Guiding Stair Descent by Young and Old Adults." *Experimental Aging Research* 31, no. 4 (2005): 441–55.

Chapman, Owen, and Kim Sawchuk. "Research-Creation: Intervention, Analysis and 'Family Resemblances.'" *Canadian Journal of Communication* 37, no. 1 (2012): 5–26.

Chemero, Anthony. "An Outline of a Theory of Affordances." *Ecological Psychology* 15, no. 2 (2003): 181–95.

Chen, Mel Y. *Animacies: Biopolitics, Racial Mattering, and Queer Affect.* Perverse Modernities. Durham, NC: Duke University Press, 2012.

Clapham, David. "The Embodied Use of the Material Home: An Affordance Approach." *Housing, Theory and Society* 28, no. 4 (2011): 360–76.

Clare, Eli. *Brilliant Imperfection: Grappling with Cure.* Durham, NC: Duke University Press, 2017.

Clare, Eli. *Exile and Pride: Disability, Queerness, and Liberation.* Durham, NC: Duke University Press, 2015.

Clare, Eli. "Notes on Natural Worlds, Disabled Bodies, and a Politics of Cure." In *Disability Studies and the Environmental Humanities*, edited by Sarah Jaquette Ray and Jay Sibara, 242–65. Lincoln: University of Nebraska Press, 2017.

Clarke, Adele, and Donna Haraway, eds. *Making Kin Not Population: Reconceiving Generations.* Chicago: Prickly Paradigm Press, 2018.

Costall, Alan. "The Meaning of Things." *Social Analysis* 41, no. 1 (1997): 76–85.

Costall, Alan. "Socializing Affordances." *Theory and Psychology* 5, no. 4 (1995): 467–81.

Costanza-Chock, Sasha. *Design Justice: Community-Led Practices to Build the Worlds We Need.* Cambridge, MA: MIT Press, 2020.

Crow, L. "Including All Our Lives: Renewing the Social Model of Disability." In *Encounters with Strangers: Feminism and Disability*, edited by Jenny Morris, 206–26. London: Women's Press, 1996.

Crutzen, Paul J. "Geology of Mankind." *Nature* 415, no. 6867 (2002): 23.

Dant, Tim. *Discourse and Material Culture.* Maidenhead, UK: Open University Press, 2005.

Davids, J. D., Evvie Ormon, Crissaris Sarnelli, and Elandria Williams. "Coronavirus Wisdom from a Social Justice Lens." Hosted by Kate Werning. *Irresistible*, March 10, 2020. https://irresistible.org/podcast/corona.

Davis, Jenny L., and James B. Chouinard. "Theorizing Affordances: From Request to Refuse." *Bulletin of Science, Technology and Society* 36, no. 4 (2016): 241–48.

Democracy Now! "Naomi Klein: 4,645 Deaths in Puerto Rico from Hurricane Maria Were 'State-Sponsored Mass Killing.'" June 6, 2018. https://www.democracynow.org/2018/6/6/naomi_klein_4_645_deaths_in.

Diamond, Elin. *Performance and Cultural Politics.* New York: Routledge, 1996.

Dilnot, Clive. "Tony Fry's Defuturing: A New Design Philosophy." In *Defuturing: A New Design Philosophy,* by Tony Fry, x–xxiii. London: Bloomsbury, 2020.

"Disability Visibility Project." Accessed March 16, 2021. https://disabilityvisibilityproject.com/.

Dokumacı, Arseli. "Disability as Method: Interventions in the Habitus of Ableism through Media-Creation." *Disability Studies Quarterly* 38, no. 3 (2018). https://doi.org/10.18061/dsq.v38i3.6491.

Dokumacı, Arseli. "On Falling Ill." *Performance Research: A Journal of the Performing Arts* 18, no. 4 (2013): 107–15.

Dokumacı, Arseli. "People as Affordances: Building Disability Worlds through Care Intimacy." *Current Anthropology* 61, no. S21 (2020): S97–108.

Dokumacı, Arseli. "A Theory of Microactivist Affordances: Disability, Disorientations, and Improvisation." *South Atlantic Quarterly* 118, no. 3 (2019): 491–519.

Dokumacı, Arseli. "Vital Affordances, Occupying Niches: An Ecological Approach to Disability and Performance." *Research in Drama Education: The Journal of Applied Theatre and Performance* 22, no. 3 (2017): 393–412.

Dolmage, Jay. *Academic Ableism: Disability and Higher Education.* Ann Arbor: University of Michigan Press, 2017.

Dolmage, Jay. "Universal Design: Places to Start." *Disability Studies Quarterly* 35, no. 2 (2015). https://doi.org/10.18061/dsq.v35i2.4632.

Dunne, Anthony, and Fiona Raby. *Speculative Everything: Design, Fiction, and Social Dreaming.* Cambridge, MA: MIT Press, 2013.

Erevelles, Nirmala. *Disability and Difference in Global Contexts: Enabling a Transformative Body Politic.* New York: Palgrave Macmillan, 2011.

Escobar, Arturo. *Designs for the Pluriverse: Radical Interdependence, Autonomy, and the Making of Worlds.* Durham, NC: Duke University Press, 2018.

Fannin, Maria. "Labour Pain, 'Natal Politics' and Reproductive Justice for Black Birth Givers." *Body and Society* 25, no. 3 (2019): 22–48.

Faraj, Samer, and Bijan Azad. "The Materiality of Technology: An Affordance Perspective." In *Materiality and Organizing: Social Interaction in a Technological World,* edited by Paul Leonardi, Bonnie Nardi, and Jannis Kallinikos, 237–58. Oxford: Oxford University Press, 2013.

Flach, John M., Pieter Jan Stappers, and Fred A. Voorhorst. "Beyond Affordances: Closing the Generalization Gap between Design and Cognitive Science." *Design Issues* 33, no. 1 (2017): 76–89.

Flanagan, Bob. *The Pain Journal.* Cambridge, MA: Semiotext(e), 2000.

Foucault, Michel. *Archaeology of Knowledge.* Translated by A. M. Sheridan Smith. New York: Vintage, 2010.

Franks, Henry. "Dyslexic Objects: Henry Franks." HenryFranks, 2015. https://henryfranks.net/Dyslexic-Objects.

Freund, Peter. "Bodies, Disability and Spaces: The Social Model and Disabling Spatial Organisations." *Disability and Society* 16, no. 5 (2001): 689–706.

Friedner, Michele. "How the Disabled Body Unites the National Body: Disability as 'Feel Good' Diversity in Urban India." *Contemporary South Asia* 25, no. 4 (2017): 347–63.

Friedner, Michele, and Emily Cohen. "Inhabitable Worlds: Troubling Disability, Debility, and Ability Narratives." *Somatosphere* (blog), April 20, 2015. http://somatosphere.net/2015/inhabitable-worlds-troubling-disability-debility-and-ability-narratives.html/.

Friedner, Michele, and Jamie Osborne. "Audit Bodies: Embodied Participation, Disability Universalism, and Accessibility in India." *Antipode* 45 (2013): 43–60.

Friedner, Michele, and Jamie Osborne. "New Disability Mobilities and Accessibilities in Urban India." *City and Society* 27, no. 1 (2015): 9–29.

Friedner, Michele, and Karen Weingarten. "Introduction: Disorienting Disability." *South Atlantic Quarterly* 118, no. 3 (2019): 483–90.

Fry, Tony. *Defuturing: A New Design Philosophy*. London: Bloomsbury, 2020.

Fry, Tony. "Design for/by 'The Global South.'" *Design Philosophy Papers* 15, no. 1 (2017): 3–37.

Garland-Thomson, Rosemarie. "The Case for Conserving Disability." *Journal of Bioethical Inquiry: An Interdisciplinary Forum for Ethical and Legal Debate* 9, no. 3 (2012): 339–55.

Garland-Thomson, Rosemarie. "Disability Studies: A Field Emerged." *American Quarterly* 65, no. 4 (2013): 915–26.

Garland-Thomson, Rosemarie. *Extraordinary Bodies: Figuring Physical Disability in American Culture and Literature*. New York: Columbia University Press, 1997.

Garland-Thomson, Rosemarie. "Feminist Disability Studies." *Signs: Journal of Women in Culture and Society* 30, no. 2 (2005): 1557–87.

Garland-Thomson, Rosemarie. "Misfits: A Feminist Materialist Disability Concept." *Hypatia* 26, no. 3 (2011): 591–609.

Garland-Thomson, Rosemarie. *Staring: How We Look*. Illus. ed. Oxford: Oxford University Press, 2009.

Genest, Gabriel Blouin. "The Body as Resistance Art/ifact: Disability Activism during the 2012 Quebec Student Movement." In *Mobilizing Metaphor: Art, Culture, and Disability Activism in Canada*, edited by Michael Orsini and Christine Kelly, 260–78. Vancouver: UBC Press, 2016.

Ghai, Anita. "Disability in the Indian Context: Post-colonial Perspectives." In *Disability/Postmodernity: Embodying Disability Theory*, edited by Tom Shakespeare and Mairian Corker, 88–100. London: Continuum, 2002.

Gibson, James J. *The Ecological Approach to Visual Perception*. Mahwah, NJ: Lawrence Erlbaum, 2015.

Gibson, James J. "New Reasons for Realism." *Synthese* 17, no. 1 (1967): 162–72.

Gibson, James J. "Notes on Affordances." In *Reasons for Realism*, edited by Edward Reed and Rebecca Jones, 401–18.

Gibson, James J. *Reasons for Realism: Selected Essays of James J. Gibson*. Edited by Edward Reed and Rebecca Jones. Milton, UK: Routledge, 2019.

Gibson, James J. *The Senses Considered as Perceptual Systems*. Boston: Houghton Mifflin, 1966.

Gilroy, Paul. *The Black Atlantic: Modernity and Double Consciousness*. London: Verso, 1993.

Ginsburg, Faye, and Rayna Rapp. "Cripping the New Normal: Making Disability Count." *ALTER: European Journal of Disability Research* 11, no. 3 (2017): 179–92.

Ginsburg, Faye, and Rayna Rapp. "Disability Worlds." *Annual Review of Anthropology* 42, no. 1 (2013): 53–68.

Ginsburg, G. P. "The Ecological Perception Debate: An Affordance of the Journal for the Theory of Social Behaviour." *Journal for the Theory of Social Behaviour* 20, no. 4 (1990): 347–64.

Gissen, David. "Why Are There So Few Disabled Architects and Architecture Students?" *Architect's Newspaper*, June 15, 2018. https://www.archpaper.com/2018/06/disability-education-of-architects/.

Glassé, Cyril, and Huston Smith. *The New Encyclopedia of Islam*. 3rd ed. Lanham, MD: Rowman and Littlefield, 2008.

Gleeson, Brendan. "Disability and the Open City." *Urban Studies* 38, no. 2 (2001): 251–65.

Goodley, Dan. "Dis/entangling Critical Disability Studies." *Disability and Society* 28, no. 5 (2013): 631–44.

Gotkin, Kevin. "The Norm___ and the Pathological." *Disability Studies Quarterly* 36, no. 1 (2016). https://doi.org/10.18061/dsq.v36i1.4281.

Grech, Shaun. "Decolonising Eurocentric Disability Studies: Why Colonialism Matters in the Disability and Global South Debate." *Social Identities* 21, no. 1 (2015): 6–21.

Grech, Shaun, and Karen Soldatic. "Disability and Colonialism: (Dis)encounters and Anxious Intersectionalities." *Social Identities* 21, no. 1 (2015): 1–5.

Grech, Shaun, and Karen Soldatic. *Disability in the Global South: The Critical Handbook*. Cham, Switzerland: Springer, 2016.

Grosz, Elizabeth. *Architecture from the Outside: Essays on Virtual and Real Space*. Cambridge, MA: MIT Press, 2001.

Grosz, Elizabeth. "Feminism, Materialism, and Freedom." In *New Materialisms: Ontology, Agency, and Politics*, edited by Diana H. Coole and Samantha Frost, 139–57. Durham, NC: Duke University Press, 2010.

Guffey, Elizabeth. *Designing Disability: Symbols, Space, and Society*. London: Bloomsbury, 2018.

Gunn, Wendy, and Christian Clausen. "Conceptions of Innovation and Practice: Designing Indoor Climate." In *Design Anthropology: Theory and Practice*, edited by Wendy Gunn, Ton Otto, and Rachel Charlotte Smith, 159–79. London: Bloomsbury, 2013.

Gunn, Wendy, Ton Otto, and Rachel Charlotte Smith, eds. *Design Anthropology: Theory and Practice*. London: Bloomsbury, 2013.

Halberstam, Jack. *In a Queer Time and Place: Transgender Bodies, Subcultural Lives*. New York: NYU Press, 2005.

Hamraie, Aimi. *Building Access: Universal Design and the Politics of Disability.* Minneapolis: University of Minnesota Press, 2017.

Hamraie, Aimi, and Kelly Fritsch. "Crip Technoscience Manifesto." *Catalyst: Feminism, Theory, Technoscience* 5, no. 1 (2019): 1–33.

Haraway, Donna J. *Staying with the Trouble: Making Kin in the Chthulucene.* Durham, NC: Duke University Press, 2016.

Haraway, Donna J. *When Species Meet.* Minneapolis: University of Minnesota Press, 2008.

Haraway, Donna, Noboru Ishikawa, Scott F. Gilbert, Kenneth Olwig, Anna L. Tsing, and Nils Bubandt. "Anthropologists Are Talking—About the Anthropocene." *Ethnos* 81, no. 3 (2016): 535–64. https://www.tandfonline.com/doi/pdf/10.1080/00141844.2015.1105838.

Hartblay, Cassandra. "Disability Expertise: Claiming Disability Anthropology." *Current Anthropology* 61, no. S21 (2019): S26–36.

Hartblay, Cassandra. "Good Ramps, Bad Ramps: Centralized Design Standards and Disability Access in Urban Russian Infrastructure." *American Ethnologist* 44, no. 1 (2017): 9–22.

Hartblay, Cassandra, Joseph D. Hankins, and Melissa L. Caldwell. "Keywords for Ethnography and Design." Theorizing the Contemporary, *Fieldsights*, March 29, 2018. https://culanth.org/fieldsights/series/keywords-for-ethnography-and-design.

Heft, Harry. "Affordances and the Body: An Intentional Analysis of Gibson's Ecological Approach to Visual Perception." *Journal for the Theory of Social Behaviour* 19, no. 1 (1989): 1–30.

Heft, Harry. "Affordances, Dynamic Experience, and the Challenge of Reification." *Ecological Psychology* 15, no. 2 (2003): 149–80.

Heft, Harry. "An Ecological Approach to Psychology." *Review of General Psychology* 17, no. 2 (2013): 162–67.

Heft, Harry. *Ecological Psychology in Context: James Gibson, Roger Barker, and the Legacy of William James's Radical Empiricism.* New Jersey: Lawrence Erlbaum Associates, 2001.

Hendren, Sara, and Caitrin Lynch. "This Counts Too: Engineering at Home." Engineering at Home. Accessed February 27, 2021. http://engineeringathome.org/manifesto.

Hill, Jonathan, ed. *Occupying Architecture: Between the Architect and the User.* New York: Routledge, 1998.

Hillyard, Alexis. "Stump Kitchen." Stump Kitchen, 2018. https://www.stumpkitchen.com.

Holbraad, Martin. "Can the Thing Speak?" OAC Press, *Working Papers Series* 7 (2011).

Holmes, Martha Stoddard. "Pain." In *Keywords for Disability Studies*, edited by Rachel Adams, Benjamin Reiss, and David Serlin, 133–34. New York: NYU Press, 2015.

Hooper, Lisa M. "Parentification." In *Encyclopedia of Adolescence*, edited by Roger J. R. Levesque, 1–10. Cham, Switzerland: Springer, 2017.

Hutchby, Ian. "Technologies, Texts and Affordances." *Sociology* 35, no. 2 (2001): 441–56.

Ignagni, Esther, Eliza Chandler, and Loree Erickson. "Crips and COVID in Canada." *iHuman* (blog), October 13, 2020. https://www.sheffield.ac.uk/ihuman/covid-19 -blog/disability-and-covid-19-global-impacts/crips-and-covid-canada.

Imrie, Rob. "Architects' Conceptions of the Human Body." *Environment and Planning D: Society and Space* 21, no. 1 (2003): 47–65.

Imrie, Rob. "The Body, Disability and Le Corbusier's Conception of the Radiant Environment." In *Mind and Body Spaces: Geographies of Illness, Impairment and Disability*, edited by Ruth Butler and Hester Parr, 25–44. London: Routledge, 2005.

Imrie, Rob. "Oppression, Disability and Access in the Built Environment." In *Disability Reader: Social Science Perspectives*, edited by Tom Shakespeare, 129–46. London: Continuum, 1998.

Imrie, Robert, and Peter Hall. *Inclusive Design: Designing and Developing Accessible Environments*. London: Spon Press, 2001.

Imrie, Rob, and Kim Kullman. "Designing with Care and Caring with Design." In *Care and Design: Bodies, Buildings, Cities*, edited by Charlotte Bates, Rob Imrie, and Kim Kullman, 1–17. Chichester, UK: Wiley Blackwell, 2017.

Imrie, Rob, and Marion Kumar. "Focusing on Disability and Access in the Built Environment." *Disability and Society* 13, no. 3 (1998): 357–74.

Ingold, Tim. "Introduction: The Perception of the User-Producer." In *Design and Anthropology*, edited by Wendy Gunn and Jared Donovan, 19–33. Farnham, UK: Ashgate, 2012.

Ingold, Tim. "Materials against Materiality." *Archaeological Dialogues* 14, no. 1 (2007): 1–16.

Ingold, Tim. *The Perception of the Environment: Essays on Livelihood, Dwelling and Skill*. London: Routledge, 2000.

Ingstad, Benedicte, and Susan Reynolds Whyte. *Disability and Culture*. Berkeley: University of California Press, 1995.

Jackson, Liz. "We Are the Original Lifehackers." *New York Times*, May 30, 2018. https://www.nytimes.com/2018/05/30/opinion/disability-design-lifehacks.html.

James, William. "Is Life Worth Living?" *Journal of Ethics* 6, no. 1 (1895): 1–24.

James, William. *The Principles of Psychology*. Vol. 2. New York: Henry Holt, 1910.

Jones, Cara E. "The Pain of Endo Existence: Toward a Feminist Disability Studies Reading of Endometriosis." *Hypatia* 31, no. 3 (2016): 554–71.

Judah, Hettie. "The Real Story behind Frida Kahlo's Style." *New York Times*, June 15, 2018. https://www.nytimes.com/2018/06/15/fashion/frida-kahlo-museum -london.html.

Kafer, Alison. "Crip Kin, Manifesting." *Catalyst: Feminism, Theory, Technoscience* 5, no. 1 (2019). https://catalystjournal.org/index.php/catalyst/article/view/29618.

Kafer, Alison. *Feminist, Queer, Crip*. Bloomington: Indiana University Press, 2013.

Kärki, Kaisa. "Not Doings as Resistance." *Philosophy of the Social Sciences* 48, no. 4 (2018): 364–84.

Kim, Eunjung. "Continuing Presence of Discarded Bodies: Occupational Harm, Necro-activism, and Living Justice." *Catalyst: Feminism, Theory, Technoscience* 5, no. 1 (2019): 1–29.

Kishore, Nishant, Domingo Marqués, Ayesha Mahmud, Mathew V. Kiang, Irmary Rodriguez, Arlan Fuller, Peggy Ebner, et al. "Mortality in Puerto Rico after Hurricane Maria." *New England Journal of Medicine* 379, no. 2 (2018): 162–70.

Klein, Naomi. *The Shock Doctrine: The Rise of Disaster Capitalism.* Toronto: Vintage, 2008.

Kleinman, Arthur. *The Illness Narratives: Suffering, Healing, and the Human Condition.* New York: Basic Books, 1988.

Knadler, Stephen P. *Vitality Politics: Health, Debility, and the Limits of Black Emancipation.* Ann Arbor: University of Michigan Press, 2019.

Kukla, Rabbi Elliot. "Disability during a Pandemic: Put a Spoon on Your Seder Plate This Year." *J. The Jewish News of Northern California* (blog), April 1, 2020. https://www.jweekly.com/2020/04/01/disability-during-a-pandemic-why-you -should-put-a-spoon-on-your-seder-plate-this-year/.

Kulick, Don, and Jens Rydström. *Loneliness and Its Opposite: Sex, Disability, and the Politics of Engagement.* Durham, NC: Duke University Press, 2015.

Kuppers, Petra. "Crip Time." *Tikkun* 29, no. 4 (2014): 29–30.

Kuppers, Petra. *Disability and Contemporary Performance: Bodies on Edge.* New York: Routledge, 2003.

Latour, Bruno. *Reassembling the Social: An Introduction to Actor Network Theory.* Oxford: Oxford University Press, 2005.

Latour, Bruno. *We Have Never Been Modern.* Cambridge, MA: Harvard University Press, 2012.

Law, John. "What's Wrong with a One-World World?" *Distinktion: Journal of Social Theory* 16, no. 1 (2015): 126–39.

Law, John, and Ingunn Moser. "Good Passages, Bad Passages." *Sociological Review* 47, no. S1 (1999): S196–219.

Leder, Drew. *The Absent Body.* Chicago: University of Chicago Press, 1990.

Levin, Mike, and Tobin Siebers. "The Art of Disability: An Interview with Tobin Siebers." *Disability Studies Quarterly* 30, no. 2 (2010). https://doi.org/10.18061 /dsq.v30i2.1263.

LeVine, Mark, and Bryan Reynolds. "Theatre of Immediacy, Transversal Poetics." In *Performance Studies: Key Words, Concepts and Theories,* edited by Bryan Reynolds, 201–14. London: Palgrave Macmillan, 2014.

Liboiron, Max. *Pollution Is Colonialism.* Durham, NC: Duke University Press, 2021.

Linton, Simi. *Claiming Disability: Knowledge and Identity.* New York: NYU Press, 1998.

Livingston, Julie. "Insights from an African History of Disability." *Radical History Review* 2006, no. 94 (2006): 111–26.

Livingston, Julie. *Self-Devouring Growth: A Planetary Parable as Told from Southern Africa.* Durham, NC: Duke University Press, 2019.

Ljuslinder, Karin, Katie Ellis, and Lotta Vikström. "Cripping Time: Understanding the Life Course through the Lens of Ableism." *Scandinavian Journal of Disability Research* 22, no. 1 (2020). http://doi.org/10.16993/sjdr.710.

Ljuslinder, Karin, Katie Ellis, and Lotta Vikström eds. "Cripping Time: Understanding the Life Course through the Lens of Ableism." Special collection, *Scandinavian Journal of Disability Research* 22, no. 1 (2020): 35–38.

Loner, David, and Maggie Rosenau. "Crip Currencies: Resources on Care Community Networks in the Age of COVID-19." *Digital Feminist Collective* (blog), July 23, 2020. https://digitalfeministcollective.net/index.php/2020/07/23/crip-currencies-resources-on-care-community-networks-in-the-age-of-covid-19/.

Lorde, Audre. *The Cancer Journals.* 2nd ed. San Francisco: Aunt Lute Books, 1980.

Loveland, Katherine A. "Social Affordances and Interaction II: Autism and the Affordances of the Human Environment." *Ecological Psychology* 3, no. 2 (1991): 99–119.

Loveless, Natalie. *How to Make Art at the End of the World: A Manifesto for Research-Creation.* Durham, NC: Duke University Press, 2019.

Mairs, Nancy. *Waist-High in the World: A Life among the Nondisabled.* Boston: Beacon Press, 1996.

Makley, Charlene. "The Political Lives of Dead Bodies." Hot Spots, *Fieldsights,* April 8, 2013. https://culanth.org/fieldsights/the-political-lives-of-dead-bodies.

Malm, Andreas, and Alf Hornborg. "The Geology of Mankind? A Critique of the Anthropocene Narrative." *Anthropocene Review* 1, no. 1 (2014): 62–69.

Manzini, Ezio. *Design, When Everybody Designs: An Introduction to Design for Social Innovation.* Cambridge, MA: MIT Press, 2015.

Marcus, Neil. "Storm Reading" (video), January 19–20, 1996. https://www.youtube.com/watch?v=XVT9eqeiDdc.

Mauss, Marcel. "Techniques of the Body (1935)." In *Techniques, Technology and Civilisation,* edited by Nathan Schlanger, 77–96. Oxford: Durkheim Press/Berghahn Books, 2006.

McRuer, Robert. *Crip Theory: Cultural Signs of Queerness and Disability.* New York: NYU Press, 2006.

McRuer, Robert. *Crip Times: Disability, Globalization, and Resistance.* New York: NYU Press, 2018.

McRuer, Robert, and Merri Lisa Johnson. "Proliferating Cripistemologies: A Virtual Roundtable." *Journal of Literary and Cultural Disability Studies* 8, no. 2 (2014): 149–69.

Meekosha, Helen. "Decolonising Disability: Thinking and Acting Globally." *Disability and Society* 26, no. 6 (2011): 667–82.

Meekosha, Helen. "Drifting down the Gulf Stream: Navigating the Cultures of Disability Studies." *Disability and Society* 19, no. 7 (2004): 721–33.

Meekosha, Helen, and Russell Shuttleworth. "What's So 'Critical' about Critical Disability Studies?" *Australian Journal of Human Rights* 15, no. 1 (2009): 47–75.

Melzack, Ronald. "Pain and the Neuromatrix in the Brain." *Journal of Dental Education* 65, no. 12 (2001): 1378–82.

Melzack, Ronald, and Patrick D. Wall. *The Challenge of Pain.* London: Penguin, 1996.

Michaels, Claire F. "Affordances: Four Points of Debate." *Ecological Psychology* 15, no. 2 (2003): 135–48.

Michalko, Rod. *The Two in One: Walking with Smokie, Walking with Blindness.* Philadelphia: Temple University Press, 1999.

Mingus, Mia. "Access Intimacy: The Missing Link." *Leaving Evidence* (blog), May 5, 2011. https://leavingevidence.wordpress.com/2011/05/05/access-intimacy-the -missing-link/.

Minich, Julie Avril. "Enabling Whom? Critical Disability Studies Now." *Lateral* 5, no. 1 (spring 2016). https://doi.org/10.25158/L5.1.9.

Miserandino, Christine. "The Spoon Theory." *Butyoudontlooksick* (blog), 2013. https://butyoudontlooksick.com/articles/written-by-christine/the-spoon-theory/.

Mitchell, Audra, and Zoe Todd. "'Earth Violence: Indigeneity and the Anthropocene.'" Accessed May 6, 2016. https://worldlyir.files.wordpress.com/2016/04 /earth-violence-text-mitchell-and-todd.pdf.

Mitchell, David T., and Sharon L. Snyder. *The Biopolitics of Disability: Neoliberalism, Ablenationalism, and Peripheral Embodiment.* Ann Arbor: University of Michigan Press, 2015.

Mitchell, David T., and Sharon L. Snyder. "Disability as Multitude: Re-working Non-productive Labor Power." *Journal of Literary and Cultural Disability Studies* 4, no. 2 (2010): 179–93. https://doi.org/10.3828/jlcds.2010.14.

Mitchell, David T., and Sharon L Snyder. "Talking about Talking Back: Afterthoughts on the Making of the Disability Documentary Vital Signs: Crip Culture Talks Back." *Michigan Quarterly Review* 37, no. 2 (Spring 1998): 316–36.

Mitchell, David T., and Sharon L Snyder. *Vital Signs: Crip Culture Talks Back.* New York: Fan Light Productions, Icarus Films, 1995. DVD.

Mol, Annemarie, Ingunn Moser, and Jeannette Pols, eds. *Care in Practice: On Tinkering in Clinics, Homes and Farms.* Bielefeld, Germany: Transcript Verlag, 2010.

Montreal in/accessible Collective. "Virtual Poster Series (ViP) #1: Traffic Lights." *Canadian Journal of Disability Studies* 2, no. 4 (2013). https://doi.org/10.15353 /cjds.v2i4.105.

Moore, Jason W. "The Capitalocene, Part I: On the Nature and Origins of Our Ecological Crisis." *Journal of Peasant Studies* 44, no. 3 (2017): 594–630.

Morris, Jenny. *Encounters with Strangers: Feminism and Disability.* London: The Women's Press, 1996.

Morris, Jenny. *Pride against Prejudice: Transforming Attitudes to Disability.* London: The Women's Press, 1991.

Muñoz, José Esteban. *Cruising Utopia: The Then and There of Queer Utility.* New York: NYU Press, 2009.

Murphy, Keith M. "Design and Anthropology." *Annual Review of Anthropology* 45, no. 1 (2016): 433–49.

Nelson, Robin. *Practice as Research in the Arts: Principles, Protocols, Pedagogies, Resistances.* Basingstoke, UK: Palgrave Macmillan, 2013.

Nixon, Rob. *Slow Violence and the Environmentalism of the Poor*. Cambridge, MA: Harvard University Press, 2011.

Noble, Wiliam G. "Gibsonian Theory and the Pragmatist Perspective." *Journal for the Theory of Social Behaviour* 11, no. 1 (1981): 65–85.

Nocella, Anthony J., II. "Defining Eco-ability: Social Justice and the Intersectionality of Disability, Nonhuman Animals, and Ecology." In *Disability Studies and the Environmental Humanities*, edited by Sarah Jaquette Ray and Jay Sibara, 141–67. Lincoln: University of Nebraska Press, 2017. https://doi.org/10.2307/j.ctt1p6jht5.8.

Nocella, Anthony, II, Judy Bentley, and Janet Duncan, eds. *Earth, Animal, and Disability Liberation*. New York: Peter Lang, 2012.

Noland, Carrie. *Agency and Embodiment*. Cambridge, MA: Harvard University Press, 2009.

Oliver, Martin. "The Problem with Affordance." *E-Learning and Digital Media* 2, no. 4 (2005): 402–13.

Oliver, Michael. "Defining Impairment and Disability: Issues at Stake." In *Exploring the Divide*, edited by Colin Barnes and Geof Mercer, 29–54. Leeds, UK: The Disability Press, 1996.

Oliver, Michael. "The Politics of Disability." *Critical Social Policy* 4, no. 11 (1984): 21–32.

Oliver, Michael. "The Politics of Disablement: New Social Movements." In *The Politics of Disablement*, edited by Michael Oliver, 112–31. London: Macmillan, 1990.

Oliver, Michael. *Social Work with Disabled People*. London: Macmillan, 1983.

Oliver, Michael. *Understanding Disability: From Theory to Practice*. New York: Macmillan, 1995.

Oliver, Michael, and Colin Barnes. *The New Politics of Disablement*. Basingstoke, UK: Palgrave Macmillan, 2012.

Parent, Laurence. "Je Me Souviens: The Hegemony of Stairs in the Montreal Metro." In *Untold Stories: A Canadian Disability History Reader*, edited by Nancy Hansen, Roy Hanes, and Diane Driedger, 207–20. Toronto: Canadian Scholars, 2018.

Paterson, Mark. "On Pain as a Distinct Sensation: Mapping Intensities, Affects, and Difference in 'Interior States.'" *Body and Society* 25, no. 3 (2019): 100–35.

Patsavas, Alyson. "Recovering a Cripistemology of Pain: Leaky Bodies, Connective Tissue, and Feeling Discourse." *Journal of Literary and Cultural Disability Studies* 8, no. 2 (2014): 203–18.

Pearson, Mike. *Site-Specific Performance*. Basingstoke, UK: Palgrave Macmillan, 2010.

Phelan, Peggy. *Unmarked: The Politics of Performance*. London: Routledge, 1993.

Pickens, Therí A. *Black Madness: Mad Blackness*. Durham, NC: Duke University Press, 2019.

Piepzna-Samarasinha, Leah Lakshmi. *Care Work: Dreaming Disability Justice*. Vancouver: Arsenal Pulp Press, 2018.

Price, Margaret. "The Bodymind Problem and the Possibilities of Pain." *Hypatia* 30, no. 1 (2015): 268–84.

Price, Margaret. *Mad at School: Rhetorics of Mental Disability and Academic Life.* Ann Arbor: University of Michigan Press, 2011.

Puar, Jasbir K. *The Right to Maim: Debility, Capacity, Disability.* Durham, NC: Duke University Press, 2017.

Pullin, Graham. *Design Meets Disability.* Cambridge, MA: MIT Press, 2009.

Rapp, Rayna, and Faye Ginsburg. "Reverberations: Disability and the New Kinship Imaginary." *Anthropological Quarterly* 84, no. 2 (2011): 379–410.

Read, Alan. *Theatre and Everyday Life: An Ethics of Performance.* London: Routledge, 1995.

Reed, Edward. *Encountering the World: Toward an Ecological Psychology.* Oxford: Oxford University Press, 1996.

Reed, Edward. *James J. Gibson and the Psychology of Perception.* New Haven, CT: Yale University Press, 1988.

Rietveld, Erik, and Julian Kiverstein. "A Rich Landscape of Affordances." *Ecological Psychology* 26, no. 4 (2014): 325–52.

Roach, Joseph. *Cities of the Dead: Circum-Atlantic Performance.* New York: Columbia University Press, 1996.

Rolfstam, Max, and Jacob Buur. "An Institutional View on User Improvisation and Design." In *Design and Anthropology*, edited by Wendy Gunn and Jared Donovan, 69–79. Farnham, UK: Ashgate, 2012.

Rose, Deborah Bird. "Shimmer: When All You Love Is Being Trashed." In *Arts of Living on a Damaged Planet: Ghosts and Monsters of the Anthropocene*, edited by Anna Lowenhaupt Tsing, Nils Bubandt, Elaine Gan, and Heather Anne Swanson, 51–63. Minneapolis: University of Minnesota Press, 2017.

Saerberg, Siegfried. "'Just Go Straight Ahead.'" *Senses and Society* 5, no. 3 (2010): 364–81.

Saerberg, Siegfried. "The Sensorification of the Invisible: Science, Blindness and the Life-World." *Science, Technology and Innovation Studies* 7, no. 1 (2011): 9–28.

Samuels, Ellen. "Six Ways of Looking at Crip Time." *Disability Studies Quarterly* 37, no. 3 (2017). https://doi.org/10.18061/dsq.v37i3.5824.

Sandahl, Carrie. "Queering the Crip or Cripping the Queer? Intersections of Queer and Crip Identities in Solo Autobiographical Performance." *GLQ: A Journal of Lesbian and Gay Studies* 9, no. 1–2 (2003): 25–56.

Sandahl, Carrie, and Philip Auslander. *Bodies in Commotion: Disability and Performance.* Ann Arbor: University of Michigan Press, 2005.

Sanders, John T. "Affordances: An Ecological Approach to First Philosophy." In *Perspectives on Embodiment: The Intersections of Nature and Culture*, edited by Gail Weiss and Honi Fern Haber, 121–41. New York: Routledge, 1999.

Sanders, John T. "An Ontology of Affordances." *Ecological Psychology* 9, no. 1 (1997): 97–112.

Sassen, Saskia. *Expulsions.* Cambridge, MA: Harvard University Press, 2014.

Scarry, Elaine. *The Body in Pain: The Making and Unmaking of the World.* New York: Oxford University Press, 1985.

Schalk, Sami. *Bodyminds Reimagined: (Dis)ability, Race, and Gender in Black Women's Speculative Fiction*. Durham, NC: Duke University Press, 2018.

Schmidt, R. C. "Scaffolds for Social Meaning." *Ecological Psychology* 19, no. 2 (2007): 137–51.

Schneider, Rebecca. "Performance Remains." *Performance Research* 6, no. 2 (2001): 100–108.

Scully, Jackie Leach. *Disability Bioethics: Moral Bodies, Moral Difference*. Lanham, MD: Rowman and Littlefield, 2008.

Shakespeare, Tom. *Disability Rights and Wrongs Revisited*. 2nd ed. London: Routledge, 2013.

Shapiro, Joseph P. *No Pity: People with Disabilities Forging a New Civil Rights Movement*. New York: Three Rivers, 1993.

Shaw, Robert, M. T. Turvey, and William Mace. "Ecological Psychology: The Consequence of a Commitment to Realism." In *Cognition and the Symbolic Processes*. Vol. 2, edited by W. Weimer and D. Palmero, 156–226. Mahwah, NJ: Lawrence Erlbaum, 1982.

Shaw, Robert, M. T. Turvey, and William Mace. Foreword to *Ecological Psychology in Context: James Gibson, Roger Barker, and the Legacy of William James's Radical Empiricism*, by Harry Heft, xiii–xiv. Mahwah, NJ: Lawrence Erlbaum, 2001.

Sheppard, Emma. "Performing Normal but Becoming Crip: Living with Chronic Pain." *Scandinavian Journal of Disability Research* 22, no. 1 (2020): 39–47.

Sheppard, Emma. "Using Pain, Living with Pain." *Feminist Review* 120, no. 1 (2018): 54–69.

Shew, Ashley. "Let COVID-19 Expand Awareness of Disability Tech." *Nature* 581, no. 7806 (2020): 9.

Shildrick, Margrit. *Dangerous Discourses of Disability, Subjectivity and Sexuality*. Basingstoke, UK: Palgrave Macmillan, 2009.

Shilling, Chris, and Philip A. Mellor. "Saved from Pain or Saved through Pain? Modernity, Instrumentalization and the Religious Use of Pain as a Body Technique." *European Journal of Social Theory* 13, no. 4 (2010): 521–37.

Siebers, Tobin. "Disability in Theory: From Social Constructionism to the New Realism of the Body." *American Literary History* 13, no. 4 (2001): 737–54.

Siebers, Tobin. *Disability Theory*. Ann Arbor: University of Michigan Press, 2008.

Siebers, Tobin. "In the Name of Pain." In *Against Health: How Health Became the New Morality*, edited by Jonathan M. Metzl and Anna Kirkland, 183–94. New York: NYU Press, 2010.

Simone, AbdouMaliq. "People as Infrastructure: Intersecting Fragments in Johannesburg." *Public Culture* 16, no. 3 (2004): 407–29.

Simpson, Leanne Betasamosake. "Dancing the World into Being: A Conversation with Idle No More's Leanne Simpson." Interview by Naomi Klein. *YES! Magazine*, March 6, 2013. https://www.yesmagazine.org/social-justice/2013/03/06/dancing -the-world-into-being-a-conversation-with-idle-no-more-leanne-simpson.

Sins Invalid. "Into the Crip Universe" (podcast). Anchor. Accessed March 29, 2021. https://anchor.fm/sinsinvalid.

Sins Invalid. *Skin, Tooth, and Bone: The Basis of Movement Is Our People, a Disability Justice Primer*. 2nd ed. Berkeley: Primedia eLaunch LLC, 2019.

Sins Invalid. *We Love Like Barnacles: Crip Lives in Climate Chaos, This October*. August 29, 2020. Performance. https://www.sinsinvalid.org/news-1/2020/8/29/we-love-like-barnacles-crip-lives-in-climate-chaos-this-october.

Snyder, Sharon L., and David T. Mitchell. *Cultural Locations of Disability*. Chicago: University of Chicago Press, 2006.

Snyder, Sharon L., and David T. Mitchell. "'How Do We Get All These Disabilities in Here?' Disability Film Festivals and the Politics of Atypicality." *Revue Canadienne d'Études Cinématographiques/Canadian Journal of Film Studies* 17, no. 1 (2008): 11–29.

Sobchack, Vivian. "Choreography for One, Two, and Three Legs (A Phenomenological Meditation in Movements)." *International Journal of Performance Arts and Digital Media* 13, no. 2 (2017): 183–98.

Stoffregen, Thomas A. "Affordances as Properties of the Animal-Environment System." *Ecological Psychology* 15, no. 2 (2003): 115–34.

Stone, Deborah A. *The Disabled State*. London: Macmillan, 1985.

Struhkamp, R. M. "Wordless Pain: Dealing with Suffering in Physical Rehabilitation." *Cultural Studies* 19, no. 6 (2005): 701–18.

Taylor, Diana. *The Archive and the Repertoire: Performing Cultural Memory in the Americas*. Durham, NC: Duke University Press, 2003.

Taylor, Diana. *Performance*. Durham, NC: Duke University Press, 2016.

Taylor, Sunaura. "Age of Disability: On Living Well with Impaired Landscapes." *Orion Magazine*, November 9, 2021. https://orionmagazine.org/article/age-of-disability/.

Taylor, Sunaura. *Beasts of Burden: Animal and Disability Liberation*. New York: New Press, 2017.

Taylor, Sunaura. "Disabled Ecologies: Living with Impaired Landscapes." Othering and Belonging Institute, March 5, 2019. https://belonging.berkeley.edu/video-sunaura-taylor-disabled-ecologies-living-impaired-landscapes.

Thomas, Carol. *Female Forms: Experiencing and Understanding Disability*. Buckingham, UK: Open University Press, 1999.

Titchkosky, Tanya. *The Question of Access: Disability, Space, Meaning*. Toronto: University of Toronto Press, 2011.

Told by an Idiot. "Let Me Play the Lion Too." Accessed February 27, 2021. https://www.toldbyanidiot.org/let-me-play-the-lion-too.

Tsing, Anna Lowenhaupt. *The Mushroom at the End of the World: On the Possibility of Life in Capitalist Ruins*. Princeton, NJ: Princeton University Press, 2017.

Tsing, Anna Lowenhaupt, Nils Bubandt, Elaine Gan, and Heather Anne Swanson, eds. *Arts of Living on a Damaged Planet: Ghosts and Monsters of the Anthropocene*. Minneapolis: University of Minnesota Press, 2017.

Turner, Phil. "Affordance as Context." *Interacting with Computers* 17, no. 6 (2005): 787–800.

Turner, Victor. *From Ritual to Theatre: The Human Seriousness of Play*. New York: Performing Arts Journal Publications, 1982.

Turvey, Michael T. "Affordances and Prospective Control: An Outline of the Ontology." *Ecological Psychology* 4, no. 3 (1992): 173–87.

Union of the Physically Impaired Against Segregation (UPIAS). "Fundamental Principles of Disability." 1976. https://disability-studies.leeds.ac.uk/wp-content /uploads/sites/40/library/UPIAS-fundamental-principles.pdf.

United Nations Environment Programme and International Livestock Research Institute. "Preventing the Next Pandemic: Zoonotic Diseases and How to Break the Chain of Transmission." UN Environment Programme, July 6, 2020. https:// www.unep.org/resources/report/preventing-future-zoonotic-disease-outbreaks -protecting-environment-animals-and

Vidal, John. "'Tip of the Iceberg': Is Our Destruction of Nature Responsible for COVID-19?" *Guardian*, March 18, 2020. http://www.theguardian.com /environment/2020/mar/18/tip-of-the-iceberg-is-our-destruction-of-nature -responsible-for-covid-19-aoe.

Warren, William H. "Perceiving Affordances: Visual Guidance of Stair Climbing." *Journal of Experimental Psychology: Human Perception and Performance* 10, no. 5 (1984): 683–703.

Warren, William H., and Suzanne Whang. "Visual Guidance of Walking through Apertures: Body-Scaled Information for Affordances." *Journal of Experimental Psychology: Human Perception and Performance* 13, no. 3 (1987): 371–83.

Waziyatawin. "The Paradox of Indigenous Resurgence at the End of Empire." *Decolonization: Indigeneity, Education and Society* 1, no. 1 (2012): 68–85.

Wendell, Susan. *The Rejected Body: Feminist Philosophical Reflections on Disability*. New York: Routledge, 1996.

Wendell, Susan. "Toward a Feminist Theory of Disability." *Hypatia* 4, no. 2 (1989): 104–24.

Wendell, Susan. "Unhealthy Disabled: Treating Chronic Illnesses as Disabilities." *Hypatia* 16, no. 4 (2001): 17–33.

Wershler, Darren. "Kenneth Goldsmith and Uncreative Improvisation." In *Improvisation and Social Aesthetics*, edited by Georgina Born, Eric Lewis, and Bill Straw, 160–80. Durham, NC: Duke University Press, 2017.

Wheeler, Elizabeth. "'Moving Together Side by Side: Human-Animal Comparisons in Picture Books." In *Disability Studies and the Environmental Humanities*, edited by Sarah Jaquette Ray and Jay Sibara, 594–622. Lincoln: University of Nebraska Press, 2017.

Whyte, Susan Reynolds. "In the Long Run: Ugandans Living with Disability." *Current Anthropology* 61, S21 (2020): S133–140.

Williamson, Bess. "Access." In *Keywords for Disability Studies*, edited by Rachel Adams, Benjamin Reiss, and David Serlin, 14–17. New York: NYU Press, 2015.

Williamson, Bess. *Accessible America: A History of Disability and Design*. New York: NYU Press, 2019.

Windsor, W. Luke. "An Ecological Approach to Semiotics." *Journal for the Theory of Social Behaviour* 34, no. 2 (2004): 179–98.

Windsor, W. Luke, and Christophe de Bézenac. "Music and Affordances." *Musicae Scientiae* 16, no. 1 (2012): 102–20.

Wong, Alice. "I'm Disabled and Need a Ventilator to Live. Am I Expendable during This Pandemic?" *Vox*, April 4, 2020. https://www.vox.com/first-person/2020/4/4/21204261/coronavirus-covid-19-disabled-people-disabilities-triage.

Wong, Alice. "Valuing Activism of All Kinds." *Rooted in Rights* (blog), April 5, 2017. https://rootedinrights.org/valuing-activism-of-all-kinds/.

World Health Organization. "ICD-11 for Mortality and Morbidity Statistics." International Classification of Diseases, 11th Revision. Accessed May 24, 2022. https://icd.who.int/browse11/l-m/en#/http%3a%2f%2fid.who.int%2ficd%2fentity%2f1581976053.

World Wildlife Fund. "Living Planet Report 2018." 2018. https://www.worldwildlife.org/pages/living-planet-report-2018.

Yi, Chun-Shan (Sandie). "Crip Couture." Crip Couture. 2017. http://www.cripcouture.org/about.html.

anthropology, 11, 284

architects, 84–86, 247, 271n5, 272–73n34, 273n36, 274n43; ADA and, 274n42

architecture, 84–86, 273n39, 284n6; redesign of, 69; toilets and, 181. *See also* design

arthritis, 12, 283n20; osteoarthritis, 19; self-management program, 151. *See also* rheumatoid arthritis (RA)

Austin, J. L., 5, 254n5

Avilés-Vázquez, Katia, 87, 92

avoidance, 19, 58, 62–63; mutual, 216; risk, 67

barriers, 116–17, 165, 253n2; to access, 18, 72; to affordance, 210; disability and, 20, 31–33; performance and, 102; within political formations, 115; removal of, 51, 53, 75; social model and, 258n60

Berne, Patty, 91, 239. *See also* Sins Invalid

Bloomfield, Brian P., 35, 255n7

body, the, 60, 69, 107, 119, 261nn22–23, 273n36; ableism and, 76; agency of, 16; in architecture, 85; automatisms, 77, 80; disability and, 22, 32; disability repertoires and, 228, 233; disability studies and, 33; disease and, 241; environment and, 34, 37, 52, 56, 59, 64, 68, 90, 188, 228; exertion and, 65; freedom and, 281n37; habitus of ableism and, 74, 84, 225; impairment and, 32, 52, 258n2; limits of, 182; mind as separate from, 36; pain and, 57–58, 108; in pain, 19, 63, 162, 212, 243; painful, 56, 59, 63; performance and, 227–28, 250, 287n30; stimuli and, 263n42; as substance, 39; surfaces of, 39, 265n69; Tswana understandings of, 277n21

body-environment relation, 18, 31–32, 50, 52, 58–60, 64, 102, 244

bodymind, 51, 253n1, 268n98

Bourdieu, Pierre, 18, 76–77, 79. *See also* habitus

Boys, Jos, 84, 137, 282n15

Butler, Judith, 202, 254n5, 287n34

cancer, 12, 139

Canguilhem, Georges, 19, 64–65, 67–68, 76, 240–41, 270n28, 290n12. *See also* disease

canonical affordances, 17, 45–46, 120, 200

capitalism, 275n9, 276n21; disaster, 21, 92, 277n29

capitalist expansion, 21, 90, 250

Capitalocene, 22, 94, 257–58n58

Capitol crawl, 116, 281n35

care, 145, 208, 212, 218, 221–23, 234, 239–40, 287n29; design and, 85; device, 11; homes, 285n8; medical, 87, 206; self-care, 129, 178; work, 92, 219; workers, 164, 167, 219–20

Chen, Mel, 66–68

choreographies, 2, 8, 111, 118, 120, 145, 224, 228; access and, 121; of the everyday, 5, 9, 105; impromptu, 114; of *namaz*, 183; of world-building, 11. *See also* danced affordances

chronic disease, 1–2, 18–20, 63–64, 66, 68–69, 216, 244, 257n48; embodiments of, 53

chronic pain, 13, 18–19, 26, 56, 60–64, 69, 244, 269n13, 269n19; embodiments of, 53; inflammatory arthritis and, 12; rheumatoid arthritis and, 60

Clare, Eli, 165, 223, 274n7, 287n30

colonialism, 90–91, 256n15, 276n21; neocolonialism, 21

colonization, 34, 93

complementarity, 24, 35, 43, 210, 244, 261n23

constraint, 10, 110, 281n37

contraction, 68, 256–57n41; of the environment, 23, 66; of positive affordances, 63

Costall, Alan, 45, 120, 265n69

COVID-19 pandemic, 19, 22, 238–39, 290n6

creativity, 15, 248, 290n6; affordances and, 6, 52, 104, 163; chronic pain and, 56; disability studies and, 115; improvisation and, 103; reciprocal relations and, 17

crip: drag performance, 287n30; futures, 27, 245, 289n20; identity, 12, 116, 165, 281n36; kin, 133; technoscience, 105, 114, 195, 254n6, 279n10, 281n36, 284nn3–4; theory, 74, 232; time, 225, 229–32, 234, 288n8

critical access studies, 74–76

danced affordances, 111, 114, 201, 240, 249

debilitation, 21–22, 88, 90, 244, 249, 277n21; the earth's, 238; regimes of, 18

defuturing, 250–51, 292n44, 292n50

depression, 12, 33

design, 5–6, 23, 84–85, 120, 134, 136–38, 164, 239, 254n6, 255n13, 272–73n34, 284n6; ableist, 133, 165; affordances and, 260n21; barrier-free, 273n39; critical, 9, 111, 280n27; cultures, 251, 291n40; for everyone, 274n41; limits of, 7; objects, 163; research, 280n33; resonant, 282n17; speculative, 84, 111; theories of, 115; of toilets, 181; universal, 279n10, 283n20

disability: activism, 91, 116, 259n6, 280n33; architecture and, 84–86; artists, 11, 105, 280n33, 290n4; as category, 12–13, 74, 88–89, 91, 275–76n9, 276n16; communities, 10, 166, 253n1; culture, 166, 259n6; food, 166–67; as identity, 12, 276n9; justice, 26, 91, 257n48, 289–90n4; as method, 11; oppression, 269n13; politics, 33–34, 69, 74, 88, 91; repertoires, 27, 118, 228–29, 233–36; as shrinkage, 53, 100, 241, 246; theory, 22

disability activists, 11, 32, 69, 89, 105, 115–16, 247, 253n4, 258n60, 259n6, 280n33, 286n21, 290n4, 291n34

disability rights, 89; discourses, 79; movement (US), 32, 74, 80, 84, 91, 116, 144, 259n6

disability studies, 5, 95, 115, 238, 259n6, 275n7, 276n21; activism and, 280n33; body and, 33; crip time and, 229; critical, 13, 23, 53, 89, 91, 260n18, 289n4; disease and, 269n23; early, 18; first wave of, 34, 90; pain and, 269n13; relation between body and environment and, 31–32; social creationist, 259n8

disablement, 1, 22, 32–33, 51, 90–91, 253n2, 277n21; of animals, 290n4; of the environment, 18

discrimination, 20, 22, 32, 79, 81, 116; systemic, 276n9

disease, 5, 8, 64–65, 67–68, 121, 232, 240–41, 269n19; disability and, 33–34, 47, 52, 234, 244, 290n12; disability studies and, 269–70n23; infectious, 238; mobility-related, 63; shrinkage and, 22–23, 282n7; symptoms of, 133; thyroid, 12. *See also* chronic disease; rheumatoid arthritis

Dolmage, Jay, 78, 85

ecological psychology, 32, 35–36, 255n7, 262n24, 265n69

ecology, 13, 46

effort, 6, 51, 104, 117, 252, 257n48; calculated, 20, 68; chronic pain and, 63

embodiment, 17, 80, 121; ableism as, 78; of chronic pain and disease, 53; disability activism and, 280n33; disabled, 84–85, 254n6, 286n21; theory of complex, 34

endurance, 51, 76

environment, 6, 13, 36–40, 44–45, 106, 201–3, 208, 210, 214, 221, 234, 237, 240, 245–49, 261n22, 266n80; body and, 34, 37, 52, 56, 59, 64, 68, 90, 188, 228; disability and, 18, 33–34, 244, 258n60; disablist, 272n34; distrust in, 270n31; habitus of ableism and, 74, 76; hostile, 67, 108; ignorance of, 279n14; impairment and, 233; invariants and, 264n53; limits of, 10; livelihood of, 284n7; materiality of, 2, 7, 43, 289n18; niches and, 46; organism/organisms and, 5–6, 16–17, 39, 41–43, 57, 64, 78, 241, 261nn22–23; pain and, 19; perception of, 16–17, 41, 57; performance and, 8; shrinkage of, 18, 20–23, 26, 53, 64–66, 68–69, 74, 100, 103–4, 182, 207, 229, 242, 244, 249; substances of, 233; surfaces of, 93, 110, 201–2, 233, 264n53; time and, 201; use meanings and, 267n89; walking and, 77. *See also* body-environment relation

environmental racism, 21, 90

Erevelles, Nirmala, 89, 271–72n13

Escobar, Arturo, 93, 114, 278n42, 292n50

ethnography, 271n6, 285n8; autoethnography, 13; of suffering, 268n6; visual, 2, 11, 14–15

exclusion, 32, 115–16; architectural, 84–85, 273nn38–39; mutual, 224

fatigue, 33, 233

fine motor skills, 121; loss of, 246, 283n20; restriction of, 123 food, 37, 43, 46, 53, 61–62, 163–65, 217, 234; cheap, 250; coral reefs and, 278n44; delivery, 290n6; disability, 166–67; insecurity, 289n2

Fry, Tony, 85, 250, 280n16, 292n44, 292n50

futures, 230, 233–34; accessible, 25, 27, 203–4, 245, 247–49, 252; alternative, 255n13; crip, 27, 245, 289n20; disability, 236, 291n28; possible, 9, 235; world, 250

Garland-Thomson, Rosemarie, 11, 52, 254n6, 268n99, 270n38. *See also* misfit; misfitting

Gibson, James, 35–41, 44–46, 208, 237, 255n7, 256n35, 263n42; action and, 78; on affordance/affordances, 6, 16–17, 26, 35, 40, 43, 46, 58, 63, 160, 207, 221, 257n46, 260–61nn22–23, 265n60, 265–66n73, 282n9; ecological psychology and, 262n24; medium and, 37, 262n39, 263n41; on mutual affordances, 209, 216; on perceptual learning, 267n84; on selective affordances, 76; substance and, 37; surfaces and, 37, 262n32. *See also* ecological psychology; invariant structures; niches; perspective structure; theory of affordances

Gilroy, Paul, 80, 292n52

Ginsburg, Faye, 216, 261n22, 265n69, 281n33, 282n14. *See also* new kinship imaginaries

Gissen, David, 85, 274n46

Global North, 32, 89, 91

Global South, 89–90, 115

Grosz, Elizabeth, 85, 274n49, 281n37

habitus, 17, 76–77; ableism and, 20, 53, 104, 117, 223; of designers, 85–86

habitus of ableism, 18, 20–21, 26, 59, 74, 76–80, 82, 103, 225; architects and, 84, 272n34; architecture and, 84–85

Hahn, Harlan, 33, 166

Hamraie, Aimi, 74–75, 84, 247, 271n13, 274n42, 280n33, 291n34. *See also* Americans with Disabilities Act (ADA); crip: technoscience; critical access studies

Haraway, Donna, 202, 251, 285n3

health, 64, 67, 239

help, 133, 144, 164, 215, 218; asking for, 72, 83, 163, 187–88, 220, 222–23, 287n29; from care workers, 167; people as affordances and, 224; stigma of, 210, 223–24

illness, 47, 214, 218, 270n23; chronic, 260n14; impairment and, 33–34, 277n21; medication and, 106; shrinkage and, 18, 53

impairment, 8, 12, 21–22, 34, 53, 69–70, 88–91, 115–16, 134, 189, 224–25, 249, 258–59n2, 275n7; access and, 106; accommodation of, 188; body-environment relations and, 60; disability and, 32–33, 90, 259n4 (*see also* social model of disability); environment and, 233; mobility, 274n39; new kinship imaginaries and, 217; nonapparent, 117; rheumatoid arthritis-related, 51; shrinkage and, 52, 69, 282n7; Tswana understandings of, 276–77n21

imperialism, 20, 90–91

improvisation, 102–3, 245, 247, 279nn5–6; of activist affordances, 26; everyday, 105. *See also* *Let Me Play the Lion Too*

Imrie, Rob, 84–85, 273n36, 274n39

Indigenous peoples, 22, 94

infrastructure, 24–25, 179, 210, 219, 249, 271n6; accessibility, 247; body and, 119; care, 220; denial of maintenance for, 88; Palestine's, 21; people as affordances and, 286–87n23; privatization of, 291n40; Puerto Rico's, 87, 92; Turkey's lack of, 24, 209

ingenuity, 5–6, 32, 51, 103, 117, 151, 194, 235; disability as form of, 105

Ingold, Tim, 201–2; on design, 120, 131, 163; dwelling perspective, 214, 234; on the environment, 64; on landscape, 191, 283n1, 284n7; on surfaces, 37; on walking, 20, 77–78

inhabitable worlds, 24–25, 203–4, 245, 247

invariants, 40, 264n53

invariant structures, 39–40, 264n53

justice, 271n13, 279n13; disability, 26, 91, 257n48, 289–90n4; disability politics and, 91–92, 275n7; environmental (ecological), 6, 26

substances, 36–41, 57, 93–94, 100, 105, 108, 118, 161–62, 195–96, 200–201, 262nn31–32, 263n41; bodies as, 208; canonical, 240; disabled people and, 244, 247; of the environment, 233; harmful, 102, 106

suffering, 33, 95, 225, 269n13; disability and, 238, 276n21; mental, 13; pain as a passive state of, 56, 268n6

surfaces, 8, 36–43, 57, 59, 67, 77, 100, 105, 118, 161, 196, 200, 264n60, 265n69; bodies and, 208; disabled people and, 244, 247; ecological laws of, 160, 262n32; of the environment, 93, 110, 201–2, 233, 264n53; injurious, 106; layout of, 261n23; oww and, 94; terrestrial, 207

Taylor, Diana, 7, 27, 228, 249, 255n12, 288n3, 292n52

Taylor, Sunaura, 165, 239, 274–75n7, 286n20, 290n4

technologies, 16, 24, 92, 179; access to, 110, 114; assistive, 195, 247, 284n4; disabled people and, 75, 110, 247, 279n10, 284n4; performance and, 249

telic demand, 57, 60

temporality, 201, 229–30, 286n19; extended, 232, 263n44; of landscape, 284n7 (*see also* Ingold, Tim); of performance, 111, 191, 200

theater, 103–4, 203–4; spaces, 100. *See also* improvisation; Told By an Idiot

theory of affordances, 13–14, 16, 32, 252, 265n69, 282n9

time, 165, 224–25, 229–33, 245–47, 289n14; environment and, 201; reduced sense of, 20; theory of affordance and, 52. *See also* crip: futurities, time

Titchkosky, Tanya, 75, 80, 82

toilets, 1, 47–48, 50–51, 181–82

Told By an Idiot (theater company), 102, 279n4. See also *Let Me Play the Lion Too*

traffic lights, 71, 81–82, 87–88, 92, 179–80

violence, 91; capitalogenic, 251; colonial, 90; colonial capitalist, 88; earthly exploitative, 250; neocolonial, 89; slow, 13, 21

walking, 20–21, 77–78, 179, 192, 194–95, 198

walkism, 21, 78, 257n53

Wendell, Susan, 33, 115, 254n6, 256n22, 260n14

Williamson, Bess, 74, 195, 247, 273n36, 279n10, 283n20, 284n4

world-making/world-building, 7, 25, 70, 104–6, 114–17, 234–44, 250, 252; activism as, 5; choreographies of, 11; crip technoscience and, 105; performance of, 104